Labour Circulation and the Labour Process

The World Employment Programme (WEP) was launched by the International Labour Organisation in 1969, as the ILO's main contribution to the International Development Strategy for the Second United Nations Development Decade.

The means of action adopted by the WEP have included the following:

- short-term high-level advisory missions;
- longer-term national or regional employment teams; and
- a wide-ranging research programme.

Through these activities the ILO has been able to help national decision-makers to reshape their policies and plans with the aim of eradicating mass poverty and unemployment.

A landmark in the development of the WEP was the World Employment Conference of 1976, which proclaimed inter alia that 'strategies and national development plans should include as a priority objective the promotion of employment and the satisfaction of the basic needs of each country's population'. The Declaration of Principles and Programme of Action adopted by the Conference will remain the cornerstone of WEP technical assistance and research activities during the 1980s.

This publication is the outcome of a WEP project.

Also published by Croom Helm on behalf of the ILO:

INDUSTRIALISATION, EMPLOYMENT AND INCOME DISTRIBUTION
Ronald Hsia and Laurence Chau

EDUCATION, INNOVATIONS AND AGRICULTURAL DEVELOPMENT
D.P. Chaudhri

INFLATION, INCOME DISTRIBUTION AND X-EFFICIENCY THEORY
Harvey Leibenstein

SOCIO-ECONOMIC GROUPS AND INCOME DISTRIBUTION IN MEXICO
Wouter van Ginneken

EDUCATION AND INCOME DISTRIBUTION IN ASIA
P. Richards and M. Leonor

INCOME DISTRIBUTION, STRUCTURE OF ECONOMY AND EMPLOYMENT
Felix Paukert, Jiri Skolka and Jef Maton

WOMEN'S ROLES AND POPULATION TRENDS IN THE THIRD WORLD
Edited by Richard Anker, Mayra Buvinic and Nadia H. Youssef

STATE POLICIES AND MIGRATION
Edited by Peter Peek and Guy Standing

AGRARIAN REFORM IN CONTEMPORARY DEVELOPING COUNTRIES
Edited by Ajit Kumar Ghose

MIGRATION SURVEYS IN LOW-INCOME COUNTRIES
Richard E. Bilsborrow, A.S. Oberai and Guy Standing

Labour Circulation and the Labour Process

edited by
GUY STANDING

A study prepared for the International Labour Office within the framework of the World Employment Programme, with the financial support of the United Nations Fund for Population Activities

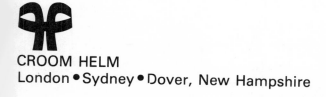

CROOM HELM
London ● Sydney ● Dover, New Hampshire

British Library Cataloguing in Publication Data

Labour circulation and the labour process.
    1. Labour mobility – Case studies
    I. Standing, Guy II. World Employment
Programme III. United Nations, *Fund for
Population Activities*
    331.12'7'0722   HD5717

ISBN 0-7099-3342-8

Library of Congress Cataloging in Publication Data
Main entry under title:

Labour circulation and the labour process.

    "A study prepared for the International Labour Office
within the framework of the World Employment Programme."
    Includes index.
    1. Migrant labor—Developing countries—Addresses,
essays, lectures. 2. Labor mobility—Developing
countries—Addresses, essays, lectures. 3. Migration,
Internal—Developing countries—Addresses, essays,
lectures. I. Standing, Guy. II. International Labour
Office. III. World Employment Programme.
    HD5856.D44L33   1984   331.12'791   84-14306

For Nancy, for courage.

Typeset by Columns of Reading
Printed and bound in Great Britain by
Biddles Ltd, Guildford and King's Lynn

Contents

Figures

Tables

Preface

Movement in distress or in search of opportunity has always characterised human development, both reflecting socio-economic, ecological and cultural change and facilitating and promoting it. A minority have moved in comfort, as a necessary part of a course of upward social mobility, cementing a niche and acquiring social skills, contacts and wealth en route. But to a much greater extent the ceaseless to-and-fro has involved suffering and degradation that has made the plight of migrants emotionally appealing throughout history. Much of the attention has been concentrated on international migrants transported to an alien culture. More recently, growing concern has been expressed for the rural dispossessed flocking into the cities and slums of industrialising economies.

Far less attention has been paid to those who have moved around, staying in numerous places for short periods, often alone or in small groups, often moving with a specific objective that they neither relish nor attain, whether their movements are from highlands to valleys, between villages and towns, between agricultural estates, mines and villages or in some less patterned way.

Despite the prevalence of various forms of labour circulation, its extent has been masked in censuses and most household surveys, whereas longer-term migration has been given considerable emphasis. Correspondingly, policies have concentrated on those movements identified in the data. Moreover, until fairly recently, analytical attention given to the massive scale of seasonal and other forms of short-term population mobility has been scant, even in critical analyses of the labour process in the contexts of agrarian transitions, industrialisation and urbanisation.

This situation deserves to be rectified, for unquestionably the social and economic aspects of these short-term movements are worth as much attention as that correctly given to the dimensions and circumstances of international migration. That circular migrants are exposed to hardships, degradation and extreme forms of exploitation is widely acknowledged. But – perhaps because by definition they have no fixed point of reference and are rarely in unions or politically integrated into civil society – relatively little effort has been devoted to remedying the worst abuses to which they are habitually exposed or to improving their access to adequate incomes and reasonable working conditions. Critical exposure of the reality of the process of circulation must remain the first objective if this situation is to change significantly.

This book focuses on one complex aspect of circular migration – the links between circulation and the transition to production based predominantly on wage labour. Complementary studies have attempted to conceptualise and suggest ways to measure various forms of population mobility, including forms of labour circulation.[1] Both are needed for integrating circulation into demographic and economic analyses of underdevelopment, for it is arguable that the lack of conceptual and empirical material reflects the rather limited treatment given labour circulation in formal analyses of labour and production processes.

Most of the following chapters are devoted to specific national or subnational contexts in which labour circulation has been widespread. Chapter 1 is a theoretical analysis situating labour circulation in the context of a growth of production based on wage labour, drawing on data and analyses from many parts of the world. It is a synthesis designed to show the close links between circulation and changing social relations of production.

Chapter 2 examines recent patterns of labour mobility in rural West Java, drawing on the author's extensive experience working in villages in Java and explaining the migration pattern in terms of structural and policy changes of recent years.

Chapter 3 is another village-based study, drawn from its author's fieldwork in the Mantaro Valley in Peru. It contrasts the experience of two villages in terms of their dissimilar socio-economic structure, and focuses on aspects of class differentiation.

Chapter 4 deals with villages in Tanzania, providing a vivid contrast with the preceding studies. Whereas the villages in the areas of Java are presented as consisting of smallholders struggling to survive through what is called 'safety-valve' migration in Chapter 1, in the Peruvian villages considered in Chapter 3 the lure and impact of a mining community is a focal point. In Chapter 4 the impact on village migration of plantation agriculture is the crux of the analysis, showing how the Ludewa District in Tanzania was converted into a labour reserve area and how official post-Independence government policies have not radically changed the situation, even though there has been a shift from longer-term circulation to seasonal migration of agricultural labourers.

Chapter 5 is a short, mainly historical analysis designed to display the roots of a particular form of West African migration, that of urban dwellers moving to labour as groundnut farmers along the Gambia River. The tracing of the historical roots of such a form of production, with its resort to sharecropping, should be regarded as an essential ingredient for policy interventions. Any attempt to change the social relations of production in the area to the benefit of those affected would have to take account of the long-term roles that the pattern of circulation has fulfilled. Another aspect of this study is that it cautions against explanations based on simple dependency theory, which has been widely used to explain recent patterns of migration in various parts of the world.

Chapter 6 examines the changing sexual incidence of population mobility in Kenya, seeing both long-term and short-term movements in terms of the changing structure of production and distribution. What this study shows is an intriguing change from migration consisting predominantly of young men to one in which young women have come to be the majority. As men have become more proletarianised as urban wage workers, women have responded by migrating temporarily from the countryside to the towns. Incidentally, the pattern observed diverges from the conventional stereotype by which men have supposedly predominated in migration in Africa. A drawback of many census-based studies of migration in many parts of the world is that they have ignored temporary moves and short-distance moves; in many countries, including India as well as Kenya, taking them into account would alter the image of mobility quite substantially.

Carol Colfer's provocative analysis of the impact of male out-migration on women 'left behind' in the forests of Kalimantan in Borneo is an attempt to balance the conventional and typically correct vision that out-migration of male workers imposes heavy burdens on women, children and elderly dependents that often undermine the viability of traditional subsistence forms of production. This study challenges some aspects of that view.

Labour circulation in northern India is examined in Chapter 8, which draws on three surveys of groups of migrant labourers, presenting a depressing picture of impoverished workers moving in a commonly vain attempt to eke out a minimal subsistence. It too is in part directed at countering a conventional view, in this case that circulation is usually a means of achieving socio-economic mobility, raising incomes and living standards in the process.

Chapter 9 focuses on the urban labour market, examining the position of temporary migrants in the construction industry in Manila and Port Moresby, and arguing that the observed mobility pattern contributes to the efficiency of the enterprises and to the continuing process of labour market segmentation.

The pattern of labour circulation examined in Chapter 10 has some resemblance to that of the Strange farmers of Senegambia covered in Chapter 5. Here, the boias-frias of São Paulo are examined as urban dwellers who congregate at dawn in the city outskirts to be auctioned as daily agricultural workers and then transported to the countryside. Nowhere could migrants be better described as the 'light infantry' of capital, though in other parts of Latin America and elsewhere comparable practices have characterised certain sectors of production.

The authors of Chapter 11 present a theoretical model designed to explain the behavioural decision-making process that leads to circulation. This chapter takes a very different approach from the underlying theoretical perspective of some earlier chapters, but can be seen as an alternative, conceivably complementary approach highlighting the crucial reality that much of the circulation is designed to minimise the risk to families and individuals of ceasing to be able to secure some minimal subsistence standard of living. A similar perspective is found in Chapter 12, which is concerned with spatial labour allocation of peasant-type households in rural Mexico, though it also incorporates structural elements to explain different patterns of migration in four areas of the country.

Finally, Chapter 13 is concerned with the usefulness of case studies of circulation for policy formulation. To illustrate their usefulness, Murray Chapman takes three studies, conducted in the Solomon Islands, Fiji and Thailand, and proceeds to show how each could be used to help local administrators make improvements to policy that would directly benefit those involved in the mobility. The important point is that for policy design to be appropriate and to have a chance of success the underlying causes of the pattern of movement must be identified, as must the perceived and longer-term implications of the movement for those moving, their families, those making use of migrant workers and their communities.

The introduction and the papers by Swindell, Colfer and Mukherji were discussed in seminars held at the World Congress of Sociology in Mexico City in August 1982. Thanks are due to Murray Chapman, who acted as chairman of the session on circulation at the Congress, and to participants in the discussion. I would also like to thank all the authors for their co-operation in redrafting and amending papers. The paper by Cheywa Spindel has been translated from Portuguese, while several other papers are linked to longer-term studies that deal with issues only briefly raised in connection with labour circulation.

Assistance in the ILO has been provided by a number of people, most of all by Mary Dominguez; it is a pleasure to acknowledge that help with thanks. Comments by readers are acknowledged in the various chapters, although the usual caveat about author responsibility should be made. Thanks are also due to Fred Fluitman, Peter Peek, Gerry Rodgers and René Wéry for commenting on the whole manuscript. Financial assistance from the United Nations Fund for Population Activities, which has funded a research programme on population mobility and employment in the ILO, is gratefully acknowledged. Among other outputs from this programme are two volumes on state policies and migration, also published by Croom Helm.[2]

It is hoped that the following contributes to an awareness of the central relevance of labour circulation to the evolving labour process in industrialising environments, in economies characterised by poverty, gross inequalities and growing unemployment.

Labour circulation deserves to be treated as not only a symptom of that process but as a problematic issue of considerable social and economic significance.

Guy Standing

Notes

1. G. Standing: *Conceptualising territorial mobility* (Geneva, ILO, 1982); idem: *Measuring population mobility in migration surveys* (Geneva, ILO, 1983). See also various chapters in R.E. Bilsborrow, A.S. Oberai and G. Standing: *Migration surveys: Guidelines for data collection* (London, Croom Helm, 1984).

2. P. Peek and G. Standing (eds.): *State policies and migration: Studies in Latin America and the Caribbean* (London, Croom Helm, 1982); A.S. Oberai (ed.): *State policies and internal migration: Studies in market and planned economies* (London, Croom Helm, 1983). See also J. Gaude (ed.): *Phénomène migratoire et politiques associées dans le contexte africain* (Geneva, ILO, 1982).

1
Circulation and the Labour Process

GUY STANDING

I. Introduction

For many communities in the world, a lifestyle of circular migration has persisted for generations, so much so that it determines the mode of existence and fluctuations in the well-being of their members. But the diverse forms of movement, and their pervasiveness, make it hard to categorise the patterns that recur. In some, the movement is close to nomadic, with those involved having no fixed point of usual residence, or even no fixed residence at all. For many peasants the movement is seasonal, with similar or complementary activities being pursued at each of the places of seasonal residence. These patterns have been common enough. But the most pervasive has been labour circulation, involving migration in search of temporary wage employment. This has taken numerous forms, which can be compressed into three main types.[1]

The first has been described as 'the first mode of subsistence', and consists of those who lack or have been deprived of essential means of production and as such would be unable to secure their reproduction in the absence of mobility. This description actually encompasses nomads, hunters-and-gatherers and shifting cultivators. But it also includes those who spend their working life on the margins of civil society as *migratory labourers*, tramping from place to place in search of 'job work', responding to news or rumours of work opportunities in some town or frontier zone or local point of industrial expansion. In some regions those involved pursue a custom-bound trail, as has been the practice of

the *torrantes* in Chile.[2] More often the tramping seems mo
haphazard, and less rooted to some set of values, norms a
codes of conduct, though even there informal moral codes a
support networks permeate their sphere of life. But in many pa
of the world stragglers dot the roadways and linger sadly und
crude cover, without hope or aspirations. For almost all of the
life is wretched, brutish and short.

The second consists of those who possess limited or part
control of immobile (and typically non-commoditised) means
production, usually land, which do not provide enough to ensu
the reproduction of their labour power, taking account
external forms of exploitation to which they might be subject.
includes peasants who cannot generate surplus on some meagr
fragmented landholding without recourse to wage employme
outside their village; they might be called the structura
underemployed rural poor. It also includes semi-proletariar
those provided by estates or plantations with usufruct rights tc
tiny parcel of land as part payment for labour. It includes sma
scale fishermen who desert the coast or river during the monso
season, being unable to fish all year round or having such lc
financial return through excessive competition or inadequa
stock that they have to spend part of the year labouring
construction sites or in docks far from home.

The third group is less homogeneous in their social relations
production but consists of those at the beck-and-call of what
euphemistically called the 'modern sector', whether in rural
urban industrial areas. These are well on the way to bei
proletarians, but they are not fully integrated into regular wa
employment. Marx called migrants 'the light infantry of industr
capital', and the image fits this group most aptly. They inclu
underemployed village youths who await information of tempc
ary work in a city in which some relative or friend is living. Th
include those directed to go to an estate, plantation or mine
work by indebtedness to some intermediary or the enterprise
question, as in the *enganche* system in rural Peru. And th
include groups like the boias-frias in Brazil who survive in t
urban slums and attend morning auctions for their labour in
traditional spot, whether being carted off to work in the fields
some distant agricultural estate or to a new township whe
construction sites abound.

Besides these three types, one can recognise others that ha

been historically important in some societies. Thus in pre-colonial eras in today's low-income countries there existed widespread *forced labour* circulation for limited periods or until certain jobs were completed; examples were *corvée* in Thailand and *kerah* in Malaysia. Under colonial regimes such forced labour multiplied, usually to work on land clearing or public infrastructure, particularly in areas of low population density. Another traditional form of circulation has consisted of moves due to social or religious obligations, as with monkship in Thailand. One might call this form of short-term movement *sociological travelling*, which includes visiting kin and strengthening reciprocal ties between villages, and which has been a highly valued mechanism in environments where the threat of famine, drought, floods or chronic harvest failure has been endemic. Such movement has been an integral part of the lives of such communities, complementing rather than competing with other activities, but reflecting ecological limitations on the economic base of village communities. As such, it contrasts sharply with patterns of temporary migration that emerged in class-structured societies, whether quasi-feudal or undergoing partial or total transformation to capitalist production, perhaps most strikingly in the colonies of Africa, Asia, Latin America and the Caribbean.

Labour circulation is a reflection of the dynamics of socio-economic change, in itself merely one form of migration or population mobility that should be approached in terms of its relationships to the process of socio-economic transition. Without wishing to erect a straw man, there has been a tendency to treat circulation in a trivial way. Repeatedly, without putting the descriptive details into an analytical framework, pages are devoted to showing that many villagers migrate more than once, as shown in place x and in place y, that those who first migrate when young are more likely to migrate again than those who first migrate when older, that many migrants retain links with their villages and like their families, and that Benito, a 22-year-old labourer, sends chocolates to his mother every third month. The descriptive detail is impressive but rarely linked to a clear analytical framework.

At the other extreme have been those who see circulation as merely a transitional 'epi-phenomenon' in the penetration of international capitalism. In contrast to the first approach, which tends to lead to marginal policy prescriptions, such as a preference for policies to facilitate circulation instead of long-term migration, the highly abstract 'holistic' approach tends to miss contradictory tendencies making circulation a theoretical problem, that might either advance rural accumulation or retard it.

Having flirted with the shadow of two straw men, a principal concern of this volume can be summarised as the relationship between labour circulation and proletarianisation. The basic premise, rather forcefully stated in the interest of brevity, is that labour migration is a necessary element of the process of proletarianisation. Circulation *per se* is an inherently unstable part of that process, which may facilitate limited accumulation while restricting the extent of proletarianisation. An implicit assumption of the analysis is that, short of revolutionary change, proletarianisation is an integral part of the transition from a relatively stagnant (economically non-advancing) structure of production and distribution to one in which accumulation can accelerate.

Before turning to more specific topics, a few words on conceptual issues are required. Proletarianisation is itself an awkward concept, either dismissed as a rhetorical word outside 'scientific' vocabulary or bandied about without much attempt to translate it into a viable analytical concept. For present purposes, it will suffice to define it as the process by which the mass of the working population become 'free' in the classic double sense, free of the means of production and free to sell their labour, *and* – which is where conventional discourse typically breaks off – a process by which workers come to have the necessary attributes, attitudes, commitment, tastes and consciousness required of a surplus-producing wage labour force.[3] In some circumstances, it might well suit the needs of the recipients of economic surplus – the estates, landlords or others – to have what has been called semi-proletarianisation, that is a situation in which the bulk of the workers have partial control over some means of *re*produc-tion. But that situation tends to be a transitional process and inherently unstable. In particular, the ability to appropriate surplus is limited, and workers with even partial control over some aspect of the production process have enhanced bargaining power and, perhaps most crucially, have been liable to identify their aspirations in terms of escape from wage labour. Above all, if accumulation is to occur on a large scale in industrialising environments a tightening and formalisation of control over the labour process is required, and for that workers must be induced to internalise behaviour required of efficient wage labourers. This brings into consideration such characteristics of wage labour as: (i) job stability and labour turnover; (ii) absenteeism; (iii) intensity of work effort, or the workers' 'effort bargain' for any wage rate; (iv) the socially accepted, or tolerated, duration of work; (v) the mechanisms of labour force stratification and control; (vi) the mobility of workers in terms of task flexibility; (vii) the acquisition, refinement, application and *re*production of skills; and (viii) the class and other forms of consciousness of workers.

In a pre-capitalist social formation, attempts to secure proletarianisation are bound to involve conflict, and one can interpret many of the authoritarian regimes in industrialising countries as involved in trying to secure that transitional process. This is not a digression, for intrinisically proletarianisation involves a series of contradictory developments, and it is the contradictions inherent in labour circulation that this introduction will attempt to stress.[4] But we must be careful to avoid deterministic, teleological reasoning. At the most abstract level, proletarianisation involves the *uncertain* conflict between at least two main groups, the outcome of which may not be full proletarianisation and the successful transition to production based on acquiescent wage labour. The first group consists of those trying to squeeze surplus out of the direct producers, using diverse mechanisms of control and relying on other changes in the labour process, as well as encouraging political developments facilitating such changes. The second group consists of the exploited and potentially exploited mass of the population. Anybody who takes account of history can see that this conflict was the reality of the history of industrialised countries and is the reality of current history in industrialising countries. And it is odd to spend time pontificating on the sending of chocolates by a temporary sojourner or on how many times the average circulant circulates, when circulation is a central feature of that historical process.

Nothing stated here should be taken as suggesting that the process of proletarianisation is one in which one class consciously sets out to secure a clearly-defined control of another or that the outcome is smooth or predictable. But the imposition of controls is the inherent tendency of transitional situations. Besides the brutality of regimes seeking to secure industrialisation by forcibly suppressing the protests and struggles of those being 'freed', in the double sense noted earlier, more subtle techniques have been used. These can be summarised as: (i) techniques to erode traditional social relations of production and distribution; (ii) dispossession of control over means of production, raw materials and output; (iii) techniques of direct coercion in the labour process; (iv) manipulation of the forms of worker remuneration; (v) manipulation of the social and detailed division of labour; (vi) generation of a relative surplus population (unemployment, etc.); (vii) destruction or erosion – or as some social scientists would put it, the disarticulation – of social and kinship support mechanisms among direct producers; (viii) use of paternalistic labour relations; (ix) inculcation of appropriate attitudes to productive labour by means of schooling and related institutions; and (x) ideological and legal 'superstructural' support, including religious dogma and civil law.

Arrayed against this battery of mechanisms, history attests to the dogged resistance and reluctant behavioural adaptation of the mass of the population subjected to the pressures of proletarianisation. Through the conflicts, there has always been an underlying current of pressure, response and mutual adaptation.[5] Arguably, this should be the core of analyses of the labour process, and as such it seems regrettable to divorce the analysis of the mobility of people as workers from that dynamic context. That is not stated polemically, but as a reaction to the tendency to analyse migration, and circulation in particular, in the classic case-study format, whereby two tendencies emerge with monotonous regularity. The first is reliance on observations of a few households or individuals, focusing on 'soft' attitudinal data, as if attitudes simply determine behaviour or that practices indicate or reflect preferences, or that behaviour yields outcomes consistent with them. That methodological quagmire is remarkable. The second tendency is that of formulating the questions to be asked, and the interpretations to be put on the data collected, on an ad hoc basis. One easily emerges with a shopping list of banal hypotheses that are scarcely linked to a theoretical perspective reflecting an identified problem.

The desire to avoid such tendencies is the principal justification for beginning with a statement of a theoretical 'position'.

The following sections are derived from that perspective, the intention being to suggest how labour circulation involves a series of unstable contradictions that link it to proletarianisation, both negatively and positively. Before doing so, it might be appropriate to add some remarks about the policy relevance of studies of labour circulation. In most of the following chapters the emphasis on policies is quite explicit, either in critically assessing past and current policies, or in tracing the implications of specific policies for migration patterns and related living conditions, or in proposing alternative policies derived from the findings of specific analyses. This is most forcefully presented in the final chapter derived from surveys in the Solomon Islands, Thailand and Fiji. However, policy implications should not be interpreted in a marginalist sense. If empirical analysis showed circulation to be an iniquitous but essential part of a labour process rooted in the social formation under review, it would be little use pretending that the situation would improve merely through attempts to control such circulation; that may indeed worsen the situation in which the migrants have to survive. That does not mean studies of short-term migration patterns and their rationale cannot have policy implications, for there is no question that ameliorative policies would be valuable in many areas. For example, labour contractors who have used diverse tactics to gain control of migrant workers need to be exposed; the functioning of labour exchanges, as examined briefly in Chapter 4, has to be monitored to see if they could ameliorate the plight of migrant labourers, reducing job-search costs, informing them of their legal rights, and so on. Such policy conclusions are useful. But ultimately identification of appropriate policy implications depends on the validity of the analytical perspective brought to bear on the phenomenon; regrettably, this point needs persistent emphasis.

II. Circulation Preserving/Undermining Pre-capitalist Relations of Production

First of all, labour circulation has been a 'safety valve', a means of preserving forms and social relations of production in rural areas, often reflecting a mode of production under stress. Thus, in the West Javan villages examined in Chapter 2, the recent upsurge in circulation has consisted of basic 'subsistence movement', whereas longer-term out-migration has been more geared to socio-economic mobility, moving up rather than preventing further decline. Circulation has often been a mechanism preserving a social mode of production, or at least reducing the immediate pressures on it.

In Melanesia, to give a simple example, village youths go to work in an urban area as a rite of passage, allowing village elders to retain control over production and avoiding disruptive competition between young male workers; temporary migration has helped prolong a form of communal production based on surplus appropriation and distribution by elders.[6] More generally, such temporary migration, commonly being selective of young men and of those with skills and aptitudes that are in some sense 'marginal' to existing labour requirements, is liable to deprive rural areas of leaders in any struggle to change traditional forms of exploitation or to prevent the encroachment on living standards by new forms.

Safety-valve circulation – or as it might be called, 'stress migration' – may reflect population pressure on resources, a growing inability to meet the demands of landlords and other exploiting elements, or a growing inability to reproduce productive forces, by maintaining land quality through proper use of fallow periods, avoiding excessive interplanting, and so on. It may also reflect landlords' attempts to squeeze out more surplus to meet growing revenue requirements. The role of population growth in this process has been essentially two-fold. Clearly, where landlords, or other groups controlling the means of production or in a position to extract surplus from the peasants, have stipulated rents and imposed local 'taxes' that to some extent have been based on the customary ability to pay, the growth in size of peasant households has reduced that ability. But there has also been an impact from the demographic expansion of landlords' households, which has increased their need for revenue to maintain the accustomed standard of living, leading to higher rents or more layers of taxes.[7] Whatever the causes, the increased exploitation or the reduced ability to pay has often induced temporary migration by one or more family members in search of extra income or simply *cash* income. The resultant movements may have been between rural and urban areas or from one rural area to another, to villages, to mines or simply in pursuit of harvests.

In some communities, the introduction of new technologies has forced defensive innovations on the part of smallholders, who have had to migrate for short periods of wage employment to obtain the cash for new implements.[8] Similarly, temporary movements may reduce household 'underemployment', allow higher per capita product and thus allow taxes or rent to be paid from remittances without the household having to sell assets or supply labour to kulaks, landlords or estates. In short, one or more members migrate to obtain monetary income to relieve temporary or longer-term stress.[9] In India, indebtedness has induced families to send wives and daughters to towns to earn money through prostitution to help them retain land.[10] In Thailand, village girls flock to work for a few months or years as masseuses and prostitutes in Bangkok to help maintain rural households.[11]

In some areas 'peasant families' have survived by what has been called 'relay migration', with different family members going to work in the city or town at different stages of the family life cycle – at one point the teenage daughter, at another the father, at another the mother, and so on. Where this represents the decomposition of the economic basis of the peasant subsistence, in the face of land fragmentation, soil erosion and related pressures, a survival strategy can entail growing reliance on family circulation and thus lead to 'expanded reproduction' of their primary asset, their children, thereby raising fertility.[12]

In central Peru it is reported that short-term migration helped maintain rural petty commodity production and 'occupational multiplicity' by strengthening reciprocal ties of labour obligations between geographically split 'household confederations'.[13] And in Kenya, among other countries, remittances from temporary migrants have helped preserve low-income rural households and small-scale landholders by slowing the growth of indebtedness and the loss of land. As in West Java, discussed in Chapter 2, this might be described as extending the involutionary process spatially. Elaborate models of behavioural decision-making emphasise that circulation is a form of risk reduction, a means of spreading the risk spatially and occupationally while maximising consumption. This theme is brought out in several chapters, formally in Chapter 11, but also in Mexican villages considered in Chapter 12 and in the West Javan villages examined in Chapter 2.

However, such examples emphasise the inherent contradictions of safety-valve migration. One should not be too categorical, but whereas temporary migration may originate as a means of preserving certain productive relations, it becomes disruptive. First, it accelerates the decay of feudal or other traditional social relations by undermining the perceived legitimacy of existing obligations. Migrants have been agents of change in their villages, exposure to an alternative environment teaching them that modes of exploitation to which their families had grown accustomed are neither just nor inevitable. Even in Melanesia, returning youths have resented the elders' control and have grown impatient of waiting for acquisition of elder status. In Venezuela, many peasant union leaders were those who had spent time in city life.[14] Pressures from return-migrants may lead to revolutionary action or, more commonly perhaps, oblige the authorities to make changes.

Such migration may accelerate the demise of landlordism by inducing defensive reactions on the part of landlords. If out-migration threatens their source of rent or related revenue and induces them to 'tighten the screws' of labour control, as an attempt to prevent the absence of workers during the harvest, that will erode the legitimacy of conventional social relationships, in so far as new forms of exploitation are added without compensating rights. That in itself will stimulate the desire to migrate. If, conversely, landlords make concessions to discourage out-migration, barriers to migration will be lowered. That can be illustrated by the classic series of changes in rental forms. The shift from labour services to produce rents and from either to cash rents increases the opportunity for all or some members of the tenant's household to absent themselves from the land. For the changes enable rent to be paid from the earnings from wage labour circulation, while some members remain to produce the family's basic subsistence and rural security.[15]

Conversely, temporary out-migration also allows landlords and other controllers of means of production to dispense with reciprocal obligations impeding their efforts – or deterring them from making efforts – to transform pre-capitalist productive relations, obligations such as loans to tide over the slack season or the implicit guarantee of employment throughout the year.

So far, emphasis has been laid on the disruptive effect of temporary migration on basically feudal social relations of production. Yet this applies just as much with petty commodity, or smallholder, production. One factor is the tendency for seasonal circulation to give way to temporary circulation that is not seasonal in character and to longer-term out-migration.[16] These changes reduce labour availability at critical seasonal periods, leading to a deterioration in the ability to reproduce means of production and maintain levels of output. The Miskito of Nicaragua provide an example.[17] In the 1960s fishermen travelled to plantations or shrimp-packing plants to supplement their traditional subsistence income. But commercial emphasis led to longer-term migration, remittances being sent to enable the family to hire wage labour. Gradually productive relations in the villages changed.

Even temporary out-migration can disrupt those relations of 'balanced reciprocity' that abound in village communities. It is possible that circulation will be perceived as a personal means of preserving a set of reciprocal relations and traditional lifestyles. But what an individual desires need not have much correspondence to what transpires. Thus, *gotong-royong* (exchange labour) in Malaysian kampongs has been based on the expectation that those involved will need the input of others later and be able to rely on it; temporary out-migration reduces the flexibility of that schema, leading to a substitution of wage labour and increased land underutilisation. And in turn the growth of wage labour further encourages out-migration.

Another element in this contradiction is that whereas temporary out-migration of young men may reflect the inadequacy of local income-earning opportunities and the need to supplement household incomes, it may actually lower household incomes. In northern India, the circulation of rickshawalas was observed to result in lower household incomes because the migrants were obliged to maintain two households, as noted in Chapter 8. More generally, such circulation leaves aged rural labour forces and households in which women and children have to assume a much greater work burden.[18] Although in certain circumstances it may not do so, as cogently argued in Chapter 7, this usually impairs the ability of families to meet formal and informal obligations and cuts them off from some reciprocal relationships. How and to what extent disruptive changes occur depends on the network of productive relations among smallholders, an avenue of enquiry that deserves to be explored. In sum, by no means can it be safely assumed that safety-valve migration results in an improvement in the living standards of rural families.

III. Circulation and Class Differentiation

Characteristic of transitions to capitalist production and proletarianisation is the process of class differentiation, in which income differentiation gives way to that based on the ownership and control of means of production. Again, the pattern of circulation may reflect a desire by the majority to reduce differentiating tendencies, but the actual implication is to accelerate them. The following indicates the main ways by which this can be expected.

Above all, temporary out-migration from rural communities reflects attempts to maintain living standards. Yet the poor are less likely to obtain high-income jobs and more likely to be obliged to use what income they do obtain to cover consumption needs, whereas members of richer households who migrate temporarily will do so to strengthen their family position in the rural areas.[19] Those acquiring relatively high incomes will be able to make technological innovations and expand commodity production, thereby differentiating themselves from those who cannot do so.

Both short-term and long-term forms of migration involve transfers that influence income and class differentiation. Assessments have been distorted by the relative neglect of money and goods taken or brought back by circulating migrants, a distortion partly due to the methodological difficulty of identifying such transfers. But there are reasons to suppose that usually patterns of transfers associated with migration accentuate inequalities and differentiation in the production process.

Remittances may appear to be equalising, information often indicating that low-income households receive transfers more often, that low-earning migrants send a greater proportion of their income back, that most remittances are small and that remittances are predominantly for consumption. But these conceal other changes they induce. First, 'attitudinal' responses on what was done with *particular* sums of money sent or brought back are not reliable guides to the impact of transfers on spending and investment.[20] Second, even if most remittances are small, that is consistent with a few large transfers, and it is those that strengthen a minority's position in the production process. In some areas the evidence clearly points to remittances accentuating such tendencies.[21] Third, even if poorer households are more likely to remit, the *net* flow may be negligible, as their initial costs of travel and job-search represent a higher proportion of the income they obtain.

Fourth, and most difficult to document though perhaps most crucial, investment by wealthier landholders is stimulated not only by actual remittances but by their availability, if needed.[22] This reduces risk, encouraging land purchase, technological change and the use of hired labour.

Fifth, in many peasant communities remittances and the cash income brought back by the migrants encourage the commoditisation of land, and thus land transfers from smallholders to richer peasants and estates. The absence of a market in land has characterised villages in which land fragmentation and generalised poverty have co-existed. In such circumstances, the influx of cash has helped undermine the social structure checking the growth of land-based differentiation.

Sixth, there is the facilitating factor of 'pooled transfers', primarily through migrant organisations. In some places, these have helped develop rural infrastructure and stimulated commercial production, enabling some petty producers to become capitalist employers. In Nigeria migrants to towns have joined 'improvement unions' to promote their home village development, in effect exhibiting 'village patriotism'.[23] Similar practices are found in Indonesia, notably among the Bawaens. But these are by no means isolated cases, having been replicated in many parts of the world.

Seventh, for richer households remittances and the benefits of temporary out-migration are partially concealed in the form of improved skills, marketing information, contacts, access to commercial credit, and so on, all of which strengthen the strong. Indeed, this applies to inter-community as well as intra-community differentiation. For to the extent that circulation from more affluent areas is more purposeful and complementary with local needs, whereas that from poor areas is done in distress to cover survival needs, it can strengthen the external links and accumulation in the former while turning the latter into labour reserve areas, unable to compete in the staple commodity markets and increasingly finding it more advantageous to supply wage labour.

Labour circulation has usually started as a seasonal phenomenon, complementing local activities by providing some income in the slack or 'dead' season, but gradually the dominant factor becomes the nexus of opportunities in the areas to which the migrants go. In 1982, when interviewing village leaders in northern Kelantan in Malaysia I found that initially men had gone to Singapore and urban areas in Malaysia in the slack season, returning for the padi harvest and transplanting seasons. But once circulation had become an established pattern, men had been leaving for two or three months at a time whenever informed of opportunities, regardless of the need for their labour in their kampong. One apparent result was increasing land underutilisation among smallholders. With chronic land fragmentation and tiny parcels one might expect land sales, land being rented out, and land consolidation. But other factors had checked those developments, notably inheritance customs, the underdeveloped market in land, and land fragmentation that minimised the exchange value of mini-plots.

Once temporary migration becomes oriented to the needs of the destination labour market rather than the needs of the community of origin, it encourages differentiation by weakening the poorer rural households, depleting them of family labour and forcing them to buy consumer goods they previously produced. Often labour shortage is scarcely visible, initially the only signs being that poorer households are precluded from new opportunities or forced to abandon secondary occupations. For some, production becomes more fragile, so that the first crisis, such as a bad harvest, drought or period of heavy rain, leads to ruin. Whenever petty commodity producers have to concentrate on one or two activities and neglect complementary activities they are on their way to joining the proletariat. The absence of one or more household members may allow exploitation to continue and preserve subsistence levels for a while, but typically it leads to inattention to repairs, inadequate land preparation and related forms of neglect, reducing yields and incomes. Thus, in parts of Africa, male out-migration has left households vulnerable, for the absence of labour has meant dilatory bush clearance and soil erosion, seriously impairing the indigenous shifting cultivation.[24] Ironically, such tendencies may be worsened by limited labour-saving innovations made to offset migration or as a result of small remittances. If they cannot afford complementary inputs, the introduction of one new input may disturb the sensitive ecological balance in the traditional cultivation. Enforced adaptation reduces household income and labour reserve, reducing the capacity to cover financial or labour contingencies without resort to moneylenders and hired labour. That in turn increases their precariousness and pauperisation.

The relatively affluent can take advantage of their neighbours' plight, aided by remittances. They may draw them into debt and eventual dispossession, reduce their opportunity for commodity exchange through their own ability to sell at lower prices or because they can oblige the poorer, more dependent villagers to buy from them. Some smallholders will be forced to lease land to them, often to become temporary out-migrants. A variant of that occurs in Mexico, where despite restrictions on land transfer under *ejido*, smallholders have leased their parcels to sharecroppers and migrated in search of wage employment.[25]

Another feature of differentiation relates to the risk-minimising behaviour of smallholder farming households, which will depend on the level of income locally, the opportunities to combine petty farming with other income-earning activities and the variability of output and income. In some circumstances, inadequate incomes and pressures on household resources may preclude circulation by family members because of the perception of risk to the investment in the costs of travel and job-searching unemployment. Such households are locked into a process of impoverishment that typically leads to dispossession of means of production and eventual permanent displacement from the local community.

Slightly higher income levels may facilitate safety-valve circulation, as seen in the Bajio region of Mexico in Chapter 12, though there circulation was also stimulated by the commercialisation of agriculture that had increased the riskiness of agricultural income and reduced local agricultural employment opportunities. A feature of differences in migration patterns across the four areas covered in that study is that circulation was made possible by the attainment of a certain level of income and a reduction in what might be called 'subsistence risk', due to slightly wealthier households having multiple sources of local income.

Differentiation is also affected by the incidence of migration, though few studies have stressed its class nature. It may be that temporary out-migration is relatively high for landlord or commercial big-farmer groups, with sons and daughters going for schooling or training, and also high for the rural proletariat and semi-proletariat (those with a tiny land parcel, obliged to work for wages to provide a subsistence income), the former being mainly rural-urban, the latter more often intra-rural. Poor peasants with mini-holdings may find it hard to realise even a distress sale of the land, especially if their land is fragmented into tiny parcels. Conversely, those in 'medium circumstances' may be most likely to make permanent moves.[26] Interestingly, a recent ILO survey in the Indian Punjab suggested that smallholders had a higher rate of 'permanent' rural emigration than landless households.[27] In Ecuador the distribution of out-migration was observed to be bi-modal, the suggestion being that the high rate in the very large landholder category was education-linked, and thus temporary, while the high rate among those with from 2.5 to 5.5 hectares was longer-term, coming from households under stress.[28] An Argentinian study also suggested the long-term out-migration was greatest from the 'middle-classes'.[29]

If middle-income groups have high long-term out-migration and others strengthen their position or survive by short-term circulation, the pattern may be explained by differentiating pressures within the rural community and the tendency of the middle peasantry to experience most a sense of decremental deprivation, arguably a powerful motivator to rebellious action or its essentially passive alternative of migration.[30] Rather than sink into the rural semi-proletariat, they migrate.[31]

Indicating a related phenomenon, a village study in Bangladesh reported that sons in low-income households were more likely to leave altogether than those in richer households, and to do so at an earlier age, depleting their households of needed labour.[32] Such findings may only be indicative of strains and currents of change induced by migration, but it is likely that circulation from higher-income households is more purposeful and planned as a long-term course of domestic expansion, while that from lower-income groups is more a matter of distress and necessity.

IV. Circulation and Rural Wage Labour Growth

While labour circulation has typically occurred in response to the lack of rural income-earning opportunities, it has facilitated and encouraged the growth of such opportunities in the form of wage labour. Rural circulation and the shift to wage labour employment have been mutually reinforcing.

In most pre-capitalist agricultural communities, kinship and family divisions of labour co-exist with forms of communal labour and exchange labour. The latter are too rarely taken into account in analysing the dynamics of decay and growth. As both communal and exchange labour depend on recognition of balanced reciprocity between petty producers, there has to be a sense of exchange equivalents for such labour relations to persist. And in the absence of major social upheavals or externally imposed changes, such labour systems come under threat when some smallholders *either* perceive a serious and long-term decline in the probability of their receiving equivalent labour services in return for their own, *or* perceive a relative decline in the efficiency of such labour inputs on their own land, *or* perceive a rising opportunity cost of their own involvement in exchange or communal labour. The influx of seasonal migrants in search of wage labour is one mechanism that alters the balance preserving such labour relations. But opportunities for smallholders themselves to go elsewhere to obtain wage work rather than commit themselves to non-wage labour locally is often a powerful factor inducing a decline in exchange and communal labour, undermining the basis of reciprocity on which they depend. Clearly, other external influences play a part, notably the growth of cash transactions and any growth in socio-economic and status differentiation. But circulation is often critical. Once such systems begin to decline, many marginal smallholders are directly threatened, because they survive by judiciously combining more than their share of labour time in such work with access to the intermediate inputs, knowledge and labour strength possessed by other village members.

Another form of change is the shift from semi-proletarian to proletarian status. In many rural areas landlords, plantations or commercial agricultural estates have overcome real or potential shortages of labour by securing attached labour forces through some non-labour tie. Classically, a small plot has been provided, for rent or as part payment for labour services. In some villages, landlords or estates retain attached labourers by means of some non-labour exchange relation – a form of labour control that may also be a mode of exploitation – notably through indebtedness, fictive kinship and related forms of patronage. These tend to be prevalent when commodity circulation and cash transactions in the community are limited.

The growth of surplus labour in such circumstances precipitates changes in the social relations of production. Surplus labour may emerge from population growth, growing land concentration, labour-displacing mechanisation or the inflow or availability of migrant wage labourers. Whatever the causes, there will be a tendency to discontinue social relations that check the mobility of local agricultural labourers. But the availability of substantial numbers of migrant labourers also enables employers to change custom-based practices and obligations. Thus, they ease a shift from non-cash payments to money wages, which is often accompanied by a fall in annual earnings, in spite of a rise in *daily* wage rates. Migrants from other villages might be used because they are unfamiliar with local customs regarding the form and level of wages and benefits, allowing the wage system to be monetised.[33]

Considering the two classical forms of agrarian transition, one can identify forms of 'external proletarianisation' and 'internal proletarianisation' of the relations of production.[34] With external proletarianisation the agrarian structure of production exhibits growing class differentiation, with the growth of a sub-class of kulaks – rich peasants or labour-hiring yeomen farmers – as well as the displacement of middle and lower strata of the peasantry through land concentration and the hiring of migrant labourers. This transition path has sometimes been called the *via campesino* or the American route. The other ideal type of transition of rural relations of production has been called the Junker route, by Lenin among others.[35] Here, traditionally entrenched landlords displace tenant landholders and resort to commercial farming themselves, expelling most of the peasants, even if they retain a core of semi-proletarian workers. Intrinsically, this process relies less on the existence of seasonal or other temporary migrant labourers, since the new commercial estates may be able to retain sufficient ex-tenants as wage labourers. However, the new social relations of production may be more easily imposed on migrants than on ex-tenants, who will be likely to resent the loss of traditional rights and informal entitlements, and the abrogation of what has been called the 'little tradition'.[36] So, in general, the availability of seasonal migrants would assist both types of transition. And to the extent migrants would be more exploited than other workers, they would actually encourage changes in the relations of production.

Rural proletarianisation reflects the erosion of pre-capitalist social relations and the growth of class differentiation. But intra-rural circulation clearly influences the shift to wage labour. In areas of in-migration it weakens the middle and lower strata of the peasantry, those who survive by judiciously combining petty agriculture, craftwork and wage labour. If cut off from wage labour opportunities, many will be forced into debt, to give up land and other means of production and to join the rural proletariat or migrate to join it elsewhere.

Migrants into villages have commonly displaced family workers, often allowing some to pursue schooling and often paid wages from remittances sent back by other family members who have left the household. Moreover, where social relations of production are custom-bound, landlords and commercial farmers have often been able to resort to wage labour efficiently through using seasonal migrants. To transform petty producers into a proletariat that can be manipulated to produce a sizeable surplus, there must be a period in which new *forms* of exploitation and oppression – represented most by the depersonalisation and formalisation of labour relations – are internalised by workers. In effect, pauperisation is a necessary prelude to proletarianisation. And for that reason alone, employers tend to use seasonal or other migrant workers who have already been reduced to 'proletarian consciousness'.[37] There are many examples in which enterprises have sought migrant labour rather than use available local workers.[38] As such, migrants have been used as an indirect disciplining factor on those not yet 'ready' for regular wage labour, while the local population's expectations and aspirations are reduced and reoriented. For example, the use of temporary migrants in construction industries is a pervasive phenomenon, migrants often being recruited in groups in rural areas by middlemen and exposed to severe working conditions and wages that urban workers would actively resent to a much greater degree.[39] Migrants hired for specified periods and brought from their villages by labour contractors are effectively controlled by their isolation from other elements of the emerging working class and by such devices as advances and the withholding of wages until the end of the seasonal period of employment. Temporary migrants into the Bombay construction industry have been manipulated in that way, being paid meagre weekly living expenses during the work period, the rest of the wage being paid on their return to the village.[40]

In this phase, the local population may exhibit signs of incipient proletarianisation through mass alcoholism, anomie, absenteeism and high labour turnover, and as such be scarcely exploitable. Migrants can be subjected to much greater control, having locally no strong support system or close ties of class solidarity. As noted with respect to the harsh superexploitation of migrants in Gujarat,

> Even under the blatantly capitalist mode of production it is difficult to see that such anonymous and ruthless treatment could be meted out to people who are part and parcel of the local society and who previously were partners in a labour system with feudal overtones.[41]

One could go further, for often temporary migrants facilitate a transition to wage labour production that would be impossible or slowed in their absence. Even so, migrant labour is unstable, for supply depends on the existence of a surplus population, and estates once dependent on such workers are vulnerable to their withdrawal.

V. Circulation and the Social Division of Labour

In petty commodity production both the detailed and social divisions of labour are restricted by its kinship orientation and are also flexible, mainly based on conventional age-sex role complementarities within households or 'household confederations', however loose the kinship community structure. Survival is ensured by 'occupational multiplicity' and a set of structured reciprocities, including simple forms of exchange labour, gang work, age sets, and so on. The managerial-authority structure is essentially an internal household or community process, and notably in a feudal setting production and distribution take place within essentially isolated units. All this changes with proletarianisation.

In particular, capitalist control requires artificial or institutional barriers to divide the labour force, imposing heterogeneity where the tendency of the labour process is towards homogeneity (the collectivisation of the mass of workers). This is epitomised by the term 'divide-and-rule' and labour force stratification. Second, the capitalist need for a committed low-cost labour supply implies a very different household or family division of labour, between those available as wage labour and those doing reproductive work. A breakdown in the flexible domestic division of labour and in the occupational multiplicity of individual workers creates a workforce more dependent on wage labour and thus more resigned to the labour relations imposed on wage workers.

How does circulation relate to this process? Perhaps foremost is the relation to the sexual division of labour, notably where men are drawn into migrating into wage labour, leaving women as well as children and the elderly with greater burdens in domestic production.[42] The most well-known examples of migration-induced redivision of labour are in sub-Saharan Africa. In Ghana, Zambia, Tanzania and in all the countries bordering South Africa, male long-term circulation has meant vast rural areas being devoted to the reproduction of labour power while urban areas concentrate on commodity production.[43] Rural women have been pushed more into the domestic economy. In some rural areas, in-migration of wage labourers has contributed to the displacement of women in productive tasks, forcing them to concentrate on domestic work. Other aspects are noted later, but it is worth stressing that not only does this pattern of circulation increase the oppressed state of women, cutting them off from access to cash and increasing their dependence on men; it also increases the oppressed state of men who have more responsibility for household income, and come under more pressure from wives and other relatives to labour regularly and docilely.

However, care must be taken not to overgeneralise or treat the issue sentimentally. If attention is restricted to the immediate impact on women left behind, more crucial social dynamics may be obscured. Women who remain in the villages while men migrate for short periods, or even for some years, do not necessarily suffer catastrophic declines in their standard of living, as Colfer implies in Chapter 7 in her analysis of the impact of male circulation from two remote villages in the forests of Kalimantan in Borneo. One should avoid romanticising women's ability to cope, just as much as one should avoid excessively sentimentalising their plight. But in certain contexts, where the village economy is not an integrated appendage to the sector into which migrant workers are drawn, the out-migration of men can facilitate a breakdown in traditional oppressive divisions of labour that restrict women to certain subordinate tasks and decision-making, enabling them to develop skills and opportunities that might otherwise be denied them.

The sexual division of labour is also inter-related with the sex selectivity of different types of population mobility. This is brought out in Chapter 6 in the context of the changing pattern of mobility in Kenya, where labour circulation by men gave way to longer-term migration coupled with circulation by women. More commonly, the development of industries based on process labour has led to the absorption of young, single women, drawn from the countryside into new areas of urban-industrial expansion. Contrary to a still surprisingly common image, in numerous countries women make up the majority of short-term and longer-term migrants, very commonly moving in search of wage labour, having been marginalised in the labour process in their areas of origin and drawn into the sort of unstable low-wage process-type jobs for which their oppressed upbringing makes them peculiarly suitable, from the point of view of capitalist accumulation. Such women migrants are particularly utilised in 'static' jobs with low costs of labour turnover, should they remain in them only for short periods. In Malaysia, electronics and textile companies have sent buses, lorries and even planes into the countryside to recruit young girls for such jobs, providing them with basic accommodation on their arrival in town. There and elsewhere migration accentuates the sexual division of labour in the industrial sectors.

Age selectivity of migration also affects the social division of labour. As circulation and other forms of migration are selective of the young, the rural labour force becomes increasingly aged, which impedes technical change and makes rural petty commodity production more fragile in its ability to adjust to adversity. This is particularly so once circulation based on seasonal labour requirements gives way to other forms of short-term or longer-term migration.

Circulation has also played its role in fostering an ethnic or racial division of labour, with some racial group in the rural areas supplying short-term labour to urban-industrial or estate areas in which another racial group makes up the core of the labour force.[44] Commonly, ties develop between specific villages and a type of job in a specific industry or establishment, with groups of workers separated into almost isolated cells in the workplace. This is observed in Chapter 3, resulting from a study of temporary migration from two Peruvian villages.[45] Often such movement involves communal migration.[46] It is not uncommon for the incoming group to receive sub-subsistence wages, on the expectation that their subsistence needs will be met through an implicit subsidy from their rural family. Such stratification allows a process of 'co-exploitation', by which *part* of the surplus acquired from the lower strata of wage workers is transferred to higher strata, and by which the immediate, perceived interests of the different strata of the labour force are divided. An illusion is fostered that one group benefits from the relative disadvantage of another; it is an illusion because ultimately this mechanism enables capital to exploit all strata of the proletariat more effectively, while weakening their collective bargaining position.

Migrants contribute to the social redivision of labour by filling jobs for which there is little upward occupational-income mobility. Such jobs do not require a stable committed labour force because there are no returns to on-the-job experience and no large recruitment, induction or training costs. This is illustrated by a study in Santiago where male migrants entered jobs with little upward mobility potential and where they seemed to experience much less upward mobility than non-migrants, even controlling for schooling differences. It was suggested that:

> The influence of migrants at the bottom may have a structural effect on the process of mobility in Santiago; the low-status migrants take over the lower-status positions in the city while the native urbanites move up the occupational ladder.[47]

Such tendencies commonly divide groups by area of origin, each identifiable by manner of dress, accent, racial mix, habits, or type of schooling.

Migrants also comprise a large component of the so-called 'informal sector', whose role in accumulation has been blurred by the rhetoric about its growth potential. Part of it consists of activities by which those involved – commonly temporary and longer-term migrants – subsidise urban-industrial labour costs by providing cheap means of subsistence, such as low-cost food channelled from migrants' home areas. It may also supply wage goods or involve subsidiary activities done for capital, such as repair work or the provision of spare parts, allowing capitalist enterprises to acquire more economic surplus, indirectly.

The 'informal sector' is a nebulous concept, embracing petty commodity or artisanal activity, street-vending, illegitimate pursuits that are merely redistributive at the margin, and outworkers whose labour is superexploited in the interest of accumulation in the 'formal sector'. In the present context, two distinctive patterns should be acknowledged. First, in many parts of the world rural producers migrate to urban areas to work in such activities to complement or supplement their seasonal or otherwise inadequate rural incomes, returning to their rural dwelling and their families to continue their agricultural work whenever needed. Second, there are those who live in or around urban areas who migrate to rural areas at certain times of the year, leaving the urban 'informal sector' to sag. This latter pattern has been studied by Swindell in Senegambia (the roots of which are explored in Chapter 5), whereby men leave the towns to become seasonal groundnut farmers working on plots lent to them by their village hosts in return for a predetermined number of days labour.[48]

A quite different practice is the use of migrants in sensitive positions of intermediate authority. This reduces confrontation between workers and employers, redirecting potential resentment to such intermediary categories. In Peru, migrants were used in such jobs as being less likely to identify with local workers doing manual work.[49] In Gujarat, distinctive groups of seasonal migrants were used as *mukadams* and others as lower categories, though in recruitment employers also stressed past diligence.[50] But there, as elsewhere, recruitment was based on spreading the geographical source of seasonal workers, as a means of reducing the likelihood of collective action to improve working conditions and pay.

The hiring of seasonal migrants as labour brokers or supervisors enables employers to avoid supervisory costs and makes it easier for them to assume a paternalistic role without resort to coercion or the acquisition of an authoritarian image. That tactic impedes the development of class consciousness, for workers identify their discontent with the strictness of the intermediaries. In some cases, it is a migrant group that acts as co-exploiter, in others local workers, such as former craftsmen undermined by the development of productive forces.[51] The place of migrants may vary even within industries, perhaps by size or type of firm. In Manila, as discussed in Chapter 9, small subcontractors in the construction industry rely on a pool of circulatory migrants, typically from the foreman's rural district. Small and medium-sized companies delegate recruitment to the foreman, but large contractors find this practice risky in case the foreman and workers develop close ties, which they can prevent by drawing labourers from different areas.

What emerges is a picture of various possibilities, any migration-related division of labour being the outcome of a process of adjustment based on the nature of previous productive relations and the specific needs of capital. But if there is no predetermined pattern, that does not mean migrants are not used to stratify and control the labour force in the interests of accumulation and proletarianisation.

VI. Circulation and the Detailed Division of Labour

The detailed division of labour is the division of work tasks within production. With the transition to capitalist production, its defining characteristic is that workers are separated from the conception and creation of the output, 'stripped of their independence and specialised to such an extent as to be reduced to mere supplementary partial processes'.[52] The role of migration in that process deserves to be stressed.

In agriculture, as in industry, the inflow of migrants has made it easier for landlords and employers to reorganise work tasks, if only because local workers wedded to traditional methods have resisted changes in routine and skill use, often responding to changes by reducing their 'effort bargain', striking or resorting to sabotage. It is also apparent that migrant landholders, being less attached to local farm techniques sometimes evolved over centuries, have been relatively innovative, introducing mechanisation and modern inputs that have drastically altered the division of labour. They in turn may force local landlords into defensive innovations so as to survive.

In urban-industrial areas, growth of capitalist production has tended to occur in new urban areas – and to do so most easily there – rather than in established cities where traditions and guild-like restrictions have impeded progressive changes in the detailed division of labour. New areas initially lack infrastructure and the means of providing even the basic needs of the essentially migrant labour force; this leads to temporary in-migration of those providing some of those needs and to temporary in-migration of workers who have to continue to rely on activities and contributions from relatives in their 'home' areas. But these are mechanisms by which circulation helps in creating an urban-industrial proletariat.

Migration concentrates workers with similar skills, and as capitalist development relies on the concentration of labour power it necessarily involves an 'urban bias', aided by State policies, whether this involves a mass rural-urban relocation of people or a mix of migration and circulation.[53] But most crucially, migration – and perhaps most of all circulation – has weakened certain labour relations impeding changes in the division of labour. Any increase in the detailed division of labour implies restricting workers' subjective involvement in production. If aware of this, workers will reduce work commitment, and if the growing division of labour also reduces potential job mobility, workers will be less inclined to refine skills. Workers experiencing a decline in mobility potential while in a job can be expected to feel a strong sense of deprivation and frustration. As a corollary, migrants will be less affected, be least resistant to changes in productive techniques and, as some evidence suggests, have a greater *belief* in workers' ability to rise in status.[54] Accordingly, employers introducing new techniques entailing a more vertically integrated structure of increasingly 'static' jobs will prefer migrant workers.

However, circular migration is unsatisfactory for employers *to the extent* that the labour supply is liable to be withdrawn at short notice, should incomes fall or type of work deteriorate. And circular migrants may not stay long enough to gain even limited skills to give a reasonable return to employers.[55] They may do so in certain industries, notably construction, and it is in these that most temporary migrants are to be found. Even there, it is doubtful whether use of circular migrants is consistent with a 'cumulative acquisition of skills'.[56] Circulation can facilitate some skill development because the security of rural residence permits a worker to have some commitment to a precarious job, as is the case in construction. But it seems more likely that skill development is limited by circulation, even if migrants return to an industry fairly regularly, as they have done in Manila, examined by Stretton in Chapter 9. A fluctuating labour supply can be expected to encourage a more refined detailed division of labour, so as to use workers with limited skills.

VII. The Inculcation of Tastes, Aspirations and Habits

Like the diversion of the population from agriculture to the towns, non-agricultural migration is a *progressive phenomenon*. It tears the population out of the neglected, backward, history-forgotten remote spots and draws them into the whirlpool of modern social life. It increases literacy among the population, heightens their understanding, and gives them civilised habits and requirements.[57]

Migrants have been agents of change through stimulating the 'taste' for industrial commodities, and various observers have favoured circular migration as a means of getting 'faster development and modernisation'.[58] In helping to homogenise social tastes, they have enlarged the home market, standardising consumption, thus benefiting mass production routines of large-scale industry. Agriculturally, return migrants – or migrants sending alternative consumer goods back to their families – have weakened smallholder production by reducing tolerance for traditional staple diets that were both cheap and relatively available. Once lured into a commercialised diet, such communities adopt new subsistence 'norms' that are hard to reverse.[59]

Remittances have influenced these developments, both by introducing external commodities and by stimulating aspirations. In some circumstances they may have perverse implications. Remittances have sometimes introduced commodities to peasant communities oriented to staple crops, and any subsequent decline in remittances may induce local farmers to shift from staple to cash crops to substitute for the lost monetary income. This seems to have been the case with the shift to copra production in West New Britain, Papua New Guinea, following a decline in migrants' remittances.[60] What such examples suggest is that even where remittances initially slow the commoditisation of production, they stimulate it indirectly, in part by influencing the pattern of consumption. From influencing consumption, they influence production.

The standardisation of 'tastes' extends to cultural matters, encouraging such phenomena as bi-culturalism, where it is likely that a loss of identity would be associated with a passive response to exploitation and oppression. Yet this does foster national integration through homogenising subregional cultures. Arguably, return migrants, having had contact with 'modern' values of smaller family size, also internalise lower fertility norms, thereby reducing population growth in their villages.[61] And, as noted in Chapter 2, in West Java return-migrants have stimulated a desire for formal schooling, which is intrinsically geared to the type of life found outside the villages. This was also observed in a study of return-migration in Nigerian villages, where they not only introduced new crops but contributed to the construction of village schools and health centres.[62]

And yet, most crucially, migrants have been agents for rural proletarianisation through a demonstration effect on the work habits of other workers. In areas previously dominated by pre-capitalist modes of production, compulsion and such devices as head taxes and restrictions on non-wage activities have typically been used to secure an 'unlimited supply' of wage labour, partly because monetary incentives in themselves are ineffectual in such communities. However, such pressure has its costs, and if workers can be induced to respond to 'modest' incentives or out of a desire to acquire more consumer goods, profits rise and the detailed division of labour can be extended more easily, simply because costs of supervision and of coercion are reduced while workers are attuned to a higher effort-bargain. Migrants make that shift in tactics more feasible. In spreading the taste for commodities, they have a demonstration effect on work habits, strengthening the response to monetary incentives and fostering a sense of work regularity, a sense of time in work (a point made famous in a celebrated essay of E.P. Thompson), and a sense of acquisitive individualism.

As long as there is a reasonable chance of realising them,

rising aspirations for 'modern' commodities will encourage workers to become a disciplined, surplus-generating proletariat. But therein lies a basic contradiction. For as a means of proletarianisation the stimulation of tastes and aspirations risks exacerbating the crisis in the labour process. Without suggesting that migrants are revolutionary in themselves, a point to which we will return, the stimulation of unrealisable aspirations can foster a sense of deprivation and frustration uniting workers in opposition to existing class relations. There is another contradictory element, which is that to the extent migrant workers in urban-industrial areas retain rural links they may also retain rural values and lifestyles inimical to effective proletarianisation. This would lead to greater coercive authority being used in the industrial labour process, which has costs, even if migrants accept it.

VIII. Circulation and the Industrial Labour Reserve

Marx described migrants as 'the light infantry of industrial capital', a reserve to be flexibly deployed wherever labour is needed to expand production. The need for a relative surplus population for proletarianisation is considered elsewhere.[63] But basically, the labour reserve can be divided into four components – the 'stagnant', 'floating' and 'latent' categories identified by Marx and what is best described as the 'employed reserve'.[64] Migrants fit into all four but mainly the latter three.

First, the *latent reserve* comprises those in rural areas who are potential migrants and others outside the urban-industrial labour force, such as 'housewives', who would enter it if required. That they are not in the active labour force does not prevent them from having effects associated with a labour reserve, notably helping to reduce urban-industrial wage rates, without imposing costs on the urban-industrial infrastructure in terms of services, housing and related amenities. And, when needed, a latent labour reserve can be converted into a floating reserve. To give a classic example, in early nineteenth-century England the rural population's mobility was restricted by the Speenhamland system of poor relief, maintaining a reserve of impoverished workers in villages and restraining movement into the new industrial towns. When new strata of urban-industrial workers were required, the

1834 Poor Law opened the floodgates of rural emigration by making life so intolerable that rural paupers migrated to any job on offer.[65]

Latent labour reserves exist in smallholding communities experiencing 'contrived stagnation' in the interest of accumulation elsewhere.[66] The classic case of a regressive decay designed to maintain and enlarge a latent labour supply was the creation of 'native reserves' in South Africa from the late nineteenth century onwards.[67] But in modified form this phenomenon has characterised most transitions to industrial capitalism, with a gradual conversion of a latent reserve into a floating or stagnant surplus population. The means by which labour reserve areas for the plantations and mines were created in parts of Tanzania are displayed in Chapter 4, which highlights the legacy of colonial policies and the difficulties of reversing long-term patterns of survival-subsistence among peasants settled in such areas.

The *floating reserve* consists of the open or job-seeking unemployed and those intermittently employed, whose wage labour is interspersed with spells of unemployment or labour force withdrawal. This category encompasses those available to replace wage labourers who are attuned by experience to wage work. Circular migrants are a prominent group in the floating reserve, as are permanent migrants, those such as the *torrantes* in Chile, whose lifestyle is almost nomadic labour. In some cases, too rarely considered, dispossessed peasants move to towns in the wake of changing agrarian relations but remain part of the *rural* labour reserve. Such patterns persist in southern Europe and elsewhere, a good example being the boias-frias in Brazil, as discussed in Chapter 10.[68] These constitute a rural labour force of mainly urban dwellers, highly exploited as seasonal workers on estates and doing casual urban jobs at other times of the year. Many come from families dispossessed of agricultural land in the wake of a shift from subsistence to export-oriented crops that, with accompanying technological changes, increased the seasonality of labour requirements.[69]

Some observers have argued that circulation is no longer viable once urban unemployment emerges, because migrants have to cling to a job once they have obtained one.[70] There may well be some change in the pattern, with wives and children visiting the urban-industrial area rather than the male migrant worker returning home periodically. But the persistence of circulation reflects the structure and nature of the urban or other wage labour market, in which migrant workers are often preferred to the urban unemployed, on grounds of familiarity, exploitability and even intentional stratification of the labour force. In short, urban unemployment does not preclude labour circulation. Indeed, in some circumstances employers will institutionalise labour instability by allowing prolonged leave, in return for a commitment to return, or by locking the migrant worker in a cycle of indebtedness. In Peru, the form of debt recruitment (*enganche*) involving cash advances to migrants has been only one extreme form of this practice.

The *employed labour reserve* is also strongly related to circular migration. This consists of extra workers hired where the scale of production and detailed division of labour allow a complementarity between the mass of workers but where the absence of just a few can affect the productivity of all. In eras of proto-proletarianisation, when wage labour commitment is limited, the employment of a reserve can be used to compensate for high absenteeism and labour turnover or erratic work intensity on the job. Indeed, pools of surplus workers may be hired for a nominal fixed cost, being paid mainly on a piece-rate basis, so earning little or nothing if 'permanent' workers are on the job or during slack business periods. In large enterprises such surplus workers may be employed on a temporary, probationary basis for many months or even years before being shifted into regular posts. In the interim, they are subject to a gradual induction process of proletarianisation, while visibly posing as a threat to other workers' jobs and incomes.

Migrants in this reserve are liable to retain links with rural areas, from which they receive a 'subsidy' and which they visit as a respite from the life of insecurity to which they are exposed. The long period of induction may weaken those links or, if not, enable employers a 'weed out' those committed to industrial wage labour. This was a feature of the sugar factory workforce in Gujarat.[71] There, many more seasonal migrants were hired than could be fully employed, at little extra cost; the surplus, all desperate for income, helped the *mukadams* increase their authority and allowed flexible adjustments to production schedules. In the textile industry in Bombay, high absenteeism (no doubt due to low wages and poor work conditions) has led to the practice of keeping a 'Badli pool' of surplus workers, accounting for perhaps 20 per cent of total employment.[72] Most are migrants with ties with their villages, returning once or more a year.[73]

Finally, there is the *stagnant reserve*, in which migrants can be expected to be less prominent. This encompasses the endemically unemployed, those reduced to a state of being unable to retain work, and those perceived as or actually 'unemployable' (in the short-run), doing what in Jamaica is aptly called 'scuffling'. This is the lumpenproletariat, in part comprising those unable to come to terms with new social and material relations, forced by repeated failure in the labour market into vagabondage, prostitution, crime, alcoholism, and long-term social illnesses. Many are part of the surplus population but scarcely part of the labour reserve.

Some have claimed that migrants make up a large part of this group, using such epithets as 'marginal mass' to describe them.[74] However, there are good reasons for supposing that most migrants avoid this category, reasons making them relatively exploitable and thus relatively likely to be employed. Often migrants are 'superexploited', paid wages below the cost of reproducing labour power, partly because they are single or unaccompanied married individuals – as in the urban areas of northern India examined in Chapter 8 – and partly because they are expected to get part of their subsistence from rural family production. Highlighted in southern Africa, this factor has been of widespread significance.[75] It has been prominent even where circular migration has originated as a means of realising surplus for landlords.

With superexploitation the migrant is paid just enough to survive the period of wage labour.[76] Some argue that for this to persist, migration must be temporary.[77] But as long as the migrant is insecure and retains rural ties, the duration of migration has no limit. Indeed, superexploitation could persist through support from relatives working in the ubiquitous urban informal sector. But whether at the expense of the rural or urban poor, the process is unstable. First, it prevents the rural community from fulfilling its role of providing social security for the old and sick.[78] It also undermines the rural economic base of reproduction and accumulation by withdrawing surplus. With the outflow, rural incomes will fall to the point that mass migration can be expected despite a lack of urban opportunities. More of the latent reserve will join the active surplus population, and the pool of urban unemployed may grow beyond that needed as a labour reserve, and pose a threat to the process of accumulation. But that does not mean migrants themselves will be at the forefront of social unrest.

Historically, migrants have been exploitable because they are not integrated into urban society, often lacking work permits or social security cards and in a weak bargaining position. For example, migrants in Rio de Janeiro receive few social benefits because they have no work cards, for which they need a birth certificate, usually unknown in rural areas; some employers have insisted on workers *not* having a work permit so as to avoid paying social security contributions.[79] Elsewhere, migrants have been hired as pseudo-apprentices.[80] Ignorant and in a precarious position, they have received little or nothing – some even paying for the privilege – and have been expected to receive subsistence from rural or urban relatives.

Migrants have relatively low wage aspirations and expectations, partly due to their age, schooling and family status, but also because their sense of deprivation reflects rural incomes and work intensity whereas the aspirations of urban workers are in terms of the incomes of the urban labour aristocracy and bureaucracy. There is some evidence that migrants not only take low-income jobs but avoid lengthy unemployment through their lower aspirations and expectations.[81] Indeed, temporary migrants may find work even more readily than other migrants, as observed in Jakarta in Chapter 2. In a recent migration survey in Malaysia it was found that almost all migrants had found work within a month of arrival and had low aspirations that made them an exploitable labour supply in many wage jobs that were by no means marginal 'informal sector' activities.[82] There are selectivity problems in interpreting the available data, but it cannot be presumed that high urban unemployment will deter rural-urban migration; for many urban jobs urban residents may be virtually excluded.

IX. Circulation and the International Division of Labour

International labour circulation is closely linked to the changing international division of labour, as is the process of internal labour circulation. Indeed, it is only on practical grounds that one could conceivably justify treating internal population mobility separately from international movements. The absurdity of the traditional research boundary can be simply illustrated by the example of West Africa, where international migration was vastly increased by the contrived fragmentation of nation states that accompanied decolonisation.

Migrant workers from the 'peripheral' low-income countries who have gone to the advanced capitalist economies, principally Western Europe, North America, Australia and South Africa, have represented a massive labour reserve. In their form as 'international labour circulants', they have provided a low-cost labour supply, the State in the country of immigration having no costs of labour reproduction to bear. Being vulnerable as aliens and ignorant of their rights as citizens, if they have had any, they have represented a highly exploitable labour supply, workers who could be used to depress wages (through a resignation to accept lower wages and through exerting pressure on average wage rates); they have facilitated an increase in the detailed and social division of labour and helped perpetuate and accentuate a stratified labour force in very much the same ways as with internal labour circulation.[83]

Migrants who have settled on a long-term or permanent basis have remained vulnerable, especially to the extent their aspirations and expectations were formed before they left their village or town in their country of origin. Nevertheless, although often resented by other workers as a perceived threat to their jobs and bargaining position, they have developed links with local communities and some identity with the class aspirations of the local working class.

International circulants are both more vulnerable and more oriented to the 'instrumentability' of work, so that they can be expected to experience less sense of relative deprivation in low-paid, narrow, static jobs. In effect, they are more likely to remain uninterested, in an active way, in efforts to secure long-term improvements in working conditions, fringe benefits and so on.[84] Their lack of political integration can only accentuate their exploitation.

In the countries from which the circulants originate and to which they return, international labour circulation has helped in the expansion of international capital by stimulating the 'taste' for imported goods, even in villages that would otherwise be regarded as isolated from the national mainstream economy, let alone the international market. And by the extensive flow of remittances they have helped commoditise many rural areas. In that regard, it is of interest to note Swindell's account in Chapter 5 of certain patterns of population mobility in West Africa, where commodity exchange was restricted by the lack of legitimate currency as an accepted medium of exchange. In recent years, remittances from international migrants – particularly from those intending to return and most of all when they return – have constituted a major source of income for certain rural areas of low-income countries.[85] As such, they have spurred changes in productive relationships, in some places helped create a viable market in land – so essential for the transition from a peasant economy to one in which there is accumulation and internal class differentation – and even enabled some countries to finance a basic change in their development strategy.[86] Circulation has also encouraged the spread of certain work habits and aspirations, through return-migrants having been habituated to disciplined (proletarianised) wage labour abroad. And the remittances have been used by those able to do so to expand production through the use of more wage labour. Finally, as the differentials between rural incomes in those countries and incomes in even the fairly low-wage sectors of the industrialised countries have been much greater than those between rural and urban-industrial areas of the industrialising economies, scope for class differentiating tendencies through the mechanism of remittances has been much greater than from internal labour circulation.

International labour circulation might be expected to reduce unemployment and 'underemployment' in low-income countries. This has been perceived in some countries, such as Jordan, Greece and some in North Africa.[87] However, it is too facile to trace a straight link between the extent of emigration and the level of unemployment. Just as in the case of internal labour circulation, the selectivity of out-migration may have an adverse effect on the productivity of household units, obliging other members to enter the wage labour market. The much mooted 'brain drain' has reportedly created structural unemployment of a particular type, and loss of skilled manual workers has even impeded expansion of key industries required to play a prominent part in development strategies.[88]

In some countries, emigration has created an absolute labour shortage, as with the temporary movement of fishermen and farmers from the northern states of Malaysia to work in the construction industry in Singapore. Often this type of typically temporary movement has set off a process of migration from lower-income countries, as in the Malaysian case where mostly illegal immigrants from Indonesia have gone to work on rubber and palm-oil estates. Or it has strengthened the pattern of labour circulation, as rural workers have taken jobs in the cities vacated by the emigrants. Such replacement migration has been particularly conspicuous in Jordan, from which many workers have gone to Saudi Arabia; Egyptians, Syrians and Pakistanis have joined internal migrants in taking urban jobs, while some of those from those other countries have taken agricultural jobs left by the rural-urban migrants.[89] Similarly, seasonal migrants from Mali have been going to work in the millet fields of Mauritania to replace the migrants who go to France.[90] In sum, there is a pattern of replacement migration, made up of a mixture of short-term circulation and longer-term migration.

In that context, the most pertinent question concerns the consequences of the depression in industrialised countries. In previous periods of recession, international migrants in many of the industrialised countries were treated as, and behaved as, a classic floating labour reserve; by various devices, they were 'sent home', while the inflow was curtailed by legislation and more strict application of rules on entry permits and the like. But the depression of the early 1980s came after a protracted period of prosperity and high levels of employment. During that period many migration streams from low-income economies had resulted in established communities in which migrants could expect income support in times of hardship, and more crucially still, many of the temporary international migrants in countries such as the Federal Republic of Germany had acquired rights to welfare and unemployment benefits. Consequently, even where they lost their jobs, the prospect of losing those benefits and being unable to return if they left the country have surely made migrants more reluctant to respond in the way they had in previous recessions, when international migration flows were less tightly regulated.[91] In earlier recessions, the full rise in unemployment had been concealed through the exodus of many of the principal victims to their countries of origin, through their non-return from visits home, and through the non-arrival of potential migrants. Probably this change has been a factor raising open unemployment in industrialised countries relative to that in some low-income countries. With the traditional international division of labour, and with low-income countries providing a floating labour reserve of international circulants, the worst signs of recessions were expected to show up in the labour markets of labour reserve countries, relieving the advanced industrialised countries of some of the stress associated with recessions. This may no longer hold.

However, in many low-income countries the growing labour force made emigration a potential mechanism to limit the rise in unemployment. Limiting migration opportunities may, therefore, have had a serious adverse impact in some labour-exporting countries. Within such countries, one can only speculate on the tensions created by the curtailment of migration opportunities and of remittances. The survival mechanisms of petty producers, and the links between international crises and transformations of productive relations in 'peripheral' economies, as well as the accumulation-decumulation process in such areas, should be major fields of research. One might surmise that if circulation is a progressive phenomenon in general, its restriction would encourage stagnation or even regression. But one should resist the temptation to perceive it in that way. There are 'ratchet effects', in that once traditional social relations of production have had their perceived legitimacy eroded they cannot be restored, or at least not without tremendous cost to the potential beneficiaries and not without serious risk to their ability to acquire surplus.[92]

A second point to bear in mind is that restricting international circulation may represent a form of 'delinking', enabling 'peripheral' economies to achieve a greater degree of indigenous capital accumulation and retention of surplus. A third factor is that the effects will depend in part on the extent of movement. Where a few return-migrants are involved, the impact on the area's social relationships and productive system is likely to be non-existent, and those returning are likely to conform to the rules set out by the local elite or abandon their links altogether if they are unprepared to accept the old way of life. But where a sizeable number is involved collective action or pressures may force changes that lead to new production relations.

Finally, a fourth crucial aspect is that the effects will depend in part on whether the migration had originated in a heavily labour surplus area or from one in which there were seasonal, structural or chronic labour shortages. One may hazard the guess that the curtailment of international circulation has had a series of linked effects that have left many of the poorer rural communities previously dependent on local circulation increasingly unable to survive by that means. The difficulty of empirically tracing those links needs to be overcome.

X. Concluding Remarks

As with most forms of migration, circulation is a progressive phenomenon in the sense that it undermines previous forms of oppression and exploitation while facilitating the growth of new forms. But migrant labourers are typically a highly vulnerable group exposed to diverse abuses and severe exploitation without recourse to protective legislation or effective countervailing power. Unionisation of migratory workers is rarely conceivable, and there have been ample instances of use of migrants, as strike-breakers or as workers ignorant of legitimate rights, to under-mine the claims of those pressing for those rights. One cannot be too sanguine about the prospects of changing that pattern. Too often, the perceived interests of employers, unions and govern-ments have been hostile to those of migrant workers, resented or exploited by a system of employment relying on their existence. In such circumstances effective protective legislation is unlikely. This makes it even more essential to engender critical analysis of their plight.

Contrary to the hopes of such observers as Fanon, migrants have proved the least revolutionary element of the emerging working class.[93] For migrants the move itself is in a personal sense revolutionary, whereas the exploitation of urban, or even rural, wage labour, with its relative freedoms, is often regarded in the context of escape from patriarchal, feudal or other custom-bound constraints. Their reference group continues to be the village population they leave behind, not the urban middle class to which they might otherwise aspire and also resent; this atavism is most likely when short-term circulation is involved.

However, even there contradictions arise. First, those mi-grants forced by economic crises to return to their 'home' areas are marginal there, separated from the social nexus and very likely to challenge social and work relations of production there, whatever those may be. Second, there is the 'second generation' effect. Wherever migrants settle and raise their children the latter will grow up in conditions of superexploitation and relative deprivation but without the sense of potential mobility experienced by their parents. They will then be more openly discontented. Third, though migrants may have low unemployment, their presence may swell the open unemployed and lumpenproletariat by displacing others. This may create a mass of urban unemployed, without rural roots to placate them.

Arguably, a protracted period of dislocation precedes proletarianisation. But this fosters a crisis if the growth of a 'marginalised' population can be pacified only with increasing brutality or transfers. Such a surplus population, without access to means of production or a regular subsistence income, threatens the fabric of accumulation, and may act as a vanguard of class opposition. Whether the class position of this mass of workers justifies optimism for effective opposition to exploitation and degradation is a matter of some importance.

Notes

1. A more taxonomic conceptualisation is suggested elsewhere. G. Standing: *Conceptualising territorial mobility in low-income countries* (Geneva, ILO, 1982). Some define circulation very broadly to include commuting, visits to relatives and even holiday trips. See, e.g., M. Chapman: 'Circulation', in J.A. Ross (ed.): *International encyclopaedia of population* (New York, Doubleday, 1982).

2. G. Falabella: 'The formation and development of a rural proletarian stratum: The case of the Chilean torrante', in A. Bhaduri and M.A. Rahman (eds.): *Studies in rural participation* (New Delhi, Oxford and IBH Publishing Co., 1982), pp. 194–213.

3. To be strictly correct, for full proletarianisation, the 'freedom' from the means of production should be extended to other aspects of the production process, such as raw materials and output. For a more detailed discussion, see G. Standing: *A labour status approach to labour statistics* (Geneva, ILO, 1983; mimeographed World Employment Programme research working paper).

4. To anticipate, by contradictory is meant a form of behaviour that is initiated to achieve one objective but which leads to quite different outcomes that undermine the basis of that objective.

5. This is implicit in one of the finest analyses of the creation of an industrial proletariat. E.P. Thompson: *The making of the English working class* (Harmondsworth, Penguin, 1968).

6. This role of temporary migration has been noted in several studies. See, for example, J. Grant and M. Zeleniez: 'Changing patterns of wage labour migration in the Kilenge area of Papua New Guinea', in *International Migration Review*, Summer 1980, vol. 14, no. 2, pp. 228-9.

7. A striking example is in Rajasthan, India, where no less than 86 different types of local tax were imposed. R. Pande: *Agrarian movement in Rajasthan* (Delhi, University Publishers, 1975), p. 22. It seems reasonable to suppose that such complex systems arise because the appropriators of surplus wish to extract as much of the surplus as possible, which was most effectively achieved through a series of layers of demands, each of which by itself was too small to cause mass resistance or permanent flight.

8. See, e.g., R.L. Curtain: 'Migration in Papua New Guinea: The role of the peasant household in a strategy of survival', in G.W. Jones and H.V. Richter (eds.): *Population mobility and development: South east Asia and the Pacific*, Development Studies Centre Monograph No. 27, (Canberra, Australian National University, 1981), p. 198.

9. J.S. Migdal: *Peasants, politics and revolution: Pressures towards political and social change in the Third World* (Princeton, Princeton University Press, 1974), pp. 118-21.

10. M.K. Pandhe (ed.): *Bonded labour in India* (Calcutta, Indian School of Social Sciences, 1976), p. 52.

11. P. Phongpaichit: *From peasant girls to Bangkok masseuses*, Women, Work and Development No. 2 (Geneva, ILO, 1982).

12. See, e.g., L. Arizpe: 'Relay migration and the survival of the peasant household', in J. Balán: *Why people move: Comparative perspectives on the dynamics of internal migration* (Paris, UNESCO, 1981), pp. 187-210. This is an empirical study of circulation from two villages in Mexico.

13. G.A. Smith: 'Socio-economic differentiation and relations of production among rural-based petty producers in central Peru, 1880-1970', in *Journal of Peasant Studies*, 1979, vol. 6, no. 3, pp. 286-310.

14. J.D. Powell: 'Venezuela: The peasant union movement', in H.A. Landsberger (ed.): *Latin American peasant movements* (Ithaca, New York, Cornell University Press, 1969), p. 83.

15. One significant change is from a situation in which most members of the peasant or servant family are obliged to provide labour services to where only one member is expected to do so. This might occur if the landlord's labour needs declined, or if he wished to reduce his reciprocal 'patronage' obligations. The family unit would typically be tied to the landlord through debt, making family migration impractical, except as a risky act of desperate flight. But the change does allow an increase in temporary migration by family members. For a brilliant empirical study dealing with this type of issue in the Indian context, see J. Breman: *Patronage and exploitation: Changing agrarian relations in south Gujarat, India* (Berkeley, University of California Press, 1974), especially pp. 187-95.

16. J. Nelson: 'Sojourners versus new urbanites: Causes and consequences of temporary versus permanent cityward migration in developing countries', in *Economic Development and Cultural Change*, 1976, vol. 24, no. 4, pp. 721-57.

17. B. Nietschmann: 'Ecological change, inflation and migration in the Far West Caribbean', in *The Geographical Review*, 1979, vol. 69, no. 1, pp. 1-24.

18. Too many studies of circulation that have stressed its 'positive' nature have neglected the impact on the 'women left behind'. For a valuable study done for the ILO, see E. Gordon: 'An analysis of the impact of labour migration on the lives of women in Lesotho', in *Journal of Development Studies*, April 1981, vol. 17, no. 3, pp. 54-76. On the possible impact on children and their work patterns, see G. Rodgers and G. Standing (eds.): *Child work, poverty and underdevelopment* (Geneva, ILO, 1981).

19. M. Lipton: 'Migration from rural areas of poor countries: The impact on rural productivity and income distribution', in *World Development*, January 1980, vol. 8, no. 1, p. 4.

20. G. Standing: *Income transfers and remittances: A module for migration surveys* (Geneva, ILO, 1982).

21. See, e.g., J. Connell: 'Migration, remittances and rural development in the South Pacific', in Jones and Richter 1981, pp. 229–55.

22. A.R. Waters: 'Migration, remittances and the cash constraint in African smallholder economic development', in *Oxford Economic Papers*, November 1973, vol. 25, no. 3, pp. 435-54.

23. A. Adepoju: 'Rural-urban socio-economic links: An example of migrants in South-west Nigeria', in S. Amin (ed.): *Modern migrations in West Africa* (Oxford, Oxford University Press, 1974), p. 135.

24. See, e.g. L. Cliffe: 'Labour migration and peasant differentiation: Zambian experiences', in *Journal of Peasant Studies*, April 1978, vol. 5, no. 3, pp. 332-3; E.P. Skinner: 'Labour migration and its relationship to socio-cultural change in Mossi society', in *Africa*, October 1960, vol. 30, pp. 373-401. On similar disintegration in Pacific economies, see, e.g., H.C. Brookfield: 'Intensification and disintensification in Pacific agriculture', in *Pacific Viewpoint*, 1972, vol. 13, no. 1, pp. 30-48.

25. K. Finkler: 'From sharecroppers to entrepreneurs: Peasant household production strategies in the ejido system of Mexico', in *Economic Development and Cultural Change*, October 1978, vol. 27, no. 1, pp. 103-20.

26. This was what Lenin observed in late-nineteenth-century Russia – V.I. Lenin: *The development of capitalism in Russia* (Moscow, International Publishers, 1960), pp. 182-3.

27. A.S. Oberai and H.K. Manmohan Singh: *Causes and consequences of internal migration: A study in the Indian Punjab* (ILO, forthcoming).

28. P. Peek and P. Antolinez: *Labour migration in the Sierra of Ecuador: Causes and incidence* (Geneva, ILO, August 1980; mimeographed World Employment Programme research working paper; restricted); P. Peek and G. Standing (eds.): *State policies and migration: Studies in Latin America and the Caribbean* (London, Croom Helm, 1982).

29. R.W. Wilke: 'Towards a behavioural model of peasant migration: An Argentine case study of spatial behaviour by social class level', in R.N. Thomas (ed.): *Population dynamics of Latin America: A review and bibliography* (Massachusetts, University of Massachusetts Press, 1971).

30. G. Standing: 'Migration and modes of exploitation: Social origins of immobility and mobility', in *Journal of Peasant Studies*, January 1981, vol. 8, no. 2, pp. 173-211. Migration, circulation and rebellion of one kind or another are alternative reactions to adversity. For peasants, when would circulation be the most likely response? First, the idea of migrating must be recognised as an acceptable response to adversity or frustrated aspirations. Second, it will be more likely if there is little class consciousness of oppression and exploitation, merely a general feeling of despair or deprivation. Collective action is more likely if peasants identify their oppression as unjust and not inevitable, which means typically that some reciprocal right will have been violated to cause a sense of social deprivation, or that they are unable to satisfy a traditional level of subsistence. The third condition favouring circulation or migration is that the rural poor must perceive little chance of collective action being successful. Fourth, circulation will be more likely than long-term or permanent out-migration if the poor can retain rights to land and other means of production during their absence.

31. It is worth noting that methodologically, cross-sectional data make it hard to state unequivocally that specific groups have high propensities to move, partly because they have only identified individual moves, partly because data on class status are not collected, and partly because a change of class status may well precede actual migration.

32. M.T. Cain: 'The household life-cycle and economic mobility in rural Bangladesh', in *Population and Development Review*, September 1978, vol. 4, no. 3, pp. 421-38.

33. See, e.g., B. Dasgupta: 'New technology and agricultural labourers in India', in S. Hirashima (ed.): *Hired labour in rural Asia* (Tokyo, Institute of Developing Economies, 1977), p. 21.

34. A related distinction can be made between 'internal peasants' and 'external peasants' – C. Kay: 'Agrarian change and migration in Chile', in P. Peek and G. Standing (eds.), *State policies and migration* (London, Croom Helm, 1982), pp. 35-80.

35. V.I. Lenin, *The development of capitalism in Russia* – see especially the Preface to the second (1908) edition.

36. See, e.g., J.C. Scott: *The moral economy of the peasant: Rebellion and subsistence in South-East Asia* (New Haven and London, Yale University Press, 1976).

37. This is not the same as class consciousness, whereby the proletariat identifies itself as a 'class for itself'.

38. For example, J. Breman: 'Seasonal migration and co-operative capitalism: The crushing of cane and of labour by the sugar factories of Bardoli, South Gujarat', in *Journal of Peasant Studies*, October 1978, vol. 6, nos. 1 and 2, pp. 41-70, and January 1979, pp. 168-209.

39. See, e.g., M. Bellwinkel: 'Rajasthani contract labour in Delhi: A case study of the relationship between company, middleman and worker', in *Sociological Bulletin*, 1973, vol. 22, pp. 78-97. In Kuala Lumpur in 1982-3 it was widely recognised that many construction workers were short-term illegal immigrants from Thailand and Indonesia.

40. Breman, 1974, p. 104. With the deductions of advances and the interest and their living expense payments, they have often had little to receive. Incidentally, to refer to such mechanisms as a labour 'contract' is mischievous; there is no redress before the law, and the exploitation is based on power, control and ignorance.

41. Breman, 1979, p. 185.

42. This has sometimes led to changes in inheritance customs, as in central Peru – Smith, 1979, p. 299. Research in 1982 in Malaysian kampongs affected by heavy short-term male out-migration suggested that Muslim inheritance customs had been modified in some places to give equal or fairer shares to women. The proportion of work done by women had increased in recent years.

43. See, e.g., N-K. Plange: ' "Opportunity cost" and labour migration: A misinterpretation of proletarianisation in northern Ghana', in *Journal of Modern African Studies*, December 1979, vol. 17, no. 4, pp. 655–76; Cliffe, 1978; P. Raikes: 'Rural differentiation and class formation in Tanzania', in *Journal of Peasant Studies*, April 1978, vol. 5, no. 3, pp. 308-10; Gordon, 1981.

44. See, e.g., N.E. Whitten: 'Jungle Quechua ethnicity: An Ecuadorian case study', in H.I. Safa and B.M. DuToit (eds.): *Migration and development: Implications for ethnic identity and political conflict* (Paris, Mouton, 1974), p. 163; P. Peek and P. Antolinez: 'Migration and the urban labour market: The case of San Salvador', in *World Development*, April 1977, vol. 5, no. 4, pp. 291-302.

45. See also J. Laite: *Industrial development and migrant labour* (Manchester, Manchester University Press, 1981), p. 45.

46. See, e.g., J.A. Kirchner: *Sugar and seasonal labour migration: The case of Tucuman, Argentina*, Research Paper No. 192 (Chicago, University of Chicago, Department of Geography, 1980), p. 6.

47. D. Raczynski: 'Migration, mobility and occupational achievement: The

case of Santiago, Chile', in *International Migration Review*, Summer 1972, vol. 6, no. 2, p. 196.

48. See also K. Swindell: *The Strange farmers of The Gambia: A study in the redistribution of African population*, Monograph No. 15 (Swansea, Centre for Development Studies, 1981), pp. 63-81.

49. Smith, 1979, p. 309.

50. Breman, 1979, pp. 186-7.

51. This is the classic case. E.J. Hobsbawm: 'The labour aristocracy in 19th-century Britain', in E.J. Hobsbawm: *Labouring men: Studies in the history of labour* (London, Weidenfeld and Nicolson, 1964).

52. K. Marx: *Capital* (New York, International Publishers, 1967), vol. I, p. 338.

53. See Peek and Standing, 1982 for analyses of such policies.

54. For instance, a study in a Paris car factory found Breton migrants had such beliefs much more than city-born workers – A. Touraine and O. Ragazzi: *Ouvrier d'origine agricole* (Paris, L'Ecole des hautes études, 1961).

55. For example, Textor's early study of pedicab drivers in Bangkok found very few learned new skills during their stays in the city – R.B. Textor: 'The northeast samlor driver in Bangkok', in UNESCO: *The social implications of industrialisation and urbanisation* (Calcutta, UNESCO, 1956).

56. M. Chapman: 'Policy implications of circulation: Some answers from the grassroots', in Jones and Richter, 1981, p. 78. This conclusion is drawn from Alan Stretton's work in Manila. In five Malaysian kampongs in April 1982, all with heavy temporary out-migration of men into construction jobs, all village headmen were convinced that most workers returned having gained no skills. Data from the pilot household survey supported that view.

57. Lenin, 1960, p. 576.

58. S. Goldstein: *Circulation in the context of total mobility in Southeast Asia* (Honolulu, Papers of the East-West Population Institute, No. 53, August 1978), p. 45; G. Hugo: *Population mobility in West Java* (Yogyakarta, Gadjah Mada University Press, 1978).

59. Anecdotally, in research in Guyana in 1977-8 it intrigued me that villages had grown accustomed to imported condensed milk, the taste for which had apparently been spread by return migrants; a government attempt to expand dairy farming foundered because of the unwillingness of consumers to shift back to ordinary milk.

60. J. Grant and M. Zelenietz: 'Changing patterns of wage labour migration in the Kilenge area of Papua New Guinea' (Toronto, 1979; mimeographed).

61. See, e.g., A. Simmons, S.D. Briguets and A.A. Laguian: *Social change and internal migration: A review of research findings from Africa, Asia and Latin America* (Ottawa, International Development Research Centre, 1977).

62. Adepoju, 1974.

63. Standing, 1981.

64. For Marx's categories, see *Capital* vol. III, pp. 640-2.

65. E.J. Hobsbawm: *The age of revolution: 1789-1848* (London, Abacus, 1977), p. 188.

66. This is the pivot of my analysis of migration in Guyana – G. Standing: 'Contrived stagnation, migration and the state in Guyana', in Peek and Standing, 1982, pp. 251-319.

67. See, e.g., B. Magubane: 'The "native reserves" (Bantustans) and the role of the migrant labour system in the political economy of South Africa', in Safa and Du Toit, 1975, pp. 225-67.

68. See also, among others, D. Goodman and M. Redclift: 'The Boias-Frias:

Rural proletarianisation and urban marginality in Brazil', in *International Journal of Urban and Regional Research*, 1977, vol. 1, no. 2, pp. 248-64. Similar groups exist in other parts of Latin America. In Chile suburban communities of migrant labourers have greatly expanded in recent years, notably in the export-oriented fruit-growing regions, according to Rigoberto Rivera (personal communication).

69. W.S. Saint: 'The wages of modernisation: A review of the literature on temporary labour arrangements in Brazilian agriculture', in *Latin American Research Review*, 1981, vol. 16 no. 3, p. 100.

70. A. Gilbert and J. Guglar: *Cities, poverty and development: Urbanisation in the Third World* (Oxford, Oxford University Press, 1982), p. 82.

71. Breman, 1979.

72. Ambekar Institute for Labour Studies: *An inquiry into the effects of demographic characteristics of work behaviour* (Bombay, ILO, 1980; mimeo.).

73. In Kingston, Jamaica, in 1974 I found one multinational with average daily absenteeism of about 20 per cent, for which account had been taken through the hiring of probationary workers, most being migrants – G. Standing: *Unemployment and female labour* (London, Macmillan for the International Labour Organisation, 1981).

74. See, among others, A. Quijano: 'The marginal pole of the economy and the marginalised labour force', in *Economy and Society*, November 1974, vol. 3, no. 3, pp. 393-428; A.G. Frank: *Capitalism and underdevelopment in Latin America* (New York, Monthly Review Press, 1969). One analysis described migrants as 'a large lumpenproletariat', claiming that 'the mass of rural migrants is not absorbed into urban-industrial employment' – Safa, in introduction to Safa and Du Toit, 1975, p. 6.

75. H. Wolpe: 'Capitalism and cheap labour power in South Africa', in *Economy and Society*, 1972, vol. 1, no. 2, p. 434; M. Legassick and H. Wolpe: 'The Bantustans and capital accumulation in South Africa', in *Review of African Political Economy*, September-December 1976, no. 7, pp. 87-102. This was even the rule of wage policy in the Solomon Islands.

76. This wage Meillassoux called 'salaire d'appoint', labelling the difference between that and the cost of reproducing labour power as interest ('rente de travail') – C. Meillassoux: *Femmes, greniers et capitaux* (Paris, Maspero, 1975).

77. T.J. Gerold-Scheepers and W. van Binsbergen: 'Marxist and non-Marxist approaches to migration in Tropical Africa', in W. van Binsbergen and H.A. Meilink (eds.): *Migration and the transformation of modern African society, African perspectives*, No. 1 (Leiden, Afrika-Studiecentrum, 1979), p. 26.

78. D. Clarke: 'Social security and age subsistence: Parts of the predicament in Zimbabwe', in *South African Labour Bulletin*, 1977, vol. 3, no. 5.

79. J.E. Perlman: *The myth of marginality: Urban poverty and politics in Rio de Janeiro* (Berkeley, University of California Press, 1976), p. 158.

80. See, among others, E. le Bris: 'Migration and the decline of a densely populated rural area: The case of Vo Koutime in Southeast Togo', in Binsbergen and Meilink, 1979, p. 122.

81. See, e.g., G. Standing: 'Aspiration, wages, migration and urban unemployment', in *Journal of Development Studies*, January 1978, vol. 14, no. 2, pp. 232-48.

82. G. Standing: *Migration in Peninsular Malaysia* (Kuala Lumpur, ILO-EPU, 1983).

83. The classic historical case of the inter-relationships between international migration and the changing division of labour in industrial production is the USA.

84. Piore argued that migrants with short time-horizons would feel they have less to lose from joining strikes; the opposite seems much more likely, for they

would fear deportation, victimisation, and so on – M.J. Piore: *Birds of passage: Migrant labour and industrial society* (Cambridge, Cambridge University Press, 1979), p. 113.

85. See, among others, I. Gilani, M.F. Khan and M. Iqbal: *Labour migration from Pakistan to the Middle East and its impact on the domestic economy* (Washington, DC, IBRD, 1981); C. Murray: *Families divided: The impact of migrant labour in Lesotho* (Cambridge, Cambridge University Press, 1981).

86. C.W. Stahl: 'Labour emigration and economic development', in *International Labour Review*, December 1978, vol. 116, no. 4, pp. 869-99. In Upper Volta, the Yemen Arab Republic and Jordan, for example, international remittances have covered over a third of all imports and been equal to over 10 per cent of the gross national product. It has been estimated that in 1978 all international remittances associated with migration amounted to about US$ 24 billion – G. Swamy: *International migrant workers' remittances: Issues and prospects*, IBRD Staff Working Paper No. 481 (Washington, DC, World Bank, 1981).

87. See, e.g., F.X. Kirwan: 'The impact of labour migration on the Jordanian economy', in *International Migration Review*, Winter 1981, vol. 15, no. 4, pp. 671-95; D.G. Papademetriou: 'European labour migration: Consequences for the countries of worker origin', in *International Studies Quarterly*, September 1978, vol. 22, no. 3, pp. 377-408.

88. See, among others, W. Glaser: *The brain drain: Emigration and return* (Oxford, Pergamon Press, 1978).

89. I. Sirageldin, J. Socknat, S. Birks, B. Li, and C. Sinclair: *Manpower and international labour migration in the Middle East and North Africa* (Washington, DC, IBRD, 1982).

90. E. Dussauze-Ingrand: 'L'émigration Sarakollaise du Guidimaka vers la France', in Amin, 1974, pp. 239-57.

91. An irony of tighter controls is surely that they make it more likely that the migrant labour supply will not fall as much when excess supply is greatest.

92. This theme is one brilliantly suggested by Barrington Moore and Habermas in their respective ways – B. Moore: *Injustice: The social bases of obedience and revolt* (London, Macmillan, 1978); J. Habermas: *Legitimation crisis* (London, Heinemann, 1976); see also T. Gurr: *Why men rebel* (Princeton, Princeton University Press, 1970).

93. For Fanon's view, see F. Fanon: *The wretched of the earth* (London, MacGildoon and Kee, 1965) p. 104. Hobsbawm suggested that rural migrants in Latin American cities would not identify with working-class politics but would follow a populist leader, showing the pervasive influence of their experience of patronage and personal dependence – E.J. Hobsbawm: 'Peasants and rural migrants in politics', in C. Veliz (ed.): *The politics of conformity in Latin America* (London, Oxford University Press, 1967), pp. 60-1.

2
Structural Change and Labour Mobility in Rural Java

GRAEME HUGO

I. Introduction

In a paper entitled 'Movement of people within Java' published in 1916, Meijer-Ranneft stressed the critical significance of structural changes wrought by Netherlands colonial exploitation in explaining population movements in rural Java.[1] He showed how the transformation of Java's social, economic and political structure under the impact of Netherlands colonisation, which had reached unprecedented scale and intensity at the time at which he wrote, reshaped the scale, nature and impact of contemporary population mobility. Half a century later, the scale and pace of structural change in rural Java has been no less dramatic. Indeed the 1970s was a decade of enormous change in rural Java. It encompassed the introduction and rapid spread of high-yielding varieties of rice and associated inputs of fertiliser, pesticide and machines; major changes in the organisation of labour and patterns of access to employment in agriculture; a period of harvest failure more widespread than at any time since the expulsion of the Netherlanders; massive improvements in transport and a reduction in geographical isolation; unprecedented penetration of rural areas by consumer goods and pressures; major attempts by the national government to initiate rural development via a series of integrated five-year plans; and large increases in government expenditure from foreign exchange surpluses from oil and gas exports. Associated with these changes have been significant social changes and shifts in power relationships within Java's villages. Patterns of population mobility in rural Java have also undergone dramatic change, but there have been few attempts to build upon Meijer-Ranneft's work and investigate the complex interactive relationship between the transformation of population movement patterns and contemporary changes in rural society.

The aim of this paper is to review some of the major structural changes that have occurred in Java in the last decade and explore the ways in which they have reshaped patterns of population movement. However, an attempt is also made to examine the impact this movement has had on economic and social changes in rural areas influenced by it. The paper initially briefly describes some of the major structural changes which have occurred within Java's rural areas over the last decade, pointing out their effects on the availability of, and access to, employment. Structural changes examined include changes in agricultural methods and practices, increased commercialisation and capitalist penetration, changing transport patterns, and changes in traditional modes of organisation within rural areas. The ways in which these have operated to change employment patterns are explored. Particular attention is focused on temporary mobility as one of the survival strategies long employed by Javan rural dwellers to cope with poverty associated with limited resources and unequal access to those resources. The paper attempts to explore how these structural changes have operated so as to increase the importance of temporary movement vis-à-vis other survival strategies traditionally practised in rural society. However, the relationship between structural change in rural areas and temporary labour movements is a complex interactive one, and the latter part of the paper focuses on the impact of the increased volume of movement within the village. Using case study results, the flow of remittances associated with this form of mobility is measured and their impact is explored. Other ways in which this movement impinges upon village labour conditions are also examined using the case study material. The paper concludes by attempting to derive some more general findings out of the largely case-study-based analysis. In particular, the implications for development and social change in villages generally are spelled out and related to current and possible rural development strategies in Java.

The study is based predominantly on material and experience collected in a series of detailed village-based studies in Java, and draws upon this experience in an attempt to clarify how macro-social and economic processes, such as capitalist penetration and commercialisation, are acting at local levels to shape population movement trends and patterns.

II. Study Area and Data Sources

In 1980, Java had a population of 91.3 million and an average population density of 690 persons per square kilometre.[2] Since some 83 per cent of households relied on agriculture for all or part of their livelihood, Java is rivalled only by some districts in China, the Ganges Valley and the Nile Valley as the most densely populated agricultural area in the world.[3] It is a region of enormous population pressure upon resources and employment. Arief, taking as a poverty line the equivalent cost of 20 kg of rice per capita per month, estimated that, in 1976, 61 per cent of Java's rural population was receiving an income below that level.[4] In this study we focus predominantly upon the province of West Java, which covers most of the western third of Java and in 1980 had a total population of 27.45 million persons, 79 per cent of them living in areas designated as rural.[5] Some 88 per cent of households relied on agriculture for all or part of their livelihood, but only 53 per cent owned or rented agricultural land, of whom half operated less than 0.25 of a hectare. West Java adjoins Indonesia's rapidly growing capital city of Jakarta, which in 1980 had a population of 6.5 million, and itself contains Indonesia's third largest city of Bandung (1.46 million residents in 1980). By any criteria the province must be regarded as poor. In 1976, 25 per cent of urban dwellers and 41 per cent of rural dwellers were in poverty.[6] The province had a male infant mortality rate of 172, there were 0.32 doctors per 10,000 population, and 39 per cent of persons aged 10 years and over were illiterate.[7]

A range of sources of data is used in addition to the 1971 and 1980 Indonesian Censuses, national socio-economic surveys and other secondary data. Most important are a series of intensive village-level studies undertaken by the author alone or with colleagues in several parts of West Java during the 1970s. These include:

1. A 1973 study of 14 villages selected so as to be representative

of major source areas of movers from rural West Java to the cities of Bandung and Jakarta. In each village structured interviews were conducted with 100 randomly selected households and 10 formal and informal leaders, while a range of secondary data was also collected. The methodology and some of the findings of these studies are reported in detail elsewhere.[8]

2. A 1979 study of two villages. One was selected to represent communities that had adopted most of the new agricultural technology and methods associated with the 'green revolution', while the other had experienced little such change.[9] In each village a random sample of some 200 households was interviewed, as was a panel of formal and informal leaders.

3. A 1980 study of 16 villages in one region of Kabupaten Sukabumi (see Figure 2.1) which were to be influenced by the proposed development of an irrigation scheme.[10] Some 540 randomly selected households were interviewed, together with a number of key respondents.[11]

The locations of the villages are indicated in figure 2.1. Among other useful sources of village-level information relating to labour mobility in West Java, the most important are two sample surveys undertaken in the Banten and Priangan areas (see Figure 2.1), where a total of 940 households were interviewed.[12] The pre-eminent work of agricultural change and rural development in West Java has been that of the Agro-economic Survey of Bogor, West Java, based largely on repeated surveys of 26 villages over the 1968-81 period.[13] Six of those villages are located in West Java.

III. Structural Change in Rural West Java During the 1970s

1. Changes in Agriculture

Any discussion of recent change in rural Java must begin with a consideration of wet rice (*sawah*) agriculture which regulates much of village life and provides the bulk of the population's food and employment. From 1968 to 1978 rice production in Java increased by an annual average of 3.6 per cent (4.7 per cent between 1968 and 1974).[14] This was only partly achieved by horizontal expansion, and indeed the area planted to wet rice

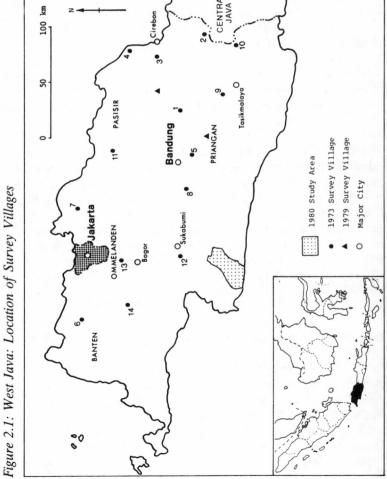

Figure 2.1: West Java: Location of Survey Villages

increased by only 0.7 per cent per annum over that period.[15] While all the survey villages reported increased rice production of the order outlined above, only a few had experienced some lateral extension of *sawah* lands in the decade preceding the survey, and in no case was the extension greater than 10 per cent. Clearly, the bulk of the increased production was achieved *in situ* via intensification of wet rice agriculture. Geertz argued that for generations Java's massive population growth has been accommodated via a series of economic and social adjustments he called agricultural involution.[16] The first element in the involutionary process is the capacity of *sawah* productivity to be increased almost indefinitely by increasing labour inputs devoted to 'pre-germination, transplanting, more thorough land preparation, fastidious planting and weeding, razor blade harvesting, double cropping, more regulation of terrace flooding and the addition of more fields at the edges of volcanoes'.[17] He argued that this not only furnished an increasing supply of food for the burgeoning population but also provided them with employment, since the intensification demanded much greater labour inputs. Complementing this set of labour absorptive/increased productivity strategies was a set of social adaptations, whereby the work and food generated by them were made accessible to all sections of village society (though by no means equally so). This was achieved via a complex of inter-group relations best summed up in the term 'shared poverty'. In addition to the strong family ties, these include such traditional practices as landowners permitting anyone wishing to to participate in the harvesting of rice fields for a traditionally determined share of the amount they harvest. In addition, in the villages strong *bapak/anak buah* (patron/client) relationships welded bonds of mutual responsibility between rich and poor. In West Java these traditional authority relationships have been explored in detail at the village level by Jackson, and include such elements as access to land and employment of the client as either a sharecropper or wage labourer, insurance against unpredictable calamities such as drought, and loans to pay off money lenders.[18] In return, the client owes a debt of moral obligation (*hutang budi*) to the patron.

It is apparent, however, that the increased output of the last decade has been achieved quite differently, with much of the intensification being associated not so much with increased labour but with increased use of other inputs. To be sure, the area of *sawah* with reliable dam and river-fed water supply (as opposed to rain-fed systems) has greatly increased with the rehabilitation of existing irrigation systems and the development of new dams.[19] Among the latter, the most notable is the Jatiluhur dam, which transformed more than a quarter of a million hectares from a single *sawah* crop each year, which every few years was wiped out by flooding or insufficient rain, to an assured double cropping system. Indeed, in some areas three crops per year are being achieved with the assistance of the new high-yielding varieties of rice which have a shorter growing period than traditional strains. More important in the increased production has been the rapid spread of high-yielding varieties, increased fertiliser use and adoption of improved cropping patterns and techniques. In the early years of the decade the government introduced the *Bimas* programme.[20] This provides credit for farmers and encourages the adoption of high-yielding varieties of rice, proper fertiliser application, improved cultural and irrigation practices and control of pests and diseases. The *Bimas* programme was confined to the best irrigated areas. However, it is apparent from Table 2.1 that the adoption of HYV was not restricted to such areas, although there has been much greater acceptance in villages with good irrigation systems. The table also indicates that the other inputs of the Green Revolution have gained a high acceptance in the survey villages, especially manufactured fertilisers. This represents a major change in the villages, since both fertiliser and pesticide were rarely used 15 years ago. These changes are not involutionary, since they increase productivity by capital rather than by labour intensification. Moreover, it is the better-off land operators who are most able to afford optimum applications of fertiliser and pesticides.

2. *Impact of Change Upon Rural Employment*

What are the implications of these changes for local job opportunities? In the early 1970s planners initially believed that introduction of the HYV would have an essentially involutionary effect by not only greatly increasing production, but also increasing village employment opportunities. A study of the Agro-economic Survey's panel of villages in Java during the 1969-70 wet season supported this belief. It was found that the average labour use (in man-days) per hectare of *sawah* was 228.9 for local unimproved varieties, 237.7 for national improved varieties and

Table 2.1 *West Java Survey Villages: Proportion of Land Operators with Irrigated 'Sawah' and Using High-yielding Rice Varieties,[a] Fertiliser and Pesticide, 1973, 1979, 1981*

Village	Per cent of land operators			
	With irri- gated *sawah*	HYV	Using pesticide	Fertiliser
1 1973 study	74	83	89	96
2	70	83	81	97
3	93	86	100	100
4	17	28	48	60
5	100	30	38	90
6	7	27	15	34
7	0	15	6	1
8	49	14	23	82
9	99	67	43	97
10	84	88	50	93
11	5	7	10	40
12	98	34	58	99
13	55	39	53	49
14	39	22	38	31
15 1979 study (Garut)	30	95	91	100
16 1979 study (Majalengka)	16	7	66	94
1981 study sample	38	61	28	58
1981 study leaders	29	79	69	85

Note: a. This table indicates the proportion of land operators who planted *some* HYV in the year preceding interview. It does not represent the percentage of all land under the HYV since most operators only planted them on part of their land.
Source: Field surveys, 1973, 1979, 1981.

284.5 for the IRRI and Pelita HYV.[21] This represented a statistically significant increase in the amount of hired labour used when the HYV are planted, although not in the labour inputs of the land operator's family. However, subsequent rounds of the Agro-economic Survey and field work in the study villages revealed some of the disturbing tendencies towards concentrating labour and capital in the hands of the rich and dissolving traditional rural livelihood systems which have been found in other developing countries experiencing the Green Revolution. In West Java these changes can be summarised as follows:

(1) In some villages some landholders have replaced the traditional unlimited access to participate in the harvest, mentioned above, with more formalised labour arrangements which have labour-displacing effects. Under one system known as *ceblokan* a group of women transplants and weeds a plot of *sawah* for a landowner (for no payment except meals) in return for the sole right to harvest it.[22] More widespread is the *tebasan* system, whereby the landowner sells his rice to a *penebas* (middleman) a week before the harvest and the latter becomes responsible for harvesting and selling the crops. The *penebas* can then limit the number of people participating in the harvest and is also able to pay them less than the traditionally determined share of the crop.[23] In other cases, the less extreme situation exists of landholders limiting participation in their harvest to people of the same village, or limiting the number of outsiders or the number of participants regardless of their origin.[24] These systems clearly represent a more 'commercial' orientation of landholders, in that their share of the harvest is likely to be greater under the *tebasan* system than under the traditional *bawon* system whereby any neighbour or itinerant landless labourers could participate in the harvest. This penetration of commercialisation has thus initiated a breakdown of traditional obligations between landowners (especially large landowners) and landless and other poor groups, denying the latter access to one of their few village sources of income. The spread of commercialisation is clearly associated with the greater use of manufactured inputs (fertiliser and pesticides) and the extension of credit facilities and consumerism into Javan villages, which has occurred apace in recent years. As Hayami and Hafid point out, these changed labour arrangements did not necessarily reduce the work required for the harvest.[25] However, several other studies have suggested that the numbers gaining work in the harvest are significantly less under the *tebasan* system than under the *bawon* system. Their data indicate a 12 per cent difference, although the findings of Collier *et al.* and Utami and Ihalauw suggest greater differences.[26] It also has been found by the Agro-economic Survey that contract (*borongan*) labour groups were also used for agricultural tasks other than harvesting, thus denying many landless workers access to other

agricultural employment.[27] As Collier concluded, these changes in cultivation practices suggest that the preferred equilibrium between labour supply and labour absorption under agricultural involution 'is giving way to a condition where the values of efficiency and profit assume a much more pronounced role in the economy of agricultural production'.[28]

(2) A second noticeable trend in areas of West Java where HYV have been introduced is the changeover from traditional stalk-by-stalk harvesting using an *ani-ani* to the use of sickles.[29] This more efficient method reduces the man-hours required to harvest a hectare of padi from more than 200 to around 75.[30] The enormous labour displacement associated with this change is obvious. In most of the survey villages the sickle replaced the *ani-ani* as the major tool used in padi harvesting during the 1970s. The adoption of the sickle was encouraged by the adoption of the HYV because the mature HYV rice plants are shorter than are the local varieties. Associated with this has been a changeover to payment by wages or a modified version of the traditional *bawon* (share) system. Under the *bawon* system, the rice (with stalks intact) was tied in bundles (*ikat*), and harvesters ensured that their share comprised the heaviest bundles. The HYV, however, are threshed in the field and the share weighed out in grain, so that there is an effective reduction in the harvester's payment. Collier *et al*. made a careful analysis of these changes and estimated that they represent employment decreases of from 18 to 60 per cent.[31] But harvesting costs of landowners were reduced by around 40 per cent.

(3) A third trend is toward agricultural mechanisation, or more particularly the proliferation of *hand tractors* and, to a lesser extent, four-wheeled mini-tractors, a trend that has become especially strong in rural Java since 1975. One study in the early 1970s showed that the use of mechanical ploughs on 20 hectares of *sawah* in a Subang (West Java) village would displace between 2,000 and 5,000 man-days of labour.[32] At the time of the 1973 survey, tractors were encountered in only one survey village, although they were very much in evidence in the better-off areas of the province such as Cianjur and Subang. Since 1975, however, it is clear that their use has become much more widespread. It was reported that there were 109 hand tractors in Kabupaten Indramaya in 1977 and 215 in Kabupaten Krawang in 1979, and these are by no means the most heavily

'tractorised' areas.[33] Several public figures have advocated a more rapid introduction of tractors, 'referring to a shortage of agricultural labour in rural areas.[34] Recent detailed studies of the impact of agricultural mechanisation in West Java have conclusively shown that while promotion of tractorisation may be advisable where scarcity of labour is a barrier to increasing production (mainly outside Java), in Java they have seriously depleted employment opportunities.[35] The impact of hand tractors is most eloquently indicated by a 43-year-old agricultural labourer in a village boasting 45 tractors, a man interviewed in a popular Indonesian journal (*Tempo*, 28 July 1979): 'Sejak adanya traktor banyak orang yang menganggur di desa ini' (Since the tractors, there have been many people unemployed in this village). Other work-providing stages in the agricultural cycle are also being subject to mechanisation in Java, with labour-displacing results. Collier, for example, has pointed to the growing use of mechanical threshers.[36] In the study areas, the use of Japanese rotary weeders (*landak/caplak*) has become much more widespread, and one study has indicated that eight man-days of weeding with the *landak* replaced some 20 woman-days of handweeding.[37]

(4) A more ubiquitous change in the 1970s was the almost complete changeover to milling rice with mechanical hullers rather than the traditional hand-pounding, whereby women could supplement their families' incomes. In 1973 there were hullers in ten of the survey villages, and all had been purchased within the past three years. In the later surveys 70 per cent of villagers reported using mechanical hullers to mill their rice. One study demonstrated that the replacement of hand-pounding with hullers had resulted in a massive loss of wage labour and a considerable redistribution of income in favour of large landowners and rice traders.[38] Singarimbun, in revisiting his 1969 study village of Srijarjo in 1975, graphically observed the impact of the construction of three rice hullers in the interim:

> most of the women who formerly worked in this industry have lost a major source of income. When I asked five of them what alternative employment they would seek, they answered that there was no alternative work for them. 'Then what will you do?' I asked. 'We will eat more carefully', they replied.[39]

Collier reported a study in West Java indicating that 3,701 labourers were displaced by each mechanical huller, which would suggest that in all Java in 1971 some 7.7 million part-time workers were displaced.[40]

Clearly, these tendencies are working against labour absorption traditionally associated with agricultural involution. As Collier observed,

the imperatives of efficiency and profitability are beginning to exact their toll in the erosion of traditions where elasticities in the production function allowed for high rates of labour absorption within the rice producing sector . . . which seems to be exhibiting a marked tendency towards exclusion rather than absorption in responding to a burgeoning workforce.[41]

Other rural changes also appear to have had labour-displacing effects. First among these was the widespread harvest failures of the mid-1970s that were associated with drought and infestations of the brown planthopper (wereng), to which the HYV then in use had no resistance. During this period

labour markets were unable to respond adequately to the reduced demand and many landless labourers and marginal farmers were unable to secure sufficient employment. There was an acceleration of land sales from marginal farmers, often to those outside the village.[42]

In 1977 in Kabupaten Krawang, traditionally a major rice-producing area, some 80,000 people were reported as severely affected by the drought and 11,000 in dire need of food aid. In one sub-district alone, 9,280 of the normal 22,370 population migrated to find work elsewhere.[43]

Yet another labour-displacing development was observed in one of the 1973 survey villages where, under a government programme to promote national sugar production, 25 per cent of the village's prime sawah land was rented out to grow sugar. The land was rented for 18 months, and the landowners were paid Rp. 100,000.[44] However, while this one crop of sugar was produced, three crops of sawah with a monetary value of some five times this figure could have been grown by the landowner. His loss was minor because he was freed from all overheads by the sugar enterprise, but the impact on local landless labourers was considerable, since the volume of work available to them from one sugar crop was much smaller than that associated with three *sawah* crops.

In Java the rural non-farm sector has traditionally played an important but often overlooked role in rural employment generation. These activities usually involve the provision of goods and services to other villagers. These include village administration workers and small-scale traders operating out of a small stall or on an itinerant hawking basis. Many of the stalls and shops are operated as subsidiary activities by villagers engaged in farming. In addition, most villages have some form of small-scale industry usually practised by farmers seeking extra income and whose 'chief investments are labour, skill, inventiveness, zeal and so on – but no capital'.[45] However, it is clear that the penetration of rural areas by consumer goods manufactured in large cities or overseas has sounded the death knell to many such locally based activities, which cannot compete on scale, quality or cost terms. In 1948, Aten made an inventory of rural industries in Kabupaten Sumedang, West Java in which he identified 74 separate types of enterprise, 3,778 enterprises employing 5,395 people.[46] Field checking in the *Kabupaten* in the 1970s indicated that there had been a massive substitution of locally manufactured goods (usually produced by one-person operations using traditional methods) by cheaper, mass-produced goods manufactured in the Jakarta urban region, another major city or overseas. The local employment-displacement effects are again all too obvious.

3. *Local Employment and Survival in Rural Java*

In sum, the evidence from villages studied in West Java was that many of the changes impinging upon wet rice agriculture and local rural manufacturing were displacing labour, far from accommodating population growth. This can be demonstrated with reference to the concept of *cukupan* (to have enough) which Penny and Singarimbun found to have a very specific meaning in the village of Srijarjo (Yogyakarta).[47] In the West Javan villages, interviews with respondents involved in a grim day-to-day struggle to provide sufficient food for their families indicated that they become very aware of the threshold between enough and not enough. The almost universally acknowledged definition of *cukupan* in the villages was 250 kg of *gabah* (unhusked rice separated from stalks) for each adult person each year. This is similar to the Srijarjo definition of 1.2 tons of rice or its equivalent per family per year. They suggested that to obtain this a family would need to operate 0.7 ha of *sawah* and 0.3 ha of *pekarangan* (house garden).[48]

In Table 2.2 a value of 1 in the first column represents a situation in which there was sufficient land available in the village for each household to be *cukupan* from land within the village. It can be seen that in none of the villages was there enough agricultural land to provide for the subsistence of all resident households. Agriculture, which dominates the local economic

Table 2.2 *West Java Survey Villages: Sufficiency of Agricultural Land Operated by Sample Households, 1973, 1979, 1980*

Village	Sawah/ pekarangan per house-hold (ha)	Households not operating any sawah (%)	Households with insufficient land for subsistence (%) Movers[a]	Stayers
1 1973 study	.82	1	15	20
2 "	.43	24	59	74
3 "	.5	43	51	68
4 "	.43	31	74	79
5 "	.71	45	71	84
6 "	.45	35	87	89
7 "	.60	34	69	88
8 "	.31	27	84	86
9 "	.58	20	82	49
10 "	.56	54	82	70
11 "	.46	38	85	89
12 "	.50	33	73	81
13 "	.45	55	85	89
14 "	.30	66	96	98
15 1979 study (Garut)	.31	35	78	
16 1979 study (Majalengka)	.12	33	61	
1980 study	.34	13	78	

Note:a. Mover households in the 1973 study were those from which at least one person had moved out of the village to seek work, either permanently or on a temporary basis.
Source: Field surveys, 1973, 1979, 1980.

base of the villages, was clearly insufficient for all resident households to attain *cukupan*. However, distribution of the available land is far from equal. Thus Table 2.2 shows that in most villages less than two-thirds of households operated any *sawah* and more than three-quarters of all households had insufficient land to attain *cukupan*. This pattern of only a minority of rural households owning and/or renting sufficient land to provide subsistence is by no means confined to the survey desa. Table 2.3 presents data from the 1980 census showing that 88 per cent of West Javan households had some involvement in agriculture, but 34 per cent were completely landless while 26 per cent owned or rented less than a quarter of a hectare of agricultural land.

Table 2.3: *West Java: Households According to Whether or Not They Rely upon Agriculture for Their Livelihood, 1980*

Household type	No. of households	%
Operating less than 0.25 ha	1,603,354	26
Operating 0.25-0.49 ha	888,073	15
Operating more than 0.5 ha	754,737	13
Total operating agricultural land	3,246,164	54
Total landless agricultural labourers	2,095,146	34
Total non-agricultural households	759,403	12
Total	6,100,713	100

Note: 'Operating' includes both owning and renting.
Source: 1980 census.

Further evidence of the failure of village agricultural systems to absorb population increases was provided in the 1973 survey by responses to the question of whether or not it was more difficult to obtain work than a decade earlier. The results presented in Table 2.4 show that less than a quarter of respondents reported the existence of a 'static expansion' involutionary situation, and in most villages at least half of the respondents reported greater difficulty in finding work than they had encountered 10 years ago. Moreover, the reasons given for this (Table 2.5) pointed to a failure of local agriculture to absorb population increases, with more than half of the responses being

Table 2.4: *West Java Survey Villages: Degree of Difficulty Experienced in Obtaining Work, by Mover and Stayer Households Compared to 10 Years Ago, 1973*

| Village | Degree of difficulty in getting work compared to 10 years ago (%) | | | |
	Greater	Same	Less	No.
1	54	8	38	88
2	44	16	40	94
3	48	17	35	88
4	54	20	26	79
5	32	23	45	87
6	58	13	29	91
7	67	8	25	95
8	61	11	20	92
9	55	19	26	92
10	61	11	28	87
11	44	16	40	89
12	41	17	42	93
13	56	20	24	97
14	61	14	25	86
Mean	52.8	15.4	31.6	

Source: Field survey, 1973.

expressed precisely in these terms. A further third considered there had been an absolute reduction in local agricultural job opportunities, while a small number gave such reasons as local environmental deterioration and disease infestation. Slightly less than a third of respondents indicated they found less difficulty in finding a job than a decade ago. However, Table 2.5 indicates that this improvement was almost entirely due to increased job opportunities outside the village and access to them being enhanced by upgrading of the transport network.

It is clear that during most of the 1970s employment opportunities for many rural West Javans were insufficient to ensure survival. The strategy that many had adopted to cope with this was to seek work in off-farm activities, in many cases outside their home village. But before examining this movement, it is necessary to consider one other structural transformation that swept rural Java during the 1970s.

Table 2.5: *West Java Survey Households: Reasons Given by Respondents Finding Greater and Less Difficulty in Finding Work than They Had a Decade Ago, 1973*

	Leaders No.	Leaders %	Movers No.	Movers %	Stayers No.	Stayers %
Reasons for greater difficulty						
Population increase had been too great	51	58	140	51	225	55
Reduction in agricultural work opportunities	27	30	99	36	135	33
Problems with local agriculture	5	6	18	6	31	9
Other	6	6	20	7	16	4
Total	89		273		407	
Reasons for less difficulty						
More work available outside of the village	34	57	101	62	153	67
Improved transport between village and city	18	30	45	27	59	26
Improvements in local agriculture	3	5	1	1	5	2
Other	5	8	17	10	10	5
Total	60		164		227	

Source: Field Survey, 1973.

4. 'Revolusi Colt' – The Transformation of Physical Accessibility in Rural Java

The term *revolusi colt* (literally, minibus revolution) is often heard in Java, and refers to the veritable revolution which occurred in the provision and availability of transport during the 1970s. There can be no doubt that the extension of roads and proliferation of vehicles of a multitude of types, especially minibuses and buses, into hitherto isolated rural areas led to greatly increased personal spatial mobility for a wide spectrum of Indonesia's rural dwellers and greatly increased penetration of rural areas by consumer goods and government agencies. By the 1980s there were very few villages in West Java without a regular minibus link with the outside world. Between 1970 and 1980 the number of kilometres of asphalt roads in Indonesia nearly trebled, from 20,444 to 56,665 km. In West Java the roads

Table 2.6: *West Java – Jakarta: Number of Registered Motor Vehicles, 1970 and 1980*

	1970	1970	Per cent increase	Average annual per cent increase
Jakarta				
Passengers cars	87,009	220,872	154	9.7
Buses	5,080	29,546	482	19.2
Trucks	19,013	75,219	296	14.8
Motorcycles	110,980	428,909	286	14.5
Total	222,082	754,546	–	–
Persons per vehicle	20.6	8.6	–	–
West Java				
Passenger cars	34,219	122,910	259	13.6
Buses	1,898	10,997	479	19.2
Trucks	10,727	91,864	856	23.4
Motorcycles	54,078	329,354	509	19.8
Total	100,922	555,125	450	18.6
Persons per vehicle	214.3	49.5	–	–

Source: Biro Pusat Statistik: *Statistik kendaraan bermotor dan panjang jalan, 1974* (Jakarta, 1975); idem, 1981.

maintained by national, provincial, and *kabupaten* officials increased from 7,878 to 11,533 km, and this does not include local roads that had undergone major extension and upgrading.[49] The most striking indication of the change in accessibility and the breaking down of village isolation lies in statistics relating to the numbers of registered motor vehicles.[50] Table 2.6 shows the massive increase that occurred between 1970 and 1980 in the number of motorised vehicles in West Java, a growth almost ten times the rate of population growth. The reduction in the number of persons per vehicle from over 200 to fewer than 50 within a decade is indicative of how far-reaching transport changes have been. The figures for Jakarta are also included, since many of the public transport vehicles registered in Jakarta actually provide services between that city and West Javan localities. It is unfortunate that minibuses are not separated from other passenger cars in the statistics since it was the 'colt' type of vehicles that had the major impact in making previously remote villages accessible to the outside world in recent years.[51] The impact on population mobility of this massive increase in vehicles, and the major reductions in persons per vehicle, is greater than the figures would suggest, because a very substantial proportion of the growth of four-wheeled vehicles has been in those utilised within the public transport sector. This means, as anyone who has observed the buses and minibuses packed with people plying Indonesian roads will testify, that the increased spatial mobility which a substantially increased vehicle fleet affords is being spread much more widely than the owners of those vehicles.[52]

The importance of this breaking down of village isolation in enhancing and initiating social and economic change in rural Java must be stressed. The 1980 Sukabumi study was conducted in one of the more remote areas of the province (Figure 2.1) and only 10 of the 16 villages sampled had road access at the time, with roads to all but two of those dating only from 1972, 1976 or 1979. A substantial majority of residents sampled nominated improved accessibility as the *most* important change in their community during the previous decade.[53] The implications of the improved accessibility have been little studied.[54] Leinbach found, in a 2,500 interview survey, that construction of feeder roads generally produced improvements in income because of new accessibility to markets, increased spatial mobility, increased penetration of the village by traders of all kinds and government officers, increased availability and acquisition of information such as that regarding off-season employment, credit and crop prices and increased employment from road construction and maintenance.[55] The transport revolution certainly facilitated an increase in the magnitude, distance, and periodicity of rural population movement and changed its composition in Java during the 1970s. However, there is little known of the long-term structural impact of these major changes in the transport system. Elsewhere, some of these questions are considered in more detail, but they predominantly related to which groups in the village are gaining most from the improved accessibility.[56] We also know little of the information flows and social impact of increased penetration of consumerism and ideas from the major urban centres. In this regard, it is notable that the proliferation of public transport in Java has been matched by a huge intensification of the impact of mass media. In the 1980 census in Indonesia, among urban households 57 per cent owned radios and 29 per cent television sets, while the equivalent figures for rural households were 36 and 4 per cent.[57] In the two villages studied in 1979 in West Java

Table 2.7: *West Java Survey Villages: Mass Media Exposure (%)*

Indicator	1973 survey			1979 survey	1981 survey	
	Leaders	Stayers	Movers		Leaders	Others
Never read newspapers	24	82	70	60	27	51
Listen to radio daily	73	34	47	56	67	39
Never watch television	48	83	63	27	25	42
Watch television at least weekly	5	1	1	30	11	4
Never been to the cinema	41	65	56	76	95	97

Source: Field surveys, 1973, 1979, 1981.

47 per cent had radios and 6 per cent had television sets, while in the 1981 Sukabumi study in a poorer and less accessible area 37 per cent had radios and 2 per cent television sets.[58]

The influence of mass media, especially transistor radios and battery- or generator-operated television sets, in influencing social and economic change in rural Java is too frequently overlooked. Table 2.7 indicates how ubiquitous radio listening is in Java and also how significant television has become. There can be no doubt that the rapid increase in media penetration of rural Java has greatly expanded awareness of opportunities outside the village and has been an element in an increased pace of commercialisation, social change and challenge to traditional institutions and customary ways of living. It should also be mentioned that one of the major achievements of the Independence period in Indonesia has been in the spread of education to rural areas. While illiteracy levels remain high, the massive effort to spread education into villages was a major force for social change among the young in rural Java in the 1970s.

5. Changing Distribution of Wealth and Power in Rural Java

While aggregate indications point to real improvements in rural Java, changes reviewed earlier suggest that the benefits of expanded agricultural production afforded by the Green Revolution have been unequally distributed. The larger landholders have been better placed to gain access to credit and manufactured inputs of the new rice agriculture, while many of the new agricultural technologies and processes outlined earlier have reduced the proportion of production that has to be spent on labour. For the landless and near landless, which Table 2.3 show to make up the majority of West Java's rural households, the evidence shows a reduced access to agricultural employment and income opportunities and to traditional labour-intensive rural industry. Data relating to income and land ownership in Java are generally scarce, unrepresentative and unreliable.[59] But there is evidence that larger landholders have been able to improve their relative position even further by utilising their expanded income to increase their landholdings at the expense of smallholders and to invest in high-capital, high-return enterprises such as mini-buses and hullers. As a result, there is considerable 'evidence of a widening gap between rich and poor'.[60] The situation has thus led to a consolidation and perhaps enhancement of the economic position of rural elites, who not only have acquired greater control of the land but other non-agricultural rural-based activities.[61] There is evidence that there has been significant change in the power structure in rural Java, involving a shift in favour of the richer landed groups. As Husken summarised the situation in his study village:

> The landlords are becoming 'entrepreneurs' not only in agriculture but outside of it . . . they have introduced new rice hullers; purchased 'Colts' (pick-ups adapted for public transport that visit all the main villages in the district; acquired diesel-powered generators, the electricity from which they sell to other villagers and engage in trade in agricultural produce.[62]

It has been suggested that the enhancement of the rural elite's economic position has in some cases been accompanied by abandonment of the obligations they have traditionally provided to the village poor and landless, whereby they provided income-earning opportunities, however small. However, the Alexanders have argued that the notion of shared poverty in traditional Javan villages has been exaggerated, and have demonstrated that the degree of economic equality in the past has been overstated.[63] However, if many of the practices and obligations that ensured survival (albeit at the most marginal of levels) of the poorest groups during crises have been abandoned, it would represent a major change in inter-class relationships within the village.

Another change relating to power within rural Java was the greatly increased involvement of government institutions in the villages in the 1970s. The *Bimas* programme has involved a spread of agricultural technicians and other government functionaries to villages. Various rural works programmes were introduced to provide food and/or cash to rural dwellers in return for labour on local infrastructural projects.[64] The successful family planning programme and a range of other government activities meant that villages had more government officers visiting and living within them. Besides being agents of change in themselves, these activities strengthened village links with the outside world. On the other hand, many of the traditional informal institutions that previously provided some welfare and security to the landless and near-landless farmers have been greatly weakened in many villages. Collier *et al.*, for example, maintained that:

Informal agricultural institutions (*bawon, ngasak, sakap, lumbung desa, simpan pinjam*) that have in the past provided food security, income and perhaps welfare to the landless and marginal farmers will not be functional in case of natural calamities in the future.[65]

5. Conclusion

The 1970s were thus years of major improvements in rice production with the per capita availability of the staple food in Java increasing from 108 kg per person per year in 1970 to 136.4 in 1980. The benefits of this increase were not shared equally in rural Java. There was a relative decline in the demand for agricultural labour during the decade, even though there was an increase in the numbers actually working in the agricultural sector.[66] There was almost certainly an increase in landlessness and greater dependence upon wage labour. However, the available evidence suggests there was no decline in the level of real wages in rural areas,[67] so that as Jones pointed out, 'Labour absorption appears to have kept pace with labour supply'.[68] There are a number of reasons for this.[69]

One major element in maintaining, and in some cases enhancing, the welfare of rural households was the participation in a range of off-farm employment, involving some members of those households in moves beyond (and in many cases, far beyond) the village. In most cases, this movement did not involve a definitive break with the village but the establishment of a pattern of a circular migration. It is to this mobility that we now turn.

IV. Labour Mobility in Rural West Java

1. Introduction

As rural Javans have for so many generations lived in areas experiencing enormous population pressure upon available employment and subsistence resources and have experienced recurring food crises, it is to be expected that many will have responded to that pressure by moving on a permanent or temporary basis to less critical areas. However, Javans have been stereotyped as being highly immobile, rarely moving beyond the confines of their village of birth.[70] This has been partly a function of census data detecting only permanent and long-distance migration.[71] But it also reflects an unquestioning acceptance of the veracity of Geertz's theory of agricultural involution, and frequently a naive interpretation of it. The elegance of the involution argument has led to other survival strategies adopted in traditional Java being largely overlooked. These include deliberate attempts to control fertility and a wide variety of population movements. Indeed, in Java population mobility during the pre-Independence period occurred at much higher levels and with a greater degree of complexity than suggested by most commentators.[72] The mobility of the West Javan population in the pre-1800 era was such that the historian Haan characterised them as 'wanderers'.[73] Nevertheless, the village studies and other evidence point to mobility of rural dwellers during the 1970s attaining unprecedented levels and complexity.

2. Levels and Types of Labour Mobility in West Java

According to the 1980 census, only 2.6 per cent of the population of West Java migrated within the past five years. But the census definition of migration excluded people migrating within the province, who outnumbered interprovincial migrants by at least six to one. More importantly, it excluded all moves where the mover did not settle permanently at the destination or was absent for less than six months. Hence it took no account of the bulk of non-permanent mobility, which has been shown to be of much greater numerical significance than migration as conventionally defined.[74] Several types of temporary movements were identified as being of major significance within West Java.[75] These included daily commuting over distances of up to 50 km, either involving participation in full-time employment or irregularly to engage in work supplementary to village-based jobs. More distinctive is circular migration, whereby movers do not change their usual place of residence in the village but are absent at an urban destination for longer than a single day. Such movement can also be associated with permanent full-time employment at the destination, but usually it involved non-permanent work in the so-called urban 'informal' sector. Circular migrants usually maintained some village-based employment, and the frequency with which they moved to the city and returned to the village was determined by the distance and the travel costs, their earnings at the destination and the availability of work in the home village. In the survey villages, most of this non-permanent movement focused on urban areas, especially the major metropolitan centres of Jakarta and Bandung. All commuters and most circular migrants retained their village of origin as their official residence, leaving their wives (most such movers being men in West Java) and children behind. Circular migrants rarely owned or rented an urban dwelling, often sleeping in barracks, in rooms rented with fellow village migrants, at their workplace, in unfinished buildings or even in the open. While much of the temporary movement was rural-urban in direction there were also flows to other rural areas, where employment opportunities were available.[76] Much, though by no means all, of this circular mobility was seasonal, occurring in the extended periods of limited job opportunity in the village between planting and harvesting rice during the wet season and during the dry season. There was also significant long-distance circular migration from West Java to other islands to work on plantations or on oil/mineral development projects, often under contract` and involving absences of up to two years.

One of the most striking features of the labour mobility detected in the survey villages was its recency. Information from many sources during fieldwork strongly indicated that the contemporary scale and periodicity of commuting and circular migration was a recent phenomenon. In most villages studied, there were well-established precedents of temporary labour migration in colonial times. But the current pattern was highly dependent upon and shaped by the major structural changes that had occurred in the village. In the 1973 study, for example, in all but one of the fourteen villages more than half of the current circular migrants had begun that pattern of movement since 1970.[77] Moreover, this could not be explained simply in terms of most movers being new entrants to the workforce, since the survey data indicated that a majority of recent circular migrants were established members of the village workforce when they adopted that mobility strategy. In the more recent surveys more than half the movers commenced their current circular movement pattern within the past five years. By the 1980s it was not unusual to find villages in West Java in which a high proportion of households had at least one member working outside the village. The villages studied were selected partly because of their high levels of out-migration and had more than half their households receiving income from outside the village. However, even in the Agro-economic Survey it was found that seasonal and semi-permanent migration had become so well established that between 27 and 41 per cent of respondent households had members working outside the village.[78]

3. Causes of Increased Labour Movement Outside the Village

The fact that this upswing in labour movement out of rural Java, especially temporary moves, was contemporaneous with the structural changes mentioned earlier points to the forces impelling the movement. Increased concentration of agricultural land, increased landlessness and reduced access to agricultural labour opportunities exerted strong pressures on those groups to seek alternative sources of subsistence. The reasons reported for both temporary and permanent migrants leaving the village were almost entirely work-related. However, in all the survey villages there were clear differences in the emphases of the employment-related responses for commuters and circular migrants compared with longer-term migrants. Almost all temporary migrants referred to the lack of *any* job opportunities in the village, especially at particular times of the year. Their movement was a response to this pressure. In many cases respondents reported that their movement was essential to provide basic survival needs for their family, so that it could be described as 'subsistence movement'. The almost universal response to the question of why they left the village was *mencari nafkah*, which means to search for subsistence. While the lack of local job opportunities was also the most frequent response for persons *migrating* to a city, unavailability of educational institutions and job transfer were also important. This reflected not so much the lack of *any* job opportunities in the village for these people but the lack of what are considered *suitable* opportunities. Hence in most villages children wishing and financially able to attend upper secondary school are forced to move to a larger centre. Moreover, villagers completing secondary school are 'educated to migrate', in that the jobs to which they have been encouraged to aspire are concentrated in urban areas. Jobs in the public service and army are much sought after and involve transfer from the village. There is a greater tendency for migration to occur as a family group, compared to the dominance of individual breadwinners in temporary movement. And a small number of migrants gave as their main reason for leaving the need they felt to broaden their horizons, whereas this was not mentioned by any of the temporary movers, whose responses almost all indicated the dominance of economic necessity.

Detailed examination of land ownership patterns of households with members engaging in some form of work outside the village indicates that they tended to have a greater proportion who were landless or near landless than those with no members engaging in temporary labour mobility. Similarly, a much greater proportion of these 'mover' households reported that they had found there had been no improvement in village job opportunities over the last decade and expressed dissatisfaction with available village work. Of course, a shortage of agricultural employment, especially during certain phases of the agricultural cycle, was not new to many West Javans, and households have allocated their available labour over a wide range of off-farm activities. The mid-1970s situation has been summarised thus in a World Bank report:

Although two-thirds of rural households report that they depend primarily on agriculture for their incomes almost 17 per cent of these supplement their income from non-agricultural sources. In all some 45 per cent of rural households derive at least part of their income from activities outside of agriculture, with over 25 per cent wholly dependent on non-agricultural incomes.[79]

Moreover, multiple jobholding among individuals in rural Java is commonplace. A study of all Java in 1958, for example, found that a quarter of rural Jarvans had more than one occupation.[80] In the survey villages, more than a third of the workforce had more than one job.

In the 1970s, structural adjustment within agriculture exerted increased pressure upon many households to earn at least part of their income outside local agriculture. But this cannot be accepted as a comprehensive explanation of the upswing in population mobility out of West Javan villages during the 1970s. It is clear that the changes outlined earlier in education and information were important in informing villagers of possible income-earning opportunities at places, especially cities, quite distant from the village. Moreover, the transport revolution *facilitated* movement to such places, in that it allowed individuals to range over a wider area in search of employment and made it possible for families, in seeking subsistence levels of income, to allocate their labour over a wider geographical area and often over a wider variety of income-earning sectors, especially in urban areas. However, all this assumes that such opportunities existed in urban areas for rural Javans. Yet the high unemployment that prevailed in urban Java during the 1970s, and the low and stagnating urban wages would appear, on the surface, to have presented a discouraging picture to prospective migrants.[81] On the other hand, the 1970s was a period in which Indonesia had substantial foreign exchange surpluses from gas and oil exports. Much of that went into expansion of government programmes and in increased expenditure on consumer goods among those groups who prospered during the period. So these developments favoured employment growth in urban rather than rural areas. Moreover, an examination of government expenditure indicated that there was a tendency for government policies to favour concentrated urban development and for investment in agriculture and the rural sector to be limited.[82] Osborn pointed out that in *Repelita-I* (the first five-year plan), despite the dominance of the rural population and the fact that agriculture was the leading economic sector, 'roughly 40 per cent of . . . expenditures can have been said to have gone to urban and urbanizing services'.[83] He showed that in *Repelita-II* more stress was given to agriculture, but it 'continues to apply project predominance in the urban and urbanizing field'. This pattern was maintained in the planned expenditure for *Repelita-III*, in which, as Booth and Tyabji showed, in comparison with *Repelita-II*,

> Rather less resources as a proportion of the total will be devoted to sectors such as agriculture, transport, regional development and government capital participation in businesses, while more will go to industry, mining and energy, transmigration and defence.[84]

Jakarta, in particular, has attracted a disproportionately large share of investment,[85] and the proximity of West Java to the national capital has resulted in its becoming a major destination of movers, both permanent and temporary, from rural parts of the province. Urban investment has thus greatly increased, and with it urban labour markets have expanded. However, competition for work in the urban sector has also increased greatly, though many rural West Javans have been able to penetrate urban labour markets. As will be shown, this has often been possible because they were able to enter the labour markets at the margins, working periodically in informal-sector activities, often in low-productivity jobs, working long hours for very low returns. They have not become fully proletarianised but, via circular mobility strategies, have maintained a major stake in their villages.

4. Gaining Access to Employment Outside

Examination of the urban employment patterns of movers out of the West Javan survey villages shows major differences between permanent and temporary migrants. First, a third of permanent migrants to Jakarta took longer than a fortnight to obtain their first job, while more than 20 per cent took longer than a month. Somewhat larger proportions of migrants to Bandung and other centres were able to find work more quickly. But all temporary migrants found work within two weeks of arrival in the city. This difference is related to the fact that permanent migrants generally came from more prosperous backgrounds than short-term movers, so that their families were better able to support them through a period of unemployment. They were also more likely than temporary movers to have relatives in Jakarta with whom they could live during this period. Permanent migrants have also generally had more formal education than temporary movers and hence have had stronger aspirations for 'formal-sector' jobs. Thus, even though entry into the informal sector may be earlier, permanent migrants are more willing and able to forgo such opportunities and wait for a more desirable job. This points to the second major difference – some two-thirds of permanent migrants entered formal-sector activities, while this was so for only one third of temporary migrants (and nearly half of those worked as day labourers). The majority of temporary migrants worked in the labour-intensive, low-productivity, small-scale non-wage sector of the urban economy. The flexible time commitments, whereby the worker decides the days and hours of work, mean that such employment is much more compatible with circular migration than the six-day-week, regular working hours regimen characteristic of the formal sector. However, this does not explain the different levels of participation in formal and informal sector activities, though it relates to different degrees of difficulty in gaining access to the two sectors. Most temporary migrants have little margin to be selective about the job they take in the city and are prepared to accept low incomes in low-status, heavy, time-consuming activities. The necessity for some income gains them access to the margins of the workforce as pedicab drivers, cigarette-butt scavengers,[86] kerosene and water carriers, day labourers, and so on. The low overheads of circular migrants allows them to compete successfully for such work and keep the incomes received from it very low.

Access to many occupations, particularly informal activities such as small-scale selling and trading, is usually gained via kinship and friendship linkages. In his study of migration of the Frafras to Accra-Tema in Ghana, Hart noted,

> few will apply for a job where they have no particularistic relationship, such as a previously employed kinsman . . . Information about vacancies tends to travel along informal social networks rather than through employment exchanges and nepotism is not unknown in Ghana.[87]

Such a statement could be equally applied to movers from the

West Javan survey villages. Jackson, in his study of patron/client relationships among Sundanese in Bandung, has shown how these traditional authority linkages have been modified in the urban context.[88] Whereas the village *bapak* supplied access to land and agricultural employment to his *anak buah*, other informal methods develop in urban areas, whereby access to jobs is provided within the national and government bureaucracies, nationalised enterprises and private business.[89] Such activities operate not only between patrons and clients, but also within overlapping kinship and friendship networks. It is common knowledge, for example, that *koneksi* (connection), preferably of a family nature, is an all important requirement for access to many lucrative jobs in Pertamina, the government oil monopoly. One often finds kinship bonds between the top echelons of provincial government departments, and even access to the army is eased by *koneksi*. Some examples of this phenomenon in the survey villages are discussed elsewhere.[90]

Informal links are particularly important in gaining access to informal-sector employment. This applies whether a worker is completely self-financed or relies on merchandise and equipment from a middleman. Traders from one survey village who went to Jakarta to sell groundnuts gave newcomers hints about selling, suggesting likely selling areas. The same applied to street barbers from another village who may also have been given assistance in buying their chair, mirror, scissors, clippers and razor. But many bazaar jobs involve dealings with some middleman. Few *becak* (pedicab) drivers, for example, own their own *becak*, but hire them on a 12- or 24-hour basis. Similarly, most hawkers have to obtain their goods from merchants. In such circumstances, a mover is unlikely to gain access to such occupations unless he has capital, though if he is known to the merchant, goods can be obtained on credit. Migrants from particular villages and areas establish relationships with particular middlemen, so that kinsmen and friends whom they recommend are also able to gain employment. The middleman in return gets a reliable, continuous supply of labour to sell his goods. Thus bread sellers from one village had developed a virtual monopoly on their trade in Jakarta because they had special arrangements with bakeries. People from elsewhere found it very difficult to enter this section of the market.

It is clear that *koneksi* had a critical role in gaining

Table 2.8: *West Java Survey Villages: Occupational Specialisation in Urban Areas of Movers in the Workforce*

1973 survey village	No.	Main occupation	%	Second occupation	%	First two occupations
1	74	Groundnut hawker	65	Government/army	15	80
2	55	Cooked food/cigarette hawker	35	Day labourer	22	57
3	91	Cooked food hawker	43	Jewellery hawker	21	64
4	70	*Becak* driver	57	Day labourer	16	73
5	82	*Becak* driver	41	Factory worker	34	75
6	100	Labourer	35	Hospital worker	13	48
7	87	Kerosene hawker	32	Household domestic	15	47
8	77	Airline/hotel worker	32	Household domestic	10	42
9	87	*Kelontongan* hawker	60	Government/army	12	72
10	88	Driver	27	Government/army	26	53
11	87	*Becak* driver	38	Construction worker	20	58
12	92	Carpenter	49	Government/army	28	77
13	99	Barber	31	Bamboo worker	20	51
14	104	Bread hawker	42	Driver	32	74

Source: Hugo, 1975, p. 546.

employment within both the informal and formal sectors, and this had led to a considerable degree of occupational clustering among movers from each of the survey villages. For example, Table 2.8 shows that in most villages covered by the 1973 survey, more than half of the permanent and temporary migrants to cities worked in one or two occupational niches. This is a manifestation of the fundamental importance of chain migration – because of the strength of family/local ties, most movers were channelled into a narrow range of occupational and residential situations. The origins of such specialisations lie in the essentially random experiences of pioneer migrants,[91] the fact that their villages of origin had long traditions of skill in particular crafts or stressed entrepreneurial values. The resultant labour segmentation eases entry into the urban labour market for villagers with an appropriate network of contacts but it excludes those with no such contacts. This is especially so for more remunerative and secure occupations, so that movers without connections are forced to seek work in the marginal activities mentioned earlier.

5. Temporary Versus Permanent Labour Migration

It is clear from fieldwork that much of the increased movement out of West Javan villages during the 1970s was of a temporary nature. Moreover, there was little evidence from the villages that circular migration and commuting were seen as a transitory phase in which movers 'test' the urban environment before settling permanently in the city. In the 1973 study, only 1.6 per cent of the temporary movers indicated an intention to eventually settle in an urban area, while 93.2 per cent intended to remain in the village and 5.2 per cent were undecided. In the 1979 study, 8.5 per cent had intentions of eventual relocation, 89.4 per cent intended to remain in the village and 2.1 per cent were undecided. The indications were that many movers had little choice in the selection of a temporary rather than a permanent move strategy.[92] More than half the movers gave as a reason for not settling in the city the high cost of living and of housing in the city, and many respondents stated that they could not support their family on their urban earnings alone and were forced to retain sources of income that required residence in the village. It should also be borne in mind that the movement frequently results from a household or family decision rather than of the mover himself or herself and that the mobility is seen as part of a household allocation of labour to ensure survival. In the past, most of this labour was deployed in the village (although sometimes in non-agricultural activities) or in nearby areas.[93] The reduction of job opportunities in the wake of the structural changes mentioned earlier forced families to extend the area over which their labour was deployed, and the circular migration and commuting associated with this was facilitated by transport improvements. There were two basic strategies. In some cases, particular household members were assigned to work almost entirely outside the village, returning only briefly for regular visits and to deliver their earnings. In other cases, households maximised their incomes by encouraging some members to work in the village at times of peak labour demand, such as planting or harvesting, but to seek work in the city or elsewhere at other times, leaving other members to cope with limited village labour needs. By leaving dependents in the village, the movers effectively reduced the cost of subsistence in the city or other destination, not only because accommodation, food and transport costs were usually greater there (especially in the city) but also because an individual could put up with cheaper and less comfortable conditions than his family would require, thus cutting personal costs to a minimum. By earning in the city and spending in the village, the mover maximised consumption. This latter aspect (especially accommodation costs) was of basic importance to most commuters, who tended to engage in village work much less than did circular migrants.

A second dimension to the predominance of temporary mobility is that it spreads the risk for village households. The village studies indicated this was important among mover households, who considered it imperative to keep their village options open, so that the risk of not being able to earn subsistence was reduced by spreading it between a range of village and city income-earning opportunities. Moreover, there were several village support systems that could be mobilised in times of economic or emotional need, namely the nuclear and wider family, the tradition of *gotong royong* (mutual self-help) in the village community and the traditional *bapak/anak buah* (patron/client) relations. In most cases such support was not available in the city, so that if a mover maintained a stake in his village he did not cut himself off from what was often the only available support in times of dire need.

This discussion should not be interpreted as indicating that households and individuals in West Java had a vast choice in deciding their labour allocation. In fact, the decisions were made within severe constraints. Village options had been reduced for the majority of the population who did not own means of production. For many, work outside the village was an absolute necessity for survival.

6. The Impact of Increased Labour Migration on the Village

The relationship between structural change and population movement is not a simple uni-directional one. Structural adjustments could be and were initiated at places of origin and destination in one or more of three ways:

1. Adjustment to the permanent or temporary absence of out-movers.
2. Adjustment to the permanent or temporary presence of in-movers.
3. Adjustment to the reciprocal flows of money, goods, information, ideas and attitudes initiated along the linkages established by movers between origin and destination.[94]

These impacts are manifold and cannot be dealt with in detail in the space available here.[95] We will therefore focus on the impact of the increased mobility on income, although it impinged on many other elements of the village, such as agricultural productivity, employment, traditional roles (especially of women), health, welfare and social change.[96] The raison d'être of most circular migration and commuting was to enhance the income of their village-based families. Hence all temporary movers remitted money and 81.1 per cent brought back goods, often in the form of gifts for their families. In West Java, the nuclear family was the 'unit of most decisions about consumption, savings and investment and the unit of most production'.[97] Therefore, it is essential to consider the impact of remittances on household, rather than individual, incomes.

In the West Java studies, some inter-village differences in the relative importance of remittances in the total income of their households of origin were observed according to the type of mobility that predominated in the villages. First, since there was little seasonal or day-to-day fluctuation in rates of rural-urban commuting, most commuters were employed on a full-time basis in urban areas, and 60 per cent of the income of their households of origin consisted of remittances. Circular migrants were more likely to be employed in the village during part of the year, and their urban participation was thus more intermittent. Even so, their remittances still accounted for nearly half of their households' total income on average. Yet, as argued elsewhere, most examinations of remittances concentrate on those of permanent migrants, ignoring those of temporary movers.[98] Among permanent migrants, 52 per cent had brought back or sent money in the year prior to survey and 62 per cent had brought or sent goods. On average, these remittances made up 11 per cent of the incomes of migrants' households of origin.

The major use of remittances was the purchase, at comparatively cheap village prices, of the basic necessities of life, namely food and, to a lesser extent, clothing. Schooling expenses were also significant, as were ceremonies, especially for circumcision and marriage, and the purchase of consumer goods, such as pressure lanterns and radios.

Among circular migrants, the average proportions of income earned in the city remitted ranged from 21 per cent to 44 per cent. These ratios were particularly high considering the meagre levels of urban earnings. In fact, most circular migrants accepted absolutely minimal living conditions in the city in order to maximise the amount remitted and the frequency with which they could return to the village. The study of the West Javan villages indicated it was absolutely critical to the wellbeing of many village households for remittances to continue.

The social implications for the village of the dominance of non-permanent movements between village and city should also not be ignored. The fact that such mobility often involves prolonged and regular separation of husbands from wives and children means that 'loss' of migrants affects not only the social organisation and structure of the community but the family during the crucial stage of the family life-cycle when household heads are fertile and economically active. The findings of the village surveys concerning the role of rural-urban population mobility in bringing about social change in the village were somewhat inconclusive. However, it is clear that return-migrants themselves, and the advice they gave, were highly respected in the village, giving them a potentially important role as agents of change. Moreover, movers were generally more 'modern' than non-migrants and there is little doubt they had been important contributors to the creation of positive attitudes towards education. On the other hand, there is little evidence that movers had challenged the traditional authority structure in the village.

Lipton quoted studies, many from Africa in situations with little population pressure on resources, to support the view that out-migration leads to reduced agricultural productivity and a deterioration of the agricultural system.[99] However, in the densely-settled survey villages, where the marginal productivity of labour was virtually zero except for short periods of peak labour demand such as the harvest season, there was little evidence of such a pattern. In recent years there have been some reports in West Java of labour shortage during these periods of peak demand, although Sinaga suggested that these were restricted to 'occasional spots in Java . . . but they can be solved (as they have always been solved in many regions) by increasing spatial mobility of labour'.[100] For example, in the rich agricultural areas surrounding the city of Bandung it was reported that in 1981 there was a deficit of labour during peaks of the agricultural cycle because labourers at newly-constructed factories on the outskirts of Bandung were being paid at least Rp. 1,400 per day, whereas agricultural labourers received only Rp. 750.[101] Collier *et al.* also reported some labour shortages and an improvement in real wages in agriculture in their study villages in the good seasons of the 1979-82 period.[102] They considered such advances were associated with ideal weather conditions for rice production in this period and a growing availability of off-farm out-of-village employment. They also suggested that any continuation of this progress depended on 'favourable weather for rice production and part on substantial government revenues flowing into the construction, service and industrial sectors of the national economy'.[103] It seems the labour shortages were occurring in the richest agricultural areas, where up to three rice crops per year were being grown. However, in the villages under consideration here there was little evidence of *sawah* being neglected because of labour shortages.

7. Conclusion

It is difficult to generalise about structural changes in rural West

Java during the 1970s, since the period encompasses an initial period of increase in agricultural production benefiting mainly those with access to land, a period of crisis during the *wereng* infestation, and more recently a period of unprecedented increase in agricultural output when it seems some of the benefits accrued to the poor.[104]

There is no doubt that participation of rural-based Javans in off-farm employment, most of it outside the village and much of it in cities, increased greatly over that period. Associated with this has been an upswing in labour mobility, much of it of a non-permanent kind. The implications are many, not the least being a blurring of the distinction between urban and rural labour markets and a strengthening of the links between them, since individuals frequently participated in both or the family's workforce was deployed so as to spread it between both. This also means that major shifts and policy measures in the urban sector will also impinge on the village economy. It is frequently vital to the welfare of village households that access to income-earning opportunities in cities is preserved. For example, in the early 1970s legislation was enacted in Jakarta to restrict the areas where pedicabs and street-hawkers could operate. As the bulk of the workers affected were circular migrants the dwindling remittances to their villages along the north coast of West Java had a devastating effect. Of course, the reverse also applies; major shifts in rural areas are being felt in urban labour markets. For example, the failure of the harvest in Krawang due to drought and *wereng* infestation in 1977 caused a huge influx into Jakarta of people seeking work, such that the city authorities had to build barracks to accommodate them and take other welfare measures.

Structural changes in agriculture resulted in major increases in production but displaced labour, so that the landless and near landless that made up more than half of households dependent upon agriculture have experienced reduced access to employment opportunities in this part of the rural economy. Their response has been to spread their labour over a wider area, a process facilitated by the improved transport system. Most have not become proletarianised residents of urban areas because they cannot earn sufficient in either the village or the city to support their families, so that participation in both labour markets via circular migration has become necessary for the survival of such families. As a result, the wellbeing of villagers in West Java, especially the landless, has increasingly become dependent on urban sources of income, making that wellbeing rather fragile. It depends on continued prosperity and expansion of the urban economy, but the downturn in national foreign exchange earnings due to reduced world oil and gas prices seems likely to have especially detrimental consequences in the cities. In rural areas, the recent sequence of excellent seasons has maintained demand for agricultural labour, which has somewhat disguised (together with the increased out-migration) the fundamental changes displacing agricultural labour. The onset of less favourable weather conditions in 1983 will have reduced the work available for the landless, notwithstanding the reports of labour shortage in 1981 and 1982. This occurred in a context in which many of the institutions and mechanisms that have assured the security and survival of the poor of village Java, albeit at a very marginal level, have been weakened.

The outlook for the landless circular migrants is therefore a cause for concern. This is especially true in view of the harsh demographic realities of the growth of Java's workforce, which will double within a few decades and during the 1980s increase by around one quarter of a million workers each year.[105] Some commentators have seen the recent expansion of circular mobility as offering a long-term solution to the employment problems of rural Java. Collier et al., for example, saw

some basis for hope that rural society in Java is becoming one marked by a small proportion of commercial farmers and agricultural labourers with reasonable living standards, and a much larger proportion, perhaps a majority, of villagers earning a substantial share of their family incomes from construction, services or the industrial sectors of the economy.[106]

Such a vision of the future would assign circular migration a significant role in the support of the landless and near-landless of rural Java. However, the extent to which circular labour mobility constitutes a satisfactory long-term solution to village poverty and maldistribution of wealth must be open to question. There is some evidence that circular mobility functions as a survival strategy for landless families, and like other such strategies, is a mechanism whereby the poor are able to obtain just enough to survive at a bare subsistence but not improve their level of living. Is the upswing in circular mobility simply a means whereby the involutionary struggle of the rural poor in Java has been extended over a wider spatial area? Is it simply a stop-gap measure that will maintain, or perhaps exacerbate, current rural inequalities, whereas only a more fundamental restructuring, and policies that direct more resources toward the landless would really help the poor in the long term? Unfortunately, our knowledge of circular mobility and its short-term, let alone longer-run, implications is too limited to address these questions, and research directed toward elucidating the complex relationship between structural change and population mobility in rural Java should be a major priority.

Notes

1. J. Meijer-Ranneft: 'Volksverplaatsing op Java', in *Tijdschrift voor het Binnenlandsch Bestuur*, 1916, vol. 49, pp. 59-87, 165-84.

2. The 1980 census information quoted here is drawn from Biro Pusat Statistik: *Penduduk Indonesia 1980 Menurut Propinsi dan Kabupaten/Kotamadya* (Jakarta, 1981).

3. K.J. Pelzer: *Pioneer settlement in the Asiatic tropics* (New York, American Geographical Society, 1945), p. 162.

4. S. Arief: *Indonesia: Pertumbuhan ekonomi disparitas pendapatan dan kemiskinan massal* (Jakarta, Lembaga Studi Pembangunan, 1979), p. 79.

5. Elsewhere it has been argued that the distinction between urban and rural is a very blurred one in Indonesia – G.J. Hugo, S. Suharto and H. Sigit: *Migration, urbanization and development in Indonesia* (New York, United Nations, 1981), p. 9.

6. World bank: *Employment and income distribution in Indonesia* (Washington, DC, 1980), p. 84.

7. Biro Pusat Statistik: *Social indicators, 1978* (Jakarta, 1979).

8. G.J. Hugo: 'Population mobility in West Java, Indonesia', PhD dissertation, Department of Geography, Australian National University, Canberra, 1975; idem: *Population mobility in West Java* (Yogyakarta, Gadjah Mada University Press, 1978).

9. This study was conducted with Dr I.B. Mantra of the Population Studies Centre, Gadjah Mada University, Yogyakarta, and Dr A.D. Saefullah, Population Studies Centre, Pajajaran University, Bandung.

10. A kabupaten is a regency – a large administrative unit which in Java has an average population of 950,000 persons.

11. The main results have been published elsewhere. G.J. Hugo: *Cikaso Irrigation Project pre-feasibility study, May 1982*, vol. 5: *Sociological study* (Bandung, West Java Public Works Department, 1982) (hereafter referred to as Hugo, 1982a).

12. A.D. Saefullah: *Mobilitas tenagas kerja dan ciri-ciri ketenaga kerjaan*

wilayah pembangunan Banten dan Sukabumi (Bandung, Population Studies Centre, Pajajaran University, 1981); idem: *Mobilitas tenaga kerja dan ciri-ciri katenaga kerjaan pada wilayah pembangunan Priangan Timur* (Bandung, Population Studies Centre, Pajajaran University, 1982).

13. W.L. Collier, W.G. Soentoro, E. Pasandaran, K. Santoso and J.F. Stepanek: 'Acceleration of rural development in Java', in *Bulletin of Indonesian Economic Studies*, 1982, vol. 18 no. 3, pp. 84-101 (hereafter referred to as Collier *et al.*, 1982a).

14. Between 1978 and 1981 rice production increased from 17.5 to 22 million metric tons. The per capita availability of rice in kg/person/year increased from 98.4 to 108 between 1960 and 1970 and to 149.3 in 1981. W.L. Collier, W.G. Soentoro, E. Pasandaran, K. Santoso and J.F. Stepanek: *Accelerating rural development in Java from village studies to macro perspective of rural Java*, Occasional Paper, Rural Dynamics Study, Agro-economic Survey, No. 6 (Bogor, Indonesia, 1982), p. 10 (hereafter referred to as Collier *et al.*, 1982b).

15. L.A. Mears: *The new rice economy of Indonesia* (Yogyakarta, Gadjah Mada University Press, 1981), p. 21.

16. C. Geertz: *Agricultural involution: The processes of ecological change in Indonesia*: (Berkeley, University of California Press, 1963).

17. Ibid., pp. 77-81.

18. K.D. Jackson: 'Urbanization and the rise of patron-client relations: The changing quality of interpersonal communications in the neighbourhoods of Bandung and the villages of West Java', in K.D. Jackson and L.W. Pye (eds.): *Political power and communication in Indonesia* (Berkeley, University of California Press, 1978), pp. 343-94; idem: 'Traditional authority and national integration: the D'Arul Islam rebellion in West Java', PhD dissertation, Massachusetts Institute of Technology, Boston, 1971.

19. World Bank, 1980, p. 29.

20. *Bimas* means 'mass guidance' and is the name given to the Indonesian National Government's agricultural extension programme for rice.

21. W.L. Collier and Sayogyo: 'Employment opportunities created by high-yielding rice varieties in several areas on Java', in *Ekonomi dan Keuangan Indonesia*, 1972, vol. 20, p. 4.

22. W.L. Collier, J. Colter and C. Saleh: 'Observations on recent rice problems at the farm level in Subang Kabupaten, Bogor', in *Agro-Economic Survey Research Notes*, No. 12 (Bogor, Indonesia, 1972), pp. 5-6.

23. W.L. Collier, G. Wiradi and K. Soentoro: 'Some recent changes in rice harvesting methods', in *Bulletin of Indonesian Economic Studies*, 1973, vol. 9 no. 2, pp. 36-45; W. Utami and J. Ihalauw: 'Some consequences of small farm size', in *Bulletin of Indonesian Economic Studies*, 1973, vol. 9 no. 2, pp. 46-56.

24. Y. Hayami and A. Hafid: 'Rice harvesting and welfare in rural Java', in *Bulletin of Indonesian Economic Studies*, 1979, vol. 15, no. 2, p. 95.

25. Ibid.

26. W.L. Collier: 'Agricultural evolution in Java', in G.E. Hansen (ed.): *Agricultural and rural development in Indonesia* (Westview, Boulder, 1981), p. 159; Utami and Ihalauw, 1973, p. 55.

27. Collier, 1981, p. 168.

28. Ibid., p. 161.

29. The *ani-ani* is a small blade held in the fingers and used to cut rice stalk by stalk. It is the traditional method of harvesting used in Java.

30. Collier *et al.*, 1973, p. 42.

31. Ibid., pp. 43–4.

32. W.L. Collier, J. Colter and C. Saleh: 'Observations on recent rice problems at the farm level in Subang Kabupaten, Bogor', in *Agro-economic Survey Research Notes*, 1972, no. 12, p. 3.

33. R. Sinaga: 'Implications of agricultural mechanization for employment and income distribution: A case study of Indramayu, West Java', in *Bulletin of Indonesian Economic Studies*, 1978, vol. 16, no. 2, pp. 102-11 and *Tempo*, 28 July 1979.

34. Ibid, p. 102.

35. Ibid.; Collier, 1981, p. 164; J. Lingard and A.S. Bagyo: 'The impact of agricultural mechanisation on production and employment in rice areas of West Java', in *Bulletin of Indonesian Economic Studies*, 1983, vol. 19, no. 1, pp. 53-67.

36. Collier, 1981, p. 163.

37. R. Sinaga: *Rural institutions serving small farmers in the village of Sukagalik, Garut Regency, West Java*, paper prepared for ESCAP Expert Groups Meeting on Rural Institutions Servicing Small Farmers, Bangkok, December 1976, p. 6.

38. W.L. Collier, J. Colter, Sinarhadi and R. d'A. Shaw: 'Choice of technique in rice milling – a comment', in *Bulletin of Indonesian Economic Studies*, 1974, vol. 10, no. 1, pp. 106-120.

39. M. Singarimbun: 'Srijarjo revisited', in *Bulletin of Indonesian Economic Studies*, 1976, vol. 12, no. 2, pp. 117-25.

40. Collier, 1981, p. 166.

41. Ibid., p. 171.

42. Collier *et al.*, 1982a, p. 86.

43. G. Sacerdoti: 'Help for Java's drought victims', in *Far Eastern Economic Review*, 1977, vol. 98, no. 43, pp. 48-9.

44. Rp. 500 = US$ 1, approximately.

45. A. Aten: 'Some remarks on rural industry', in *Indonesie*, 1952-3, vol. 6, p. 331.

46. Ibid., pp. 330-45.

47. D.H. Penny and M. Singarimbun: *Population and poverty in rural Java: Some economic arithmetic from Srijarjo*, Cornell International Agricultural Development Monograph No. 41 (Ithaca, Cornell University, 1973), p. 2.

48. With dry land being given a value 0.4 that of *sawah* and *pekarangan* – ibid., p. 8.

49. T.R. Leinbach: 'Transport evaluation in rural development: An Indonesian case study', in *Third World Planning Review*, 1983, vol. 5, no. 1, pp. 23-35.

50. For a detailed discussion of the accuracy of these data, the growth of Indonesia's motor vehicle fleet and the implications of that growth, see G.J. Hugo: 'Road transport, population mobility and development in Indonesia', in G.W. Jones and H.V. Richter (eds.): *Population mobility and development*, Development Studies Centre Monograph No. 27 (Canberra, Australian National University, 1981).

51. This includes not only minibuses but also sedans, jeeps, taxis, oplets and bemos.

52. The 1980 census also showed that one in three Indonesian households owned a bicycle.

53. Hugo, 1982a, p. 170.

54. The main studies are by Leinbach and Hugo. See, e.g., T.R. Leinbach: *Feeder road impact within the rural works program* (Jakarta, 1978; mimeographed); idem: *Rural transport, trip characteristics and information channels: Some observations from the Indonesian Rural Works Program* (Lexington, University of Kentucky, 1979; mimeographed); idem, 1983; Hugo, 1981; idem, 1982a.

55. Leinbach, 1983, pp. 30-3.

56. Hugo, 1981.

57. G. McNicoll: 'Recent demographic trends in Indonesia', in *Population and Development Review*, 1972, vol. 8, no. 4, p. 817.

58. Among village-leader households interviewed, 65 per cent had radios and 10 per cent had television sets.

59. B. White: 'Political aspects of poverty, income distribution and their measurement: Some examples from rural Java', in *Development and Change*, 1979, vol. 10, pp. 91-114.

60. Collier *et al.*, p. 85; Arief, 1979.

61. White, 1979, p. 101.

62. F. Husken: 'Landlords, sharecroppers and agricultural labourers: Changing labour relations in rural Java', in *Journal of Contemporary Asia*, 1979, vol. 9, p. 149.

63. J. Alexander and P. Alexander: 'Shared poverty as ideology: Agrarian relationships in colonial Java', in *Man*, 1982, vol. 17, no. 4, pp. 597-619.

64. Leinbach, 1983.

65. Collier *et al.*, 1982b, p. 17.

66. World Bank, 1980, p. 42.

67. Indeed, in the good seasons from 1978 to 1981 there seems to have been an upturn in real wages – Collier *et al.*, 1982b, p. 50.

68. G.W. Jones: 'Population growth in Java', in J.J. Fox, R.G. Garnaut, P.T. McCawley and J.A.C. Mackie (eds.): *Indonesia: Australian perspectives* (Canberra, Australian National University, Research School for Pacific Studies, 1980), p. 578.

69. Collier *et al.*, 1982b, p. 50; World Bank, 1980, p. 45.

70. E.g., G. McNicoll: 'Internal migration in Indonesia', in *Indonesia*, 1968, vol. 5, pp. 33-9; D.W. Fryer and J.C. Jackson: *Indonesia* (London, Ernest Benn, 1977), p. 18.

71. Hugo, 1975, pp. 234-8.

72. G.J. Hugo: 'Population movements in Indonesia during the colonial period', in J.J. Fox *et al.*, 1980, pp. 95-135.

73. F. de Haan: *Priangan* (Batavia, Bataviaasch Genootschap van Kunsten en Wetenschappen, 1912), vol. I, pp. 31-2.

74. G.J. Hugo: 'Circular migration in Indonesia', in *Population and Development Review*, 1982, vol. 8, no. 1, pp. 59-84; also published as East-West Population Institute reprint no. 149.

75. For a typology of population mobility based on the West Java data, see G.J. Hugo: 'New conceptual approaches to migration in the context of urbanization: Some observations based on experience in Indonesia', in P. Morrison (ed.): *Population movements, their forms and functions in urbanization and development* (Liège, Ordina, 1983), pp. 69-114 (hereafter Hugo, 1983a).

76. S. Rusli: 'Inter-rural migration and circulation in Indonesia: The case of West Java', MA thesis, Canberra, Australian National University, Development Studies Centre, 1978.

77. Hugo, 1978, p. 142.

78. Collier *et al.*, 1982a, p. 90.

79. World Bank, 1980, p. 41.

80. Indonesia, Direktorat Tenaga Kerja: 'Labour force sample survey in Java and Madura', in *Ekonomi dan Keuangan Indonesia*, 1963, vol. 16, p. 33.

81. On urban unemployment, see G.W. Jones and C.M. Manning: *Urban employment in Jakarta, Bandung and Surabaya* (1974; mimeographed). On wage levels, see World Bank, 1980, pp. 68-9. The World Bank concludes that 'on balance it is doubtful whether urban unskilled wages in manufacturing, construction, transport or services are markedly out of line with average earnings of agricultural labourers in surrounding areas'.

82. Hugo *et al.*, 1981, p. 154.

83. J. Osborn: 'Government and urbanization in Indonesia', paper presented to 13th Pacific Science Congress, Vancouver, August 1975, p. 6.

84. A. Booth and A. Tyabji: 'Survey of recent developments', in *Bulletin of Indonesian Economic Studies*, 1979, vol. 15, no. 2, p. 34.

85. Hugo *et al.*, 1981, p. 68.

86. The tobacco is recycled in cheap cigarettes.

87. K. Hart: 'Informal income opportunities and urban employment in Ghana', in *The Journal of Modern African Studies*, 1973, vol. 2, no. 1, p. 68.

88. Jackson, 1978.

89. R.Z. Oostingh: 'The Pegawai Negri of Bandung: Structure and process in Indonesia', PhD dissertation, University of Virginia, 1970, pp. 134-42.

90. Hugo, 1978, p. 207.

91. Hugo, 1975, p. 545.

92. See, e.g., Hugo, 1978, pp. 197-9.

93. Seasonal circular migration over short distances between rural areas during the slack season in the home area to participate in the harvest elsewhere has a long history in Java.

94. G.J. Hugo: 'Evaluation of the impact of migration on individuals, households and communities', in United Nations, Economic and Social Commission for Asia and the Pacific: *National migration surveys: Guidelines for analysis* (New York, 1983; ST/ESCAP/203), pp. 189-215 (hereafter Hugo, 1983b).

95. See Hugo, 1978, Chapter 7.

96. Hugo, 1983b; A.B. Simmons: 'Hypotheses and analytic approaches for the study of the demographic and social consequences of migration', in United Nations, ESCAP: *National migration surveys: Guidelines for analysis* (New York, 1983; ST/ESCAP/203), pp. 163-88.

97. A.W. Palmer: 'Situradja: A village in highland Priangan', in Koentjaraningrat (ed.): *Villages in Indonesia* (New York, Cornell University Press, 1967), p. 315.

98. G.J. Hugo: 'Population mobility and wealth transfer in the Third World', *Papers of the East-West Population Institute*, No. 87 (Honolulu, 1983).

99. M. Lipton: 'Migration from rural areas of poor countries: The impact on rural productivity and income distribution', in *World Development*, 1980, vol. 8, no. 1, p. 7.

100. Sinaga, 1978, p. 111.

101. In the magazine *Tempo* (24 October 1981, pp. 51-2) in an article entitled 'Selamat jalan buruh tani' ('Goodbye farm worker').

102. Collier *et al.*, 1982a.

103. Collier *et al.*, 1982b, p. 74.

104. Collier *et al.*, 1982a.

105. A.M. Strout: 'Agricultural growth, employment and income distribution: Dilemmas for Indonesia's next Five-Year Plan', in *Prisma*, 1977, vol. 7, p. 11.

106. Collier *et al.* 1982a, pp. 100-1.

3
Circulatory Migration and Social Differentiation in the Andes

JULIAN LAITE

I. Introduction

The expansion of the international capitalist economy has influenced patterns of migration throughout the southern hemisphere.[1] There has been a massive migration of peasants to the cities, the concomitant of urbanisation, but there has also been considerable return migration by these people to their places of origin, either temporarily or for longer periods. This circulatory migration, coupled with other processes linked to capitalist expansion, such as proletarianisation and commercialisation, can result in an increase in socio-economic differentiation in rural areas. Patterns of circulatory migration have occurred in Africa, India and Latin America and despite important differences in their rates, structures and political environments, it is clear that many have been associated with the processes of capital accumulation and establishment of labour systems in the Third World. In turn, these processes are linked to developments in the international economy.

The presence of circulatory migration is of both theoretical and practical interest. First, through analysis of this process it is possible to shed light on the forms of rural production, their rationale and labour utilisation. The relations between different productive forms are also revealed in this way. Second, the information relating to circulatory migration is relevant to an assessment of how rural peoples will respond to policy initiatives and what form such initiatives might take. Those involved in patterns of circulatory migration do not see their interests as lying within, or circumscribed by, one economic sector. Rather, they have a range of interests across sectors and their adherence to these may frustrate policy initiatives in any one sector.

Some regions of Latin America became part of the international economy due to the Conquest in the sixteenth century. Since then capitalist institutions and production relations have increasingly penetrated the subcontinent. One such region is the central highlands of Peru, which came under Spanish domination in the sixteenth century. A mainly agricultural region, it also contains mines and towns and as such, since the Conquest, it has been linked to a wider economic system. Through both relations of exchange and production, socio-economic differentiation in the region has increased. Village economies have become commercialised in order to both buy and sell commodities, while rural labour has been a commodity used in both agrarian and urban production processes.

Circulatory migration between villages and mines in the region presumably existed during Inca times and was certainly present from the early years of Spanish colonisation. Today, migration is widespread throughout the central *sierra* of Peru. Most is the uni-directional movement of people from the countryside to towns and the capital, Lima. But there is also considerable return-migration to the highlands. Returning migrants bring with them new ideas, values and cash, all of which further socio-economic change in the rural areas. Circulatory migration supports capitalist penetration of the countryside, the commercialisation of social relations there and the tendency towards socio-economic differentiation.

A considerable debate now exists on the process of capitalist penetration of rural areas, originated by Lenin in his analysis of the development of capitalism in Russia.[2] He stressed the role played by migration in adding to differentiation in the country-side and was challenged by Chayanov, who argued that such differentiation was more due to processes internal to the peasant economy and that this economy was highly resistant to capitalist penetration.[3] In the ensuing debate the concept of the peasant economy and its relation to the capitalist economy have been important elements.[4] The former economy is distinguishable from the latter by its units of combined production and consumption, household labour and lack of market valuations. The resilience of the peasant household and extended family, plus the mutual aid practices found amongst peasants, ranging from household exchanges to communal co-operation, result in a dogged resistance by the peasant economy to capitalist transformation. Vergopolous has argued that the very persistence of small peasant ownership is due in part to the development of capitalism, although Kay's analysis of agrarian change and migration in Chile supports more the capitalist development of large-scale enterprises.[5] In Peru there is seen to be a particular Andean organisation of this peasant economy, separate from the capitalist economy.[6]

Such household structures and co-operative practices exist among peasants in the Mantaro Valley, located in the Peruvian central Andres. However, such practices and institutions do not constitute a mode of production separate from the capitalist development of the region.[7] Rather, they form part of that development. In this region it is difficult to identify social groups and institutions which operate exclusively in either agriculture, mining or commerce. Rather, families, workers, traders and agriculturalists operate across a number of sectors such that the labour systems and the process of accumulation are regional, rather than pertaining to any one sector. The region is undergoing capitalist transformation that is increasing socio-economic differentiation. Yet, the extent of polarisation in the rural economy has been limited by peasant practices and institutions. For example, there is not open and widespread conflict between agrarian classes in the villages, even though differentiation has increased. Co-operative arrangements, kin networks and rural emigration have acted to curtail conflict.

Understanding the nature of the peasant economy and the processes of differentiation and migration are important for shaping and implementing policies in rural areas. Policies oriented to transforming peasant farming into efficient monoculture may be thwarted because they cut across the grain of agrarian organisation. At present, the peasant household is maintained within a circulatory migration system because it provides foodstuffs to family migrants, is a place of productive employment for circulatory migrants and their elderly kin, and is a means of subsistence social security for the extended family. Modern capital-intensive monoculture threatens those functions. Thus policies aimed at the better marketing of peasant produce may take control of marketing out of the hands of the peasant household.

Policies oriented to industrial change in the rural areas may be neglected. Yet, because of their migration histories, villagers – seemingly peasants – are often ex-mechanics, lathe-turners and lorry drivers. Some, with savings gleaned from migration wages, will have invested in a small piece of machinery, or even a lorry, but find little government support for industrial or commercial ventures. Policies oriented to population control may also be frustrated. Limiting the number of children may mean limiting the number of economic sectors in which a family is involved, thus increasing its specialisation and dependence on any one sector.

Policies implemented at the local level will also be affected by social differentiation and national events and policies. Social differentiation may lead to one agrarian or merchant class seizing on a policy initiative and using it in their own interests. Once seen as such by the remainder of the peasantry, the policy may falter due to lack of popular involvement. At the national level, decisions may be taken to expand or limit an urban or industrial sector which will have immediate consequences for peasants attempting to market produce through, for example, new government agencies. A system of circulatory migration then is the context in which peasant households operate and which links local and national levels in Third World countries. It is such a system that operates in the Mantaro Valley in Peru.

II. The Mantaro Valley: Villages and Migration

The Mantaro Valley lies at 3,000 metres in the Peruvian Andes, is 80 kilometres long and 3-5 kilometres wide. It is some six hours' road and rail journey from Lima. Through the valley flows the broad Mantaro River, and at either end of the valley stand the towns of Jauja and Huancayo. The valley contains numerous villages and *communidades*, and the dominant economic activity is agriculture, practised under a *minifundia*, or smallholding system, centred on household subsistence farming. In 1961 some 90 per cent of the farm units in the region were under 5 hectares and the trend was towards increasing fragmentation of land ownership.[8]

Alongside agriculture there is a wide range of occupations, from pottery to lorry driving, while commercial activities are

Figure 3.1: Peru: Highland Towns and Villages the Installations of Cerro de Pasco Corporation

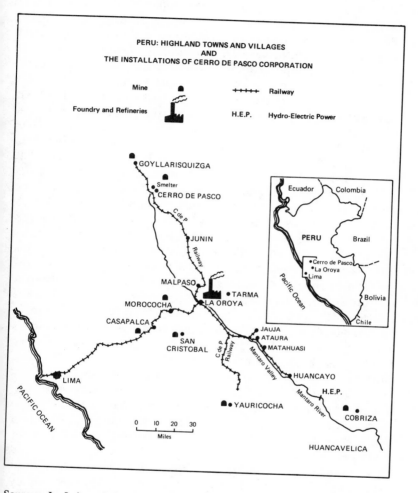

Source: J. Laite: *Industrial development and migrant labour* (Manchester University Press, 1981). Reprinted by kind permission of the publishers.

important. Much of the commercial activity is centred on the two towns, but much is also carried on in the villages, or in a network of rotating fairs. Also, around the valley, and at some hours distance from it, lie the mines and mining towns of central Peru. These mines have long been exploited by the Incas, Spanish and Americans, and all have used labour drawn from the valley.

In the agricultural economy of the valley, three major social classes exist, defined in relation to the means of agricultural production.[9] The first consists of the rich peasants who have sufficient land to produce a surplus for the market. This class is itself differentiated. Some rich peasants use household labour mainly, while others rely on hired workers; some combine their agricultural-production interests with trading, to the extent that some are mainly traders, perhaps using land and products as security against entrepreneurial ventures. Around 15 per cent of the households in the valley are rich peasant households.[10]

The second class consists of subsistence peasants. This group produces enough for household necessities, but no more. Consequently, there is little accumulation of capital among this class. To supplement their incomes members of these peasant households engage in craft work, migrate to urban work-centres or work sporadically on the land of rich peasants. The third class consists of the poor peasants, who are again differentiated. Some have small plots of land that do not meet their subsistence needs while others are landless labourers. These peasants work regularly in the fields of others, migrate to do wage labour, or work in the commercial ventures of the rich peasants as porters and labourers. Also included in this class are *comuneros* who have usufructory rights to sections of communal land. The subsistence peasants comprise between 40 and 50 per cent of valley peasant households, while the poor peasants account for 35-40 per cent.[11]

In order to assess the impact on the rural economy of capitalist expansion and migration, two villages in the Mantaro Valley were selected for analysis. Ataura and Matahuasi are two villages that lie on the east bank of the Mantaro River, some 20 kilometres apart. Ataura is small in terms of land and population, whereas Matahuasi is large, prosperous and expanding. Migrants from both villages live and work in the mines and Lima, and both villages have high rates of emigration. Of all the villages in the Mantaro Valley, Ataura has the highest proportion of its sons working in the mines, while Matahuasi has the largest number of villagers living and working outside the valley. Only just over half of the adults living in the two villages were born there.[12]

In 1971 Ataura had a population of about 1,700 and occupied around 600 hectares of land, 400 of which were viable for crops or pasture. The main occupational activity was agriculture practised within *minifundia*. Ataura was composed overwhelmingly of poor peasants. Four-fifths of the households owned or worked less than 1 hectare, and it required between 3 and 4 hectares of irrigated valley-bottom land to meet the subsistence needs of households.[13] One-fifth of the Ataura households owned more than 1 hectare, but most of them owned only between 1 and 2 hectares. Only two people in Ataura owned around 5 hectares.

In 1971 there were 107 adult men living and working in Ataura. Nearly all had some agricultural interest, but only one-third were peasants without a supplementary occupation. Around half were artisans, with shoe-making, house-building and driving being the most common occupations. Shopkeepers and professionals each made up one-tenth of the resident males respectively, the former often selling the products of their own fields, while the latter were schoolteachers or retired white-collar workers. Two-thirds of the men were independent workers, one-tenth were mainly independent, occasionally hiring out their services to others, while one quarter were dependent workers. Of these dependent workers, one quarter worked not for cash, but as *partidarios*, splitting the cost and profit of cultivation with the owner of the land. The remainder of the dependent workers worked for small concerns, the government, or private landholders. Two-thirds of all the men worked in and around Ataura, while the others worked in Jauja, Huancayo, or valley villages.

Matahuasi is a much larger village than Ataura, in 1971 consisting of some 3,000 inhabitants, and extending over some 2,000 hectares, most of which was cultivable.[14] Like Ataura, the predominant activity in Matahuasi was agriculture, but the class structure of Matahuasi was more differentiated than that of the smaller village. Nearly all of the Matahuasi households were engaged in agricultural production. One-seventh of Matahuasi households were rich peasants, controlling 4 or more hectares of cultivable land, while nearly two-fifths controlled between 1 and 4 hectares. So, a little over half of the village households were those of rich and subsistence peasants.

The other half of the households were those of poor peasants, a class internally differentiated. One group in this class were the landless labourers, who comprised one-fifth of Matahuasi's households. This group had been growing. The second group were peasants controlling less than 1 hectare, accounting for one quarter of village households. At the same time, Matahuasi has long been a recognised *comunidad*, and there was an extension of 60 hectares of communal land. *Comuneros* with usufructory rights to this land were drawn from the class of poor peasants, there being 120 households with such communal rights.

As well as Matahuasi's agrarian structure being more differentiated than that of Ataura, the larger village's occupational structure was also more complex. Although in Matahuasi most households were engaged in agriculture, only half of the heads of households were solely peasants. The remainder were shopkeepers and traders, artisans, teachers and other professionals, and unskilled workers. Each group accounted for around one-tenth of household heads. Importantly, the commercial activities in Matahuasi were on a much larger scale than in Ataura. As well as prosperous shopkeepers catering to the large population and outsiders, there were timber merchants, agricultural traders and milk producers. Some members of this commercial stratum were rich peasants with trading outlets, but others were mainly traders who maintained an agricultural base.

These two villages form part of a circulatory migration process which embraces the highlands, the mines and Lima. Seasonal migration from the poorer villages lying at the foot of the eastern valley side provide female agricultural labour to work in the fields of richer villages, as well as supplying male temporary labour to the mines of Huancavelica and the hydro-electric power station to the south. The women from these poorer villages are recruited both by large landholders and by the families of men working in urban centres, who send home cash to help with the hiring of this casual labour. The rural migrant in the urban work centre may be joined by his wife and family, and so sever his links with the land, or he may maintain his links with the land through keeping his wife and children in the village. If the urban centre is a mining town he may then go on to Lima or return to his village, and if the centre is Lima itself, then his choice is to remain there or return to the village.

The relation between this circulatory migration and rural socio-economic structures is analysed in the following through considering the effects of migration on the rural economy and then of rural structures on migration. Such an analysis then provides for the consideration of policy design and implementation. This is done through an investigation into the similarities and differences of the two villages, focusing on their economic, landholding and occupational structures, and their migration histories. The differences between the villages help to explain the different tendencies for accumulation, differentiation and polarisation within them. Both similarities and differences are related to government policies for the region and to discussion of relevant alternative policies.

III. Village Similarities

Although in both villages it is possible to distinguish between communally and privately owned land, subsistence and market-oriented peasants, and richer and poorer peasants, the basic unit of production in both and in the Mantaro Valley generally is the peasant household involved in subsistence, household farming.

It is the peasant household which controls property and organises production.[15] Usually, it consists of three-generation extended families with the senior generations owning the resources while other family members work with them. This means that while junior household members are 'landless', they do have access to land. The transmission of household property is through inheritance and there is a cycle of property dispersal and concentration. The organising principle of the household is that consumption needs must be met through the mobilisation of available family labour, recruited and removed through the cycle of birth, marriage and death that entails a constantly changing balance between the labour inputs of the household and its consumption needs.

No one household meets all its needs however, and so attempts are made to mobilise external resources while maintaining the viability of the household. These attempts include migration, co-operation with other households and the development of market orientations. Occasionally, such attempts can lead to the break-up of the household, as external demands become too great, but often they do not.

To sustain household farming there exist within the Andean peasant culture various co-operation practices that range from the lending of tools to communal village work projects. Between individual households is the practice of *uyay*, or the exchange of household labour at times of sowing and harvesting. Also between households are the systems of *minka* and *trueque*, whereby services and goods are paid for in kind. Between individuals are the practices of *al partir* and *ipoteca*, the former being the sharing of cost and profit on land, the latter the pawning of land. At the village level is the *comunidad* itself, in which peasants may engage in common agricultural or construction tasks. Such larger-scale co-operation may be religiously grounded, when it is known as a *cofradia*. Underpinning and reinforcing these economic practices are the social networks of kin, *compadrazgo* and neighbours.

The migration experiences of the two villages were somewhat similar. Both villages had a long history of external contacts and in both villages migration had been an aid to subsistence and a means of social mobility. For both Ataura and Matahuasi, contacts with the mining sector had been particularly important.

Migration presumably affected the two villages during the Inca period as the Inca State established colonies, or *mitimyes*, of foreigners throughout the valley. The immigration of Spanish settler families during the Conquest and the emigration of peasants to work in the mines was the subsequent stage of migration in the valley. In Ataura, required emigration to the mines during the seventeenth century is documented in a land dispute. As well as being required to work in the mines under the *mita* system, both Ataurinos and Matahuasinos had to do *faena* – the rendering of labour tribute without payment. For Ataurinos, this meant travelling to Jauja to clean the streets or the bull-ring, while for Matahuasinos it meant a journey to nearby Apata.

The passage of Spanish, Chilean and Nationalist armies through the villages during the nineteenth century also brought the villagers into contact with the outside world. At the same time, the villages were resting and victualling places on the main road from Cajamarca to Cuzco, for the old Inca highway ran along the valley floor. With the growth of Lima and the several attempts to colonise the jungle, even more migrants passed through the villages, leading to the prosperous *pension* trade (lodging) in Ataura and the emergence of several muleteers in Matahuasi.

The emigration of peasants to the mines also continued during the nineteenth century. At the turn of the century this flow was quickened by the expansion of the mines and the activities of labour recruiters, or *enganchadores*, who were often village notables — majors, heads of Spanish families, or shopkeepers. These notables would pay the peasants a sum of money in advance, which the peasants had to repay by working in the mines. For some peasants the *enganche* system meant cash and a work adventure. Others, however, were pressed into service through their debts in the village store. If a man died in the mine, the debt was transferred to his widow and was often paid through the seizure of land.

In the first two decades of the twentieth century emigration to the mines quickened as American investment increased output dramatically and the railway network was extended to the Valley. In Ataura, these events led to the integration of the village into the mining sector. By 1920 some Ataurinos had gained white-collar positions in the refinery built by the Americans in the mining town of Oroya.[16] These Ataurinos were able to use their positions as labour brokers to enable others to gain posts. During the 1920s mining was the largest single employer of migrant Ataurinos, although there were many in government construction work and the office work, usually in Lima. The outflow of men during the 1920s left a village consisting largely of women, children and the aged.

It was a similar story in Matahuasi. The arrival of the railway in 1910 also stimulated migration on a larger scale. As well as those in debt to *enganchadores*, several small shopkeepers in Matahuasi migrated when they found they could not compete with the larger merchants, who used the railway. Unlike the Ataurinos, the Matahuasinos went more to the mines than to the refinery in Oroya, and did not take up white-collar work. As in Ataura, due to the migration, agricultural employment declined markedly during the 1920s.

The Depression of the 1930s meant the reversal of migratory flows for both villages. The mining corporations, government and small-scale employers all laid off men, who flooded back to their villages. There, the migrants again became peasants working on their own plots of land. This situation continued until the end of the Depression, when employment began to expand in government and construction work. During the 1940s emigration again increased, and since the Second World War the rate of migration from and to both villages has been high.

Both villages have thus experienced high emigration to the mines, large-scale immigration during the 1930s and then post-war emigration to a wider range of economic sectors than before. In both cases the existence of a *minifundia* village economy, plus co-operative practices, enabled villagers to withstand the Depression and other fluctuations in external employment. However, differences in the village economies led to other differences, the consequences of which are assessed below.

In both Ataura and Matahuasi, migration has meant success for some and failure for others, depending often on the timing and place of their migration. At the turn of this century, fortunes could be made in mining, and then later as an *enganchador*. But this was before land was brought fully into the cash arena. The transformation of land into a commodity through purchases by migrants meant that land prices came to reflect migrant wage levels. Unless a migrant could move into a profitable commercial venture, the money earned from wage labour could only suffice to provide a basic subsistence for his family, perhaps with some savings put aside to purchase a small plot.

However, compared with the situation at the end of the nine-teenth century, migration in the twentieth century has had a marked impact on the structure of landholding in the two villages. During the nineteenth century in Ataura there were four landholding entities – a group of five Spanish families, the Catholic Church, the *comunidad* and the peasants themselves. The acquisition and dispersal of land were through marriage and inheritance. In one instance the vast bulk of land became concen-trated in the hands of two female cousins, who were promptly married by two brothers, so that the land passed out of the control of one family into that of another.

With the increase in migration at the end of the nineteenth century this pattern changed as land was brought into the cash arena. In Ataura this change was brought about by one man, Lucas, the illegitimate son of a Spanish descendant, who at the turn of the century made his fortune in mining. He returned to Ataura and bought out the old Spanish families, purchasing their lands, houses and mill. By 1920 he owned 20 hectares and employed three full-time labourers. However, although one of his sons continued as a farmer and expanded the amount of land, his other sons emigrated from Ataura and became professionals in Jauja and Lima. When the last son died, his sons sold the lands and themselves moved away.

Lucas's estate was sold to returning migrants, who bought not only his land, but also land from potential migrants and widows in debt to *enganchadores*. The break-up of Lucas's estate was part of the fragmentation of the blocks of land held by different groups at the end of the nineteenth century. And in Matahuasi it was a somewhat similar story. Money gained through migration, or through commercial contacts with the mines and the metropolis, has been used to purchase land. However, it is the differences between the land structures of the two villages that are of primary interest, as discussed later.

As well as affecting the structure of landholding, migration has also influenced occupational differentiation in the two villages. Two ways by which this has occurred have been through the rise of a stratum of shopkeepers and through the reinforcement of the sexual division of labour. Migration has aided the former through being a source of finance for shopkeepers and through providing them with a market for consumer goods, while the sexual division of labour has been reinforced by the absence of the menfolk.

Undoubtedly, some occupational differentiation has always existed in the two villages, due to the presence of bakers, cobblers, muleteers, and so on. But the increased range of occupations is a twentieth-century phenomenon. An example of the proliferation of commercial activities is given by the shopkeepers of Ataura. The main body of shops in Ataura flank the central square, occupying the lower sections of a house once owned by a Spanish descendant. In the first decade of the twentieth century, the house was divided into three shops by sons catering to travellers. Through the marriage of their sons the house was further divided and this process has been repeated until there are now seven shops in the old house. All the owners of the shops were the direct descendants of the original owner of the house, and they either worked in the shop themselves or let it to a trader.

In both Ataura and Matahuasi the people owning or working in shops all have long migration histories. For many of those who set up shop it was a retirement occupation, with funds accumulated from wages received during migration and invested in stock in the shop. Sometimes, the stock did not come wholly from the migrants' savings but in part from a bank loan or a forwarding loan from a wholesaler in Jauja looking for an outlet. Also, part of the stock may have been produce from the trader's own land, grown by himself or his wife while the other minded the store. Many of the shopkeepers gained experience of trading during migration, for some ran shops in the mines or in Lima, while others became friends with traders there and took their advice about opening a village shop. Aiming to capture part of an established market, the shops were all general stores, selling foodstuffs and beer.[17] And they sold to people who themselves had cash, often from wages obtained through migration.

Migration not only supported the rise of a commercial stratum, but reinforced the sexual division of labour in valley villages. This it has done in three ways. First, the absence of men meant that it was the women who were called upon to perform communal tasks. In the nineteenth century women did *faena* when the men were away in the mines. In the twentieth century, it was the women of Ataura who built the church tower and carried the stones to dam a spring. Second, the absence of men has led the women to turn more to their own company and kin. The village was a women's world organised around a range of village affairs from child-rearing to representation on the village council.

The third way in which male emigration contributed to the sexual division of labour is probably the most important, and relates to landholding and land usage. When the men were away it was the women who worked the land. They did the manual work, or contracted others to plough and harvest, with money sent to them by their migrant husbands. At the same time, women have inherited land equally with men and occasionally amassed land as the men died in mining accidents. Thus the world of women became closely related to the land, a feature with clear consequences.

Although men migrated, village women were reluctant to leave their established women's world, often staying because of their access to land. The relation of valley women to the land distinguished them from non-valley women from poorer highland areas. The valley women were marriageable prospects and so alongside the immigration to the village of returning migrants, there was a marked influx of outsiders who had married village women. These outsiders were viewed with some suspicion by the residents, who joked cagily about these men who had married their sisters and captured their land. For their part, the outsiders recognised the suspicion and tried not to aggravate it, for they were not on home ground.

So, in Ataura and Matahuasi, the effect of migration on rural socio-economic structures was to some extent similar. The economies of the two villages were similar in that they were based on subsistence households engaging in co-operative practices. They had similar migration histories, in that the mining and the metropolis had been the major destinations, while the levels of employment in both work centres had fluctuated. Money earned from migration had enabled returning migrants to purchase land, and so the larger blocks of land existing at the turn of the century have been divided up and sold. Such money had also led to the rise of commercial strata and supported the division of labour between the sexes as women used cash to recruit labour to work on the lands of emigrant husbands. At first glance, it seems possible to generalise about the effects of migration on the peasant *minifundia*. But a closer inspection of the relation between migration and the rural economy shows that differences both within that economy and in migration histories are of great significance. Those differences have important consequences for capital accumulation, social differentiation and polarisation, as the following material suggests.

IV. Village Differences

There are important inter-village variations on all the four dimensions under investigation. However, the most important concern the first two of these dimensions – the rural economy and migration history – since the other two, in landholding and occupational differentiation, follow from them. The outcome is that, whereas Ataura has been integrated into a migratory way of life, in Matahuasi migration has been integrated into a peasant/ commercial way of life. In Ataura, migration is a necessary and permanent adjunct of a small subsistence economy. In Matahuasi, migration is a source of finance on which market-oriented peasants can capitalise.

Today, the peasant economy of Ataura is small, divided, and subsistence-oriented. The scale of the economy, plus the cultural devices available, support a migrant solution to the problems facing the household. Typical agricultural scenes in Ataura are of women working the land. The wives and mothers of migrants tend several small plots, usually scattered around the village. At planting and harvest times they mobilise either another female kin member for hand-work or contract a retired migrant who has two oxen. As he ploughs, the woman brings him beer and food which they consume together, gossiping. He receives the cash rate for the job and the woman helps carry his implements back to his house. As this sort of operation does not provide a basis for capital accumulation, Ataurinos spend their working lives as migrants.

In contrast, Matahuasi has more land and more market-oriented peasants. One person illustrating this difference is Saul. He formed a link in the overall migration process from poor villages to valley emigration. Many of the able-bodied men of Matahuasi were away, while the remainder were working on their own land. So to recruit labour Saul hired a labour contractor. Together with this *contratista*, Saul went in his lorry to a poorer village on the valley slopes and picked up a gang of six women. At such times their own sowing or harvesting period was at an end, so they were free to work for Saul. He employed them on specialised tasks, such as the harvesting of oats, for village children did the easier work, and he paid the statutory minimum 40 *soles* per day per worker. The money went to the *contratista*, while Saul gave the women 2 *soles* worth of *coca* per day, plus food and drink. On top of that, he paid the team one sack of whatever they harvested, and the *contratista* an extra 5 *soles* per person per week.

Saul would have used a harvester rather than women workers to gather some crops, such as wheat, for it was cheaper. It took six women six days to harvest one hectare of wheat, which cost 1,500 *soles*, whereas a harvester could do the job in one day, for only 800 *soles* rent. The problem was that as the land was irrigated, it had ridges across it, and therefore a harvester could not be used on it. So, Saul continued to contract labour. He used the same team each year and came to know their work, while they came to know him, the land, and the assurance of payment. Usually only women came, for their husbands were working in small mines or on the hydro-electric project. But occasionally a man did come. He then worked on an individual task, never joining the women in their work. Agricultural organisation on this scale can support independent, diverse ventures, standing in contrast to the subsistence activities in Ataura.

The migration histories of Ataura and Matahuasi also differ in four main ways. First, whereas Ataura has established labour contacts with external sectors, Matahuasi has established both labour and trading contacts. Second, while these contacts for Ataura have been dominated by the mines, with Lima only lately coming into prominence, for Matahuasi, Lima has always been of great importance. Third, Matahuasi's ability to support trading links has meant that Matahuasino migrants do not take up wage employment to the extent that Ataurinos do. And fourth, while the 1930s Depression resulted in Ataurinos taking village agricultural work, some Matahuasinos moved into the transport sector, which had profound repercussions for the village economy. These differences are revealed in the following.

The Life Histories of Ataurinos and Matahuasinos

The life histories of 76 Ataurinos and Matahuasinos were collected and analysed. These 76 men comprised a one-in-7 sample of all males now resident in Ataura with migration experience (15), a 10 per cent sample of all males now resident in Matahuasi with migration experience (14), all Ataurinos resident in Oroya (22) and all Matahuasinos resident in Oroya (25).

The analysis is of the occupations and economic sectors in which the migrants had worked since they were 18 years old, and the employers they have had. The total number of years worked by all Ataurinos was 1,121, and by Matahuasinos was 1,168, in 1971. In Tables 3.1-3.3, N is the number of years worked in each category of occupation, employer and economic sector, by the whole migrant group. The chi-squared significance tests were statistically significant at the 1 per cent level.[18]

That Ataura established only labour contacts with external sectors while Matahuasi established labour and trading contacts is shown in a variety of ways. Historically, there is oral and documentary evidence of labour migration from Ataura to the mines, but little sign of trading with the mines. The reverse is true for Matahuasi. Present-day Matahuasino traders recall their grandfathers travelling to the mines to open up shops and sell village produce

Table 3.1: *Migrants' Occupational History, by Village*

Occupation	Ataura		Matahuasi	
	N	%	N	%
Peasant	213	19	140	12
Worker	369	33	506	43
Artisan	196	18	213	18
Employee	254	23	149	13
Trader	50	4	139	12
Other	39	3	21	2
Total	1,121	100	1,168	100

Chi-squared = 109.9

Table 3.2: *Migrants' Employers, by Village*

Employer	Ataura		Matahuasi	
	N	%	N	%
Self	272	24	328	28
Mining companies	613	55	491	42
Railway	31	3	166	14
Other	205	18	183	16
Total	1,121	100	1,168	100

Chi-squared = 110.9

Table 3.3: *Migrants' Sectoral History, by Village*

Economic sector	Ataura		Matahuasi	
	N	%	N	%
Agriculture	226	20	142	12
Mining	602	54	475	41
Manufacturing	27	2	77	7
Construction	84	7	91	8
Commerce	8	1	57	5
Transport	51	5	238	20
Service	52	5	66	5
Government	71	6	22	2
Total	1,121	100	1,168	100

Chi-squared = 241.9

there. Also, analysis of the life histories of migrants now living in the villages shows that whereas the Ataurinos have spent their lives as peasants or miners, the Matahuasinos have spent significantly more time as petty traders. Whereas only two-thirds of the Matahuasinos currently resident in Matahuasi had migration experience, nearly all the Ataurinos resident in Ataura had some. While half of the migrants from Matahuasi living in Oroya were traders, all the Ataurino migrants worked for the mining company of the municipality.

The dominance of the mines in Ataura's migration experience is also revealed by the life-history analysis. Half of the Ataurino migrants' lives were spent in wage work in the mining sector, while the bulk of the rest was spent on the land. The Matahuasino migrants, however, had spent only two-fifths of their working lives in the mines, the rest being divided between self-employment in agriculture, trading and transport. And the location of these latter two activities for the Matahuasinos has not only been in the highland mining areas, but also in Lima.

The ground for Matahuasino transport activities was prepared during the 1930s, although it is probable that their foundations lie in the activities of the muleteers who congregated at Matahuasi to take *colonos* down to the jungle. Whereas in Ataura returning migrants rode the Depression by taking up agricultural work, in Matahuasi some returning migrants diversified into transport, either purchasing a lorry themselves or in partnership with others, or working on lorries and buses. With the post-war boom, Matahuasinos consolidated this diversification away from mining and are now to be found in a variety of sectors, including transport. Ataurinos on the other hand re-established links with those white-collar Ataurino migrants working in the mines who had not been laid off, and once again took up industrial work.

These differences are reflected in the work histories of migrant brothers. Whereas half the Ataurino brothers had worked in Oroya, the main mining work centre for Ataurinos, very few Matahuasino brothers had done so. One-third of the Matahuasino brothers had worked in Lima, compared with only one-tenth of the Ataurino brothers. And while four-fifths of the Ataurino brothers had worked for mining companies, only one quarter of the Matahuasino brothers had done so. Thus, life-history analysis, as well as discussions with peasants, revealed distinct differences in the migration histories of the two villages.

Not only have the village migrants differed in the occupations they take up when they emigrate, but also in the occupations taken up when they return to the village. Although all try to purchase plots of land and set up shops, in Matahuasi more land is bought, and usually more is for sale and in larger units. And while the products of the villages are similar – potatoes, maize, wheat and some cows and sheep – it is the Matahuasinos who focus on pastoral activities. It is they who attempt dairy farming, rear sheep and market their products.

These differences in economic structure and migration histories have had their effects on landholding and occupational differentiation in the two villages, and thus on capital accumulation, socio-economic differentiation and polarisation in the two locations. In Ataura, the subsistence economy supports a migrant way of life, providing social security in times of economic fluctuations and retirement. In Matahuasi, migration provides funds or contacts that support commercial expansion. In Ataura, village life is integrated into a migratory lifestyle; in Matahuasi, migration is integrated into village patterns of work and life.

In both villages, migration has contributed to land turnover and alienation. In Ataura this has led to land fragmentation, whereas in Matahuasi it has led to the concentration of land and sharp socio-economic differentiation. In Ataura, there were several pressures inducing land fragmentation. The exodus of Lucas's children and grandchildren, seeking the professional occupations of their brothers and uncles, led to the break-up of his estate. The land was divided among returning miners, the mill was bought by a miner's wife, and Lucas's big house was purchased by a retired refinery worker.

At the same time, the 40 hectares of communal land pertaining to the village was lost. Refuse dumped in the Mantaro River by the refinery in Oroya made its way into the Mantaro Valley. The communal land of Ataura was located on an island in the middle of the river and was rendered completely useless by the pollution. This removal of so much land threw an even greater burden on to the land belonging to Ataura on the valley bottom. In the 1930s, the pressure was eased slightly by the sale of church land, but so great was the land pressure that this land was immediately split into small lots and sold to migrants. Thus, in Ataura there was on-going land fragmentation.

Quite the reverse was the case in Matahuasi. The sale of

church land throughout the valley in the 1930s opened the opportunity in Matahuasi for large-scale land acquisition. In Matahuasi, the amount of land released was much greater than it had been in Ataura, and its acquisition had a more marked effect on social stratification.

As the church land had been communally worked and the produce communally distributed, the villagers felt that negotiations with the church should proceed on a village basis. With many of the villagers working away, a group was elected to represent Matahuasi's interests. Realising that organised opposition from the dispersed village migrants would be sluggish, this group promptly bought the land for themselves – much of the money used in the purchase coming from working in or trading with the mines and Lima. The response of other villagers was to form a committee to contest this, and it was out of this committee that the legally recognised *comunidad* of Matahuasi was formed.

Thus, the combination of a sudden increase in the supply of land, the absence of many villagers, and the availability of cash for a few, led to the creation of the two most easily identifiable land-related strata in Matahuasi – the large, private landholders, and the members of the *comunidad*. These groups have persisted and compete for political office in the village. So, in contrast to Ataura, the landholding groups in Matahuasi are more polarised.

Differentiation in Matahuasi has occurred not only within the landholding structure but also within the occupational structure. In both Matahuasi and Ataura migration supported the rise of commercial strata, but this was much more marked in Matahuasi. Indeed, in Ataura, the commercial stratum was made up of no more than petty, often part-time, shopkeepers, and so the occupational structure may also be characterised as fragmented amongst shopkeepers, migrants, peasants, and out-workers. In Matahuasi, the occupational divisions were sharper and greater. Two case studies from each village illustrate both the differences in occupational differentiation between the villages and the relation between migration and occupational attainment.

In Ataura, during the late 1950s, Alfredo built a brick house with money he had earned from working in Oroya. He decided to become a *transportista* and, having only a little land of his own, persuaded the old village priest to lend him the money for the lorry. The priest, a descendant of the old Spanish families of Ataura, had over many years increased his wealth by surreptitious acquisition of land in the village. He now rents out this land and himself lives in Huancayo. He forwarded Alfredo the money, but insisted that, since Alfredo had no land, the house be the security for the loan. Alfredo bought the lorry, but through lack of contacts and thus contracts, the venture failed and the priest sued Alfredo for the money. The priest won the suit, evicted Alfredo, and the house now stands empty while Alfredo and his family are lodged in a small adobe dwelling nearby.

A little later, in the early 1960s, Armando returned to Ataura from the mines of Tamboraque. With the money he had earned plus a sum raised from putting their land in *ipoteca*, Armando and his brother Flavio raised enough money to put a deposit on a lorry. For three years they were *transportistas*. They hired a driver and worked carrying anything to and from Lima and the Valley. Again, the venture failed, and the brothers now regretted the inexperienced way they went into the business without the necessary contacts. The problem, they pointed out, was that with their land in *ipoteca* they had no supplementary source of income either to pay the loan interest or feed themselves when the venture was in a slack period. Unable to pay their debts, the brothers were evicted from their house in Ataura and in 1979 were working in Oroya trying to earn money to redeem their land.

These Ataurino examples are in marked contrast to the Matahuasino ones. The son of a large landowner in Matahuasi Gonzalo studied in Lima and then went to join his brother's timber business in the jungle. The two brothers supplied wood to the mines and railway, but with wood prices falling and transport costs rising they could not compete with wood grown in the Mantaro Valley itself and so they sold the business and bought some land, a house and a lorry in Matahuasi. Gonzalo's brother opened a wood-yard and Gonzalo became the transporter taking wood to the mines, then mineral from the mines to Lima, and then kerosene from Lima back to the valley. The brothers got the transport contract to the mines from their sister, who had a timber-yard in Jauja. Then Gonzalo crashed the lorry and was forced to look for wage work. His brother-in-law was a chemical engineer in Oroya, offered Gonzalo a job, and so for five years Gonzalo was employed as a white-collar worker. Later he returned to Matahuasi, to work as driver for his brother's wood yard.

Long offers a second example of *transportistas* in Matahuasi, that of Julio, who uses his lorry to transport both timber and labour.[19] Julio's father established a timber mill in the 1940s and purchased land for farming. Both mill and land are now controlled by Julio and his wife, though the father still owns both. Three operatives, one a cousin, help Julio, but it is he who drives to the mines to negotiate timber contracts with contacts established by his father. The land is worked by Julio's sister and her husband, and Julio markets some of their produce, receiving a share of the profits.

Julio's parents-in-law were themselves successful *transportistas* and Julio is developing his business in association with them. He transports temporary labour to his mother-in-law's fields at harvest time, while it is she who has the market connections in Lima for the sale of the produce. She also allows Julio to use her lorry to transport timber to the mines, enabling him to make several deliveries a week. Operating on this scale, Julio is now constantly searching for timber, and his mother-in-law is able to put him in touch with local farmers. Occasionally, Julio is further helped by his affines, who, driving lorries under the direction of their mother, work with Julio at harvest time.

Gonzalo and Julio contrast sharply with Alfredo and Armando. Through the availability of land and networks, the Matahuasinos have been able to build up independent trading relations with the mines and Lima. Migration, resulting in money and contacts, has played a part in the establishment of those relations, but in Matahuasi it was complementary to viable household economies. In Ataura, the peasant economy could not underwrite the risks of commercial ventures and there was no history of trading contacts that could be used in the setting up of those ventures.

These differences in socio-economic differentiation and available resources in the two villages are also reflected in the extent to which skills and capital gained through migration can be utilised. At first glance, both villages appear overwhelmingly peasant locations. Yet, in both villages, in the courtyards and outhouses, there stand lathes, carpenter's benches, small diesel engines and lorries. The difference is that in Ataura they are not used. Ataura's returned migrants are just as skilled, indeed more skilled, than Matahuasi's, but they do not use their trades.[20] Remaining in Ataura because their land is there, or their wife's family is there, their entrepreneurial activities are limited by the lack of market, resources and contacts in Ataura. A diesel engine providing electricity would help, but few can afford one, while general electrification is prevented by a legal battle with Muquiyauyo, a neighbouring village which has electricity but which limits its spread. The lorries in Ataura are old and rusting, for the villagers cannot afford spare parts.

As we have seen, the picture in Matahuasi is quite different. Not only do the resources of the larger village facilitate independent ventures, but perhaps more importantly returning migrants can drive merchant's lorries, get wood directly from the timber yards, or share power supplies with established entrepreneurs. One example of entrepreneurial initiative in Matahuasi arose over the supply of milk to the refinery workers in Oroya. The trade union in Oroya had demanded that the mining company supply workers with fresh milk to slake thirst while working in dusty conditions. As there were 6,000 workers, the contract for the milk supply was bound to be lucrative. Ataurinos had contacts in Oroya, but as it was in Matahuasi that dairy cattle were being raised and lorries were available, it was Matahuasinos who capitalised on this opportunity and began transporting milk to Oroya.

In the early 1970s, then, there were tendencies towards polarisation in both villages, but it is clear that these were much more marked in Matahuasi than in Ataura, producing in Matahuasi a group of richer peasants able to accumulate capital. All three agrarian classes existed in both villages, but whereas Ataura comprised predominantly poor peasants, Matahuasi contained more rich peasants. In terms of agricultural practices the rich and poor peasants were distinguishable.[21] In gaining access to land the classes differ, for the rich more often gained their land through purchases. Two-thirds of the rich had bought land compared to only two-fifths of the poor, while far more poor than rich had only inherited land. Also, while the rich gained access through renting, the poor used the mechanism of *al partir* or became members of the *comunidad*. Once access was established, landworking practices also differed, for it was the poor who had most recourse to the traditional devices of *partidarios, minka, uyay* and extended kin, while the rich used paid labour. And in the disposal of products, it was the rich who were market-oriented, often selling their dairy products, in contrast to the poor who consumed theirs. But although there were some tendencies toward polarisation in both villages, these were much more marked in Matahuasi.

The differences in the peasant economies and migration experience of the two villages thus produce differences in their landholding and occupational structures that in turn relate to different potentials for capital accumulation, socio-economic differentiation and polarisation. However, before concluding on these differences and these relations, it is necessary to assess briefly the impact of rural socio-economic structures on emigration.

Analyses of the life histories and responses of residents in the villages and of migrants in Oroya show that there was no simple 'match' between rural socio-economic structures, emigration and urban-industrial socio-economic structures. At some time or another the vast majority of both rich and poor peasants emigrated, many returning at various times to the village. All were searching for work, some to subsist, some to accumulate capital and some to practise a profession; the differences between them did not simply reflect more or less land or income.

Rather, the structure and rate of migration were influenced by the cycles of industrial production, the development of the rural economy and individuals' life cycles. The above account has suggested how the industrial economy attracted and shed all kinds of labour during the 1920s and 1930s, for example; how the rural economy, organised around the household, required sons to emigrate in search of money or to ease the subsistence burden; and how individuals faced with problems of education, marriage, or succession to the head of the household emigrated and later returned. It was not only the rich peasants who were able to move, nor was there a flight from the land by a landless peasantry.

V. Policy Implications

Earlier it was noted that socio-economic differentiation and circulatory migration would affect the shaping and implementation of policies in rural areas. Examples of these influences can be useful in assessing policy orientations.

The first is an example of policies oriented to agricultural production. While research for this study was in progress an international aid agency undertook to construct a milk purification and bottling plant in Concepcion, a small town near Matahuasi. Requiring a supply of milk, the agency representative set about persuading Matahuasinos to raise dairy cattle. The benefits would be both commercial, as they would sell milk to the plant, and dietary, since milk was a source of protein. He put his case at a meeting of the Matahuasi *comuneros* and was dismayed when they rejected his plans. In terms of agricultural economic organisation his scheme may have been more efficient, but in terms of the role of agricultural production in a migrant labour system it was unacceptable to poor peasants. Separate, family-controlled strips of land would have been combined for grazing and so would not have been able to provide journeying migrants in both village and towns with the potatoes, maize and vegetables they needed for subsistence. The scheme was more acceptable to richer farmers who were prepared to rent, or set land aside, for dairy cattle.

The second is an example of policies oriented to industrial production. While the research was in progress the Peruvian Government was building a large dam across the lower Mantaro River, to the south of the valley. This was a hydro-electric power project and many migrants from the Mantaro Valley laboured on the dam. The aim of the project was to provide electric power to Lima. Yet languishing in the valley were machines and skills accumulated through migration that could have been productive had electricity been available. Instead, government policies meant that under-resourced villages had to engage in legal battles over local supplies of electricity, which benefited nobody but lawyers.

The third example concerns the relation between local needs and national policies. When the refinery workers' trade union in Oroya put forward its demand for milk, and for meat too, the government supported the mining company's prevarication over the issues. At one point, the government argued that the meat would have to come from Argentina, and so would increase the import bill. The refinery workers based their case for milk consumption on the claim that the International Labour Organisation had recommended that milk be made available to those working in dusty conditions. Had the government supported this initiative it could have pressured the mining company into accepting, thereby improving the diet of the refinery workers and expanding the scope for commercial activities in the Mantaro Valley, so helping the agrarian initiatives under way there. As it was, the Ministry of Labour was probably unaware of any initiatives supported by the Ministry of Agriculture. Because the trade union demands were seen to be politically motivated they were resisted by the government. As the research project came to an end the government was increasing the supply of imported powdered milk to the refinery workers.

Finally, one can make an assessment of policy orientations. One major policy of international agencies in rural areas has long been birth control. It is possible to demonstrate to rural populations that large family sizes are linked to splintered landholdings and overburdened peasant households. However, in a migrant labour situation, that link may not be so apparent. Younger family members migrate to mining or to the towns, entailing something of a 'syphoning-off' effect, while older kin maintain the family land. Also, 'successful' families are seen to be those like Gonzalo's and Julio's, with offspring in different economic sectors, each helping the family during moments of economic instability. Certainly, women in both villages and refinery towns wanted effective birth control, but they were also concerned with the delivery of medical care generally. They wanted their existing children to remain alive and so remove the necessity of having any more children. In the Mantaro Valley villages there were no formally trained doctors, and so the sick must journey to town or seek the help of *curanderos*.

VI. Conclusions

It is clear that capitalist expansion and migration in the Peruvian highlands have increased rural socio-economic differentiation. During the nineteenth and twentieth centuries, the mines of the highlands and the cities of Peru expanded and attracted migrants from the Mantaro Valley. At first, the migration process was differentiated between the wealthy landowners, who emigrated to become professionals, and the peasants, who became miners and labourers. As the twentieth century progressed that differentiation increased as different social classes at different times either capitalised on migration or met failure and exploitation.

These differences were reinforced as separate villages built up strong links with particular migrant destinations.

The effects of capitalist expansion and migration on the rural economy have been marked. Land has been alienated and is now a commercial commodity. Large blocks of family, church and communal land have been broken up and valley landholding is increasingly fragmented. The old Spanish families owning large tracts of land are disappearing, being replaced by rich peasants or by subsistence peasants purchasing small plots of land. Occupational structures have become differentiated. Alongside the agrarian classes there are traders, teachers, shopkeepers, artisans and urban labourers. All of these groups use migration money, experience or contacts to pursue their occupations. Migration reinforces the sexual division of labour in the valley as women handle village affairs in the absence of menfolk.

That is to say, capitalist expansion and migration have led to the crystallisation of social classes in the valley. During the nineteenth century the class structure was based on landholding and was composed of two major classes, consisting of the Spanish descendants and the indigenous peasantry. The economic changes of the first half of the twentieth century broke down this simple division and expanded the basis of class away from access to land. Economic structures in the valley became more complex, and from that situation new classes emerged. In the agricultural sector rich market-oriented peasants have engaged in trading. Subsistence peasants remain, although increasing population and consumption demands have put subsistence households under growing pressure. Poor peasants have been unable to meet subsistence needs, and agricultural labourers have increased in number. Alongside these agrarian classes are commercial and industrial classes, both in the region and in the valley itself.

As yet, this class differentiation has not produced polarisation or overt political conflict in the villages. This is due in part to the availability of migration opportunities, the potential for social mobility and the fact that population expansion has only recently met ecological limits. It also reflects the fact that the potential for conflict is reduced in villages due to the various co-operative arrangements in Andean culture. Thus, much agrarian production is organised by households for subsistence, with households co-operating with one another. Nevertheless, it is clear that such co-operation is increasingly class-oriented. The poor peasants engage in household exchanges, relying on kin, but the subsistence and rich peasants have increasingly relied on commercial arrangements, hiring labour and purchasing land.

Thus, even though villages are distinct locations with different histories, they form part of the agrarian class structure in the valley. It would appear that the two villages, Ataura and Matahuasi, differ in their relation to the wider Peruvian economy. Ataura is a small subsistence village that cannot facilitate capital accumulation and does not contain sharp socio-economic differentiation. It is a village of dependent worker-peasants, integrated into the highland mining sector. Conversely, Matahuasi is a village that has established independent trading relations with the wider economy. It is a village that has experienced capital accumulation and growing socio-economic differentiation. But the contrasts between the two villages stem mainly from different class structures. In Ataura and Matahuasi it was the poor peasants who became dependent migrant labourers, while in Matahuasi it was the rich peasants who turned to trading.

Consequently, although there are important village differences in the valley, one cannot speak of a peasant economy distinguishable from a capitalist economy in the region. The agricultural sector in the valley has been part of the international capitalist economy since the sixteenth century. The socio-economic relations in the valley from that date have been established under the influence of the outside agencies of the Spanish State, the Peruvian State and international capital.[22] The socio-economic relations in the agrarian sector have not been established independently from within a peasant mode of production. It is not that a peasant economy has been increasingly differentiated by capitalist penetration, but rather that the valley's agrarian classes have once again been changing as the international capitalist economy develops.

Thus, the migration in this region has been not from a peasant economy to a capitalist one, but has formed part of capitalist development. Different classes in the region have produced with the resources available to them. Thus, rich peasants have used kin contacts to recruit labour and paid that labour in *coca*, while the poorest peasants have a long history as mine workers. Migration patterns have been mainly circular, though there has been a permanent exodus to the cities. In various ways, peasants have maintained their links with the land as they migrated to urban work centres. Such links are essential, providing a form of social security in an unstable economy as well as some measure of subsistence to the families of migrants. So far, this measure of support in the rural areas has been complemented by the level of employment opportunities available in the Peruvian economy. However, without economic growth migration will no longer be a solution for poor peasant workers. It would be the return of these workers to the villages that would polarise the class structure there and could precipitate political conflict. Meanwhile, in the short and medium term, an understanding of social differentiation and circular migration is crucial for any agency embarking on policies aimed at changing the socio-economic organisation of the peasantry and raising their living standards.

Notes

1. See A. Portes: *Labour, class and the international system* (New York, Academic Press, 1981); J. Laite: *Industrial development and migrant labour* (Manchester University Press, 1981); R. Cohen: *Peasants and proletarians* (London, Hutchinson, 1979).

2. V.I. Lenin: *The development of capitalism in Russia* (Moscow, Progress Publishers, 1967).

3. A.V. Chayanov: *The theory of peasant economy*, edited by D. Thorner, R.E.F. Smith and B. Kerblay (London, Irwin, 1966).

4. See T. Shanin: *The awkward class* (London, Oxford University Press, 1972); M. Lewin: *Russian peasants and Soviet power* (London, Allen and Unwin, 1966); J. Ennew, P. Hirst and K. Tribe: 'Peasantry as an economic category', in *Journal of Peasant Studies*, July 1977, vol. 4, no. 4, pp. 295-322; W. Roseberry: 'Rent, differentiation and the development of capitalism among peasants', in *American Anthropologist*, March 1976, vol. 78, no. 1, pp. 45-58; N. Long and B. Roberts: 'Peasant cooperation and underdevelopment in central Peru', in N. Long and B. Roberts (eds.): *Peasant cooperation and capitalist expansion in central Peru* (Austin, Texas University Press, 1978); T. Shanin: 'The nature and logic of tne peasant economy: A generalisation', in *Journal of Peasant Studies*, 1973, vol. 1, no. 1, pp. 63-80.

5. K. Vergopolous: 'El capitalismo disforme', in S. Amin and K. Vergopolous: *La cuestión campesina y el capitalismo* (Mexico, Editorial Nuestro Tiempo, 1975); C. Kay: 'Agrarian change and migration in Chile', in G. Standing and P. Peek (eds.): *State policies and migration: Studies in Latin America and the Caribbean* (London, Croom Helm, 1982).

6. J. Murra: *Formaciones económicas y politicas del mundo andino* (Lima, 1975); J. Golte: *La racionalidad de la organizacion andina* (Lima, IEP, 1980).

7. A. Foster-Carter: 'The mode of production controversy', in *New Left Review*, January 1978, no. 107, pp. 47-77.

8. Long and Roberts, 1978

9. Ibid.

10. Ibid.

11. Ibid.

12. Instituto Indigenista Peruano: *Movimiento migratorio en el Valle del Mantaro* (Huancayo, Peru, 1967).

13. Long and Roberts, 1978.

14. N. Long and R. Sanchez: 'Peasant and entrepreneurial coalitions', in Long and Roberts, 1978.

15. Shanin, 1973.

16. J. Laite: 'Industrialisation, migration and social stratification at the periphery', in *Sociological Review*, November 1978, vol. 26, no. 4, pp. 859-88.

17. That is, the principle of minimum differentiation operates – see R. Boulding: *Economic analysis* (London, Hamish Hamilton, 1961).

18. See M.R. Spiegel: *Theory and problems of statistics* (New York, McGraw-Hill, 1961).

19. N. Long: 'Commerce and kinship in highland Peru', in R. Bolton and E. Mayer (eds.): *Andean kinship and marriage* (Washington DC, American Anthropological Association, 1977).

20. J. Laite: 'The migrant worker', PhD thesis, Manchester University, 1977.

21. Ibid.

22. The importance of relating agrarian social structures to wider societal structures is emphasised by Ennew, Hirst and Tribe, 1977.

4

Seasonal Labour Migration in Tanzania: The Case of Ludewa District

CHRISTOPHER LWOGA

I. Introduction[1]

Using the District of Ludewa as a case study, this paper attempts to explain the persistence of labour migration in the former labour reserves in Tanzania.

Circulation of labour is not a voluntary process; it is primarily a response to economic necessity. Under ideal market conditions, demand for labour is created at the centres of production and supply of labour can be made possible through market forces. When labour supply is through the market, it means that reproduction of the labour force is also possible through the market, by the employer paying sufficient wages for the maintenance of the worker's family.

Political compulsion was used to obtain labour in colonial Tanzania precisely because market forces could not procure the required labour force for the cheap labour-intensive commercial agriculture. In pre-colonial societies land and labour were not commodities, hence subsistence producers were not compelled to sell their labour power to the plantations. Employers and labourers had to be brought together by force, and throughout the colonial period their relationship was maintained by various forms of coercion. To keep production costs down for the sake of realising high profits, cheap labour had to be employed. The cheapness of the labour force resulted from ensuring that the reproduction costs of the labour force were borne by the labourers themselves.

A combination of political and economic measures was used to ensure supply of labour to the plantations. The measures resulted in the emergence of two categories of peasants in the rural areas. These were:

(a) Peasants who produced directly for the market. There were two levels of the market, external (world market) and internal (domestic market). The external market was dominant because cash crop production was oriented to export markets. The internal market was for food crops and catered for the urban population and the plantations. A few urban centres were established primarily to serve the external market through commercial and political administration. And today the internal market remains less developed than the external one. Peasants who produced cash crops for the external market and food crops for the internal market, also produced food for their own subsistence.

(b) Peasants who had to sell their labour power to the plantations. They too had to produce their own subsistence crops.

The two categories of peasants emerged everywhere in the country at different times (with the exception of the pastoral Masai who already had a commodity that could be exchanged on the market), and with a different mixture according to opportunities available in a particular area. Where the second category of peasants was predominant, such areas came to be regarded as labour reserves. Those areas included Kigoma Region; large parts of the former Southern Highlands Province (now Mbeya and Iringa Regions); Mtwara, Lindi and Ruvuma Regions in southern Tanzania; and Rukwa Region and Singida Region.

The role of the State in production for the world market was, and still is, crucial. The role is sometimes inconsistent due to the fluctuating agricultural policy. For example, sometimes the State supports plantation production, ensuring labour supply to the plantations; at other times it favours smallholder peasant production of cash crops, thus interrupting the smooth flow of labour to the plantations. The fluctuating role of the State is seen in both colonial and post-colonial Tanzania, as is discussed in this paper.[2]

The mechanisms for creating a migratory labour force in Tanzania did not involve land alienation as in Southern Africa.

The mechanisms used were a combination of political and economic measures. Political/administrative policy forbade peasants in labour reserves from engaging in commercial agriculture by growing cash crops such as coffee, pyrethrum, tobacco and cotton.[3] In some areas in the labour reserves the failure of cash crops (encouraged by local administrative officers, often in defiance of State policy) was due to 'ineffective and misapplied' administrative efforts.[4] Economic measures involved the monetisation of the economy which made it necessary for part of the basic subsistence requirements to be met only with cash. Monetisation of the economy in itself was not sufficient to push peasants into wage employment. Initially, tax forced peasants into wage labour. Contracts of up to three years, the 30 days labour cards which took a minimum of 45 days to complete, and low wages enabled employers to hire migrant labour for long periods. As male labour supply declined, women and children were drawn into wage employment.

The area under investigation was primarily a 'labour reserve'. This status involved and entailed a slow development in infrastructural networks. Later, attempts at cash crop production proved difficult or failures. Ludewa District is one of the districts of Iringa Region in southwestern Tanzania. It had a population of 76,610 people, 40,872 of whom were men. Figures prepared by the District Development Directorate show that this population consisted of 16,002 households living in 47 villages. The total number of able-bodied persons (men and women) was 28,200.

The economy of the district is based on agriculture, the largest part of which is subsistence. In 1978-9 subsistence agriculture constituted 71.4 per cent of the GDP. The commercial sector (including cash crop production) contributed 6.9 per cent. The service sector's contribution was 0.8 per cent. The rest of the GDP (20.8 per cent) came from government. From these figures the per capita income was Tz. shs. 703, which was about 80 per cent of the regional per capita income of Tz. shs. 875.

It was estimated that in a period of five years (1976-7 to 1980-1) GDP was growing at an annual rate of 4.8 per cent, although allocation of funds to the district by government increased by 260 per cent over the same period. The reason for the poor performance in the directly productive sectors (agriculture, animal husbandry, fisheries and small-scale industries) was that the lion's share of the funds allocated to the district went to nonproductive sectors, for example, construction of the district headquarters and the district hospital and the improvement of roads.[5]

What is argued here is that Njombe District, including Ludewa which was part of it, was established as a labour reserve in the colonial era, and has remained one. But there have been changes in the characteristics of labour migration with respect to the rates of migration, its duration and destinations:

(a) the 1920s-1950s was a period of longer-term migration to sisal plantations;

(b) this type of migration declined in the second half of the 1960s for reasons external to Njombe itself;

(c) it has been partly replaced by other types of migration since the mid-1960s. Thus, it has become seasonal rather than long-term; there are different destinations, and the overall rates of migration are lower.

It is also shown in the paper that there have been various attempts to provide alternative economic opportunities to migration as sources of money, such as cash crops in the late-colonial period and since 'villagisation'. But as these have had limited effects, migration continues even if at lower rates and in different forms than in the colonial period.

II. The History of Labour Migration in Ludewa District

To understand the causes of seasonal labour migration in Ludewa District, it is necessary to go back to the colonial period when the district was regarded as a labour reservoir for the plantation economy, especially the sisal industry. At the time, Ludewa District formed the southern part of Njombe District in the Southern Highlands Province. Therefore, discussion of labour migration in Ludewa District up to 1975, when the district was created, cannot be separated from labour migration from Njombe District as it was then. All the available data on labour migration cover Njombe District as it was before it was split up, with the creation of Ludewa District (1975) and Makete District (1979). Presentation of accurate labour migration figures from Ludewa District is made impossible even now by the following factors:

(a) There is only one Labour Division Office which caters for both Njombe and Ludewa Districts, and it is situated at Njombe township. Statistics are kept by this office and they are not separated into Njombe and Ludewa statistics;

(b) The outlet to sisal, tea and sugar plantations is through Njombe; thus if there were a Labour Division Office in Ludewa District, it would have been impracticable for the majority of labour migrants to go to Ludewa to register themselves, and then traverse the route to Njombe. Furthermore, only labour migrants who seek wage employment through the Labour Division are registered. Others go directly to employment areas or are recruited in their villages by estates' employment officers and taken to the estates without registering with the Labour Division;

(c) Labour migrants who go to work for individual peasants in the neighbouring districts are not required to register themselves, hence it is impossible to ascertain how many labour migrants leave their homes in search of wage labour.

1. The Beginning of Labour Migration in Njombe District

In this section we look at labour migration between the 1920s and 1950s when work in sisal dominated the labour market. No records exist to show exactly when labour migration began in Njombe District, but it is recorded that by the mid-1920s long-distance travelling for the sake of earning cash had become regular.[6] The need to earn cash through labour migration had been brought about by several factors, notably a decline in local trade, lack of markets for local produce, the disruption caused by the German reprisal after the Maji Maji uprising, and the First World War. Decline in local trade was particularly caused by the import of industrial commodities to replace local products. Lack of markets for local produce was a result of the lack of means of transport to the markets in the north, and this factor held back development of the district for a long time.[7]

Njombe District became a labour reservoir during the German rule. This happened when more labourers were required for sisal estates in the north-eastern parts of the country and the local supply could not satisfy demand for labour. Moreover, the sisal estates were not the only centre of employment for migrant labour from Njombe District. There were also European settlers in the then Southern Highlands Province who had established commercial estates. By 1929 hundreds of labourers from Njombe

District were working for the settlers.[8]

Since the opportunities to earn cash in Njombe District were limited, labour migration became an established way of life and was accepted as part of the people's customs. By 1930 more than 4,500 peasants were working on government payrolls, either as porters or as road labourers, in Njombe District, while 6,000 were migrant workers in other districts.[9]

The majority of the peasants who left the district in search of wage employment went to the sisal estates in Kilosa and Tanga. The motivation for seeking wage employment in the sisal industry was the higher wages of 30 shillings a month in 1926, compared to 5 shillings in Njombe District.[10] The pay for sisal cutters was higher than for other field operations, and it was for this reason that many people from Njombe District preferred to take up sisal cutting.

The exodus to sisal estates is shown by a District Commissioner for Njombe who estimated in 1943 that more than 400 men left Njombe by lorry bound for Kilosa every month. He also showed that at one time 126 men were sent to sisal estates in a single day.[11]

During the Second World War when labour for the sisal industry had to be obtained through conscription, Njombe District's quota was put at 600 men per year, the highest quota in the province. It was difficult to fulfil the quota as the district had already been depleted of able-bodied men, due to recruitment in the villages by touts representing various estates. In some villages only 33 per cent of able-bodied men were at home at the beginning of the cultivating season.

The District Commissioner complained to the Provincial Commissioner about the 'unrealistic' quota, pointing out that:

Lorries from Kilosa are picking labour from Upangwa [Ludewa District]. Njombe District provides 80 per cent of labour for Mufindi tea estates . . . a large percentage of labour [is] working on sisal estates on the Central Line. A considerable number of natives also go to Tanga for work on sisal estates. Tukuyu tea estates employ large quantities of Wakinga . . . the pyrethrum estates here have 3,000 natives employed by them . . . Government is employing 500 on government works and the roads in the district. Finally this district has to supply a considerable number of porters monthly.[12]

He went on to say that labour migration in Upangwa was more depressing with only 36 per cent of men at home at any time.

The District Commissioner's complaint resulted in the ending of conscription in the district, but at the same time the district was opened to recruitment by licensed labour agents.

The migration of men to the sisal industry caused a shortage of labour within the district and in the province. In 1945 and 1946 there was a serious labour shortage in Iringa; besides the exodus to sisal, causes for the shortage included the low wages paid in Iringa and Njombe, and the increase in peasant agricultural production.[13] Shortage of men in the district led to the employment of women and children. For example, returns from one of the pyrethrum farms in Njombe District for December 1946 show that there was a total of 7,375 man-days, broken down into: 3,404 men man-days; 1,372 women man-days and 2,599 child man-days. Another farm showed a large labour force made up of 50 men, 30 women and 160 children.[14] Women and child employment was not limited to the pyrethrum estates in Njombe District. It was also widely practised on tobacco farms in Iringa.

The law allowed the employment of child labour, but on condition that 'a child labourer shall be accompanied by a parent or guardian'. One must regard child employment as socialisation of children in the labour process. The children grew up as labour migrants. They were lured away from school, growing up illiterate and believing that labour migration was the only way to earn cash. The entire family unit (man, wife and children) became labour migrants. Thus, when the children established their own families, the cycle was repeated. Reproduction of migrant labour biologically, and in respect of training and socialisation, was ensured.

The employers' concern was to employ as many children as possible. They were paid very low wages and there was no threat of them complaining or going on strike over wages or living conditions. At times up to 25 per cent of labour migrants travelling to employment centres were children accompanying relatives or headmen. Employment of women and children still goes on today in the tea and tobacco industries at Mufindi and Iringa.

A few colonial officials were willing to check labour migration and encourage cash crop production in Njombe District, but their 'local' interests were pitted against the interests of the plantation owners. These were backed by the colonial State because of the importance of the plantation sector in the country's economy.

The local officials were aware of the importance of sisal in Tanganyika's economy, but they were also aware of what famine could do to the people in their area, such as happened in Tunduru District in 1932 when the government had to spend £5,000 on famine relief. That famine had been a result of 'progressive deterioration of tribal life and consequently the decrease in cultivation caused through the overlong absence of able-bodied males from their homes in search of work at the coast'.[15] In the 1940s, the danger of deteriorating 'tribal life' was real in the Southern Highlands Province, as the Acting Provincial Commissioner pointed out in 1945. He argued against labour migration and favoured development of peasant production of cash crops: 'It is an entirely negative attitude to argue that the families of some 100,000 taxpayers who are concerned in this matter, are a permanent reservoir of labour for local tea and pyrethrum planters and for local industry'.[16] But good intentions alone on the part of local officials would not end labour migration. It was an economic issue; to commercial agriculture it concerned the supply of cheap labour; for the migrants it was an issue of meeting immediate cash needs. It could only end when alternative means of earning cash were available. This depended on agricultural policy, stabilisation of labour in the employment centres and investment in peasant agriculture – all of which seem to have gained momentum in the late 1950s.

2. Decline of Migrant Labour to Sisal Estates from the Labour Reserves

In the late 1950s changes were taking place in the sisal industry as well as in the labour-supplying areas. The latter changes involved expansion of cash crop production by the peasants, which meant new employment opportunities for migrant labour. Changes also took place in the labour force as a whole. The development of trade unionism and the nationalist movement enabled workers to voice their grievances against the colonial government and employers.[17]

What concerns us here are changes brought about by trade union action in the sisal industry, which resulted in changes in the employment structure and wage rates and increased labour productivity. Increasing productivity was achieved through increases in tasks and longer working hours, and led to the employment of a smaller labour force, making many labour migrants in the sisal industry redundant. The changes also led to employers in the industry depending on labour settled on the plantation and in the neighbourhood of the estates. The latter was an important source of casual labour, and it remains an important source of labour today. The redundant labourers returned to their villages to become smallholder cash crop producers, or they simply reverted to subsistence agriculture.

A major result of the changes was a reduction of labour supply to the sisal industry. The decline led to the closure of the Sisal Labour Bureau (SILABU) in 1965. The Tanganyika Sisal Growers' Association (TSGA) had become established in Njombe District, as in all major exporting areas. The contribution of labour power to the sisal industry by the major labour reserves through recruitment by SILABU is shown in Table 4.1.

It should be noted that the closure of SILABU in 1965 did not mean the end of labour migration or end recruiting. Labour migrants went on to look for wage employment in the sisal industry, and the Department of Labour took over the role of recruiting labour. Furthermore, not all migrants who went to sisal estates registered themselves with the Department of Labour, as was also true during SILABU days. It is therefore impossible to know how many people went to work in the sisal industry during the colonial period.

At that time, when changes were taking place in the sisal industry, Njombe District had a new District Commissioner who was keen on economic development in the district through an expansion of cash crop production. He was strongly opposed to the recruitment of labour in the district. But the Department of Labour viewed unfavourably his efforts to change the status of the district from that of exporter of labour to exporter of cash crops. For example, when the Department of Labour suggested that more labourers might be recruited from Upangwa, he vigorously opposed the idea, arguing that:

The Njombe Local Administration are now making an intensive effort to increase the wealth of the district by developing new cash crops, such as coffee, pyrethrum, wheat and peas . . . which will begin in 1959 . . . and which have the

Table 4.1: *Analysis of Labour Migration through SILABU, 1947-65, Provinces of Origin (% of total migrants, columns 4-9)*

Year	Total males[a]	Dependants[a]	Western	Highlands	Lake	Southern	Central	Ruanda Urundi	Total[b]
1947	25,557	7,111	22	42	15	17	1	2	105,326
1948	33,532	10,384	18	40	21	12	3	5	122,541
1949	38,831	15,958	14	41	16	18	6	4	134,711
1950	29,748	13,797	11	36	15	29	5	4	128,640
1951	36,310	17,757	15	43	5	29	3	4	128,656
1952	38,935	19,313	15	39	4	31	3	4	137,675
1953	36,402	17,112	16	37	8	22	3	7	145,952
1954	30,123	14,268	14	36	5	27	10	8	137,589
1955	24,865	12,076	16	34	3	36	10	9	129,843
1956	25,221	13,927	14	36	2	37	4	8	127,407
1957	25,874	13,928	15	35	2	37	2	9	125,598
1958	32,569	16,424	15	37	1	38	3	9	126,010
1959	24,325	11,768	19	4	1	36	2	6	133,216
1960	8,934	2,591	38	25	–	35	3	1	121,861
1961	3,180	627	51	33	–	35	2	–	109,809
1962	6,820	1,061	49	46	–	22	–	–	109,641
1963	3,659	331	68	32	–	5	–	–	87,933
1964	3,454	266	82	18	–	–	–	–	83,049
1965	138	12	95	5	–	–	–	–	63,066

Notes: a. Figures in columns 2 and 3 refer to migrants forwarded to sisal estates in that particular year. b. Column 10 refers to total labour force in the sisal industry in each year.
Source: P. Lawrence in L. Cliffe et al.: *Rural co-operation in Tanzania* (Dar es Salaam, Tanzania Publishing House, 1975), p. 114.

secondary object of attracting back to the district some 15,000 Africans who now find it necessary to seek work elsewhere. In the circumstances I cannot support any proposal which might aid in draining off still more of the area's able-bodied men . . . I am particularly opposed to the establishment of any Forwarding Office in Upangwa, a backward area where great efforts are to be made to develop an indigenous coffee industry.[18]

By 1961 many peasants in Njombe District, especially in the north and central areas, had taken up cultivation of cash crops as an alternative to working on sisal estates. For example, pyrethrum production by smallholder farmers had risen to 212 tons in 1960 from 2 tons in 1955; coffee had gone up from 14 tons to 562 tons; sunflower oil, from 22 tons to 900; castor oil, from 68 to 200 tons; groundnuts, from 3 to 35 tons. The total value of these main export crops produced by African smallholders had risen from £43,000 in 1955 to £118,000 in 1960, and it was estimated to rise to £263,200 by 1962.[19] However, labour migration had not ended. Peasants still went to tobacco and tea estates in Iringa and Mufindi, and to wattle and pyrethrum estates within the district.

3. Cash Crop Production and Labour Migration in Ludewa District in the Last Years of the Colonial Period

Efforts to introduce cash crops as an alternative source of cash for peasants in Ludewa District in the late years of colonial rule largely failed, while labour migration continued.

Two cash crops were introduced in Ludewa District in the late 1950s, coffee in 1956 and pyrethrum in 1959. In 1959 there were 54 peasants growing pyrethrum, and between them they had 29 acres. The number rose to 293 growers, cultivating 170 acres, in 1960 and to 731 growers, cultivating 661 acres, in 1961. Coffee was being grown further south of the pyrethrum belt and in 1958 there were 240 coffee farmers who between them had a total of 64.5 acres of coffee trees.[20]

To encourage coffee expansion, a European agricultural officer was stationed in the area and several coffee nurseries were established. By 1960 harvested coffee amounted to 118 bags (about 60 kg each). Acreage under coffee had risen to 346 acres and the number of coffee farmers to 1,133. Although many peasants had taken up coffee growing, they were not enthusiastic about it, most of them limiting themselves to about 50 or 60 coffee trees. The official explanation was that this was due to peasants' apathy, and as a result the Department of Agriculture, towards the end of 1960, removed half of the staff from the coffee area.[21]

The officials concerned did not look into other possible reasons for the lack of enthusiasm for coffee growing. One of the reasons may have been the cost of coffee seedlings. Sold at 10 cents each, it would have been difficult for many peasants to afford enough seedlings even for 1 acre (about 500 seedlings). Furthermore, investment had to be made in equipment, such as pruning scissors, hand-operated pulping machines, pesticides, and so on. Also the crop demanded much attention, thus competing with food crops. For many coffee growers one member of the household (usually the man) had to devote his entire time to looking after coffee, and during the harvesting season every member of the household had to join in the picking of the coffee berries. Lastly, while coffee was being sold through Lupembe Co-operative Society in Ubena, the growers in Upangwa obtained poor prices for their coffee, and had to pay 16 shillings each for membership in the co-operative society.[22] It should also be noted that although coffee instructors were available to advise peasants on coffee growing, no credit facilities were available for inputs. Thus, for many peasants in Ludewa District, coffee growing was not easy to start and also it was not profitable.

Meanwhile, peasants were producing surplus food crops, but there was no market for them. For example, in 1961 over 50 tons of surplus food crops could not be taken to the market for lack of transport. In these circumstances peasants in Ludewa District had to go on depending on labour migration as the only alternative means of earning cash. While agricultural instructors were exhorting peasants to take up cash crop production, the Department of Labour was issuing permits for labour recruitment in Njombe District, including Ludewa District. The colonial State's interest was to raise the quantity of export crops based on the plantation system, whose production was dependent on cheap labour. The local interest was served by raising cash crop production on smallholdings, especially after the failure of settler crops, due to the fall in price of such crops as pyrethrum. The

State's interest in raising production of the major crops, especially sisal, and the recruitment of migrants from the labour reserves, prevailed because the local authorities had failed to identify and effectively deal with the causes of rural poverty, which reinforced conditions inducing labour migration. The lack of development of communications and of material support from government in the case of Ludewa District did not encourage peasant production of cash crops.

The first Provincial Commissioner for the Southern Highlands Province had felt that no part of his province was too far from an outlet to make profitable export impossible. The first District Officer at Njombe was impressed by food production in Ludewa District (then Upangwa), but also realised there was no market for the surplus food crops.[23] That was in the 1920s and 40 years later some parts of the province were still too far from an outlet to the market for cash crops and surplus food crops; but they were not too far for labour recruitment.

Hiring by professional recruiters was stopped in Njombe District in 1957, but other kinds of hiring were allowed, notably that of 'voluntary' labourers who presented themselves at the workplace or at an office of a recruiting agency, such as SILABU. Another common method involved employers applying for Worker Recruiter's Permits and sending some of their workers to recruit in the workers' villages. This latter method was widely used in Njombe District. Records show, for example, that in a period of eight months in 1958, 115 permits were issued for the recruitment of a total of 20,080 labourers.[24] These were only for employment in Iringa and Njombe Districts. The records unfortunately do not show how many of the required labourers were actually hired.

The point is that Njombe District, until the late 1950s, was still being regarded as a labour reservoir and not as a potential exporter of cash crops.

One might be tempted to suggest that during the entire colonial period, Ludewa District was largely left in its pre-colonial situation, and that its incorporation into the world market was marginal. But that was not the case. Ludewa District was incorporated into the world market system by the early 1930s through the monetisation of the indigenous economy.

When pre-colonial social formations were incorporated into the world market system, the incorporation was not uniform.

Each part of the social formation performed a special function for the world market, according to the requirements of the colonial economic system. Therein lies the basis for socio-economic differentiation between the various regions of a country (differentiation rooted in the so-called division of labour on a world scale).

During the colonial period the areas nearer to ports of rail and road communications (with the exception of Kigoma Region) were incorporated into the world market system through the production of cash crops. This led to investment in children's education, development of social and economic infrastructure, and the development of rich and poor categories of peasants. As cash-crop production was intensified, rich peasants hired the labour of poor peasants.

Areas which could not grow cash crops, because of the distance to the markets or because they were forbidden, would not see the development of social and economic infrastructure. Their subsistence agriculture stagnated; education was non-existent, or minimal conducted by missionaries. For a long time they were excluded from the crucial decision-making positions in the economic structure of the country.[25] They only participated in the monetary sector through the sale of labour power to plantations or rich peasants.

It is by looking at labour migration as part of the complete economic system of a country that one can see it as a circulation of labour between production processes.[26] But in the type of migration discussed here, circulation of labour was, and still is, between the subsistence sector and the monetary sector. In the transformation which took place during colonial rule the previous systems of simple reproduction were undermined without being destroyed, by preserving the food production sector, necessary for the reproduction of the labour force. At the same time, as labour from the subsistence sector was withdrawn for cash-crop production, the latter was maintained by the food crop sector. The system became self-perpetuating, with the cash-crop sector being dominant because food crops could not fetch the same value on the world market as cash crops. Even when improved agricultural methods were introduced to the peasants, they were confined to cash crops. Food crop production continued by traditional methods.

Regarded in that way, labour surplus disguised underemployment and the push and pull factors per se become inadequate as explanations for labour migration. It is by analysing the incorporation of the pre-colonial economies into the world market and the linkages between the monetary sector and the so-called subsistence sector that peasant agriculture, migration patterns and rural development programmes in colonial and modern Tanzania can be understood.

III. Labour Migration in Post-colonial Tanzania

In this section we discuss the end of the short period of relatively abundant labour supply to the sisal industry, the continuing demand for labour from Njombe District (including Ludewa) and the development of seasonal labour migration.

The independent trade union movement, which played such a major part in the stabilisation of labour in the sisal industry in the 1950s, ended in 1964 when the government dissolved the Tanganyika Federation of Labour (sisal workers being represented by the Tanganyika Sisal and Plantation Workers' Union) and replaced it with the government-controlled National Union of Tanganyika Workers (known as NUTA). From then onwards, workers lost their power to negotiate directly with employers, and working conditions deteriorated. For example, a negotiated agreement on productivity reached between NUTA and employers in the sisal industry on 30 October 1964 increased the tasks of sisal cutters; these were impossible for many of the labourers to fulfil, making work in sisal even more difficult.[27]

1. Labour Shortages and Demand for Labour from Njombe District

After Independence in 1961 the Tanzania Government took steps to end labour migration, both from outside and within the country. The reason was the government view that labour migration was responsible for the economic and social stagnation of the labour reserves. But no measures were taken to ensure labour supply to the plantations from other sources. Conditions in the labour reserves had not changed, that is, peasants in the labour reserves could not earn cash within their localities, for cash-crop production had not become widespread. Labour migration continued because for peasants in the labour reserves wage labour was necessary to meet their subsistence requirements, complementary to subsistence agriculture. Their going into wage labour was not due to compulsion, because throughout the colonial period conditions had been created for the emergence of 'free labour', partly separated from the major means of livelihood – the land. Ownership of land was not sufficient for the subsistence of the part-peasants and part-wage-earners in the labour reserve.

Besides the sisal, tea, pyrethrum and tobacco industries, other employment centres had been established in the 1960s, such as the Wattle Company within Njombe District and Kilombero Sugar Company in Morogoro Region. Rich peasants in commodity-producing areas too became employers of migrant labour.[28] The migrant labourers were employed in commodity production as well as in production of subsistence crops. It was in the 1960s that the pattern of migration began to change from long-term to seasonal. Also, although there was a labour surplus in the sisal industry (following labour stabilisation), enterprises in Iringa, Mufindi and Njombe had labour shortages. By 1966 the problem was serious, especially in the tobacco industry which in November of that year alone required 5,000 labourers, when there were a total of 9,550 labour vacancies in the wattle, pyrethrum, tobacco and tea industries.[29]

In order to meet their demand for labour, tobacco farmers resorted to employing children, also from Njombe District. Some farmers sent lorries to Njombe to collect the children, some of whom were less than 10 years old. Between 1960 and 1977 the child labourers were paid 1 or 2 shillings per day. The rates laid down by the government for labourers in agricultural enterprises were 8.85 shillings a day for adults and 7.60 shillings a day for youths under the age of 18 years, but tobacco farmers were paying adult workers 5 shillings a day.[30] That partly explains the labour shortage problem in the tobacco industry in Iringa at that time. In 1977 the Area Commissioner for Njombe District estimated that annually about 40 per cent of primary school children in the three divisions in Ukinga (new Makete District) left school to seek wage employment.[31]

Demand for labour in tobacco production fluctuates according to season, the peak periods being the planting and harvesting/-sorting seasons. For the large farms, of about 200 acres, about 500 man-days per month are required in the peak period and 100 man-days per month in the slack period. The peak in tobacco farming coincides with food production, and fewer labour migrants look for wage labour at that time. For example, between January and March 1978, tobacco farmers required a total of 877 workers for harvesting and curing tobacco leaf, but only 18 were recruited in Njombe and a few more in Iringa. On the other hand, during slack periods in peasant agriculture labour is often available for wage employment. For example, between October and December 1978 the tobacco estates were able to recruit 655 labourers from Njombe, although this figure was 135 below the required labour force.

The marked decline of labour supply to the traditional centres of employment (the sisal, tobacco and tea industries) in the 1970s is shown in Table 4.2. In the 1977-8 season total labour requirements by tobacco estates, as submitted to the Labour Division at Iringa, were 40,355 man-days per year. This figure did not include labour for eight estates that had not submitted their labour returns to the Labour Division. In interviews with Labour Division officials, we were told that the required labour would be recruited in Njombe.

The seriousness of the labour problem in the tobacco industry in Iringa District has forced some tobacco growers to abandon their farms, whereas others have gone into mixed farming of tobacco and maize, the larger part of their farms being given to maize production. According to Labour Division officials, the reason for this is that with maize production all processes can be mechanised, which means that only a small labour force is required.[32]

The labour shortage caused a decline in tobacco production from 4,261,685 kg in 1976-7 to 2,300,000 kg in 1980-1 – and a further decline was expected in 1981-2.[33] Naturally, the falling tobacco production has caused concern for the government. Tobacco farmers in Iringa (who are of Greek origin) produce 80 per cent of the crop from Iringa Region. The government had to intervene to ensure an adequate labour supply to the tobacco farmers. This was done after village governments (grassroots-level State apparatuses officially known as 'village governments') in the districts of Njombe, Mufindi and Makete (the latter being formerly Njombe West and the major supplier of labour to the tobacco farms) had resolved to stop peasants from going to work as labour migrants.

Table 4.2: *Decline of Labour Supply from Njombe District, 1977-9*

Date	Tobacco Required	Tobacco Recruited	Tea Required	Tea Recruited	Wattle Required	Wattle Recruited	Sugar Required	Sugar Recruited	Sisal Required	Sisal Recruited
Jan.-Sept. 1977	NA[a]	NA	NA	NA	NA	NA	642	264	850	107
Jan.-Dec. 1978	1,351	683	40	None	NA	NA	1,200	254	2,250	28
Jan.-June 1979	NA	NA	200	None	100	4	NA	NA	Unlimited	None

Note:a. NA – not available

Source: Compiled from *Quarterly Reports* (Njombe, Labour Division).

Thus to ensure a continued supply of labour to the tobacco farms, the government turned away from its earlier stand of opposing labour migration from the former labour reserves to active recruiting for the tobacco farmers through the Labour Division. A special form for labour recruiting for the tobacco farms was devised by the Labour Division and distributed in villages in Makete District. The form says in part: 'I certify that the workers named below have my approval to go to Iringa to work on tobacco farms and that they are not school children.' The form, having been filled in in quadruplicate, has to be signed by the Village Chairman or the Ward Secretary and then submitted to the District Labour Officer and the District Secretary of the National Organisation of Tanzania Workers (JUWATA) for approval. The village governments' opposition to labour migration has thus been effectively silenced.

The village governments have opposed recruitment drives by trying to check migration by exhorting would-be migrants not to migrate and by fining the returning migrants. It should be noted that recruitment is not controlled by law; that is, recruited migrants are not bound by any contract. They are free to take up employment as casual labourers or as permanent workers. On the other hand, the law requires an employer to engage on permanent terms casual labourers who have worked continuously for three months. But most labour migrants do not like to stay in wage employment for long periods. For example, many of the labour migrants who go to work on tobacco farms in Iringa do so for only about two months before returning to their villages.

The government's position as regards labour migration, especially the efforts to maintain the labour reserve status of the former labour reserves, contrary to the opposition to labour migration shown in the late 1960s, has been caused by the decline in production of plantation crops, especially sisal. For example, in its labour recruiting drive in 1970, the Labour Division issued permits for recruiting labour in Njombe (including Ludewa and Makete) District for sisal, tobacco and tea estates. Since the officials in Njombe District were known to be opposed to recruiting labour in the district, the Labour Division used 'nationalistic sentiment', pointing out that peasants were free to go to work anywhere in the country, and that by refusing permission for labour recruitment in the district, the national economy would be adversely affected.[34] Other examples of the

State's intervention in the procurement of labour on behalf of employers include the authority given in 1978 to the Minister of Labour and Social Welfare by Parliament to authorise recruitment of labour from 'anywhere in the country', which in reality means the former labour reserves. In 1979 the government, in a bid to get away from its earlier opposition to labour migration, rationalised the recruitment of sisal cutters in former labour reserves by arguing that sisal cutting was no different from any other kind of employment, such as working in a textile factory. This was after the Member of Parliament from Kigoma Region (an important former labour reserve) had opposed recruitment of sisal cutters from former labour reserves.[35] In 1981 the Tanzania Sisal Authority, in a move to counter opposition from the labour supply areas to recruitment, offered to pay Tz. shs. 600 per year to the village concerned for each recruited labourer if the labourer worked for an average of 23 days per month.[36] But despite such government intervention, labour supply to sisal and tobacco industries has continued to decline.

Although labour migration cannot be ended solely by political and administrative measures, in that the uneven development of the rural areas still pushes peasants to search for wage labour, attitudes to labour migration have been changing. Wage rates, working and living conditions and ideological exhortations against labour migration, have each played a part in shaping peasants' attitudes towards labour migration. It is true that economic reality obliges them to earn cash as labour migrants, but they do not have to earn it in the traditional employment centres, which are no longer predominant in the labour market.

2. Economic Development and Seasonal Labour Migration in Ludewa District, 1975-81

The creation of Ludewa District in 1975 was meant to enhance economic development in the area and check labour migration. Before its creation, when administration of economic development was run from Njombe, political division of the then Njombe District was based on tribal lines. At the top of the ladder were the Wabena in the northern and central parts of the district. They were followed by the Wakinga in the western part. The Wapangwa in the southern part of the district were at the bottom of the ladder, and probably the most backward.

For many years labour migration was the major source of cash income for the peasants in Ludewa District, especially in the 1950s and 1960s. The high rate of migration is shown in the figures in Table 4.3 from the sample villages covered by our research.[37]

Table 4.3: *Rates of Migration from Sample Villages in Ludewa District, 1940s-80 (%)*

Date	Mapogolo	Milo	Maholong'wa
1940s	3.9	9.4	14.3
1950s	42.3	37.5	50
1960s	27	31.3	25
1970s	23	21.8	10.7
1980	3.8	–	–

Note: The figures were restricted to the heads of household in the sample villages.

Participation in wage labour since the late 1960s has no longer been achieved through political or administrative coercion, although sometimes recruiting agents have had to go into villages to prod peasants into wage labour. The market forces of supply and demand are operative and peasants choose when and where to sell their labour power and when to withdraw from the labour market. This is a result of the fact that cash income from either surplus food production or wage labour taken separately, is not sufficient for the subsistence of the family unit.

Another relevant development is the intensification of cash-crop production, both in the traditional cash-crop growing areas and the former labour reserves. The expansion has meant more use of wage labour in crop production. The use of wage labour by individual peasants is not limited to cash crops. Migrant labourers from Ludewa District cross into Songea and Mbinga Districts each year in search of wage employment. Those from Ludewa find jobs as farm labourers for both cash and food crops. Those from Njombe District are mainly engaged in brick-making, although others work as farm labourers; and many girls end up in Songea and Mbinga towns as barmaids. Men from Makete District go for lumberjack employment, sometimes as many as 40 being employed by one individual in Mbinga or Songea.[38]

Migrant labourers from Ludewa District have at times gone to

Usangu Plains in Mbeya Region, where they have been employed by individual peasants in rice growing; others have been employed by the Mbarali Rice State Farm as casual labourers. There are also movements within the district, especially to the newly-established district headquarters at Ludewa Minor settlement.

District officials at Ludewa have been alarmed by the labour movement to the neighbouring districts, and measures to try to prevent migration have been taken. They include an imposition of fines on returning migrants by their village governments. But this measure alone has not been effective in checking labour migration. While interviewing migrant labourers from Ludewa at Mgazini village in Songea District during this research, we were told that most migrants would rather risk emigration than remain at home without cash, although they might not return home with sufficient savings for the fine.

Although labour migration still takes place in Ludewa District, the rate of migration (especially to sisal estates) is lower than during the colonial period. It is true though that employment centres such as the sisal and sugar industries still regard Ludewa as a labour reservoir, and from time to time recruiters go into the district to recruit labour, sometimes unsuccessfully. For example, in 1975 a recruiter from sisal estates in Tanga found it difficult to recruit workers, and comparing the situation to recruitment in the 'old days', lamented:

It used to be that a recruitment officer need only book into a hotel [presumably at Njombe township], and people would readily come to him for jobs in sisal. Now we have to roam in order to recruit, almost begging for workers.

The officer was able to recruit 400 labourers, but after only a few days most had left for a local tea estate where work was much lighter. Those who remained specified that they only intended to stay for three months at the most and then return home.[39] At other times, recruiters have successfully recruited large numbers of labourers in Ludewa District, as in 1977 when recruiters from Mtibwa sugar estates in Morogoro Region were able to engage about 80 men at Maholong'wa and a nearby village, and in 1978 when recruiters from the same estates recruited many youths in several villages, including Maholong'wa. The recruiters had gone to the district with several large lorries kept at Mlangali, the area divisional headquarters, while smaller lorries were used to bring the labourers from the villages.[40] In all such trips, recruiting officers are taken to the villages by labourers already employed by the estates.

It is not possible to say conclusively 'who migrates'. For example, not every peasant in the labour reserves has been a labour migrant. Not all migrants come from the poorest group of peasants. Similarly, in the traditional cash-crop areas, not every peasant produces cash crops. It seems that to become a labour migrant or a cash-crop producer depends on what opportunities are available. Where there are fewer opportunities, the peasants' condition becomes more depressed, as we see from the three sample villages. However, there is no doubt that where cash-crop growing has flourished, labour migration has declined.

In one of the villages, Mapogolo, pyrethrum is the major cash crop, followed by maize which is the major staple crop in the northern and central parts of the district, where the majority of the population is concentrated. The second village, Milo, is a mission station, several miles south-east of Mapogolo. Although pyrethrum thrives well here too, peasants have become disillusioned with the crop and concentrate on maize as a cash crop. The third village, Maholong'wa, is about 12 miles east of Milo and at a lower altitude than the other two. Coffee does well there, but before the villagisation programme in 1974 production was only on a small scale, and was completely disrupted during the villagisation programme. Village interviews revealed that there were no coffee plots in the new village and that only a few peasants had continued to look after the few trees they had in their old villages. The village had 10 bags of coffee (about 600 kg) from the 1979-80 season, which had not been collected by the Tanzania Coffee Board, allegedly because the quantity did not warrant the board sending a vehicle to the village to pick them up. Another village between Milo and Maholong'wa had 20 bags, which had not been collected for the same reason.

The first two villages (Mapogolo and Milo) are included in the National Maize Project, which is aimed at producing sufficient maize through peasant farming for the country's requirements. The project involves several regions of the country and is supported by funds from the World Bank. The Tanzania Development Bank facilitates the implementation of the project by supplying inputs (hybrid maize seed, fertilisers and insecticides) to the villages on credit, at the lending rate of 8 per cent interest on outstanding credit. To qualify for a loan from the TRDB, a village must show increases in marketed maize in previous seasons, and any village which has had a default in payment is disqualified from further loans. The village distributes the inputs to peasants, usually on credit, and according to individual peasants' requirements, with payment due when the crop is harvested.

Marketing is dependent on the ease with which the authorities can reach a village. The quantity of marketed crops is dependent on soil fertility, and with hybrid maize the use of chemical fertilisers is essential. Poverty and lack of communications seem to reinforce each other, and that is the position in which peasants at Maholong'wa village find themselves.

This village had the highest rate of seasonal labour migration. For example, close relatives of the sample heads of households who were in wage employment as migrant labourers at the time of this research (April–June 1981) were 30 per cent for Mapogolo, 47.1 per cent for Milo and 54.5 per cent for Maholong'wa. Yet the distinctiveness of Milo village, as a result of the mission influence, is also notable. The village had the highest number of migrants in white-collar jobs (29.4 per cent compared with 13.3 per cent for Mapogolo and 15.1 per cent for Maholong'wa); the highest number of children with secondary education (14.7 per cent compared with 3.3 per cent for Mapogolo and none for Maholong'wa); and the highest number of household heads' children in white-collar employment (41.2 per cent compared with 6.7 per cent for Mapogolo and 12.1 per cent for Maholong'wa). Milo was also the only village whose migrants had been employed as domestic servants in hotels or European households, and had fewer migrants working in the sisal industry (only 21.9 per cent as against 61.5 per cent for Mapogolo and 71.4 per cent for Maholong'wa).

Throughout the colonial period the Milo mission was the educational centre for those of the Anglican faith in Upangwa. The people who benefited most were those from Milo village itself and to a lesser extent those from the neighbouring villages, from where children could walk to school at Milo and return to their homes daily.

There are three options for peasants in the former labour

reserves to earn cash income. One is to produce for the market, either cash crops or surplus food crops. The second is to combine subsistence farming with wage labour. The third is to break completely from the land and join the bureaucracy with secure employment and provision in the event of unemployment due to illness or old age through pension schemes and the National Provident Fund.

The third option can only be achieved through education. A white-collar worker becomes a migrant too, although not necessarily seasonal or oscillatory, in that most of the white-collar workers do not work in their own districts. Furthermore, on retirement not all return to their villages. Their break with the so-called traditional society is complete and their children are brought up in an urban environment, completely dependent on wages for their livelihood. Both the white-collar workers and the migrant labourers earn cash income, but in different ways. For the socio-economic system to function, it needs the services of both the white-collar workers and the migrant labourers, but the system offers differential rewards to the two categories of worker according to their position in the socio-economic structure. For example, the higher status and rewards of the white-collar workers in relation to the migrant labourers is due to the fact that the former have to be trained for a long time, and must be stabilised in the urban centres where they work. Conversely, migrant labour is illiterate or semi-literate, unskilled, easily replaced, can be paid at its individual reproduction cost and need not be stabilised at the place of employment.

3. Incentives and Organisation of Production

It is essential to consider how production for the market is organised in the villages in Ludewa District, for this has contributed to the perpetuation of labour migration.

For peasants whose villages qualify for loans from the TRDB, disengaging from labour migration should be easier than for peasants who lack access to agricultural inputs. But a change from labour migration to crop production is not only conditional on access to agricultural resources. Incentives for production are equally important.

Productive conditions are governed by the purpose of production. For example, in a society where production is determined entirely by the producer's subsistence needs, the producer exercises control over production and disposal of produce in circumstances set by the vagaries of weather and kinship obligations. The producer chooses what and how to produce. Mutual aid in the form of reciprocal labour exchange forms an important supplement to household labour. But where production is determined by market conditions, the need for the State to earn foreign exchange as well as to feed the urban population leads to control being imposed on the producers, as is the case in Tanzania. Kinship obligations and reciprocal labour exchanges are replaced by market transactions. Peasants have little control over what, when, where, how and how much to produce. Production is increased by the use of either incentives or coercion. In Ludewa District coercion has been used extensively to oblige peasants to produce for the market, especially after the villagisation programme. For example, in addition to subsistence food crops, including maize, which under the National Maize Project ought to have been regarded as a major cash crop in the district, peasants have been required to produce either coffee, tobacco, pyrethrum or cashew nuts, according to the suitability of the area. Minimum acreages have been prescribed for each peasant.

At present, villages included in the NMP produce maize through a system known as *virobo*, from the Kiswahili word *robo* meaning a quarter. Under this system each able-bodied peasant is required to cultivate a quarter of an acre of maize. At harvest time maize worth Tz. shs. 250 (for 1980 and 1981) is surrendered to the village government. Alternatively, a peasant can pay the government that amount in cash. Any surplus maize from the *virobo* is retained by the peasants. This system was introduced when communal farming proved a disaster.

The village government plays the role of landlord in what looks like a feudal system of exploitation. The village government distributes land, sometimes also regulating its use, especially where block farms are established; it distributes agricultural resources on credit, on behalf of the TRDB. But the payment the peasants make is not land rent, as land is not an exchangeable commodity and payment is not dependent on land productivity. Whether or not peasants harvest any maize on the *virobo*, they have to make the payment, so long as they get inputs for the *virobo*. They cannot opt out of the system, which is compulsory for every member of the village. In this way, the government is assured of revenue even though peasants may not always get cash returns for their labour.[41] The system also ensures a minimum maize production in the worsening terms of trade against the peasants. Consumer goods as incentives for production are in short supply, and when they sometimes appear on the shelves of the village shops the price is usually beyond the reach of most peasants.

The NMP has plunged many peasants into debt, which in turn has reduced the number of potential users of fertilisers and hybrid maize seeds. The TRDB figures show that one of the villages in the sample, Mapogolo, owed Tz. shs. 502,297.45 and Milo owed Tz. shs. 213,551.85.[42] Maholong'wa was among the villages which by the time of this research had not yet qualified for a loan from the TRDB. This means that according to the TRDB, the quantity of maize produced at Maholong'wa in the past was not sufficient to warrant the village's being considered for a loan. In its report on crop purchases covering the period 1976/7 to 1980/1, the Ludewa District branch of the National Milling Corporation asked the Department of Agriculture, the government and party leadership in the district to find other means to enable the 10 villages (including Maholong'wa), which did not qualify for a loan from the TRDB, to obtain agricultural inputs.[43]

The unequal access to resources between villages and between households enables some households to concentrate on agricultural production and pushes others into labour migration. The lack of access to resources by peasants in Maholong'wa village is reflected in the low maize production, as shown in Table 4.4.

The point of discussing production in the villages is that the organisation of production as an alternative to labour migration does not encourage peasants, especially youths, to remain at

Table 4.4: *Production of Maize in the Three Villages in 1979 and 1980 as Percentage of District Population*

	Mapogolo	Milo	Maholong'wa
1979	13.1	2.4	0.6
1980	17.1	5.3	0.1

Source: Prepared from reports on crop purchases by the National Milling Corporation, Ludewa District.

home. In all three villages in the sample, youths expressed their detestation of pressure by the village governments to satisfy the conditions of production; to escape from the pressure, youths resorted to labour migration. This illustrates how labour migration can be a result of pressure rather than an individual's rational decision. As life in the village becomes more of a drudgery some peasants join the seasonal migration flow while others resort to passive resistance to the pressure to grow cash crops or participate in nation-building projects.

The pressure to grow cash crops is a result (as well as meeting foreign exchange needs) of the official view equating coffee, tobacco, cotton and other 'non-edible' crops with development. Rungwe (in Mbeya Region), Kilimanjaro and West Lake Regions are seen as examples of development based on coffee production. In those regions, the major food crop is bananas, a perennial crop; it is intercropped with coffee. As the major food crop in the coffee-growing areas is bananas, a perennial crop, peasants in those areas can devote most of their time to coffee production, though bananas are also a major cash crop.

The situation is different where the major food crops are cereals. Cash crops and food crops must compete for time, good land, inputs and labour. In some areas, such as Mbinga, coffee growers have increasingly had to purchase food from maize-growing areas. When there is not enough food on the market, or in times of high inflation, the price of food goes up tremendously, pushing marginal cash-crop growers into food production.[44] It is interesting that during the fieldwork, labour migrants from Maholong'wa village who had formerly gone to work at Litembo, the major coffee-producing area in Mbinga District, had stopped going there because of the frequent shortages of foodstuffs.

Maize production in Ludewa District could easily replace the crops peasants are forced to grow. Compared to other major crops produced there, maize and beans (staple food crops) have become dominant since the district was created, as is shown in Table 4.5.

Control of peasant labour is not limited to the production of cash crops. Village projects – such as construction of classrooms, civil servants quarters, building Party offices, and maintenance of roads – are implemented using unpaid peasant labour. These projects are usually undertaken during the agricultural slack period. For many peasants, these nation-building projects have

Table 4.5: *Production and Sales of Major Crops in Ludewa District, 1975-80 (tons)*

Crops	1975/6		1976/7		1977/8		1978/9		1979/80	
	1	2	1	2	1	2	1	2	1	2
Maize	6,461.6	2,016	4,400	1,868	5,312	2,400	6,780	1,566.9	21,875	288.45[a]
Beans	102.9	92.6	96	84.4	106.3	95.8	220.9	95.8	1,780	113.1[a]
Pyrethrum	132.3	132.3	321.4	321.4	82.2	82.2	67.3	67.3	46	46
Tobacco	4.8	4.8	26.8	26.8	16.5	16.5	25	25	22.9	22.9
Coffee	17.1	17.1	13.5	13.5	15.6	15.6	15.8	15.8	15.6	15.6
Cashew nuts	6.2	6.2	NA	NA	12.9	12.9	51.9	51.9	NA	NA
Sunflower	59.6	14.9	6.0	1.5	1.6	0.4	15	3.8	135	3.4[a]

Notes: 1 – Produced; 2 – Marketed. NA – Not Available. a. Sales up to October 1980. It was estimated that maize sales would reach 4,000 tons for the year.

Source: District Development Plan 1981-2, Ludewa District.

lost the appeal they held a few years after Independence, and are now regarded as compulsory labour for the government.

In all the three villages labour migration still takes place, the destinations including Tanga sisal estates (although only a few migrants, especially from Maholong'wa, now go to work in the sisal industry), Mtibwa Sugar Estates, Kilombero Sugar Company and the villages in Songea and Mbinga Districts. Employment figures from Kilombero and Kibaranga Sisal Estate (the largest sisal estate owned by the State) show that the former labour reserves are still major contributors of labour to the sisal and sugar industries. For example, in a sample survey of 100 cane cutters at Kilombero Sugar Company in 1978, it was found that all had come from the former labour reserves of Iringa, Mbeya and Ruvuma Regions, and 82 per cent of the labourers were seasonal migrants. In the 1980/1 cane harvest, the seasonal migrant labour force made up 78.9 per cent of the entire labour force in the harvesting department. And in a sample of 60 permanent labourers in the company in 1981, the regional distribution of the source of labourers was as shown in Table 4.6.

Table 4.6: *Distribution by Region of Origin of Permanent Labourers at Kilombero Sugar Company, March 1981*

Region	Percentage
Mbeya	38.4
Iringa	25.0
Morogoro	23.3
Ruvuma	8.3
Lindi	3.4
Dodoma	1.6

The age of the labourers ranged between 18 and 52, the majority (73 per cent) being between the ages of 23 and 37. The relatively low ages contrasted sharply with those of labourers at Kibaranga Sisal Estate, where youths are not attracted to work on sisal. Out of 40 labourers (our sample, that is all permanent labourers settled on the estate) in the age range 19-57, the majority (72.5 per cent) were aged between 38 and 52 and a further 22.5 per cent were aged between 31 and 37.

In April and May 1981 Mtibwa Sugar Estates recruited 250

labourers through the Labour Office at Iringa; 300 were recruited at the same time for Kilombero Sugar Company; but only 50 were recruited for the Amboni Sisal Estates, a private company in which working conditions were said, even by the labourers, to be the best in the sisal industry. There was no breakdown to show the districts of origin of the labour migrants.

The national political campaign against large-scale use of hired labour in agriculture was tempered by the President in 1981 when he said that large-scale farmers were welcome in Tanzania, provided they did not encroach on village land and uproot villages for cheap labour. He pointed out that by 'allowing a capitalist to open a large plantation in a village, you create a landless class of people. If you uproot villagers for a capitalist, what will you do with them?' But he also said that the government did not deny the large-scale farmers the right to employ labour, provided the labourers were adults.[45]

Let us now look at why labour migrants from Ludewa have been preferring employment with individual peasants in Mbinga and Songea Districts rather than with traditional employers, notably the sisal estates.

One reason is the nature of work and living conditions in the sisal estates. Most migrants from Ludewa worked as sisal cutters doing arduous and even dangerous work. Living conditions in the plantations were bad. Furthermore, despite the monthly wage rates promised to labourers when they were recruited, real wages were dependent on completion of daily tasks, which for sisal cutters were 110 bundles of 30 leaves each. In 1979-80, a labourer had to complete the daily task for 26 days each month to earn the minimum wage of Tz. shs. 380.

In working for individual peasants, on the other hand, labour migrants lived with their employers and were provided with food in addition to the negotiated wages, which were usually based on piece rates. Often work on the farms was similar to work in the labourer's own village, making it less of an ordeal than sisal work. In real terms therefore, a labourer earned more by working for individual peasants than on sisal estates. Another point is the distance to the estates. It takes two or three days to walk to Songea or Mbinga Districts, but it takes much longer to travel to sisal or sugar estates, and the migrant labourers had to pay their own fare. Since wage employment was supplementary to subsistence agriculture, the migrants wanted to earn as much as possible in the short period they were away from their homes. The majority of the migrants arrived in Mbinga and Songea Districts in June (the start of the harvesting season in their villages in Ludewa District), and stayed at work until September or October, when they returned to their villages to prepare fields for planting.

IV. Conclusion

It has been argued that in the absence of opportunities for earning cash income within the labour reserves, migration has become a necessary supplement to subsistence agriculture. This is so because reproduction of the migrant labour force is not possible through the market. In local wage employment, wage rates are low and in peasant production the terms of trade are unfavourable.

Persistence of labour migration relates to what is taking place in the monetised sector of the economy. Most significantly, in Tanzania little restructuring of the economy has taken place. Cash-crop production has continued to be dominant over food production and industrialisation. Production in commercial agriculture remains labour-intensive, with a need for only cheap manual labour. The use of wage labour by individual peasants, albeit contrary to policy objectives, indicates the expansion of the 'rich peasant' stratum, thus furthering class differentiation. The withdrawal of labour from the migrants' households and home areas exacerbates rural poverty, the fundamental causes of which have not been altered. And the declining purchasing power of the peasants would have the effect of regenerating labour migration. Effectively checking labour migration from the former labour reserves would mean restricting migration generally and would therefore threaten labour supply to plantations as well as to individual peasants.[46] This will not be allowed to happen, despite acknowledgement by economic planners that labour migration leads to the persistence of poverty and stagnation in the rural areas.

The change from long-term to short-term migration has simply made migrant labour cheaper. This is because, as with all migrant labour, the employer pays less than the wage necessary to support a worker and his family. He pays wages just enough to enable the migrant worker to survive for the period of wage labour. Also availability of land in the villages of migrant labourers makes them prefer seasonal work to permanent low-range employment.[47]

The occasional shortage of labour on plantations arises from the State's, and individual employers' unwillingness to hire labour at higher wages, so accepting lower profit margins. As President Nyerere sees it: 'Peasants do not want to be employed even in State farms. Today you can't just recruit a peasant for cheap labour. We are not ashamed of this, we are happy.'[48]

Besides using migrants as a source of labour, plantations also use casual labour from the villages surrounding the plantations. Casual labour is even cheaper than migrant labour, but its availability is unreliable. The villagers sell their labour to plantations only for a day or two at a time. At the Kilombero Sugar Company it was observed that casual labour was available for weeding on sugar plantations only when there was no wage employment with individual peasant rice growers. At the Kibaranga and Mjesani sisal estates in Tanga, casual labourers preferred to sell their labour to individual peasants and petty traders in the village near the estates. They earned more in a day that way than the Tz. shs. 15 paid by estates for cutting 110 bundles of sisal.

The continuation of the labour-intensive plantations means a continuing demand for manual labour. The stabilisation process of the 1960s led to changes from long-term to short-term migration, and to the decline in labour supply to the sisal industry, in which production is now almost entirely dependent on the dwindling (through desertion and old age) of the stabilised labour force. Labour recruitment for sisal estates has been largely unsuccessful. On the other hand, long-term employment is not liked by migrants, as was found at the Kilombero Sugar Company. At the end of the 1980 cane harvest season, the Company advertised 400 permanent jobs to the 1944 seasonal labourers who had been engaged in the harvesting. Only 40 migrants took up the jobs. While interviewing permanent labourers in March 1981, 23 per cent of the labourers in the sample said they would revert to seasonal migration at the end of the 1981 cane harvest season (December 1981). The major reason given for wanting to revert to seasonal migration was that as permanent labourers they spent almost their entire wages on food (and rent for those not housed in Company houses), leaving very little money, if any at all, for saving. Furthermore, monthly deductions (sanctioned by law) were made by the employer from the wages as compulsory contributions to the National Provident Fund and subscriptions to the National Organisation of Tanzania Workers (JUWATA), thus lowering take-home pay. Seasonal migrants earned the same wages as permanent labourers (as wage rates are based on piece rates), but they joined neither the NPF nor the JUWATA; most of them were also provided with free accommodation by the Company.

If the existing organisation and conditions of production of cash crops in the villages in the former labour reserves are not changed to provide local opportunities for the peasants, especially for youths, it is likely that seasonal labour migration will continue to be the major source of cash income for a long time.

Notes

1. I should like to thank the following people for their comments: Ray Abrahams, Professor John Barnes, Henry Bernstein, Sandy Robertson and Guy Standing.

2. See also J. Lonsdale and B. Berman: 'Coping with the contradictions: The development of the colonial state in Kenya, 1895-1914', in *Journal of African History*, 1979, vol. 20, no. 4, on the contradictory role of the state in colonial Kenya.

3. See, for example, J. Illiffe: 'Wage labour and urbanisation', in M.H.Y. Kaniki (ed.): *Tanzania under colonial rule* (London, Longmans, 1979); C.M.F. Lwoga: 'Integration of labour reserves into cash crop production', MA dissertation, University of Dar es Salaam, 1977; E.K. Lumley: *Forgotten mandate* (London, Hurst & Co., 1976), especially pp. 25-7, 68-9.

4. P. Raikes: 'Rural differentiation and class-formation in Tanzania', in *Journal of Peasant Studies*, 1978, vol. 5, no. 3, p. 293.

5. District Development Plan 1981/2, Ludewa District.

6. J.D. Graham: 'Changing patterns of wage labour in Tanzania: A history of the relations between African labour and European capitalism in Njombe District 1931-1961', PhD dissertation, North-western University, 1978, p. 45.

7. Ibid.

8. Ibid., p. 49.

9. Ibid., p. 60.

10. Ibid., p. 64.

11. The Tanzania National Archives (TNA), File 178/22/5.

12. Ibid.

13. TNA, 178/9/35.

14. Ibid.

15. District Commissioner for Njombe appeal to the Provincial Commissioner

against labour conscription in Njombe District, TNA 178/22/5.

16. TNA, 178/L.1/5/III.

17. For further details, especially on the development of working-class consciousness in the sisal industry and the development of nationalist feelings in Njombe District, see respectively D. Bolton: 'Government labour and employers in the Tanzanian sisal industry 1930-1976', PhD thesis, Birmingham University, 1980; and Graham, 1978.

18. TNA, L.1/5/III.

19. TNA, 178/A3/17/III.

20. Ibid.

21. Ibid.

22. Ibid.

23. Graham, 1978, p. 98.

24. TNA, 178/L.1/5/IV.

25. *The Daily News*, May Day supplement, 1 May 1978, p. xxii.

26. See, for example, P. Corrigan: 'Feudal relics or capitalist monuments? Notes on the sociology of unfree labour', in *Sociology*, vol. 11, no. 3, September 1977; and L. Malaba: 'Supply, control and organisation of African labour in Rhodesia', in *Review of African Political Economy*, vol. 8, no. 18 (1981), pp. 7-28.

27. See, for example, Bolton, 1980.

28. Raikes, 1978, p. 301.

29. TNA, 576/L.1/9.

30. B.C. Nindi: 'Agricultural change and class formation in Iringa District, Tanzania', PhD thesis, University of Hull, 1978, p. 241.

31. Ibid., p. 240.

32. Interviews, Iringa, April 1981.

33. *Uhuru* (the Kiswahili daily newspaper), Dar es Salaam, 13 April 1981.

34. TNA, 576/L.10/15/III.

35. *The Daily News*, Dar es Salaam, 25 June 1979, p. 1.

36. *The Sunday News*, Dar es Salaam, 11 October 1981.

37. Data were collected from three villages in the northern part of the district from which the rate of labour migration to sisal estates was very high during the colonial period.

38. Interviews, Songea and Mbinga, July and August 1981.

39. Bolton, 1980, p. 463.

40. Interviews, Mlangali Division, Ludewa District, June 1979.

41. See, for example, peasants' participation in communal farming in which they received minimal or no cash returns in C.M.F. Lwoga: *Labour migration and peasant production for the world market in Tanzania*, seminar paper (Cambridge University, African Studies Centre, February 1980).

42. Interview, Tanzania Rural Development Bank, Njombe Branch (which caters also for Ludewa District), June 1981.

43. The National Milling Corporation's reports for 1976/7 to 1980/1 Ludewa District.

44. Field research, Mbinga, July and August 1981. For an example of competition between food and tobacco production at Urambo, Tanzania see J. Boesen and T. Mohele: *The success of peasant tobacco production in Tanzania* (Uppsala, Scandinavian Institute of African Studies, 1980), p. 48.

45. *The Daily News*, Dar es Salaam, 6 June 1981, p. 3.

46. See, for example, G. Standing: 'Migration and modes of exploitation: Social origins of immobility and mobility', in *Journal of Peasant Studies*, vol. 8, no. 2, January 1981, pp. 173-211.

47. Ibid.

48. *The Daily News*, Dar es Salaam, 6 June 1981, p. 3.

5
Pre-colonial and Colonial Labour Migration in West Africa: The Gambia and North-west Nigeria

KENNETH SWINDELL

I. Introduction

The sudanic zone of West Africa is a major source of labour-migrants whose seasonal and permanent movements towards the coast are an established part of the region's economic structure. Migrant workers are absorbed by the commercial crop zones of Senegambia, Ivory Coast, Ghana and southern Nigeria, while towns provide alternative objectives for those in search of temporary or permanent employment. Several explanations have been advanced for the emergence of a highly mobile labour force, which involves the movement of at least two million workers each year; but all of them stem from the effects of European contact and intervention.

European contact through commercial trading interests has a long history in West Africa reaching back to the fifteenth century, while colonial rule was established in the late nineteenth century and lasted until the 1960s. European contact led to the differential development of the coast and the interior with the subsequent redistribution of the labour force, albeit in many cases on a seasonal basis. Labour migration has been explained as the means of attaining an equilibrium between regions of different economic potential, and the response by West Africans to economic opportunities in the more developed areas.[1] Migration has also been attributed to the incorporation of African indigenous economies into the world capitalist economy, a view strongly advocated by Amin, based on dependency theory and the notions of peripheral capitalism.[2]

Central issues for dependency theorists are the deformation

and destruction of indigenous economies as they are incorporated into the world capitalist economy. For them, capitalist penetration sweeps away pre-capitalist social relations, and their incorporation into the world system condemns backward countries to structural underdevelopment from which they cannot escape other than by socialist revolution.[3] Furthermore, capitalism has its origins in production for exchange centred on Europe and reaching back to the fifteenth century.[4] Thus, international trade initially geared to European interests distorted the peripheral regions through the development of unequal exchange and the transfer of surplus to the metropolitan regions. Frank and Wallerstein maintain that capitalist transformation is universally complete, making it impossible for the peripheries to repeat the autonomous development experienced by the developed countries.

Amin has applied dependency theory to the underdevelopment of Africa, and as an explanation of labour migration.[5] For Amin, Africa's dependency was completed through colonialism, which distorted traditional society to the point of being unrecognisable, lacking autonomy and functioning as a provider of primary products for the world market.[6] The methods of reducing African peripheries to 'dead-ends' were trade monopolies, taxation, political support for elites and chiefs in areas providing labour reserves, political support for useful interest groups, and forced labour. In West Africa, colonial trade gave rise to a polarisation of dependent peripheries and developed areas at the regional level, the corollary of coastal wealth being the poverty of the interior. Therefore, Amin argues, the mass movement from the hinterland reflected the logic of colonial trade and the need for cheap labour on the coast where agrarian capitalism had developed. In other words, migration from the interior was a result of colonial policies, especially taxation, and these continued after Independence to the detriment of the source areas, which have been marginalised for the benefit of the cash-crop zones and the towns. Migrants are an impoverished proletariat with low status and wages, and part of the unequal exchange between the coast and the interior.

To what extent labour migration was and has continued to be a result of colonial rule, and whether colonial rule went through phases involving different types of migration, are some of the issues discussed in this chapter. There is also the question whether taxation was the chief means of achieving a mobile workforce, and whether there was actually a quick and total transformation of pre-colonial economies. These issues are explored in the context of regional flows of seasonal labour into Senegambia and from north-western Nigeria. The former comprises wet-season migrant groundnut farmers, the latter a dry-season exodus of agricultural and general labourers. There are of course other important migratory flows of labour in West Africa, notably the Mossi from Upper Volta, and during the past 15 years there has been a huge movement of workers into Nigeria since the oil boom, only recently reversed in dramatic form. But the Gambian and Sokoto material is important, because of its historical depth, and provides a useful test-bed for issues concerning the origins and development of migration. In addition, it suggests that notwithstanding the structural changes in the political economy of West Africa associated with European intervention, there were important geographical and temporal variations in the course of events and their outcome.

The Gambian migrant farmers form one of the oldest migratory labour systems in West Africa, as they were coming into Senegambia as far back as the 1850s. The material collected in north-western Nigeria from Sokoto shows that while pre-colonial mobility of labour existed, the British presence extended and inflated the system. But how were changes introduced? Issue is taken with the notion of taxes and currency as critical causes, and more consideration is given to the erosion and abolition of domestic slavery, which undermined the relations of production. But was there a sudden transformation and dislocation of the indigenous economy by European contacts, or was there gradual change by adaptation and devolution? Such considerations of continuity and discontinuity are central to the following discussion.

II. Migrant Groundnut Farming Along the Gambia River: Its Origins and Development

Migrant farmers have been associated with the Gambian groundnut trade almost since its inception. By the mid-nineteenth century migrants were leaving the upper Senegal and Niger valleys to cultivate groundnuts along the riverine and coastal margins of Senegambia, where they became known as Strange

Farmers, navétanes, or Tillibunkas. These long-distance migrants from the interior played a vital role in the development of the groundnut trade, and present an interesting case of pre-colonial labour migration that was part of the growth of legitimate trade in West Africa.[7]

Currently, between 20,000 and 40,000 Strange Farmers are seasonally employed within The Gambia. About one quarter of these men come from western Mali, another quarter from the Fouta Djallon in Guinea, while most of the remainder are drawn equally from Senegal and within The Gambia itself. A minority come from Guinea-Bissau, Mauritania and Upper Volta. A Strange Farmer is usually an unmarried man, or one about to take a second wife, who moves from his own village just before the onset of the rains to look for land on which he can grow groundnuts. He attempts to find a farmer who will take him into his household, provide him with food and lodging and a piece of land, in return for which the stranger works under his host's direction for between two and four days of the week, sometimes giving him a tenth of his crop; the rest of the time the stranger cultivates his own groundnut farm provided by the host. At the end of the farming season the stranger sells his crops to the buying agents, takes his money and goes home, though he may look for dry-season employment in neighbouring villages or towns.

The first reference to groundnuts being cultivated by long-distance migrants occurs in the Annual Report on The Gambia for 1848.[8] According to Governor MacDonnell, groundnuts were being cultivated not so much by the inhabitants of the petty kingdoms along the Gambia, but by 'Tillibunkas and Sera Woollies coming from 500 to 600 miles from the interior' (Figure 5.1). These migrants were young men drawn towards the river, where a stay of two or three years farming groundnuts would enable them to acquire imported goods that could be taken back into the Sudan. But the Tillibunkas and Sera Woollies were also involved in general trading within Senegambia which included making speculative purchases of cattle up-river and then driving them into the market at Bathurst. Other migrants from the Sudan combined farming with hiring themselves out as mercenaries to the several warring factions in Senegambia.[19]

Apparently, these longer-distance periodic movements were matched by seasonal local movements, inasmuch as in Bathurst

Figure 5.1: Western Sudan and the Guinea Coast

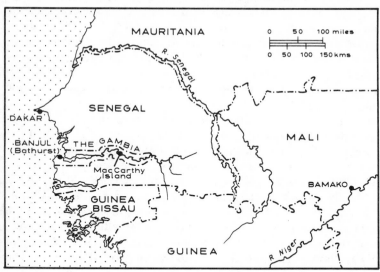

'the farming mania' took hold of the liberated Africans and
Jollofs, who 'although they could earn one shilling per day in
town, readily quit the colony with the onset of the rains, hiring
land from the Mandingos, to enable them to produce a crop of
groundnuts ready for sale at the end of the year.'[10]

The presence of traders and migrant farmers from the interior
is also described in a mid-nineteenth-century report on the state
of French factories and forts in the Casamance.[11] This provided
an interesting gloss on the development of legitimate commerce,
and observed that the ending of the slave trade provided an
incentive for erstwhile slavers to develop new forms of enterprise, which they found in the cultivation of groundnuts. Bocandé
commented on the inhabitants from the interior entering the
groundnut trade, and on the 'caravans de travailleurs' who came
into the Casamance in the rainy season to cultivate groundnuts
on land around the European trading posts.

The system of providing several days of labour on the farm of
a local host is described as the means whereby migrants obtained
board and lodging, but the organisation of migration was in the
hands of merchants and traders. Merchants or chiefs from the
interior assembled groups of both free workers and domestic

slaves and brought them into the groundnut areas. Slaves could no longer be regarded as one form of merchandise transporting another, and their owners had come to realise that their labour represented a considerable asset. Although groundnuts could be grown in the interior, the loads porters could carry in no way recompensed the merchants or chiefs for the cost of feeding them en route; so the workers had to be brought to the most economic point of production.

By the mid-nineteenth century the groundnut trade rested partly on the efforts of indigenous farmers, or at least on their slaves, together with the important contribution made by long-distance migrants from the interior. The inception of the groundnut industry owed much to the migrants, though it is frequently assumed that long-distance seasonal and periodic labour migration from the interior to the coastal regions was a direct product of colonial intervention in the late nineteenth and early twentieth centuries, especially related to the growth of railways and ports, and to the introduction of head taxes. The evidence cited above strongly suggests the importance of pre-colonial labour migration associated with legitimate trade. Nevertheless, one may still question whether there were pre-conditions for these early migratory movements, which were not only over long distances, but of a seasonal nature. If the mid-nineteenth-century reports are correct, then men drawn from the interior readily entered the groundnut trade as seasonal or periodic cultivators.

In The Gambia, the river had formed an important route and trading axis for many hundreds of years prior to the development of the groundnut trade. The evidence collected by Mauny, especially on the Dyula, shows the extent to which these merchants were operating across the Sahara, within the Sudan and between the interior and the riverine coastlands.[12] It was not unusual for men to join trading caravans on a limited basis for as long as was needed to acquire sufficient money for bridewealth or for consumer goods. In other words, they were motivated in much the same way as are Strange Farmers and other migrants today.

One of the principal commodities transported upriver was salt, while in the seventeenth and eighteenth centuries there was the counter-movement of slaves brought down to the coast for export via Bathurst, James Island, Corée and St Louis. There were also movements of gold, cloth, fish, hides and beeswax along a trade axis extending from the lower Gambia to the Upper Niger. The use of slaves as porters was an additional benefit. The accounts of Mungo Park frequently refer to slave caravans (coffles), and his writings and the evidence of other travellers indicate that this business was primarily in the hands of Sera Woollies.[13] Slaves were used to transport goods westwards because they could carry loads at no extra cost; after the sale of the slaves, donkeys were used to transport return goods eastwards.[14]

These caravans were in fact seasonal circulatory movements of traders and groups of merchants who operated during the dry season to avoid the disadvantages of wet-season travel encountered in this part of West Africa. While waiting for slaves to be taken on board ship, or in the hope of a better price, the merchants were not averse to setting the slaves to farming, and this may also have been the case with porters not being sold. Curtin draws attention to the advantages enjoyed by African merchants over their European counterparts through their ability to offset 'storage costs' of slaves by setting them to grow their own subsistence.[15] The possibility of staying from one season to the next by 'renting' land from local chiefs probably represented the antecedents of the Strange Farmers as periodic migrants.

Although the foregoing evidence is scanty, one may reasonably suppose that the patterns of group movement and labour circulation within Senegambia and western Mali were longstanding features of social and economic life before the introduction of groundnuts, the coming of Europeans, and colonial rule. It would seem these early movements of traders, cattlemen, miners and warring factions facilitated subsequent migratory movements associated with the economic opportunities presented by the era of legitimate trade and commercial cash cropping. The historical antecedents are not peculiar to Senegambia; the use of pre-existing routes by migrants has also been observed in Ghana and the Ivory Coast.[16]

III. The Origins of the Strange Farmers System

The presence of migrant farmers within Senegambia led to the development of a complex set of arrangements between migrants and their hosts, which also involved village headmen, chiefs, and eventually the British and French authorities. MacDonnell's report of 1848 not only stressed the importance of strangers in groundnut cultivation, but noted that they were hiring land from the local chiefs, – that is, 'they were paying custom'. In his final report of 1851 he also referred to the practice of strangers paying their landlords a share of their groundnut crop at the end of the season. Thus the Strange Farmer was in effect 'renting' land from the local chiefs.

The practice of hosts taking a 10 per cent levy from the crops of their Strange Farmers had a parallel in the treatment of certain domestic slaves, who were required to contribute a similar amount from their personal farms. This raises the issue of the relationship between the Strange Farmer system and domestic slavery. Although strangers were a major source of labour from the inception of the groundnut trade, local farmers played an important role too, and it seems that their slaves provided a great deal of labour. The Colonial Office correspondence after the Protectorate was set up makes frequent reference to the importance of slaves in the economy. The system of domestic slavery was widespread throughout the Sudan, where slaves worked for so many days for their owners, with the rest of the time being spent on their own plots. This continued through the nineteenth century and was not affected by the abolition of the Atlantic slave trade.

Stratification in Senegambia engendered four castes, the royal-commoner and three specialist castes all of which had slaves, whose status reflected that of their owners. Weil pointed out that the condition of slavery was not the same as its status, and it appears from Colonial Office correspondence that the Travelling Commissioners and the Governor were both aware of this difference.[17] All slaves were important as means of production, but they were used in different ways. For example, administrative slaves, publicly owned but under the king's direction, had to devote two mornings to the king's farm, during which time he had to feed them. But personal slaves of all the upper castes worked six mornings per week for eight hours, gradually reduced to five mornings per week by the latter half of the nineteenth century. If the slaves lived *within* the owner's compound, they had to be fed every day, even if they worked on their own plots.

The accounts given by the Travelling Commissioners and by Weil present an unmistakable parallel with the Strange Farmer system.[18] Weil's analysis also shows that in the 1890s the royal-commoner caste began to decrease their overheads by reducing the number of work-days of slaves to whom they had access, whereas personal slaves began to work for four days for their owners. Furthermore, the colonial period brought taxes that increased the cost of slaves, since yards were taxed according to buildings and inhabitants. In 1902, W.B. Stanley, the Travelling Commissioner for Upper River Division, observed that the suppression of the domestic slave trade under the gradualist measure of 1894 had improved the lot of the remainder and that slaves worked four or five days a week instead of the six days formerly required.[19]

The abolition of domestic slavery in 1884 by the British contributed to the growth of labour migration and led, in Weil's opinion, to the emergence of ex-slaves as the market-oriented class of farmers. But in the light of the foregoing evidence, Strange Farmers did not simply appear with the erosion of domestic slavery, for they were associated with the initial growth of the groundnut trade. Although some may have been slaves controlled by traders, free men were also migrant farmers.

The conditions governing domestic slaves and Strange Farmers were clearly similar, the one providing a pattern for the other. Once domestic slavery had been eroded, the Strange Farmer system provided Gambian hosts (as it still does) with an ideal mechanism for obtaining extra labour without recourse to the payment of cash wages or a share of the crop. Within the Gambian context, offering land to strangers made sense; it was the bottleneck in the supply of labour which impeded the expansion of production, not land shortage. Therefore, the seasonal demand for labour in Senegambia was of a high order in the groundnut areas, and by the early twentieth century the annual number of migrants in Senegambia was about 100,000 producing groundnuts for themselves as well as assisting on their hosts' farms.

The Strange Farmers were an integral part of the successful development of commercial groundnut farming, by producing groundnuts on their farms and providing extra labour for Gambian farmers. This dual role of migrant farmer and farm labourer continued through the colonial period and persists today.[20] Several categories of Strange Farmer can be recognised, but of particular interest are the changes within the migrant labour system. From a system based on the 'renting' of land from local chiefs, closely associated with the activities of long-distance traders, there was a shift towards a system based on labour-sharing with individual host farmers. It seems that this was related to the suppression of domestic slavery and tax reforms, both of which altered the Strange Farmer system and the supply and mobility of labour. Technical innovations played a minor part in the expansion of groundnut production; perhaps the greatest innovation was the adaptation of traditional labour practices to fit a new type of domestic economy in which slavery was declining, and in which groundnuts played an increasingly important role.

The Strange Farmers practise one of the oldest circulatory labour migration systems in West Africa, but there are other larger movements of circulatory labour, which developed mainly in the twentieth century. It is to such a migrant system that we now turn, by examining the development of circulatory labour from north-western Nigeria during the early years of the twentieth century. This provides useful contrasts with the Gambian case, as it is an area of out-migration rather than a receiving area. Migration primarily occurs during the dry season and is not specific to one crop. None the less, there are similarities, especially the importance of the decline in domestic slavery.

North-western Nigeria forms the core of the former Sokoto Caliphate, the largest and most populous state in nineteenth-century West Africa. The Caliphate was established in 1806 after the successful Fulani *jihad* of Usuman dan Fodio, a notable Islamic teacher and reformer. Sokoto exercised control over the former Hausa estates and commanded a huge population from which it received tribute.[21] The British conquered Sokoto in 1903, after which its size was greatly reduced to that of a colonial province; now it is one of the 19 Federal States of Nigeria.

By the 1950s, some 250,000 men a year were leaving Sokoto Province, which had a population of some 3 million.[22] The predominant flows were towards the cocoa-farming areas of Ghana and south-western Nigeria, and towards the towns of the eastern and western regions (Figure 5.2). These movements have been cited as examples of colonial-inspired labour migration, representing a sharp contrast with the mobility associated with the trading diasporas of the Hausa of northern Nigeria, which spread over much of West Africa. But is this too simple an

Figure 5.2: Dry Season Migration from Sokoto Province, 1952-3

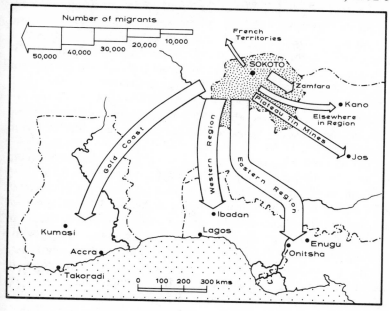

explanation? While there may have been considerable adaptation and change as a result of the colonial presence, there was not necessarily an abrupt discontinuity. By looking at the Sokoto area in the opening decades of the twentieth century we may identify the origins of circulatory migration. In contrast to the Gambian example, information comes from former migrants, and these oral histories provide insights into the nature of migration in the early twentieth century, and show how it differed from Prothero's survey in the 1950s.[23]

IV. Dry-season Migration from Sokoto: Destinations, Occupations and Rewards, 1900-33

According to accounts of former migrants, men from Sokoto engaged in a wide variety of dry-season occupations and activities, involving them in long-distance treks.[24] In the early twentieth century, men appear to have been interested in either labouring jobs or droving, both of which allowed them to engage in trading, which for some was their principal dry-season occupation. Daily-paid labourers worked in construction, well-repairing and water-carrying; others were firewood-cutters, while the droving of cattle, sheep and horses was common, together with employment on camel trains, which plied between the major urban centres of Hausaland. Drovers were paid by merchants, or state office holders with access to large areas of farmland around Sokoto. Very few took jobs in agricultural areas beyond Sokoto, although a few men had been to Zungeru to help with yam-lifting (Figure 5.3). The patterns of migration were very different from those recorded in 1952-3 (Figure 5.2).

The majority interested in dry-season jobs as labourers seem to have been employed in building and repairing, which led them towards the larger towns of Hausaland; only a minority spoke of dry-season work in Ilorin and even Accra. But the foci of attraction were Kano, Zaria and Katsina, in that order, and almost all informants spoke of having worked in Kano at some time or other. Kano was the great metropolis and trading centre of the central Sudan, providing a wide range of employment during the dry season, with goods to be brought back home on the proceeds of three to four months' work there. But all informants cited the advantages of turning at least part of their earnings (on average at least one-third) into goods that could be resold at a profit. In particular, cloths, caps and gowns were bought for personal consumption or for resale in Sokoto, where the black Kano cloth commanded a good price. Cloth from Kano could be resold at double the price, while gowns and turbans fetched over three times the price.

Although Kano and the northern Hausa towns were most attractive for dry-season employment, other centres in the south also provided employment opportunities, especially for droving and trading. Those who went to work in Accra and Ilorin used their money to buy kola (*cola nitida* or *cola acuminata*), which they resold in Jega or Sokoto. Migrants who brought kola from Accra could expect a handsome profit, and Lugard's Annual Report for northern Nigeria in 1905-6 observed that whereas kola was 4s per thousand in Ashanti, it fetched 4s per *hundred* in Jega.[25]

These movements of dry-season workers in the early twentieth century reflected the powerful regionalisation of the economy of the central Sudan as it had developed in the mid-nineteenth

*Figure 5.3: Dry Season Migration from Sokoto Province
in the Early Twentieth Century*

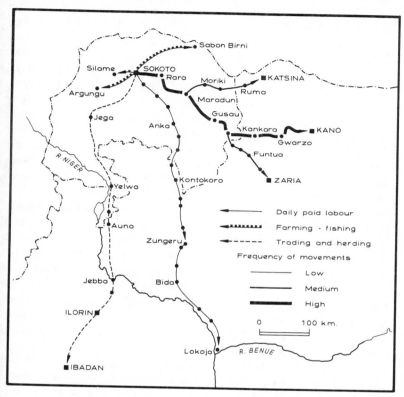

century. Late nineteenth-century descriptions point to four
distinctive economic regions within the Sokoto Caliphate, which
was arguably the largest and most populous State of nineteenth-
century West Africa.[26] The core industrial region was the textile
belt stretching from Zaria to Kano, and although the Sokoto
region was the centre of political and religious influence,
economically it was at the periphery. Thus, Sokotoans interested
in trading and dry-season occupations were drawn towards the
more economically developed areas within the Caliphate, where
they could also take advantage of the differential exchange rates
and purchasing power of the cowry currency.

Within the Sokoto Caliphate of the late nineteenth and early twentieth centuries there was a common currency based on silver and cowries, but the cowry's purchasing power showed remarkable regional variations that did not escape the notice of the migrant worker or trader. There was a substantial variation in the cowry exchange rate against the silver coinage; for example, in 1902, 1 shilling was worth 4,000, 2,500, 2,000, 2,000 and 1,200 cowries in Ilorin, Lokoja, Zaria, Kano and Sokoto, respectively. The migrant worker gained a distinct advantage when employed in Lokoja or Zaria, if savings could be brought home in cowries, or used to buy trade goods. However, because the inflation of the cowry currency during the century meant that by 1900 even relatively small earnings amounted to a huge number of cowries, goods were increasingly preferred. Bringing cowries home was less of a problem for those who took donkeys with them, and they were able to hire them out in Kano and Zaria, mainly for transporting building materials. Pack animals could also be used to carry food en route and thus reduce incidental expenditures.

The labourer's average daily wage at the beginning of the twentieth century was about sixpence a day, or fourpence to fivepence if the employer provided food. Some men increased their daily wages by taking evening work in the markets as porters. These rates compare with those paid by the British in the first decade of colonial rule, and on this basis dry-season migrants earned approximately £1.10s net of food and lodging for a four-month spell, which was worth two or three times as much if trade goods were bought from earnings for resale in Sokoto.

The striking thing about all the migrants' accounts was their interest in trading goods on the return journey to Sokoto. In this respect they resembled the professional long-distance traders (*fatake*), who moved goods between different economic regions. But, unlike the professional trader, the dry-season labourer or drover had to sell his labour to acquire capital to engage in trading. Multiple occupations characterise an economy with imperfect specialisation of labour between farm and factory, town and countryside; in the Sokoto case, farmers became labourers or drovers, then traders, and back to being farmers in the space of a few months.[27]

In the light of these accounts from the early twentieth century, it is necessary to consider the suggestion that the trading and droving activities of the Hausa-Fulani in the nineteenth century were distinct from migration that developed under colonial rule.[28] The inference from the data is rather different, and suggests that at least the two systems overlapped. In the nineteenth century small farmers with surplus crops, as well as larger merchants, entered dry-season trade, and this continued into the early twentieth century. On the northern margins of the Caliphate, farmers traded grain, potash and cloth in the Zinder, Kano and Damgarum areas, and Baiers believes this was part of the surge in commercial activity along the desert edge in the nineteenth century.[29] At that time, there was also a growing Hausa involvement in coastal trade.

However, it is difficult to estimate to what extent freeman farmers became hired labourers attached to drovers and traders during the dry season, as well as finding seasonal jobs in other sectors of the nineteenth-century economy. While the bulk of the labour force in agriculture, commerce and transport was family-based (including slave labour), marginal additions were required in the dry season, to meet the growth in trade and transport. As slave labour was largely immobilised, not easily expanded on a seasonal basis, as well as being required for intensive irrigated farming during the dry season, it seems that the seasonal labour market attracted freeman farmers, especially those without access to irrigated farms or trading surpluses. According to Lovejoy, many small merchants engaged in the kola trade employed up to 50 permanent workers, but additional men were also required on a temporary basis.[30] Baiers, investigating trading families in central Niger, showed how at times they needed extra employees to expand their firms quickly under very competitive conditions; frequently they would take on sons of friends – especially when their own children were not old enough – together with slaves who had purchased their freedom.[31] Slaves did not become seasonal labour migrants, but those who had been with families for some years, or been born into them, did become part-time craftsmen, traders and brokers, hiring labourers in their spare time on a daily basis within their local area.[32] In this manner, the more fortunate slaves were able to purchase their freedom, a practice allowed under Islamic law.

One crucial aspect of the pre-colonial West African economy was the organisation and supply of labour. Hopkins believes that there was a long-established labour market, but that it took the form of slave labour rather than wage labour as a result of relative costs.[33] This view has been challenged by Goody who thinks there is no evidence for an alternative to slaves, because if land was in surplus, as is generally agreed, then the only way to get individuals to work was as slaves rather than as hired labour.[34] Both views ignore the possibility of slaves and freemen being employed on a *casual* basis in an economy where the population and movement of goods were seasonally determined and required occasional additions to the labour force. There were differences between slaves and freemen engaging in casual labour, as the former were more immobilised and confined to local opportunities. Also, opportunities for slaves may have differed between those belonging to small domestic production units and those working on settlements owned by emir officials and 'big men'. The latter had access to a large slave-labour force, which they used for dry-season irrigation of the *fadamas*, whereas small freemen farmers had limited use for their slaves in the dry season.

In the period under discussion (1900-33), the evidence of former migrants from Sokoto shows that small farmers took labouring jobs during the dry season combined with trading, which is distinct from a situation where farmers either became traders or hired labourers, as they did in the 1950s. Farmers becoming drovers, and/or labourers and then traders, represented an intermediate or transitional phase in the development of the migrant labour force. Also, the patterns of movement differed from those observed in the 1950s; the predominant movement into the northern Hausa towns – especially Kano – was a feature of the early twentieth century and surpassed the southward movements which were so strong in 1952. But of more importance than destinations is the question of how the volume of migrants reached levels of 250,000 per season, recorded by Prothero in 1952-3, an order of magnitude that seems highly unlikely in the early twentieth century. In essence, it was the establishment of British rule that led to changes in levels of migration, and it is to these that we now turn.

V. Currency and Taxation

It has been frequently asserted that the imposition of taxes and a new currency played a substantial role in the development of West African labour migration, which was part of the transformation of the domestic economy, through its incorporation into the world trading economy, which led to an economic imbalance between the coast and the interior. Given the high degree of population mobility in pre-colonial times in both Senegambia and Nigeria, attention must be focused on the role of taxation and currencies, inasmuch as they may have been responsible for the increased *volume* and changed *direction* of migration.

The economies of pre-colonial West Africa were sufficiently developed to require the use of a circulating medium of exchange and units of account.[35] But there was no standard unit of exchange. Metal rods, cloth and coins were found in different parts of West Africa, and along the Gambia River in the 1850s the French 5-franc piece was the common medium of exchange. Cowries were widely used as small change in central Sudan, while higher units of account were of gold and silver, notably the Maria Theresa dollar used in trans-Saharan trade. From 1820 to 1840, along the Niger River and the Yoruba coast there was monetary stability, when 2,000 cowries were equivalent to one silver coin in Kano. But after 1845 the palm-oil trade expanded, which European merchants facilitated by massive imports of the larger East African cowry. Inflation followed and the exchange rates against coin became a function of the transport costs of moving large quantities of cowries, which were reflected in the rates between the coast and the interior. Exchange rate differences allowed traders from the north to benefit, as goods could be sold at inflated prices in the south, and as the above account indicates, migrant workers were aware of these advantages.

The introduction of British coinage led to a further depreciation of the cowry currency, although the effects were delayed in Sokoto, where monetary control was not established until 1903. Then the import of Maria Theresa dollars was prohibited, and in 1904 imports of cowries were stopped. Cowries continued to be used at fixed rates of exchange with the British shilling, but by 1912 the British currency had become dominant. The rapid change to the new coinage was brought about by the insistence that taxes be paid in coin; the money supply was boosted by the payment in coin of government workers, who were assuming an important proportion of the paid labour force, especially with the building of the railway. But the introduction of British coinage was not innovative in the face of well-established cowrie-silver currencies; it was an attempt to standardise the currency, stimulate trade and facilitate taxation.

Much has been made of the imposition of taxes by the colonial authorities and their insistence of payment in the new coinage as a prime mover in the development of migrant wage-labour. But in common with currency, taxes were not a colonial innovation; migrant groundnut farmers were taxed in the 1860s in Sene-gambia and there was a well-established tax system throughout the Sokoto Caliphate in the nineteenth century. What then was the fiscal position when the British arrived in Nigeria, how was it altered, and with what effects?

In discussing taxation in the Sokoto Caliphate, a distinction must be made between what was obtained in the metropolitan emirates of Sokoto and Gwandu, and in the tributary emirates of the former Hausa states such as Kano and Zaria. Taxation in what became Sokoto Province under the British was minimal compared with the elaborate system of the former Hausa states taken over and modified by the Fulani after the *jihad*. The political, administrative and military fabric of Sokoto rested on revenue from the tributary emirates, whereas local taxation was limited to that required by religious observance and sanctioned by Koranic law. A basic tax or tithe was levied on crops (*Zakat*) and on cattle (*jangali*); such taxes were widespread throughout the Sudan and were generally used locally.

In addition to tithes, there was a comprehensive system of taxation outside the urban centre, paid in kind – millet, guinea corn and cattle – or in cowries; the form of payment depended on a combination of the proximity of a community to commercial centres (in which case cowries were more likely), and the central authorities' needs at the time for grains or cash.

A major concern of Lugard when he became Lieutenant-Governor of northern Nigeria was the establishment of a new system of taxation and tax collection. His objective was to replace the existing taxes by a single tax based on the annual value of production, which by 1906 was fixed at 10 per cent. It was not a land tax, but a tax on 'income'; under the 1906 legislation it was extended to include craftsmen as well as agriculturalists. The unit of taxation was the village; the heads and elders, together with the assistant residents of a province, assessed the type of land, land use and standard of cultivation, counted the human and animal populations and arrived at an assessment. Once the assessment was approved by the resident and Lieutenant-Governor it was up to the village head to levy the tax from individuals according to their means and capacity to pay.

According to the assessment for Sokoto Emirate in 1906, the average tax per adult was 10 shillings and 7 pence. In one sense this is misleading, since tax was levied according to the means of each village community, which varied across the province, while in Sokoto city a poll tax was levied of sixpence per adult male. These levels of taxation should be compared with the daily wage paid by government at this time of sixpence per day, which accords with similar amounts received by informants from private employers in Kano and Zaria. As a dry-season's work yielded between £1.5s and £1.10s, which could be *trebled* through trading, it is hard to believe that taxation in the early years of the twentieth century (albeit *de novo* for Sokotoans) was primarily the engine of growth in migration.

The situation had changed by the early 1930s, by when taxation had risen while the system was being maladministered and abused by district heads. There was a large rise in taxation after 1910, with the worst increase between 1920 and 1933.[36] During this period taxes at least doubled within Sokoto province. Furthermore, the development of indirect rule had increased the local power of district heads, who discriminated in the allocation of land tax among their people and exacted customary labour from ordinary freeman farmers, who had to do unpaid work. In 1933, the British authorities took steps to improve the situation, stopping customary labour except for public works, but the heads responded by trying to exact more taxes in compensation.[37]

By the 1930s, labour migration began to take on a different aspect and there was a rapid increase in the number of migrants to meet new demands for taxes and a rising demand for labour in the south. The railway reached Sokoto Province in 1927 and was linked with Port Harcourt, which facilitated not only an influx of Ibo migrants into the north, but a flow of Sokotoans southwards. The swelling migration from Sokoto was not just a product of taxation, or of increased job opportunities, but the ability of a large section of the population to enter the wage-labour market with the erosion of domestic slavery. This issue is one we encountered when discussing the Strange Farmer system in The Gambia, and it is one to which we return as it is crucial to an understanding of the development of a large mobile labour force.

Hitherto, slave labour was largely immobilised, but this was radically changed by abolition, an event that undermined the foundation of the pre-colonial economy, where control and access to labour were vital.

VI. Labour Migration and the Decline of Domestic Slavery

It is hard to tell what proportion of the West African population were slaves in the nineteenth century. Estimates vary from a quarter to a half; in Sokoto early explorers and colonial officials suggested it might be as high as four-fifths. The establishment of Sokoto town as the centre of the Caliphate in 1809 led to a huge influx of freemen settlers and slaves. This build-up of manpower continued through the nineteenth century and created the present intensively cultivated close-settled zone from the empty marshlands of the pre-*jihad* Hausa states.

It seems slaves were not simply a means of prestige through larger kinship groups, but economic assets where power and influence were vested in those who controlled manpower; this was true of rulers, who derived their income from agriculture and trade, as well as of smaller farmers.[38] The relations of dependence implied reciprocity; slave owners protected their manpower resources not out of benevolence but of necessity, while slaves had access to farmland on which they worked for three to four days per week. Once the connections of power, dependence and control of production are understood, the striking changes initiated by the erosion and abolition of domestic slavery become comprehensible.[39] The colonial authorities introduced abolition measures in the early twentieth century, and the significance of this was not lost on the new rulers or the ruled. Abolition was a gradualist measure, for the colonial authorities were aware of the risk of disrupting the economic system, especially where export crops were already established. Lugard's Memoranda for northern Nigeria show his concern over the effects of sudden changes in the established system of labour control and allocation.[40]

The authorities in French Sudan were similarly dubious about abolition because, like Lugard, they feared an influx to the towns of vagrants and unemployed. The British and French authorities soon realised this was not the case and that they constituted the making of a daily paid labour force to meet the demands of the expanding colonial economy. However, it seems that development occurred by indirect means rather than by design.

Full abolition was not achieved until 1936, when the Abolition Ordinance was no more than a formality. But the process was started in 1904 with an ordinance abolishing the legal status of slavery, but not slavery as such. The ordinance recognised slaves before the law and freed their children, though it was not illegal to own slaves. But realising that slavery had a limited future, owners began to assert their rights over land formerly farmed by slaves.[41] Although the British forbade slaves from settling on land to which they had no customary title, owners were suspicious that this situation might change, and accordingly secured rights to land. At the same time, owners were faced with increased overheads, for under the 1903 General Tax, slaves became subject to assessment.

Parallel to these developments, increasing numbers of slaves secured their freedom, usually by self-redemption under Islamic law through the local Alkalis' courts, which fixed amounts to be paid and the period of repayment, extending up to 10 years. Many former slaves stayed as clients or 'tenant' farmers of their former owners, no longer working for them but paying a tenth of their produce as rent. But their changing relationships with former owners involved less reciprocity. Under domestic slavery, slaves were given food from the common granaries in the dry season, when many were employed full-time on irrigated farms, but this was discontinued once freed slaves severed links with owners; newly-independent households were responsible for dry-season food. After abolition, there were opportunities for ex-slaves to work on dry-season *fadama* farms as labourers, but these compared poorly with the prospects of working in Kano or Zaria (and subsequently the export-crop areas) which had the added incentive of trading on the return journey. Although dry-season labour migration may have been established among the Hausa-Fulani before colonial rule, with slavery's decline it assumed a heightened significance; migration was boosted by the changed conditions in the supply of dry-season grain, as well as the opportunity costs of local dry-season employment. Former owners of slaves were also affected, as they lost labour resources – especially for irrigated farming –, faced higher taxation, and were drawn into migratory labour in increasing numbers.

VII. Conclusions

One of the issues raised by the Gambian and Sokotoan cases is the extent to which labour migration can be explained as a direct result of European intervention, and the incorporation of the African domestic economy into the world capitalist economy. For example, it has been contended that European intervention virtually destroyed indigenous economies and marginalised the Sudan for the benefit of the coastal economy, which led to the extraction of seasonal surplus labour. Furthermore, direct and indirect coercion (forced labour, taxes, new currencies) were the means whereby Africans were brought into the exchange economy based on overseas trade.[42] Given their widespread advocacy, this chapter has tried to examine these assertions in the context of the Senegambian and Sokoto regions in the nineteenth and early twentieth centuries.

It is apparent from The Gambia and Sokoto that the view that taxation was a primary stimulus to migration needs some qualification. When discussing taxation, as well as the influence of other factors, it is necessary to introduce some periodisation. In Sokoto, the situations before and after 1933 were different, not only with respect to taxation, but in the extent to which domestic slavery had declined. In The Gambia, the Strange Farmer migrations cannot be viewed simply as a result of taxation and the differential development of the coast and interior by the colonial powers. Indeed, the control of groundnut production and labour movements outside the tiny colonial enclaves of Bathurst and MacCarthy Island was minimal until the Anglo/-French boundary agreement of 1889.

Therefore, if we are adequately to understand the impact of the colonial period when European intervention was at its height, it is vital to know more about the nature and dimensions of the pre-colonial economy and society, including systems of production as well as exchange. In the central Sudan, the pre-colonial economy was complex, highly commercialised and characterised by merchant capital. Even if self-sufficient production units were preponderant, there were still sectors where both inputs and outputs were commoditised. Small-scale farmers with surplus grain or animals for sale were involved in the circulation of commodities, nor were their farming systems aimed at livelihood to the exclusion of profit.

In the late nineteenth century there was a strong economic regionalisation in the central Sudan, as well as between the coast and the interior, which sustained a hierarchy of trading networks. Sokoto and its region were the political and religious centre of the largest and most populous State in West Africa, and were sustained by a diverse agriculture, trade, high population densities and the extraction of surpluses from the 'periphery' in the form of taxes and tribute. Domestic and plantation slaves provided surplus labour, and the split-time systems not only allowed the reproduction of the labour force through its own efforts, but the means whereby slaves acquired personal effects and income. In the subsequent migrant-labour system, the distribution of time between working for strangers in the south and at home on the family farm was essentially an adaptation of the former split-time system characteristic of domestic slavery; except for the distance and mobility it was almost a case of 'plus ça change'.

In the pre-colonial period, both Senegambia and the central Sudan displayed a high level of regional interdependence as well as diverse interest groups. Dependence was not simply a product of colonial rule or of European intervention; one of the problems with the dependency thesis lies in its definition, and 'attempts to give the concept empirical anchorage show that states of dependence differed so greatly spatially, temporally and analytically, that the term is less a key than a label covering a bundle of assorted symptoms'.[43] Similar problems are encountered when using terms such as 'pre-industrial' and 'pre-capitalist' to describe West African economies during the nineteenth century and earlier.

It is debatable whether the advance of European capitalism (either in the colonial or pre-colonial periods) totally transformed local economies as they were incorporated into the world capitalist system.[44] Rather there were incorporation and partial transformation of earlier structures.[45] Centre-periphery models and dependency theories tend to ignore the dynamics within the peripheries – the activities of groups of chiefs, indigenous traders, European merchants, farmers, and even slaves. In northern Nigeria, groundnuts became a basic commercial crop despite the British interests in cotton production, as local farmers and merchants perceived a better return from the former.[46] In The Gambia it was ex-slaves who became the new capitalised class of groundnut farmers, often to the exclusion of former owners and traditional rulers.[47] Indeed, stress on colonial and imperial forces as the main agents of change overlooks the internal social and cultural factors that interacted with them to produce historical specific outcomes.[48] Migration into Senegambia in the nineteenth century and from the Sokoto region in the early twentieth century accords with this view, and this analysis has stressed an overlap of systems of population mobility and different levels of continuity and discontinuity. If the colonialists did administer a sharp shock to the socio-economic system, it was in their attempts to end domestic slavery.

What is less certain is the net benefit of migration in the latter compared with the earlier colonial period. If we accept oral and written accounts from Sokoto in the early 1900s one has the impression of a migratory system conferring considerable benefits on the dry-season worker. Migrants were not simply interested in maintaining linkages with their villages and farms by earning cash to help in times of need; they had more positive attitudes leading to the accumulation of cash for forward trading ventures on their way home, or in their local towns. Regional specialisation in the late nineteenth-century and early twentieth-century economy allowed migrant workers to take advantage of the differential price structure between coast and interior, and within the central Sudan, underscored by the variation in the purchasing power of the cowry currency. Migrants from Sokoto sold their labour during the dry season in places where goods could be profitably brought back on their return journeys. As the economy became more 'open' and communications more developed, the range and availability of local and imported goods improved. In the later colonial period it was the diminution of regional inequalities, not the reverse, which reduced the advantages enjoyed by migrants who became traders.

In Senegambia regional differences remained quite sharp during the twentieth century largely because The Gambia was a British enclave within French territories. Differential policies of taxation, the relative purchasing power of the currencies and different groundnut purchasing schemes gave an impetus for border trade and migration into The Gambia. Indeed, the regional distinctions within this part of the western Sudan became even more marked after Independence, with the development of quite different and sometimes 'closed' political economies in

Senegal, Mali and Guinea. However, in the twentieth century labour migration did undergo changes, especially in the French territories, the source areas of Gambian migrants. The French from 1929 to 1946 tried a variety of measures to affect the flow of migrants into the groundnut areas; force was followed by persuasion, and encouragement was succeeded by discouragement. But this is a later aspect of the history of migration and should not be confused with the earlier period.

In conclusion, the development of labour migration has a complexity that belies some of the more rhetorical statements about its origins. European intervention did not necessarily precipitate a radical transformation; there was adaptation and change in West African economies and one must distinguish the early years of colonial rule from the later periods and what happened after Independence. While not denying the role of external forces and relations with the urban centres, there was a response and series of interactions in the periphery which had their own internal dynamic and specific historic outcomes. To ignore this is to miss a richness of detail in a search for bald generalisations, and to endow Africans with a passivity that is neither true of the past nor of the present.

Notes

1. E.J. Berg: 'The economics of the migrant labour system', in H. Kuper (ed.): *Urbanisation and migration in West Africa* (Berkeley, University of California Press, 1965), pp. 160-80.

2. S. Amin: 'Underdevelopment and dependence in Black Africa', in *The Journal of Modern African Studies*, 1974, vol. 10, no. 4, pp. 503–24; idem (ed.); *Modern migrations in Western Africa* (London, Oxford University Press, 1974).

3. P.A. Baran: *The political economy of growth* (New York, Monthly Review Press, 1957); A.G. Frank: *Latin America: Underdevelopment or revolution?* (New York, Monthly Review Press, 1969).

4. Ibid.

5. Amin, 1974.

6. Ibid., pp. 519-20.

7. The abolition of the Atlantic slave trade occurred in West Africa during the early nineteenth century, although it was not entirely suppressed until much later. The term 'legitimate trade' is used to define commercial transactions outside slaving, which developed in the nineteenth century, gradually replacing slavery.

8. The European partition of Africa took place after the Berlin Conference of 1844-5, but before this there were small colonial enclaves along the West African coasts and rivers. In The Gambia in 1848, the Crown territories comprised Bathurst (now Banjul) and Cape St May at the mouth of the Gambia River, with MacCarthy Island forming another enclave in mid-river. While these tiny

possessions gave support to British traders along the river, they exercised no control over taxation or law beyond their immediate bound.

9. *Annual Report of The Gambia, 1851* (London, CMD, 1963), paragraphs 36 and 52, p.361.

10. Ibid., p. 52.

11. E.B. Bocandé: *Rapport sur les ressources que présentent dans leur état actuel les comptoirs établis sur les bords de la Casamance*, Paris, 1856, Imprimerie Administrative de Paul Dupont 15-16, enclosure with CO 87, no. 52, 24 July 1861.

12. R. Mauny: *Tableau géographique de l'Ouest Africain au moyen âge* (Dakar, 1961), Memoires de l'Institut Française d'Afrique Noire, no. 61.

13. M. Park: *Travels in the interior of Africa performed in the years 1795, 1796 and 1797* (Edinburgh, Adam and Charles Black, 1878), pp. 56-65.

14. P.D. Curtin: *Economic change in pre-colonial Africa* (Wisconsin, University of Wisconsin Press, 1975), pp. 168-73.

15. Ibid.

16. J. Rouch: 'Migrations from French territories into Ghana', in *Africa*, 1958, vol. 27, p. 156.

17. P. Weil: *Agrarian slavery and capitalist farming in a West African society*, 75th Annual Meeting of American Anthropological Society, Washington, DC, 1975.

18. Ibid.

19. G. Denton: Despatch to the Secretary of State for the Colonies, CO 87, No. 85 of 3 June 1902, Enclosure No. 4.

20. K. Swindell: 'Family farms and migrant labour: The Strange Farmers of The Gambia', in *Canadian Journal of African Studies*, 1978, vol. 12, pp. 3-17.

21. M. Last: *The Sokoto Caliphate* (London, Longman, 1967).

22. R.M. Prothero: *Migrant labour from Sokoto Province, northern Nigeria* (Kaduna, Government Printer, 1959).

23. Ibid.

24. The estimated age of informants ranged from 74 to 95 years; ages were calculated on the basis of chronologies used in the 1963 census. Nineteen men were interviewed, each on several occasions, and their accounts span from 1900 to 1927, during which they all spent more than one dry season away from home. In total, the histories of 59 migrations were recorded.

25. F.D. Lugard: *Political memoranda* (London, Frank Cass, 1970), 3rd edition, p. 247.

26. P.E. Lovejoy and S. Baiers: 'The desert-side economy of the Central Sudan', in *International Journal of African History Studies*, 1975, vol. 13, pp. 551-81; P.E. Lovejoy: 'Plantations in the economy of the Sokoto Caliphate', in *Journal of African History*, 1978, vol. 19, no. 3, pp. 341-68.

27. Multiple occupations involving off-farm employment are common in present-day West Africa. For example, in Senegambia migrant groundnut farmers become dry-season factory workers, followed by a spell of petty trading on their return home. Migrant farming combined with trading is particularly advantageous where political balkanisation has led to a differential in purchasing power among the several currencies in use, together with the different type of goods available in one country compared with another. See K. Swindell: 'From migrant farmer to permanent settler: The Strange Farmers of The Gambia', in J.I. Clarke and L.A. Kosinski (eds.): *Population redistribution in Africa* (London, Heinemann, 1982), pp. 96-100.

28. M. Adamu: 'The Hausa factor in West African history', PhD thesis, University of Birmingham, 1974.

29. S. Baiers: *An economic history of central Niger* (Oxford, Oxford Unversity Press, 1980).

30. P.E. Lovejoy: 'Inter-regional money flows in the pre-colonial trade of Nigeria', in *Journal of African History*, 1974, vol. 15, no. 4, p. 574.

31. Baiers, 1980, p. 63.

32. M.G. Smith: *Babo of Karo: A woman of the Muslim Hausa* (London, 1954), pp. 38-43.

33. A.G. Hopkins: *An economic history of West Africa* (London, Longman, 1973), p. 26.

34. J. Goody: 'Slavery in time and space', in J.L. Watson (ed.): *Asian and African systems of slavery* (Berkeley, University of California Press, 1980), pp. 16-42.

35. M. Johnson: 'The cowrie currencies of West Africa', Parts 1 and 2, in *Journal of African History*, 1970, vol. 11, no. 1, pp. 17-49, and vol. 11, no. 3, pp. 331-53; Lovejoy, 1974.

36. P. Tibenderana: 'The administration of Sokoto, Gwandu and Argungu Emirates under British rule, 1900-1946', PhD thesis, University of Ibadan, Nigeria, 1974.

37. Ibid.

38. P. Hill: 'From slavery to freedom: The case of farm slavery in Nigerian Hausaland', in *Comparative Studies in Society and History*, 1976, vol. 18, pp. 395-426; R. Law: 'Trade, slaves and taxes: The economic basis of political power in pre-colonial Africa', seminar paper presented at the Centre of African Studies, University of Edinburgh, 1974.

39. F. Cooper: 'The problem of slavery in African studies', in *Journal of African History*, 1979, vol. 1, pp. 103-25.

40. Lugard, 1970, pp. 223-4.

41. Tibenderana, 1974.

42. Amin, 1974,; D.D. Cordell and J.W. Gregory: 'Labour reservoirs and population: French colonial strategies in Koudougou, Upper Volta, 1914-1939', in *African Historical Demography* (University of Edinburgh, 1981), vol. 11; V.J. Piché, S. Gregory and S. Coulibaby: 'Vers un explication des courants migratoires voltaiques', in *Labour, Capital and Society*, 1981, vol. 13, no. 1, pp. 77-103.

43. A.G. Hopkins: 'On importing Andre Gunder Frank into Africa', in *African Economic History Review*, 1975, vol. 2, no. 1, p. 16.

44. Frank, 1969, p. 225.

45. P. Ehrensaft: 'Semi-industrial capitalism in the Third World: Implications for social research in Africa', in *Africa Today*, 1971, vol. 18, no. 1, pp. 40, 67.

46. H.S. Hogendorn: *Nigerian groundnut exports: Origins and early developments* (Oxford, Oxford University Press, 1979).

47. Weil, 1975,; A. Jeng: 'An economic history of the Gambian groundnut industry, 1830-1925', PhD thesis, University of Birmingham, 1978.

48. N. Long: 'Structural dependency, modes of production and economic brokerage in rural Peru', in I. Oxaal, T. Barnett and D. Booth (eds.): *Beyond the sociology of development* (London, Routledge and Kegan Paul, 1975), pp. 253-83.

6

Social Relations and Geographic Mobility: Male and Female Migration in Kenya

VEENA THADANI

I. Introduction

It is usually acknowledged that the ultimate if not immediate determinants of migration reside in particular paths to, or strategies of, development. But the means by which development strategy influences patterns of migration remain obscure. For example, reference to the movement of labour from 'overwhelmingly stagnant subsistence agriculture' to a 'growing commercialised industrial centre' suggests an inevitable progression from economic backwardness to growth and modernity.[1] Such an approach has tended to eclipse the mechanisms and structures by which changes occur in the organisation of both production and labour.

Issues of divergent interests and group conflict, of power and control, of the appropriation and allocation of resources (including labour) — that is, the social relations — characterise the inter-relations between development strategies and patterns of labour migration.[2] The aim here is to explore those elements as manifest in the organisation of production and labour in Kenya between 1900 and 1970, encompassing the colonial era (1896-1963) and post-Independence years. The conflict was between African communities — largely self-sufficient, 'natural economies'[3] — and the colonial administrative and productive 'apparatus' marked by profoundly differing interests and asymmetrical relations. The colonial regime's pursuit of economic growth and capital formation — to provide revenue for local administration and imperial interests[4] — required the mobilisation of resources, land, labour, and capital from local communities. The diversion of resources to immigrant groups — most evident in the appropriation of land for settlers and in the often draconian measures to induce labour migration — altered the material base of local communities and their systems of production.

Changes in the organisation of production and labour allocation were a result of this 'articulation'[5] between the indigenous modes of production and the capitalist model, under colonial aegis. The migration pattern that developed in Kenya (as in southern and central Africa, though not in other parts of East Africa) had its origins in the collision of two modes of production and in the development policies of the early 1900s. The pertinence of these early labour movements and their origins lies in their relationship to current patterns of migration. Analyses of current trends alone have left submerged the roots of these patterns and, by confining explanation to the near-at-hand, have drawn a fragmentary picture.

Both historical and contemporary trends reveal a pattern of migratory behaviour in response to the demand for labour generated by development activity. The picture indicates a reversal in the pattern of movement from the early to the more recent period, a reversal that is, none the less, rooted in social relations that have remained essentially unchanged.

Early labour movements were confined largely to men and involved circular migration between centres of wage employment and the rural community; women were relatively immobile.[6] More recent wage-labour movements indicate the relative stability of men in urban wage employment and the circulation of women between urban and rural areas. High urban unemployment in recent decades has brought about the 'stabilisation' of the male labour force — long an issue of concern to employers and in migration studies. Earlier patterns of male circulation have been altered by the migrants' apprehension that a job relinquished may not be easily replaced. With male workers unable to return to their rural households with customary frequency, the circular movement of women between urban centre and rural homestead has replaced the circulation of men.

The origins of these patterns can be traced to development policies. The different ways in which labour movements were shaped and resource transfers exacted is illustrated with reference to the patterns of female mobility — a subject consistently overlooked. The analysis highlights the tangible, if less visible, patterns of resource transfer that underlie both the initial immobility and later circular mobility of women, with an emphasis on relations of production rather than relations of patriarchy.

II. Determinants of Migration: Perspectives and Frameworks

The organisation of labour and, subsumed within it, issues of labour migration, involve far-reaching questions related to the organisation of production. Discussion of the mode of production, and in particular of the means by which African production has been integrated into the world economy, usually proceeds along two divergent paths. In one view, the period of colonialism provided the investment and enterprise, the social and material technology, essential for the transformation of small subsistence economies into market-oriented, surplus-producing, expanding economic systems.[7] These resolutely non-Marxist scholars emphasise the receptivity of African cultivators to new opportunities and methods, the adaptation of traditional social institutions — such as networks of family, kin and patron-client relations — to new forms of production, and the mobilisation of labour.[8] The 'dependency' theorists offer an opposing view, arguing that colonial investment in the interests of the 'mother country' undermined indigenous enterprise, and thus impaired growth and transformation — a pattern that persists in the post-colonial era as dependent development and 'perverse growth'.[9]

Explanations of labour migration reflect these competing conceptions. In one view, migration is a response to opportunities for income and employment, prompted by the pursuit of self-interest and maximising rationality. Implicit if not explicit cost-benefit calculations are believed to determine decisions about economic opportunities.[10] Economic explanations of circular migration embodying these micro-economic decision-making models therefore centre on the individual migrant or his household, and are concerned with motives, perceptions, calculations, and volition. The emphasis is accordingly on perceived conditions, in the community of origin and centres of wage labour. The impetus to circulation, in particular, is explained in

terms of the psychological and material security of the traditional
social system that impels a pattern of return, and the conditions
of employment — such as wage rates, housing, and the absence
of welfare benefits — that preclude a permanent shift to centres
of wage labour. The accent is on the advantages that individual
migrant households derive from participation in both spheres —
domestic production and wage employment. As Elkan concluded
in his pioneering work on circular migration in East Africa, this
dual strategy of subsistence production and wage labour enables
the household to maximise its earnings.[11] The spotlight is on the
household's maximising rationality; the environment within
which individual decisions are made tends to be eclipsed, serving
merely as a distant backdrop that, as it were, sets the scene.

But it is these conditions — the pervasive, but more remote
social forces — that the structuralists argue shape labour
mobility. The penetration of capital, the incorporation of
production systems within an initially imperial and subsequently
world system, and the dispossession or dislocation of agricultural
producers are all seen as elements of an overall design in the
allocation of factors of production — a pattern that determines
the flow of human labour. The subversion of traditional systems
of production and the resultant development of a dual economic
system, with enclaves of capital-intensive production amidst areas
of stagnant or declining production, create the conditions for
labour migration. As Amin stated, 'The decision of the migrant
to leave his region of origin is . . . completely predetermined by
the overall strategy determining the "allocation of factors" ', that
is, by the strategy of development.[12] He dismissed 'rational
choice' as a mere rationalisation of behaviour within a system and
determined by the system. The structural conditions that shape
migratory behaviour completely overshadow the individual
migrant's decisions.

The perspective adopted here interweaves elements of both
orthodoxies. Eschewing the dichotomy between assumptions of
individualistic opportunism ('free will') and structural determinism, it focuses on the interplay between opportunity and
constraint, that is, on the limits that structural constraints place
on individual opportunity. There can be little doubt that
indigenous small-scale producers responded with optimising
rationality to the economic opportunities generated by development activity. Possessing meagre material resources that they

could ill afford to put at risk, their responses represented an approximation to 'rational' economic behaviour. But the environment narrowed their options. Restrictions on independent production (for example, of coffee) in order to 'induce' the flow of labour for colonial agriculture were one mechanism whereby certain options were made available and others foreclosed. The emphasis is on both the mechanisms that shape the possibilities and prohibitions, and the response of the household, in terms of allocation of labour, to the opportunities and restrictions with which it was faced.

III Household Production and Labour Allocation

Although pre-colonial African society was far from a collection of autarchic communities, the creation of a peasantry[13] — the subordination of communal cultivators in a wider economic, social and cultural system — is usually seen as 'the result of the interaction between an international capitalist economic system and traditional socio-economic systems', within a colonial context.[14] What characterised both the communal cultivators and the emergent peasantry was the reliance on certain rights in land and family labour for security and subsistence.[15] Incorporation in a wider system resulted in the shift from the use of land and labour as 'natural' capital — that is, as means of providing basic necessities — to its investment as capital for 'commodity production' as a means of generating profit.

Inherent in the transformation of these 'natural' economies to commodity production — and often the principal commodity was labour itself — was the change in patterns of social reproduction that had maintained the system. Household production,[16] which had ensured both the needs of subsistence and regeneration, was transformed by the demands of labour and revenue. The diversion of male labour and other resources to meet the needs of the colonial economy, by such well-known means[17] as the imposition of taxes necessitating a cash income, the use of forced labour to build the colonial infrastructure, and coercive recruitment of labour for plantations and mines, induced adjustment in the domestic community as it adapted to incorporation and its effects.

The structure and weight of the demands on the domestic

community shaped the patterns of production and labour deployment. The withdrawal of labour and its transfer to the dominant commercial sector, in a system of rotating migration, augmented the resources of the latter at the expense of the domestic community. But the domestic production system, though undermined by the periodic engagement in wage employment, was preserved because this partially proletarianised workforce was dependent on both wage labour and domestic production. Thus the incorporation of domestic communities into the wider network of the colonial capitalist system simultaneously undermined and preserved indigenous production systems.[18]

This preservation of the labour-exporting community and expansion of the labour-importing economy suggests mutually beneficial effects of incorporation. The domestic subsistence economy is invigorated by the deployment of labour in both domestic production and wage employment through such devices as seasonal migration; it is also revitalised by wage incomes and other resources remitted by returnees.[19] The impairment of village capital formation, such as well-digging, hut repair, and maintenance activities in general, is not deemed appreciable nor is the decline of 'leisure' among those engaged in both spheres of production.[20] Based on the premise of opportunity — that migration occurs because needed income either cannot be earned or earned without more intense labour input — such arguments do not deal with the issue of costs as successfully as that of benefits. Life-cycle (rather than working-span) analysis of the costs of labour reproduction and migration in its economic and social context falls largely outside the purview of these analyses.

The costs, largely hidden, of migrant labour include those of both production and reproduction. Domestic production provides a supplement to wage income and allows artificially low wage levels since 'that which the family earns from its own little garden or field' can be deducted from wages and the price of labour correspondingly reduced.[21] Domestic production also provides upbringing and maintenance of workers in childhood and old age, thereby shunting the costs of reproduction of labour from the wage sector to the domestic sector.[22] Meillassoux suggested that circulating migrants are, in this way, subject to a pernicious form of 'super-exploitation', through appropriation of the product of the domestic community in addition to surplus value generated through labour. He argued further that circular migration thus forms the basis of an especially advantageous arrangement for the capitalist sector, and its persistence ensures the continued accrual of economic benefits.[23]

An accurate assessment of the advantages and costs of a system of circulating labour hinges on the relative roles of domestic production and wage income in the maintenance of the domestic community. The impetus to migration, the conditions that shape the supply of labour, particularly the supply price of labour, and the impact on the domestic community lie at the crux of this assessment.

IV. Wage Incomes and Labour Supply

Subject to specific, government-enforced demands of taxation and of labour that could only be met by participation in a market economy, the essentially non-monetised domestic community could, in theory, engage in either the sale of agricultural produce or the sale of labour.[24] In fact, the option was largely foreclosed by measures designed to compel the sale of labour.

The demand for labour early this century, up to the 1930s, was a pressing concern. The growth of settler farming,[25] the government's railway and road construction projects, and its need for porters and carriers in its forestry, agricultural, police and public works departments created a demand that far outran the voluntary supply of labour.[26]

Although the result should have been an increase in the price of labour, political and other factors hampered the use of wage rates to alter both the conditions of supply of, and the demand for, labour. Employers were unanimous that the supply of labour varied inversely, rather than directly, with wage rates. An incorrigible leisure preference of local workers was believed to account for the fact that higher wages did not bring about an increase in the supply of labour.[27]

But the unresponsiveness of labour to the inducement of higher wages — a belief rarely tested — had its source in factors other than the 'limited wants' or 'leisure preference' of African workers.[28] Unlike the situation in Europe — the expropriation of the peasantry and the proletarianised conditions of the labouring classes — peasant communities in Kenya were more or less self-sufficient. A wage income was not essential until made so by explicit administrative and economic arrangements. Moreover, labour conditions provided substantial disincentives.[29] The costs to workers of wage employment included ill-treatment, appalling housing and feeding, harsh discipline, and medical neglect. Abuse and brutality were not rare.[30]

An increase in wages that ameliorated these conditions or outweighed the costs would have endangered the profitability of settler farming.[31] This could not be countenanced in a regime in which the interests of the administration dovetailed with those of the settlers.[32] Since a rise in the supply price of labour was not believed viable, from the settlers' point of view, nor effective in increasing supply, vigorous government intervention in the recruitment and discipline of labour appeared to be the only means of closing the gap between demand and supply.[33]

This intervention included both indirect measures, such as taxation, the reduction in the native 'reserves', and prohibitions on the commercialisation of domestic agriculture, whose effects were to compel the local population to seek wage employment, and more forceful measures, such as conscription.[34] Informal conscription had early on been used by the government to meet its own needs for porters and road-builders.[35] Private employers, who were in effect the government's competitors for labour, demanded that conscription methods be extended to procure labour for them too, and at 'standard' rates. Since the territory's prosperity depended on the viability of settler enterprise, the local authorities had few qualms about complying with the settlers' demands. The outcry against forced labour[36] — the British Government issued an edict in 1908 and in 1921 that conscription for private employers be discontinued — led to a shift in policy from 'force' to 'encouragement', a shift in rhetoric widely recognised as a euphemism.[37] The mere existence of possible compulsion tended, of course, to depress wages below the level that would have existed in a free market.

A hut tax, and later a poll tax to reach youths who were not yet householders, were imposed to raise revenue and to 'induce' the supply of labour.[38] A circular and short-term pattern of migration emerged as the only viable means of meeting the demands placed on the indigenous population.

These tax measures were reinforced by land policies that created African 'reserves'. The choicest areas, the fertile highlands located near the railway, were exclusively assigned to settler farmers. Neither Africans nor Asians were permitted to hold land there.[39] In addition, the settlers insistently advocated a reduction in the native reserves, not because they desired the land, but to compel the local communities to earn their subsistence by wage labour. As a prominent settler (Lord Delamere) stated, 'If the policy was to be continued that every native was to be a land holder of a sufficient area on which to establish himself, then the question of obtaining a satisfactory labour supply could never be settled.'[40]

The settlers' privileged access to land did not in itself imply the inadequacy of the indigenous population's land to maintain a viable agricultural economy. In north-eastern Tanganyika, for example, the Chagga lost much of their land to German settlers and were confined to a crowded Kilimanjaro. By growing Arabica coffee, a lucrative cash crop, they were able to maintain their economic autonomy, despite the demand for labour from neighbouring settler communities.[41]

But in Kenya, much of the indigenous population was not permitted to enhance the productivity or profitability of their domestic agriculture,[42] since any improvement in the indigenous economy would inevitably diminish the supply of labour or raise its price.[43] Lord Lugard, an early architect of colonial policy, was explicit in this regard:

> The requirements of the settlers, to put it bluntly, are incompatible with the interests of the agricultural tribes, nor could they be otherwise than impatient of native development as a rival in the growing of coffee, flax and sisal.[44]

Thus, coercion, in the form of tax and land policies and the prohibition of the commercialisation of indigenous agriculture, effectively precluded the operation of market forces in the determination of wage levels.[45] At the same time, this coercion guaranteed a cheap labour supply by consigning the population to wage labour.[46]

The level of earnings, of course, determines the possibility of maintaining domestic communities through wage income transfers. Despite the paucity of direct quantitative evidence for the period preceding the mid-1950s, overall trends in the purchasing power of wages — and hence in potential savings and remittance ratios — of the majority of workers is not difficult to discern. The wages of the skilled or privileged minority — the clerks, headmen, chiefs, artisans — exceeded those of the large majority by sometimes dizzying multiples, reflecting the differentiation within the workforce.[47] For them, the settler economy offered an opportunity for upward mobility and the accumulation of resources by enlarging rural holdings and expanding agricultural production.[48] They therefore had ample opportunity for savings and investment. But for over 90 per cent of the mostly unskilled migrant labour force, wages were pegged at a level minimally sufficient for the needs of single workers, and at a subsistence level lower than that in the domestic 'reserves'.[49] For those at the lower end of the spectrum, the tangible advantages of migration and wage employment were markedly less evident. In 1927 a Labour Commission reported that the wage earnings of a typical worker were subject to a direct tax of about 30 per cent and an indirect tax averaging about 20 per cent. It concluded that after outlays for taxes and minimal living expenses, most workers very rarely had anything left of their earnings.[50] In 1939, the Nairobi Municipal Native Affairs Officer reported that the earning power of cash wages of more than half the workers was below the minimum necessary for a single man taking into account only the bare needs of food and housing.[51] Conditions in Mombasa, which provided some of the highest wages in the country, were no different; wages of unskilled workers were entirely spent on urban living, leaving none for saving or the support of rural households.[52] In a survey by the East Africa High Commission's Statistical Department in 1950, wages of unskilled workers in the urban areas were found to leave many men with little to eat for the last few days of the month. The 1954 Carpenter Committee Report similarly noted the inability of workers to survive without borrowing money, thus placing themselves in a recurrent monthly cycle of debt.[53]

At this level of wage incomes, savings or transfers to support rural households were impossible. The 'tradition of a subsistence wage', as it came to be called, was based on the premise that the worker, and more importantly members of his household, had recourse to traditional subsistence agriculture.[54] Domestic production was an essential supplement to wage income, thus subsidising the wages.[55] In addition, the domestic agricultural sector also underwrote the old age and unemployment provisions of the low-wage employment sector, which discharged its redundant or retired workers and returned them to their traditional communities, through the pass system that ensured that those not employed returned to the reserves.

One of the earliest studies to document the direction of net flows between the two sectors was a 1957 income and expenditure survey of 748 urban households in Nairobi and 298 rural households, summarised in Table 6.1. The net investment by urban male wage-earners in their home farms is tabulated by income group. As column D indicates, for over 70 per cent in the lower-income groups that was negative or negligible investment. One third of the workforce, in the next to lowest income group, invested an insignificant amount; the rural household was essentially self-sustaining, providing a necessary supplement to wage income. At the lowest level of income, also a third of the workforce, the pattern of disinvestment suggests a net outflow from the subsistence to the wage employment sector, a clear subsidy to this segment of the urban migrant workforce.[56]

Table 6.1: *Urban-rural Transfers by Income Group*

A Income group (shillings per annum)	B % distribution of Nairobi workforce	C Average income of group	D Net investment in rural farm of money wages per annum (%)
0-1,799	34.1	1,693	−4.25
1,800-3,599	38.6	2,583	0.62
3,600-5,399	17.3	4,330	1.51
5,400-7,199	6.9	6,126	10.15
7,200-8,999	3.1	8,179	7.00

Source: Adapted from M.W. Forrester: *Kenya Today* (The Hague, Mouton, 1962), pp. 75-6 and Tables I and II, p. 119.

The virtual employer monopoly over the conditions and supply price of labour ensured the maintenance of this pattern of resource flow to the low-wage economy. The 'standard rates' system, by which provincial labour boards set wage rates, enabled the employers, represented on the boards, to impose a fairly effective check against any rise in wage payments, either in cash or kind, while arguing that wage levels offered 'fair recompense',[57] in line with the low standards of efficiency and high rates of turnover of migrant labour.[58] This monopoly thus perpetuated a cycle of low wages, circulation of labour between wage employment and subsistence production, and consequent low levels of skill, experience and productivity.

Labour that was both unskilled and impermanent was caught in the familiar low-level equilibrium trap. Employers were disinclined to invest in the training of an impermanent labour force, which therefore remained unskilled. But while the absence of a stable labour force hampered industrial enterprise,[59] it offered the advantage of a lowered wage bill, with correspondingly higher profits. Flexibility in retrenchment was another advantage of a circulating workforce, which could be released and returned to the villages if demand declined. The costs of retrenchment were thus shifted to the domestic community.[60]

Wage levels were immune even when they might have been expected to rise sharply, such as during the labour shortages that punctuated the period up to the 1950s.[61] Moreover, the slow upward swings in wage levels that occurred in boom periods, such as those following the world wars, did not compensate for the rise in food costs and taxation. Thus real wages were remarkably stable from the early 1900s to the 1950s, a pattern broken only by a drastic decline during the Depression and a second sharp fall (the result of inflation) in the period 1940-52.[62]

Although wages rose in the 1950s, due in part to protective legislation, for the majority of the labour force at the lower end of the scale in both rural and urban areas (and there was a vast differential between them) earnings did not remotely approach the 'family' wage recommended by the 1954 Committee on African Wages.[63] Stressing the need to improve labour conditions as a necessary means of enhancing efficiency and productivity and creating a stable workforce, the Committee recommended an increase in wages that would allow workers to maintain their families in the urban areas and to sever ties with their domestic communities.

The implementation of this proposal was impeded by new pressures in the late 1950s and 1960s. A fall in levels of employment and higher rates of population growth[64] resulted in a growing 'reserve army' of unemployed that tended to depress wage levels, especially among the unskilled.[65] It was indeed the orthodoxy in the 1960s that rising wages created a privileged elite of urban workers and were responsible for the slow growth of formal employment.[66]

Declining employment was related to several factors. As Independence and African majority rule approached, the 'run-down' of the capitalised agricultural sector, owned and operated by the immigrant settler community, resulted in a considerable reduction in employment opportunities. This decline in the 'large farm sector' coupled with the success in industry of the policy to raise labour productivity and economise on wages slowed the growth in total employment. Indeed, total African employment only surpassed its 1955 level in 1968.[67]

Falling employment levels were affected by, and shaped, changes in patterns of labour migration. The increased stabilisation of the workforce in the late 1950s and early 1960s, on which enhanced productivity depended, reduced employment opportunities more than the fall in level of employment would suggest. In turn, the shrinkage of opportunities contributed to the decrease in labour turnover. Fear of unemployment had the effect of 'freezing' labour mobility, causing a sharp drop in labour turnover.[68] The 'reserve army' faced a choice: either to cling to employment or to abandon it with little chance of finding it again.[69] Short-term circular migration thus gave way to patterns of semi-permanent, life-cycle migration. The inability of low-paid wage workers to return to the rural community with customary frequency induced a pattern of female circulation between the rural community and the centres of wage employment of their menfolk.

These patterns of stabilisation of male wage labour and circulation of female labour differed significantly from that envisaged by the Carpenter Committee. In its view, the premise of a stable labour force was based on a level of income that permitted workers to reside with and maintain their families, divorced from dependence on domestic production in the rural community. However, the stabilisation that accompanied declining employment and rising unemployment was, for all but a privileged few, achieved by a perpetuation of the 'dual domestic economy' in which domestic production provided an essential supplement to wage income.

The lowest income-earners — agricultural workers, workers in the rural non-agricultural sector, in the urban informal sector, and unskilled workers in the formal sector — making up over 60 per cent of the workforce,[70] received wages which fall below the minimum necessary to support a household.[71] Evidence of this comes from a remittance study of urban workers that provided corroboration, in the 1970s, of Forrester's picture of the 1950s. The patterns, as revealed in Table 6.2, remain largely unchanged.

Using data from a 1974 nationwide household survey, Knowles and Anker presented evidence of the net transfers received by the 20 per cent of urban households at the lowest levels of income.[72] They concluded that 'the lowest income group, comprising about one-fifth of all urban households, are net receivers of transfers, which amount to almost one-half of the total receipts of these households'.[73]

The domestic sector thus continues to sustain the young, the old, and the ill-paid in wage employment. Labour stabilisation has been achieved at wage rates below the cost of the reproduction of labour power. The benefits to the wage sector accrue not only from the provision of subsistence and support systems, but also from the lower costs of social infrastructure — housing, schooling, health and other utilities — costs avoided by the workers' households residing in the village rather than in town.

V. Domestic Production and Female Labour

The domestic community relied for its self-provisioning on subsistence agriculture. But little agreement exists on how agricultural output was maintained in the face of male out-migration. Some have assumed a drop in output proportionate to the extent of male labour migration.[74] Others suggest that if migration was limited to less than 25 per cent of adult males, production in the domestic community would be largely unaffected.[75] Another view, based on an analysis of short-term seasonal migration, is that domestic production was maintained by the partial — and timely — withdrawal of labour during the slack agricultural season. Return to the domestic community for the active season ensured participation in domestic production, in addition to periodic spells in wage employment. This pattern of seasonal migration divided the community's forces — and maximised its returns — between the domestic and capitalist sectors of production.[76]

Table 6.2: *The Distribution of Transfers by Income Group*

N = 479	Income (Kenyan shillings per annum)						Total
	0-2,499	2,500-4,999	5,000-7,449	7,500-9,999	10,000-14,999	15,000+	
Urban							
1. Transfers sent	-138	-423	-753	-541	-515	-868	-524
2. Transfers received	655	246	145	374	213	545	371
3. Net transfers received	516	-177	-608	-167	-302	-323	-153
4. Proportion of households	0.202	0.238	0.194	0.123	0.079	0.163	1.000

Source: Adapted from J.C. Knowles and R. Anker, 'An analysis of income transfers in a developing country: The case of Kenya', *Journal of Development Economics*, 1981, vol. 8, p. 212.

The view that male out-migration caused a proportionate fall in agricultural output is based on a zero sum assumption of the productive capacity of the domestic community. Besides being mechanistic, it overlooks arrangements in the traditional patterns of the division of labour, arrangements permitting an array of compensatory mechanisms.[77] The idea that a balance could be struck between wage work during the 'slack' season and domestic production during the active season is of limited applicability; such a tidy solution existed only where there were distinctly different operations in the two sectors.[78] In Kenya, however, the capital sector was also involved in agricultural production, and the active season in both domestic and capitalist farming operations coincided,[79] so that a seasonal pattern of circular migration based on the domestic agricultural cycle could not therefore be accommodated.[80] Moreover, the extent of male migration among agricultural groups was over 55 per cent of the adult male population by 1923; the period of migration had also increased to over six months a year.[81]

Rather, the domestic community could accommodate out-migration of male labour, and even sustain the later semi-permanent, or working-life migration and a 'stabilised', though not fully proletarianised, workforce because of the traditional domestic division of labour.[82] These traditional patterns — the widespread practice of female farming and the relatively minor role of male labour in agriculture — permitted the diversion of so large a part of the workforce without the wholesale destruction of domestic systems of production.[83]

The prevalence of female farming systems was the foundation of the widely-held view among employers that for men village life entailed only a few weeks' work a year, alternating with long periods of sitting in the sun and beer-swilling. In an account of the Kikuyu of colonial Kenya, Leakey described the essentially preparatory and limited agricultural activities of men — clearing virgin forest (of which there was little) or of the brushwood that covers it if it has been fallow, breaking up the surface in preparation for cultivation, and keeping birds and animals away from ripening crops (in which the whole of the community is involved).[84] Agricultural production was based largely on the labour of women engaged in the planning of maize, millet, beans, and other crops, hoeing, weeding, harvesting, and in the storage and care of food. Men did on occasion assist women in agricultural activities, and some crops, such as sugar cane, yams and bananas, were grown exclusively by men.[85] Pruning trees, building the framework of huts (thatching and plastering were left to women), fencing gardens and villages, herding cattle and goats, and special trades — such as smithing, chair-making, wire pulling, wickerwork for grain stores — were among the activities of men. In addition, men were the warriors and protectors, activities essential to the community, but not at the core of agricultural production.[86]

Community organisation reflected this division of labour. Homesteads scattered across the country comprised gardens and huts of the wives of the household head, with each wife apportioned a plot on which to maintain her own granary and from which she provided for the needs of her children. A Land Commission estimated that the average Kikuyu woman during 1921-31 cultivated about 1 acre, in several scattered plots, the precise acreage and spread being, according to Kenyatta, in accord with 'her capacity for cultivation'.[87] Traditional indicators of wealth — land, livestock, and women — bear testimony to the central role of women in the domestic economy. Traditional practices such as 'bride-wealth', paid by the groom to the bride's kin for the loss of a food producer, reflect the value attached to women's role in both production and reproduction.

The increased effort required of women as a result of the transfer of male labour from the domestic sector into wage employment is well documented. In one of the earliest ethnographic accounts of the Kikuyu, it was observed that coercive labour recruitment had the 'drawback that it results only in added labour on the part of the women'.[88] Leys drew the attention of labour policy-makers to the excessive share of the cultivation work thrown on women with 'the absence in the agricultural tribes, of more than half the able-bodied male population',[89] and recent studies have amplified the changes wrought by labour migration. Women's role in agriculture has expanded to include not only soil preparation and cultivation of certain crops once considered to be men's, but also the care of animals and livestock, traditionally male activities.[90]

Scattered references to resistance by women suggest some hardship caused by the labour intensification required to maintain domestic production. According to one report, the women of Busoga refused to cultivate their farms, causing a serious food shortage.[91] A similar incident was reported in Kitui, in Nyanza district, in the western part of the country.[92]

Several factors besides the massive and prolonged absence of male labour contributed to the increase of female labour in agriculture. Population growth, combined with land and development policies, exacerbated the pressures on domestic production.[93] Whereas in the past, the availability of open, unsettled, and largely uncontested land made the accommodation of population growth a simple matter of extending the frontiers of settlement, this was no longer an available option. Colonial settlement policies had introduced a new and formidable landholding group, the European settlers, who had the backing of a powerful state.

The creation of reserves for Africans was not based on an assessment of the needs of African economies, nor their methods of land use. The boundaries confined indigenous groups and prevented both the traditional drift of these groups across the country and the cycle of land use and regeneration.[94] The replacement of a long-fallow system of land use with a shorter fallow system, and of single- with double-cropping, reflected the need for more intensive production to maintain subsistence levels.[95] The pressure to maintain these levels in the face of depleted soil fertility, inhibition of traditional solutions, and administrative indifference to traditional agriculture, required a greater expenditure of primarily female labour, while generating the symptoms of agricultural malaise, soil erosion and declining yields.[96] A 'squeeze' on household production resulted from these twin factors of declining agricultural productivity and decreasing returns to labour.

Agrarian malaise also intensified the impetus to labour migration. Cause and consequence were inextricably related as increasing subsistence pressure made wage employment a necessary alternative to smallholder agriculture and domestic production. The labour situation was altered (as we have seen) from one of shortage to one of oversupply, directly beneficial to the colonial economy. But the system of circulating labour in a low-wage economy could only be maintained if the reserves supported the workers' wives and families. Continuing agricultural deterioration, if unchecked, could lead to pauperisation and a large-scale exodus.[97] A genuine proletariat and the transfer of its subsistence needs from the reserves to the wage bill of the settler economy, would have seriously undermined settler enterprises.[98] African agriculture could not be allowed to deteriorate to such a point.

The need to increase domestic production for the market also provided a stimulus to production in the reserves. The depressions of 1921-2 and 1929-34 had severe repercussions on Kenya's export-oriented economy. The drop in export production in the settler economy led to a sharp reduction in area cultivated and wages.[99] In its vigorous effort to shore up the settler economy, the government provided a variety of subsidies, loans, refunds, and rebates.[100] But while the government's revenue needs were increased by its greatly enhanced support of the settler economy, its revenue base — wages paid to Africans — was diminished by the general wage cut, to the tune of about 40 per cent. The expansion of domestic production for the market offered a potential solution to the problems of both export production and revenue needs.

The enunciation of a 'dual policy' committed to the parallel and complementary development of African reserves and European settled areas owed much to these considerations.[101] But although it seemed to indicate a major shift in official policy from the earlier exclusive development of the settler economy, the 'dual policy' did not translate into a vigorous government initiative.[102] The domestic economy remained virtually untouched by efforts to change or develop it.[103] Technological and financial investments required to transform domestic agriculture were not made; tax revenues generated in the reserves were rarely invested in the agricultural development of the domestic economy.[104] Other features of the colonial economy also impeded the development of the domestic economy — restrictions on the growth of certain particularly profitable or easy-to-cultivate crops, protectionist measures that provided the privileged settlers with a subsidy at the expense of the domestic economy, and the transfer of land and labour from the domestic to the settler sector.[105]

Although the transformation of domestic agriculture, the smallholder economy in particular, was largely prevented, a limited amount of commercialisation of African agriculture did take place. Expansion of maize production, confined mainly to the less densely populated areas of the reserves, was an example of commercialisation, albeit limited by the degree of subsistence pressure in the reserves.[106] Efforts to promote cotton production in Nyanza Province proved singularly unsuccessful, due in large part to the uninterest of indigenous producers in non-food-crop production.[107] However, government attempts to expand the acreage under mimosa (wattle) cultivation provide perhaps the clearest example of the limited objectives of the plans to promote agricultural production in the reserves. In the belief that 'costless' (i.e., female) household labour would enable the cultivation of the mimosa tree at a price competitive in a world market of falling prices, the government launched a drive to promote its production. Though of no direct consumption value — the bark was sold to extract factories, the wood served building and fuel purposes — the mimosa tree provided domestic producers, divested of land and labour, the advantage of non-labour-intensive cultivation and a yield per unit of land exceeding any available alternative. Although the production of maize or beans would have been more profitable, smallholders faced with the growing shortage of land and labour were in no position to opt for more attractive alternatives.[108]

The opposition to systematic investment in, or transformation of, domestic agriculture was based largely on the fact that such pursuits would reduce the availability of men for wage labour.[109] It was as wage earners rather than independent market producers that domestic communities best served the needs of the settler economy, as a labouring proto-proletariat rather than a true proletariat or cash-cropping peasantry. A delicate balance was maintained with a domestic sector plagued by deteriorating conditions — intensified inputs and declining returns — but still self-supporting and sufficiently viable to generate a supply of labour. Domestic production was thus undermined, but also preserved, and not merely to nourish the reproduction of a wage-labour force, as Meillassoux has argued, for the intensification of production served to preserve the emasculated domestic sector. Far from being strangulated or destroyed, domestic production was intensified by the often prolonged absence of male labour.[110] The basis of intensified production in the domestic community was an accentuation rather than a restructuring of traditional patterns of labour allocation.[111] As men began leaving for longer periods, the domestic community became steadily more dependent on the labour of women in agriculture.

VI. The Origins of Circular Migration: From Male to Female Circulation

The argument so far accounts for the structural conditions that preserve the relations between the domestic and wage sectors. But it has not considered how circulatory migration systems arise. Regional imbalances that occur with the 'unequal' penetration of capital and associated development activity are usually seen as the cause of migration; centres of economic growth are seen as the foci of labour mobility. This view highlights the spatial; the location of capital is seen to shape the flow of labour, particularly when centres of investment are within zones of relative underinvestment and underdevelopment. Other aspects of investment-generated activity, such as economic growth strategy, fall outside the purview of this perspective. In Kenya, however, these aspects were predominant; the economic and socio-political development strategy was the prime factor shaping the pattern of circular migration.

The debate that raged in other colonial territories over the relative advantages of indigenous peasant agriculture or an economy based on an expatriate farming class was barely heard in Kenya.[112] The Kenyan strategy was borrowed from South Africa and southern Rhodesia, where expatriate agriculture played a dominant role.[113] The West African model of peasant production, in which the surplus product of peasant producers was channelled into an export trade, was not considered feasible, because of the primitive agricultural techniques of indigenous producers, among other reasons.[114]

Whereas a system of peasant production would have dispersed the settlers among indigenous cultivators, drawing more heavily upon their labour than upon their land, the strategy in Kenya entailed extensive alienation of land and labour, and the creation of a dual society. The strategy of a dominant settler economy was based on the assumption of a distinct settler community in a separate territory — creating a patchwork of 'settled areas' and 'native reserves' with differing economic and social systems.[115]

Strict separation of the indigenous and immigrant communities was not feasible as the procurement of labour from the reserves for expatriate agriculture was essential.[116] The system of migrant labour was a consequence of this growth strategy, based on expatriate enterprise, local labour, and the separation of the indigenous and immigrant communities. Men went to work for short, but gradually lengthening, periods on farms and in towns, leaving their families to support themselves in the reserves, to which the men would fairly frequently return — a circular pattern of movement between the reserve and settlement areas. Legal measures were introduced to prevent the abandonment of 'the native tribal home' by women and children, while the residence of men in their place of employment was permitted for limited periods only, thus institutionalising this pattern.

The extent of circular migration was not the same among all groups, for while the claims to land and labour were common to them all, the nature of the claims differed. Among the Luo and Luhya in the west, for example, claims to manpower weighed heavier than claims to land. The Kamba in the south-east contributed relatively little labour, but suffered loss of land. The claims on the Kikuyu were the heaviest, involving, land, labour, and capital.[117] Differences in their resource base, and consequently in their ability to meet the demands imposed upon them without submitting to wage labour, were the principal feature distinguishing the resilience of the various communities to the encroaching settler economy. The relatively wealthy Kamba, with an economy based on agriculture and pastoral farming, were able to capitalise their extensive livestock herds. Tax demands could thus be met without resort to wage labour.[118] The western Kipsigis' expansion of maize production, made profitable by the adoption of the plough in place of the hoe, provided another alternative to wage migration.[119] The grain-producing economy of the Kikuyu did not lend itself, in the absence of technological inputs or marketing support, to the accumulation of durable savings; for them the pull of wage employment to meet taxes and the need for cash were not easy to resist.

VII. Summary

Although the claims of Kenya's settler economy were most tangibly evident in the flow of labour, land alienation, and the imposition of taxes, these were by no means the only exactions. Others included a government policy of low prices for domestic producers and similar measures favouring one sector at the expense of another.[120] The emphasis on these modes of resource reallocation and on their role in the creation of social overhead capital left another model relatively unnoticed.

The very immobility of a segment of the labour force itself constituted a mechanism for the transfer of resources. 'Bachelor' wages paid to migrants in wage employment allowed little surplus for the support of rural households. The domestic community, compelled to sustain itself while being divested of a substantial proportion of its labour resources, sought to preserve itself through the intensification of female labour in agriculture. Thus, domestic production based on female labour preserved the rural community. It also provided the structural support for a low-wage economy by externalising the settlers' labour costs and by absorbing the costs of labour force renewal. The growth and dynamism of the settler economy owed much to these resource flows, as did the impoverishment of the domestic community.

Times have changed, but the pattern of labour circulation has not. New mechanisms and structures of economic segmentation have preserved the resource flows from the domestic to the capitalist economy. The shift from male to female circular migration permitted the stabilisation of the male labour force. But stabilisation — at wages that usually do not provide a 'family' wage sufficient to support the workers' households — has not produced a stable domestic pattern. It has in fact reinforced earlier patterns of a residentially separate household. The rural families of urban workers, producing the bulk of their own subsistence, also contribute to the maintenance of future and former workers. These labour reproduction costs, formerly externalised from the settler to the domestic economy, are now borne by the rural wing of a bifurcated household. This translates into a reduction in the wage bill of the urban economy[121] and a saving on social infrastructure and urban amenities made unnecessary when the workers' families reside in the countryside. The conditions accompanying the stabilisation of the male labour force reflect the persistence of old patterns of exchange — a return to labour below the cost of its reproduction.

The dissolution of the system of reserves and settled areas with political independence and the transfer of land to the peasantry under various settlement schemes also contained within them mechanisms of resource transfer reminiscent of earlier times.[122] The price of land for even the most underprivileged smallholders was set at full 'market' valuation. Land purchase and agricultural 'development loans' resulted in a debt burden so high that the smallholder was left with a return not even covering the most essential subsistence expenditures. Over 70 per cent of net farming income of the smallest settlers was required for debt repayment, much of it to foreign creditors, since foreign loans to the government underwrote about half the costs of settlement.[123] The surplus of small-scale peasants' surplus, used for debt and interest payments, thus returned to the former settlers (for the land purchased from them[124]), via the institutions of both the local and foreign governments — a pattern expected to continue to at least the end of the century.[125] Peasant agriculture, unable to retain the surplus that could be the basis of its own accumulation and regeneration, remains locked in a pattern of stunted growth.

Appendix

Secondary sources for the patterns of migration described here are as follows.

(1) Most accounts of the colonial period indicate that labour recruitment was confined largely to men. The sources used here include Clayton and Savage, 1974; Hay, 1976; Leys, 1973; Leys, 1974; Lonsdale and Berman, 1979; Kitching, 1980; Wolff, 1974.

The restriction of women to the reserves was inherent in the separation of indigenous and immigrant groups. Until the mid-1940s, even most domestic jobs were closed to women and it is only since 1952 that women have been permitted to join the labour force in Nairobi.[126]

The focus on circular migrants excludes an important segment of the population — resident labourers or 'squatters'. Squatting allowed Africans to reside on the land of the settler farmers. In return for rent paid in labour (or money), squatters had access to a small plot for private cultivation. Apart from the requirement to work for the settler for 180 days a year, squatting permitted Africans to maintain their customary way of life and avoided the break-up of the domestic unit. 'Kaffir farming', as it was called — absentee immigrant landlords subsidised by the rent paid by African tenants — came to a virtual halt in the 1930s.[127] No official assessments of the size of the squatter population exist; according to one estimate, about 20 per cent of the total agricultural labour force were squatters.[128]

The similarity between squatters and migrants lay in the fact that neither group had permanent ties in their place of work. For both groups, unemployment, ill-health, or retirement meant a return to the reserves. A wife resident in the reserves was frequently the means for squatters to retain their stake in their home communities.[129] Unequal sex ratios were common among both migrants and squatters.[130]

(2) Evidence for the bifurcated household and the separation of its members between the rural farm and urban wage employment is to be found, among others, in one study that notes that the movement of men to the city and the residence of the wife in the rural areas (to tend the family farm) was not unusual 'judging by adult male/female ratios in many Kenyan districts'.[131]

Another study presented data on the pervasiveness of this pattern of dual households, emphasising the need to see the rural and urban units as part of a single social field.[132] Moock's study of 'occupational and residential dualities' and Abbot's analysis of change and stress among rural Kikuyu women ('Full-time farmers and weekend wives') provide further confirmation of these patterns.[133]

(3) In addition to references cited in the text on the stabilisation of the wage-labour force, male immobility is discussed in Moock, who cites the case of migrants unable to return to their village to attend important home affairs for fear that it would cost them their jobs.[134]

Kitching drew on the 1962 Annual Report of the Labour Department, commenting on how explicitly the report dates the increased stabilisation of the migrant labour force to the late 1950s and early 1960s, when 'it was reported that many more workers feared to leave their jobs in case of displacement'.[135]

(4) The circulation of women between town and country is described by Abbot:

Many of the wives travel to the cities to visit their husbands, but their frequency of travel is conditioned by the requirements of the agricultural cycle, the number and ages of their children, financial considerations, and whether or not their husbands want them to visit.[136]

In her study, Obbo coined the term 'shuttlers' for women who 'constantly move backwards and forwards between town and country':

> Their commitments as agricultural producers and mothers were perceived as situated in the villages but their duties as wives required that they periodically visit their migrant husbands in the towns. Being in town also served as a break from the rural agricultural work and domestic chores. The majority of Luo women came to visit their husbands three times a year, each trip lasting about a month. The visits coincided with the times when planting, weeding and harvesting had been completed.[137]

Confirmation of this pattern is found in Ross and Weisner: 'many wives come to Nairobi for short stays between planting seasons, when there is little farm work to be done';[138] and by Parkin: 'there is the constant switching of children and wives between town and country residences'.[139]

Notes

1. J.C.H. Fei and G. Ranis: *Development of the labour surplus economy: Theory and policy* (Homewood, Illinois, Irwin, 1964).
2. Although acknowledgement of these social conflicts has led to the adoption of the goal of equity with growth among development theorists, it is rarely combined with an analysis of the exercise of economic and political power in the design of development strategy. The ILO report, perhaps the best-known document of this genre, reflects this in its proposals for income redistribution — ILO: *Employment, incomes and equality* (Geneva, ILO, 1972). See also C. Leys: *Underdevelopment in Kenya: The political economy of neo-colonialism, 1964-71* (Berkeley, University of California Press, 1974), pp. 258-71.
3. The term 'natural' economy is used to convey the dominance of production for use rather than for exchange or accumulation. This is not to suggest that pre-colonial African societies resembled autarchic, 'primitive communalist' systems. Exchange relations — simple exchanges between local producers and more specialised long-distance trade — were developed in pre-colonial Africa. Diversity and differentiation in pre-colonial modes of production were evident in the emergence of class relations. See, e.g., R. Sandbrook and R. Cohen (eds.): *The development of an African working class: Studies in class formation and action* (Toronto, University of Toronto Press, 1975).
4. For a discussion of advantages the British economy derived from its colonies and the economic rationale that lay behind Britain's imperial expansion in East Africa, see R.D. Wolff: *The economics of colonialism: Britain and Kenya, 1870-1930* (New Haven, Yale University Press, 1974), especially Chapters 1 and 2.

5. The encounter between modes of production rarely results in a linear evolution or a predictable transition from pre-capitalist to capitalist forms. It has usually involved a complex pattern of interaction, encirclement, and partial incorporation — hence the 'articulation' approach of those who analyse the networks between and among modes of production. A collection of essays on the concept of articulation is H. Wolpe (ed.): *The articulation of modes of production: Essays from Economy and Society* (London, Routledge and Kegan Paul, 1980).

6. For the sources of these and other labour movements described below, see the appendix to this chapter.

7. B. Warren: *Imperialism: Pioneer of capitalism* (London, New Left Books, 1980).

8. A.G. Hopkins: *An economic history of West Africa* (London, Longmans, 1973); P. Hill: *Studies in rural capitalism* (London, Cambridge University Press, 1970).

9. See, e.g., A. Yansane (ed.): *Decolonisation and dependency: Problems of development of African societies* (Westport, Connecticut, Greenwood Press, 1980), and M.A. Klein (ed.): *Peasants in Africa: Historical and contemporary perspectives*, Sage series on African Modernization and Development, vol. 4 (London, Sage Publications, 1980).

10. The approaches of Gugler, Mitchell, and Parkin exemplify this perspective among anthropologists, and Todaro among economists — J. Gugler: 'On the theory of rural-urban migration: The case of sub-Saharan Africa', in J.A. Jackson (ed.): *Migration* (Cambridge, Cambridge University Press, 1969); J.C. Mitchell: 'The causes of labour migration', in *Bulletin of Inter-African Urban Studies*, 1959, vol. 6, no. 1; D. Parkin (ed.): *Town and country in central and eastern Africa* (London, Oxford University Press, 1975); M.P. Todaro: 'Income expectations, rural urban migration and employment in Africa', in *International Labour Review*, 1971, vol. 104, no. 5, pp. 387-413.

11. Explanations of circular migration have also been sought in institutional and structural factors, and in socio-cultural and socio-psychological factors affecting household economic strategies and patterns of labour allocation. The object of circular migration has been accounted for in terms of 'target income' related to 'limited wants', or the opportunity to escape the obligations of extended family systems and the demands of kin on both labour and income. But these accounts, besides being limited to particular segments of the pool of potential migrants, do not address the origins of patterns of circulation. For a review of this literature, see Mitchell, 1959.

12. S. Amin (ed.): *Modern migration in Western Africa* (London, Oxford University Press, 1974).

13. The literature abounds with controversy over the use of the term 'peasant' to describe rural cultivators in 'traditional' Africa. See, e.g., L.A. Fallers: 'Are African cultivators to be called "peasants"?', in *Current Anthropology*, 1961, vol. 2. But as Derman argues, pre-contact Africa contained more aspects of a peasantry than is sometimes acknowledged — W. Derman: 'Peasants: The African exception?', in *American Anthropologist*, 1972, vol. 74.

14. J. Saul and R. Woods: 'African peasantries', in T. Shanin (ed.): *Peasants and peasant societies* (Harmondsworth, Penguin, 1971), pp. 104-5.

15. Ibid.

16. The phrase is from Fegan. The household is viewed as a small diversified conglomerate engaged in varied productive activities shared among its members on the basis of traditional criteria of sex and age — B. Fegan: 'Folk-capitalism: Economic strategies of peasants in a Philippines wet-rice village', PhD dissertation, Yale University, 1979.

17. E.J. Berg: 'The development of a labour force in sub-Saharan Africa', in

Economic Development and Cultural Change, 1965, vol. 13, no. 4, part I, pp. 394-412.

18. C. Meillassoux: *Maidens, meal and money* (Cambridge, Cambridge University Press, 1975).

19. J. van Velsen: 'Labour migration as a positive factor in the continuity of Tonga tribal society', in A. Southall (ed.): *Social change in modern Africa* (London, Oxford University Press, 1961); W. Watson: *Tribal cohesion in a money economy* (Manchester, Manchester University Press, 1958).

20. Berg, 1965.

21. F. Engels: 'The housing question', in K. Marx and F. Engels: *Selected works*, vol. 1 (Moscow, Foreign Language Publishing House, 1962), p. 553.

22. Dr Norman Leys, an outspoken critic of the colonial administration of which he was a part, was among the first to observe that the 'native reserves' in Kenya bore the costs of child-rearing and welfare, to the benefit of employers — N. Leys: *Kenya* (London, Frank Cass and Co., 1973; 4th edn), pp. 314-40, 394-5.

23. For a discussion of the continual re-creation of the subsistence economy in the face of the eroding tendency of capitalism, see V.I. Lenin: 'The development of capitalism in Russia', in *Collected works*, vol. 3 (Moscow, Foreign Languages Publishing House, 1960), pp. 40-1.

24. Saul and Woods, 1971, p. 107.

25. The development of a settler community was actively fostered in the East African Protectorate, established in 1895 under direct British rule. It was believed that European settlement, and an export trade based on the agricultural production of European farmers would make the railway built to establish control over the Nile's headwaters profitable. This project had little to do with Kenya, but was to have profound repercussions on its future because its geography, in particular its highlands, made it the most attractive of the four East African countries for extensive European settlement. In Uganda, Tanganyika, and Zanzibar, European settlement was limited; but many Europeans settled in the Kenyan highlands, a temperate climate within the tropics.

26. On the continuing problem of labour shortages up to the 1930s, see M.H. Ross, *Political integration of urban squatters* (Evanston, Illinois, Northwestern University Press, 1973), p. 220; J. Middleton: 'Kenya: Changes in African life, 1912-1945', in V. Harlow and E.M. Chilver (eds.): *History of East Africa*, vol. 2 (Oxford, Clarendon Press, 1965), p. 354; R. van Zwanenberg: *Colonial capitalism and labour in Kenya, 1919-39* (Nairobi, East African Literature Bureau, 1975), especially Chapter 4; S. Stichter: 'The formation of a working class in Kenya', in Sandbrook and Cohen, 1974; Wolff, 1974, pp. 92-6.

27. Commissioner Charles Eliot, the protectorate's second chief officer responsible for labour policy, stated: 'To raise the rate of wages would not increase but would diminish the supply of labour. A rise in the rate of wages would enable the hut or poll tax of a family or tribe to be earned by fewer external workers, and as the payment of this tax is avowedly the reason for what labour we have seeking employment it follows that if we increase the rate of remuneration of the individual we decrease the number of individuals necessary to earn a given sum' — speech reported in *East African Standard*, 8 February 1913, cited in Leys, 1974, p. 202.

28. The debate over the 'backward-bending supply curve' of labour in Africa has been extensive. For a recent review of the literature dealing, in part, with the 'fallacy of limited wants', see G. Ellis: 'The backward-bending supply curve of labour in Africa: Models, evidence, and interpretation — and why it makes a difference', in *The Journal of Developing Areas*, 1981, vol. 15, no. 2, pp. 251-73.

29. Berg amplifies the deterrents — the long and sometimes dangerous journey, the adjustment to unfamiliar rhythms of work, surroundings, diet, and

co-workers, the restraints on 'quitting' (whip lashes and incarceration for 'desertion'), and others. Ignoring completely the fundamental facts of direct and indirect coercion (evident in penal employment legislation and the registration system), he marvels at the numbers of 'volunteers' — Berg, 1965, p. 339.

30. M.P. Miracle: 'Interpretation of backward-sloping labour supply curves in Africa', in *Economic Development and Cultural Change*, January 1976, vol. 24, no. 2, pp. 399-406. Detailed documentation is contained in East African Protectorate: *Native Labour Commission, 1912-1913: Evidence and report* (Nairobi, 1913), and in M.H. Ross, 'Politics and urbanisation: Two communities in Nairobi', PhD dissertation, Northwestern University, 1968, pp. 95-6.

31. C.C. Wrigley: 'Kenya: The patterns of economic life', in Harlow and Chilver, 1965, p. 230; Leys, 1974, p. 29.

32. The community of interest between private settlers and colonial officials was most apparent in the tax, land and labour policies. By 'encouraging' Africans to work for settlers, the administration ensured its own tax revenues while satisfying the settlers' need for labour. Government revenue in turn provided settlers with direct and indirect services and subsidies. Revenue from taxation was thus largely expended on expatriate enterprise. Munro estimated that in one district — Machakos — revenue raised by taxation exceeded expenditure in the district by 84 per cent in 1913-14 and 92 per cent in 1921 — J.F. Munro: *Colonial rule and the Kamba: Social change in the Kenya Highlands, 1889-1939* (Oxford, Clarendon Press, 1975), pp. 93-4.

33. Measures to discipline workers included universal fingerprinting, severe punishment for desertion, vagrancy regulations, a Masters and Servants Ordinance (1910) and a Natives Registration Ordinance (1915), and a pass system that allowed identification of troublesome workers or deserters — Ross, 1968, pp.186-90.

34. E. Clayton and D.C. Savage: *Government and labour in Kenya, 1895-1963* (London, Frank Cass, 1974). Conscription included both communal and compulsory labour. The former, usually unpaid, involved work on a project that benefited the local community, such as clearing ditches or bridge repair. Compulsory labour evolved from communal labour schemes and was undertaken for essential State services — building railways, docks, major roads. It was badly paid, and refusal to work was penalised. The system developed fully after the First World War, and although it had completely disappeared by 1939, following pressure from the British Government and the ILO, it was revived during the Second World War — Clayton and Savage, 1974, p. 131.

35. Wrigley, 1965, p. 231.

36. The use of compulsion by private employers was seen as slave labour — J.W. Cell (ed.): *By Kenya possessed: The correspondence of Norman Leys and J.H. Oldham, 1918-1926* (Chicago, University of Chicago Press, 1976).

37. In practice, the edict left recruitment largely unchanged. As Wrigley remarks, 'the distinction between command and persuasion was, in the circumstances, a very fine one . . . Thus the settlers could not be sure of their labour supply, but neither could the Africans be sure of their freedom' — Wrigley, 1965, p. 231.

38. See Ross, 1973, Chapter 9, for an account of the direct and indirect taxes imposed to 1926, their relative impact on the indigenous populations, and comparative investment in the two sectors. A prominent member of the administration, Sir Charles Eliot, stated the intent of taxation: 'We consider that taxation is the only possible method of compelling the native to leave his reserve for the purpose of seeking work. Only in this way can the cost of living be increased for the native, and as we have previously pointed out it is on this that the supply of labour and the price of labour depend' — Leys, 1973, p. 202.

39. Colonial land policy (and settler demands) have received much scholarly attention — G.H. Mungeam: *British rule in Kenya, 1895-1912* (Oxford, Clarendon Press, 1966); M.P.K. Sorrenson: *The origins of European settlement in Kenya* (Nairobi, Oxford University Press, 1968).

40. Leys, 1973, p. 6.

41. E.A. Brett: *Colonialism and underdevelopment in East Africa: The politics of economic change, 1919-1939* (New York, NOK, 1973), pp. 172-3.

42. Wolff, 1974, pp. 139 ff. For example, coffee, so important to the settler economy, could not be grown in the reserves. By the Coffee Plantations Registration Ordinance of 1918, every grower was to be licensed and licences were not permitted to be issued to African growers (see Wrigley, 1965, p. 246; Brett, 1973, pp. 175-7). Justifying the prohibition, the East Africa Commission (1925) concluded: 'There is no doubt that the present difficulty in obtaining labour in Uganda . . . is due to the high prices which the Uganda native is at present obtaining for his cotton crop' — Wolff, 1974, p. 141.

43. Possession of the means of production provided the means to resist the sale of labour. A settler of the time wrote: 'it stands to reason that the more prosperous and contented is the population of the reserve the less the need or inclination of young men of the tribe to go out into the labour field' — Lord Oliver: *White capital and coloured labour* (London, Hogarth Press, 1929), p. 214.

44. Lord Lugard: *The dual mandate in tropical Africa* (London, Frank Cass, 1922), p. 397. Referring explicitly to 'antagonistic' interests, Lugard elsewhere observed that the 'foreign estate owners . . . — unless artificially protected — cannot compete with the native grower, who has no "overhead charges" to meet and can work in his own time, in his own way, for his own profit, and with the assistance of his family' — Lord Lugard: 'The white man's task in Africa', in *Foreign Affairs*, October 1926, p. 69.

45. The pass system, under which a certificate was issued at the time of a worker's registration and upon which employers recorded wages earned and taxes paid, also depressed wages by preventing workers from changing employment — Wolff, 1974, p. 120; Clayton and Savage, 1974, p. 148.

46. As Kitching put it, 'the broad relationship was one in which the smaller the holding and the smaller the cash and subsistence income it gave, the lower the point on the wage range which would attract a man into the wage labour force' — G. Kitching: *Class and economic change in Kenya: The making of an African petite bourgeoisie, 1905-70* (New Haven, Yale University Press, 1980), p. 278.

47. Ibid., p. 255.

48. Ibid.

49. van Zwanenberg, 1975, p. 37.

50. Wolff, 1974, p. 119; Leys, 1973 (1st edn 1926), p. 302. The Committee on African wages (The Carpenter Committee) reported that the minimum wage had been derived from a formula of a professor at the University of Cape Town based on the barest minimum for an unmarried employee's food, clothing, fuel, and a small addition for petty expenses such as beer or a bus ticket. It was pointed out that the minimum wage usually became the actual wage, and as most workers were married, wages were far from adequate; they were insufficient to cover living costs of even a single man living in the city — the housing allowance, for example, paid — at best — for a bed space in a crowded room — Clayton and Savage, 1974, pp. 368 ff.

51. van Zwanenberg, 1975, pp. 39-40.

52. Clayton and Savage, 1974, p.284. They cite a memorandum to the Labour Commissioner on African workers on strike in Mombasa in 1947: 'We would like to know how it is expected one with a family to live on a wage, let us say for instance of Shs. 80 (we quote Shs. 80 because majority of us earn far less than

that sum); while he has essentially to occur such expenses as food Shs. 40; sundry expenses (soap, water, paraffin, fuel, letters, etc.) Shs. 15; house rent (average) Shs. 10, furnitures and utensils Shs. 10 per month. Clothes? Saving? Families at home who look upon workers for substantial help?' — ibid.

53. *The pattern of income and consumption of African labourers in Nairobi, October and November 1950, 1951* and the Committee on African Wages, 1954, cited in Clayton and Savage, 1974, pp. 368 ff.

54. Lord Hailey: *An African survey* (London, Oxford University Press, 1957), p. 701.

55. Hay emphasised the dependence of wage workers on domestic production, as opposed to the conventional notion of the reliance of rural households on remittances. 'African families were expected to meet all their staple food requirements through their own production; and the artificially low wages paid to African workers meant that in many cases rural families had to supply foodstuffs to labor migrants in the towns as well' — M. Hay: 'Luo women and economic change during the colonial period', in N. Hafkin and E. Bay (eds.): *Women in Africa* (Stanford, Stanford University Press, 1976), p. 87.

56. Forrester's measure of 'investment' in the traditional sector includes taxes and school fees. 'Disinvestment' includes food brought to town for own consumption, the proceeds of farm produce sold and used for consumption expenses, withdrawal of savings, dependence on the State. By comparing the two, Forrester arrives at a net investment percentage. Thus the lowest income group invested 1.66 per cent in the rural farm and took out 5.91 per cent from it, a net dissaving of 4.25 per cent. For the next income group, there was an investment of 4.99 per cent and a disinvestment of 4.37 per cent, a net investment of 0.62 per cent, not considered a 'worthwhile' level of investment — M.W. Forrester: *Kenya today: Social prerequisites for economic development* (The Hague, Mouton, 1962), pp. 120-1.

57. Critics of the employers' position argued that the 'fair recompense' proposition did not take into account the relative values of workers' output and returns to employers. As van Zwanenberg attempts to document, they believed the level of wages was much lower than the marginal productivity of labour — van Zwanenberg, 1974, pp. 37-41. The excessively high profit expectations, relative to risk and capital outlay, lay at the crux of the issue — Clayton and Savage, 1974, p. 315.

58. Wolff, 1974, pp. 96-7, on the complaints of settlers about the workers' manifold shortcomings and 'incompetence'. Employer sentiment about wage levels changed little over the half-century of colonial rule. In 1955, the Rural Wages Advisory Board issued a report reverting to the argument that increases in productivity and efficiency should precede an increase in wages or improvement in conditions. The similarity in its theme and recommendations to those of the Barth Commission of 1912-13 was so embarrassing to the government that the report was never published.

59. Depending on the nature of unskilled work, the advantage of greater labour stability differed in different enterprises. In oil mills or timber yards, for example, stability was probably of less importance than in enterprises like tobacco or tea packing, where the greater use of mechanical equipment required a labour force with some experience. Similarly, risky enterprises such as petrol depots, required greater experience and thus a stable labour force.

60. P. Gutkind and I. Wallerstein (eds.): *The political economy of contemporary Africa* (Beverly Hills, Sage Press, 1976), p. 46.

61. The labour shortage up to the 1930s, remedied in the decade of the Depression by both a fall in demand and an increase in supply, re-emerged in the 1940s — particularly in the post-war period — with increased wartime

conscription, a large increase in immigration and, as a result, in the demand for labour — Clayton and Savage, 1974, pp. 110-245. The shortage of the early 1950s was largely artificial and short-lived; the mass repatriation and internment of the Kikuyu, Embu and Meru to their districts during the Mau Mau emergency created first a shortage and then a flood of surplus labour as they returned in 1958 to join the growing ranks of jobseekers.

62. Clayton and Savage, 1974, pp. 148-73; Leys, 1974, pp. 94-5; Kitching, 1980, pp. 274-6.

63. The Carpenter Committee, set up in response to the alarm caused by Mau Mau to investigate African wage levels, recommended a fundamental change in the minimum wage formula from one based on the needs of single males to one based on the needs of family men, to enable workers to maintain their families in the city. The Committee recommended a 'family' minimum wage two and a half times the bachelor rate, accompanied by a similar increase in the housing allowance. Its most controversial proposal was that minimum wage protection be extended to the capitalised agricultural sector. Clayton and Savage, 1974, pp. 374-5 discusses the criticisms the report received from employers opposed to higher wages and the failure to implement the proposals.

64. On the basis of the 1969 census, the ILO projected a 3.3 per cent rate of population growth per annum; the expansion of wage employment was estimated to be 1.9 per cent per year in the 1960s — ILO, 1972, p. 7.

65. Leys, 1974, p. 179.

66. This view — if employment was to be increased, wages had to be held down — was reflected in the tripartite agreements after Independence in 1964, and in 1970, when the government hoped to secure a standstill on wage increases and a ban on strikes — ILO, 1972, pp. 529-43.

67. Kitching, 1980, pp. 289, 380-6.

68. Parkin, 1975, p. 154.

69. Gugler, 1969, p. 146.

70. The ILO report gave an 'approximate' estimate of the size of various income groups, permitting one to estimate the proportion of households constituting the 'working poor' in rural and urban areas — ILO, 1972, p. 74. The 'working poor' were defined as those 'working for excessively low incomes' and the 'modest minimum' as one 'which would generally be considered (i.e. by most people in the country) to correspond to the minimum standard needed to avoid real poverty and deprivation' — ibid., p. 60. The 'working poor' accounted for 62 per cent of the labour force.

71. For discussions of these labour market conditions (high unemployment and wages below the minimum necessary to support a family in town), see ILO, 1972, pp. 60-3; Leys, 1974, pp. 178-83. Leys emphasised that 'wages were clearly based on the assumption that their families produced their own subsistence from cultivation, and as one moves down the scale of wages this assumption becomes more and more obvious' — ibid., p. 183.

72. J.C. Knowles and R. Anker: 'An analysis of income transfers in a developing country: The case of Kenya', in *Journal of Development Economics*, 1981, vol. 8, pp. 205-26.

73. Ibid., p. 223. It is often argued that rural areas are net losers when all income flows are considered — see M. Lipton: 'Migration from rural areas of poor countries: The impact on rural productivity and income distribution', in *World Development*, January 1980, vol. 8, no. 1, pp. 1-24. It has been the conventional wisdom that a high proportion of migrants remit money home, and do so regularly. Johnson and Whitelaw suggested that the average proportion of income remitted was 21 per cent for a 1971 sample of 'low and middle income' earners in Nairobi. In a 1968 survey of recent migrants to eight of Kenya's largest

cities, Rempel, Harris and Todaro obtained an average of 13 per cent. The average income in the former study was 4,938 Kenya shillings per annum, and in the latter 3,969 — both considerably higher than the lowest income group (less than 2,500) in the Knowles and Anker study. If allowance is made for the income differences in the sample populations, the results are broadly consistent. There is a tendency for transfers to increase with income. See G. Johnson and E.W. Whitelaw: 'Urban-rural income transfers in Kenya: An estimated remittance function', in *Economic Development and Cultural Change*, April 1974, vol. 22, no. 3, pp. 473-9; H. Rempel and R. Lobdell: 'The role of urban-to-rural remittances in rural development', in *The Journal of Development Studies*, April 1978, vol. 14, no. 3, pp. 324-41.

74. A. Southall: 'Alur migrants', in *Economic development and cultural change: A study of immigrant labour in Buganda* (Cambridge, Heffer and Sons, 1953); Meillasoux, 1975.

75. Clayton and Savage, 1974, p. 43.

76. Meillassoux, 1975.

77. Compensatory mechanisms include intensification of labour, use of previously unused labour, extension of work periods, more intensive use of land by reducing the fallow period, and co-operative work arrangements.

78. In Ghana and other West African societies, migration was commonly limited to the dry seaon of the domestic agricultural cycle. Cash-crop production and subsistence production with differing cycles permitted the rotation of labour between the two sectors. Reference to some West African examples are contained in E.J. Berg: 'The economics of the migrant labor system', in H. Kuper (ed.): *Urbanization and migration in West Africa* (Berkeley, University of California Press, 1965).

79. Wolff, 1974, p. 97; Clayton and Savage, 1974, p. 25.

80. Leys, 1973, p. 192.

81. Stichter, 1975, p. 27.

82. The practice in most of tropical Africa to take wage employment for some time and then to return to peasant holdings has been termed 'semi-proletarianisation' — G. Arrighi and J.S. Saul: *Essays on the political economy of Africa* (New York and London, Monthly Review Press, 1973), pp. 13-14. Leys suggested that it may be more appropriate to speak of the peasantisation of wage employment rather than the proletarianisation of the peasantry (Leys, 1974, p. 308). The point made in the text differs from these conceptions in that it does not focus exclusively on the dual engagement of males in peasant production and wage labour, but it suggests a differentiation *within* the household, with female labour in peasant production and male labour in wage employment.

83. For an early account of women's predominance in hoe agriculture, see H. Baumann: 'The division of work according to sex in African hoe culture', in *Africa*, 1928, vol. 1, no. 3, pp. 289-319. A more recent analysis based on the *Ethnographic Atlas* suggests that women play a major part in cultivation in 53 per cent of the societies of sub-Saharan Africa — J. Goody and J. Buckley: 'Inheritance and women's labour in Africa', in *Africa*, 1973, vol. 43, no. 2, pp. 108-21.

84. L.S.B. Leakey: *The southern Kikuyu before 1903* (New York, Academic Press, 1977), pp. 10-12.

85. J.M. Fisher: *The anatomy of Kikuyu domesticity and husbandry* (London, Department of Technical Co-operation, 1962), p. 229.

86. Ross, 1968, p. 461.

87. J. Kenyatta: *Facing Mount Kenya: The tribal life of Kikuyu* (Nairobi, AMS Press, 1938), p. 177.

88. W.S. Routledge and K. Routledge: *With a prehistoric people: The*

Kikuyu of East Africa (London, Edward Arnold, 1910), pp. 38-40.

89. Leys, 1974, p. 304.

90. Fisher, 1962, pp. 238, 280; S. Abbot: 'Full-time farmers and weekend wives: Change and stress among rural Kikuyu women' PhD dissertation, University of North Carolina, 1965, p. 28; see also Hay, 1976, Kitching, 1980. In her study of Luo women, Hay suggested that female agricultural labour was intensified only after 1945. Earlier, Luo migration was limited to unmarried males who were relatively uninvolved in domestic agricultural production. Luo patterns of migration were quite atypical in this regard. Also atypical is Hay's suggestion that Luo women reduced their labour in agricultural production and turned increasingly to trading activities. Kitching also noted the intensification of female labour in agriculture. His focus, however, was exclusively on the 'petite bourgeoisie', an exceedingly narrow segment of the population — less than 10 per cent in the colonial period and roughly 15 per cent thereafter — who were in better-paid employment and whose households could depend on remittances to increase the scale of their agricultural output by expanding the area under cultivation and hiring labour to compensate for absent male labour. The emphasis here is on households at the lower end of the wage structure — 85-90 per cent of the population — for whom these were not available options.

91. J. Roscoe: *Twenty-five years in East Africa* (New York, Negro Universities Press, 1969 (1921)), p. 244.

92. Reported by Sir Edward Denham, Acting Governor, in his report entitled, 'Kenya, towns in the native reserves and native development in Kenya', in Clayton and Savage, 1973, p. 162.

93. The first census on the region was taken in 1948. The demographic history of the first half of the twentieth century is thus based on an 'informed guess', according to R.R. Kuczynski: *Demographic survey of the British colonial empire* (London, London University Press, 1948-50), 3 vols. The early decades saw a fall in the African population — Leys, 1974, pp. 297-300; Wolff, 1974, pp. 106-7; Kitching, 1980, p. 21. The beginning of an upward trend is usually dated from about 1923 and is attributed to the gradual spread of modern medicine and a reduction in internecine warfare. Kuczynski estimated the annual rate of growth of the Kikuyu population at about 1.6 per cent in the inter-war decades, attributable to an improvement in rail and road transport that alleviated food scarcities due to drought and reduced famine-related deaths.

94. The Kikuyu, for example, before their restriction to the reserves, moved from north to south, clearing the forest, cultivating the land for a few years, and moving further southward when soil fertility was depleted — Wrigley, 1965.

95. On over-cropping in the Kikuyu reserves and the conditions of agricultural deterioration see M.P.K. Sorrenson: *Land reform in the Kikuyu country: A study in government policy* (Nairobi, Oxford University Press, 1967), pp. 34-47; Wolff, 1974, pp. 141-3; Hay, 1976; Wrigley, 1965, p. 254.

96. Evidence of the declining productivity of smallholder agriculture is fragmentary, as production data are scarce. Declining yields before 1930 and in the 1940s was suggested by Clayton and Savage, 1974, pp. 110, 150, 242; and Hay, 1976. On the causes of low productivity, see H. Fearn: *An African economy: A study of the economic development of the Nyanza Province of Kenya, 1903-1953* (London, Oxford University Press, 1961).

97. A junior official warned of the possible effects of colonial land policy on the Kamba and Kikuyu: 'The native population is increasing rapidly and the reserves will shortly overflow. We shall thus create by degrees a large native pauper population which if brought into existence will become a danger' — cited in Munro, 1975, p. 190.

98. Population growth resulting in increasing landlessness, declining soil

fertility, and growing unemployment also threatened the ability of the reserves to ensure subsistence — Leys, 1974, pp. 63 ff. The attempt to stem this decline in the reserves resulted in the formulation in 1954 of 'A plan to intensify the development of African agriculture in Kenya', better known as the Swynnerton Plan, after its author, the Secretary of Agriculture. It involved consolidating land into single holdings and issuing land titles. The provision of credit lay behind the emphasis on individual tenure. '. . . agricultural credit could hardly be issued to individuals if the title to land was to be vested in some vague entity called the kinship group, the community, or the tribe. Yet credit was essential if farming was to be adequately capitalized and improved' — Sorrenson, 1967, pp. 60-1. By the late 1950s, the programme had been carried through in Kikuyu country. Extension services and credit were provided and the ban on coffee was lifted. The result was a 'dramatic' increase in output from smallholdings — Leys, 1974, p. 53. For the impact of individualisation of land tenure on women, see A.P. Okeyo: 'Daughters of the lakes and rivers: Colonization and the land rights of Luo women', in M. Etienne and E. Leacock (eds.): *Women and colonization: Anthropological perspectives* (New York, Praeger.), 1980), pp. 186-213.

99. Wrigley, 1965, pp. 248-50.

100. Indeed, the extent of government assistance to settlers was among the highest in any colonial experience — Wolff, 1974, p. 88.

101. The 'dual policy' was derived from the 'dual mandate', the idea that 'Europe is in Africa for the mutual benefit of her industrial classes and of the native races in their progress to a higher plain' — F.D. Lugard: *The rise of our East African empire* (London, Blackwood, 1893), vol. 1, p. 617. The origins of the 'dual policy' have also been attributed to non-economic causes. Munro saw it as a response to the public criticism over the colonial government's commitment to settler enterprise and neglect of the indigenous sector — Munro, 1975, p. 186. The 'dual policy' served to maintain this pattern in the intersectoral allocation of resources.

102. Leys, 1973, p. 14; G. Bennett: 'Settlers and politics in Kenya, up to 1945' in Harlow and Chilver, 1965, p. 301; Clayton and Savage, 1974, pp. 150-2; Wrigley, 1965, p. 244; Munro, 1975, p. 167.

103. This is not to suggest that the commercialisation of African agriculture did not occur — only that the process bypassed the large majority of small-scale producers. In an extensive survey of this commercialisation, Kitching outlined the variety in its shape and scale in different parts of the country — Kitching, 1980, pp. 57-107. The mirage created by his account is however dispelled by his remark that only a 'tiny minority' were in this upwardly-mobile category (considerably less than 10 per cent of the population) but that the 'statistical dominance' of the poorer groups 'should not be allowed to mask the structural importance of the elite' — ibid., p. 97.

104. Wolff, 1974, pp. 141-3; Clayton and Savage, 1974, pp. 145-6, 168-9. The use of tax revenues to subsidise the settler economy impeded investment and accumulation in the indigenous sector — Wolff, 1974, p. 143; Munro, 1975, pp. 94-5.

105. Wrigley, 1965, pp. 236-7.

106. Kitching, 1980, p. 73.

107. Ibid., p. 29.

108. The story of mimosa cultivation in Kenya, based on M.P. Cowen's 'Wattle production in the Central Province: Capital and household commodity production, 1903-64', is recounted, in part, in Kitching, 1980, pp. 62 ff., from which this account — different in interpretation to Kitching's — is drawn.

109. Wolff, 1974, p. 82.

110. The 'strangulation' and 'destruction' of domestic production have been suggested by Wolff, Bernstein and Meillassoux — Wolff, 1974, Chapter 5; H

Bernstein: 'African peasantries: A theoretical framework', in *Journal of Peasant Studies*, 1979, vol. 6, no. 4, pp. 421-43; Meillassoux, 1975.

111. Lonsdale and Berman argued that East Africa's forms of production were 'restructured' during the colonial period — J. Lonsdale and B. Berman: 'Coping with the contradictions: The development of the colonial state in Kenya', in *Journal of African History*, 1979, vol. 20, p. 488.

112. The only experiment in peasant production — cotton in Nyanza — was a complete failure and stifled peasant expansion — Lonsdale and Berman, 1979, p. 498.

113. Brett noted that an expatriate farming class was dominant in temperate zones — South Africa, southern Rhodesia, Algeria and the regions of northern Rhodesia, Nyasaland, Tanganyika and Kenya; with some exceptions, cash-crop production by peasants prevailed in the rest of the continent — Brett, 1973, p. 44.

114. The introduction of Indian peasant farmers was considered and a small beginning made, but later discontinued. Indian labour was brought in for the construction of the railway built to establish control over the headwaters of the Nile. Smallholdings, whether Indian or African, were not looked upon as an economically advantageous basis for development. Those in favour of them argued that they were inexpensive, based entirely on household labour, involved little capital and minimum immigration. Proponents also argued that the characteristic feature of the household economy — a fall in price tending to produce more intensive labour and greater output — made it economically promising, implying the applicability of Chayanov's model of the domestic mode of production to African 'primitive agriculturalists'. This was merely the converse of the backward-sloping supply curve of labour argument used by settlers to keep down wages — R.L. Buell: *The native problem in Africa*, vol. I (New York, Macmillan, 1928).

115. Emphasis was placed on the maintenance of traditional authority structures for fear that the breakdown of 'native' institutions might lead to disruption.

116. As one settler stated, 'The ideal reserve is a recruiting ground for labour, a place from which the able-bodied go out to work, returning occasionally to rest and to beget the next generation of labourers' — M.A. Buxton: *Kenya days* (London, Arnold and Co., 1927), p. 10.

117. Munro, 1975, pp. 95-6. In 1927, the Chief Registrar of Natives recorded the percentage of men in wage employment: among the Kikuyu from Kiambu, 73 per cent; among the Kamba of Machakos, 20 per cent — Clayton and Savage, 1974, p. 150.

118. Munro, 1975.

119. Kitching, 1980, p. 55.

120. Leys, 1974, p. 172.

121. A foreign-dominated urban sector, moreover. The growth of commerce and industry and the increase in investment between 1964 and 1970 were entirely foreign-owned and controlled, as were banking, finance, insurance and the tourist trade. Joint ventures between foreign companies and government-owned development corporations were the exception, accounting for about 9 per cent of the equity in new foreign investment — Leys, 1974, pp. 118-47.

122. Various settlement schemes were introduced during the transition to Independence: in 1960 the 'Harambee' (Kenyatta's slogan, roughly translated as 'all pull together') Scheme; in 1961, the Million Acres Scheme; and, in 1965, a Squatter Settlement Scheme. The schemes specified plot size and income for the various social groups. Leys analysed the 'crucial role' of the schemes 'in effecting the transition to political independence without radical economic change' and the role of the high-density settlers, 'drawn from the country's most impoverished and underprivileged classes, yet . . . expected to pay the full cost to Kenya of an asset

transfer which underwrote the profitability of the rest of the economy' — Leys, 1974, pp. 73, 82.

123. About K£20 million was paid to expatriate settlers for land purchase; grants from Britain were supplemented by loans from the World Bank, the Commonwealth Development Corporation, and Britain — J.W. Harbeson: 'Land reforms and politics in Kenya, 1954-70', in *Journal of Modern African Studies*, 1971, vol. 9, no. 2, pp. 231-51.

124. Debt and interest payments were made to the Kenya Government, which in turn paid the British Government, which had bought out the expatriate settlers — Leys, 1974, p. 83. As Leys acerbically points out, referring to the agricultural surplus extraction over several decades, 'If anything was owing to anyone for the land, they might be excused for thinking that they had by and large paid it' — ibid., p. 95.

125. Ibid., pp. 78-83. Kitching estimated that close to one million of 1.2 million smallholdings were untouched by Kenya's so-called 'agrarian revolution'. Despite land reforms and new farm enterprises introduced under settlement schemes, only 12 per cent of land in smallholdings was under high-value cash crops such as maize. Constrained by limited capital resources, these smallholders continued their 'traditional' patterns of land use for basic food crops and pasturage — Kitching, 1980, pp. 315-79. Officially-accepted explanations attributed the causes of agricultural 'backwardness' not to the underlying patterns of resource transfer but to systems of land tenure, or 'values' that emphasise social insurance and the collectivity, inhibiting individual enterprise — See for example, J.C. de Wilde: *Experiences with agricultural development in tropical Africa*, vol. I (Baltimore, Johns Hopkins University Press for IBRD, 1967).

126. F. Furedi: 'The African crowd in Nairobi: Popular movements and elite policies', in *Journal of African History*, 1973, vol. 14, p. 277.

127. Clayton and Savage, 1974, p. 175; Kitching, 1980, p. 50.

128. Clayton and Savage, 1974, p. 363.

129. Clayton and Savage, 1974, p. 129.

130. Middleton, 1965, pp. 346-7.

131. R. Anker and J.C. Knowles: 'Labour force participation of married women in Kenya', in G. Standing and G. Sheehan (eds.): *Labour force participation in low-income countries* (Geneva, ILO, 1978), pp. 144-5.

132. M.H. Ross and T.S. Weisner: 'The rural-urban migrant network in Kenya: Some general implications', in *American Ethnologist*, 1977, vol. 4, no. 2.

133. J.L. Moock: 'The content and maintenance of social ties between urban migrants and their home-based support groups: The Maragoli case', in *African Urban Studies*, Winter 1978-9, vol. 3; Abbot, 1965.

134. Moock, 1978-9, pp. 18-24.

135. Kitching, 1980, p. 387.

136. Abbott, 1965, p. 58.

137. C. Obbo: *African women: Their struggle for economic independence* (London, Zed Press, 1980), p. 75.

138. Ross and Weisner, 1977, p. 365.

139. Parkin, 1975, p. 149.

7

On Circular Migration: From the Distaff Side

CAROL COLFER

I. Introduction[1]

There has been a recent recognition that development efforts have tended to leave women behind, to neglect their interests in favour of men's. A spate of research has been undertaken to decide how best to rectify this situation. Some of this has shown that in the tropics, food production is very often primarily the responsibility of women and that men are often absent from villages for long periods engaging in wage labour.[2] These two factors constitute a potent argument in favour of providing agricultural services, inputs and knowledge to *women* farmers, particularly in light of various credible predictions about coming global food shortages.

The analysis reported here was undertaken because of the paucity of data available on the specifics of male circular migration (or migration with the intent to return home) and its impact on the women who remain in the villages tending the farm. Partially because of the difficulty of studying such topics with the data available from traditional censuses, there is very little information available on traditional patterns of circular migration, and even less on its impact on the home communities and on women's roles.[3] The pattern of male absence and regular female productive activity[4] among the Kenyah of East Kalimantan (Indonesian Borneo) presented in this paper, suggests that increased efforts must be undertaken to provide agricultural aid to the people who are steadily and reliably involved in food production: the women.

My overall purpose in presenting these findings is, first, to indicate the context and importance of circular migration in Kenyah tradition; second, to show the implications of such migration for women's productivity and general competence at subsistence; and third, to provide a better understanding of the changes in circular migration patterns as the people have moved out of the remote interior to areas that have better access to cities and sources of wage employment.

1. Research Context

The research reported here was conducted within the framework of a project entitled 'Interactions between People and Forests in East Kalimantan', began in October 1979, and was designed to gather ecological and ethnographic information of relevance to policy-makers in the area. Our research design differed from a standard ethnographic approach in that we first isolated problematic human actions, such as 'cutting down the forest', or, more specifically, 'illegally removing ironwood', and then data collection was organised around these actions. So the community was not the unit of study, though participant observation within a community provided the starting point for the research. The interacting causes and effects of relevance to the particular action under study were then traced outward as far as possible, leading to nearby lumber camps where wage-labour opportunities were available, to the provincial capital where timber-related decisions were made, to the international timber market where prices were determined. This strategy, reported in more detail elsewhere, proved a very productive one.[5] The relevance of this particular study of circular migration related to the possible fertility-regulation functions of such migration, possible importance of frequent male absence for female status and productive activity in the forest, and the frequent involvement of male circular migrants in forest-clearing activity.,

Our research approach was implemented in four settings:

— the Apo Kayan, a remote interior region near the Malaysian border, where Kenyah Dayaks practise a relatively traditional form of shifting cultivation;
— the Telen River basin, a lowland area closer to the coast, where Kenyah Dayaks practise a transitional mix of shifting cultivation, wage labour and trade;

— the Samarinda-Balikpapan Road, a coastal boom area subject to a large influx of migrants from other regions;
— a mobile investigation of the riverine marketing system for minor forest products.

The research involved a ten-month ethnographic study of the Uma' Jalan Kenyah River, as well as a one-month visit to these people's home village, Long Ampung in the Apo Kayan.

2. Long Ampung — The Remote Interior

Long Ampung is a village of approximately 500 Uma' Jalan Kenyah Dayaks who live in five longhouses clustered along the Kayan River. Journeys out of Long Ampung are by foot or by canoe, though an airstrip is under construction. A day's walk upstream and downstream are small airstrips serviced sporadically by Mission Aviation Fellowship, a Christian missionary air service; but use of the plane is expensive and access uncertain. Almost all needs are met locally, with the exception of goods carried home on men's backs in arduous foot and canoe journeys lasting one to three months.

The Apo Kayan region, where Long Ampung is located, is a sparsely populated, tropical rainforest characterised by biotic diversity, hilly topography, and many rivers. In the late 1960s and 1970s, because of its inaccessibility, the Indonesian Government followed a policy of encouraging resettlement of the Dayaks in lowland areas closer to the coast, government services, and markets. But military concerns have gained pre-eminence in the past few years, and there has been an attempt to persuade the local population to remain in the area for reasons of border security.

Beginning in 1963, a group of Long Ampung's people decided to move down into the lowland regions. A small group of about 15 men and women made a trek down towards the coast and chose Long Segar as the site for a new village. Between 1963 and 1972, many more people came from Long Ampung, resulting in a Long Segar population (including natural increase) of about 1,000 in 1982. In the same period groups moved to other sites closer to the coast, resulting in six satellite villages.[6] Discussions with old people suggest that prior to government attempts to stabilise the area's population, beginning in the 1920s with Dutch and Christian missionary penetration, the people moved more frequently. Better and more land, increased availability of game, bad omens or fires in current dwellings, and a desire to rejoin loved ones, were common reasons for moving. The major current reason is better access to trade goods, education, and medical services in the lowland regions. 'Push' reasons expressed for leaving Long Ampung during the past two decades include a reduction in the availability of accessible fertile land (phrased as 'having to walk too far to our ricefield'), religious differences, conflict over rights to a honey tree and a related political dispute, and the comparatively hard life in the remote interior.[7]

3. Long Segar — A Village in Transition

Long Segar is on the Telen River, only two days and nights by riverboat, ten hours by speedboat, or half an hour by plane from the provincial capital (Samarinda). Education, some medical care, trade goods, markets, wage labour and usable land are all available in the near vicinity. Rice hullers, outboard motors, and chainsaws greatly reduce the amount of human energy required for subsistence (as well as significantly increasing the disruptive human impact on the surrounding forests).[8]

Like Long Ampung, Long Segar is in a tropical rainforest. The forest is less diverse biotically there, the landscape is flatter, the weather hotter, and floods and short-term droughts represent more significant dangers to crops. A multinational timber company holds a 20-year lease for timber harvesting of the primary forest in which Long Segar is located. The people have so far been able to co-exist fairly amicably with the company, despite the fact that Kenyah subsistence relies on swidden cultivation — a practice that does not endear them to timber companies generally.

The Indonesian Government's Directorate General of Forestry designated Long Segar a formal resettlement project in 1972, along with Long Noran (an Uma' Kulit Kenyah village half an hour downstream) and Kernyanyan (a neighbouring Muslim Kutai village). This made the population eligible for various kinds of government assistance, including money, materials and tools for house construction, extension services, additional schoolteachers and various agricultural inputs and training. And it made them comply with various government regulations, such as a particular village layout and specifications for individual houses rather than longhouses.[9]

4. Methods

Participant observation was the primary method used in the Long Segar study, but a variety of more focused and quantitative studies was undertaken, as appropriate directions and important information needs were assessed. The frequency with which men left the village, the impact of this on the lives of the women (including their increased involvement in rice and vegetable production and an expected lowered fertility), and the potential impact on the forests all prompted an investigation into male migration.

The complexity of the factors influencing human interaction with the forests, coupled with a desire to address a variety of these factors, precluded a full-scale investigation of migration *per se*. The topic was considered in the context of a complete household survey, which included additional interviews with all adult women in both Long Segar and Long Ampung. The household survey included enumeration of all household members by age and sex, reproductive histories of all women, and a variety of agricultural, medical, and mortality questions. The women's interview schedule included a number of questions on decision-making (agricultural, migration, financial), reproductive preferences and attitudes about birth control, and complete migration histories of all their husbands.

The household and women's interview schedules were both pre-tested and revised twice, in Long Segar before the survey was launched, in Long Ampung in May and June 1980. The only adjustment, deriving from a difference in the Long Ampung conditions, was that two financial decision-making questions had to be reworded slightly, since money was very rarely used, in contrast to the situation in Long Segar.[10]

The purpose of the interviews was explained to the people of Long Ampung at a meeting of all household heads on the veranda of a longhouse, by Lee Ndjau (the project's Kenyah research assistant, born in Long Ampung, resident of Long Segar) and by myself, and we conducted all interviews in people's homes or on the verandas of the longhouses, in the Kenyah language. The people of Long Segar were already familiar with the research and its goals, so no special meeting was called. Lee Ndjau conducted interviews in Long Segar in June and July 1980.

Adult women were defined as women who had ever been

married, had a child, or who were generally considered old enough to be married. In Long Segar, 3.5 per cent of the women interviewed were between 15 and 19 years of age; and in Long Ampung, 12.5 per cent were in that age range. This difference reflects more unmarried motherhood in Long Ampung, as well as the effects of higher educational opportunities (grades 7-9) in Long Segar than in Long Ampung. At the other extreme, 25.3 per cent in Long Segar and 23.2 per cent in Long Ampung were aged 50 or over.

All interviews were conducted in the Uma' Jalan Kenyah language. The fact that Lee Ndjau was a popular, native son whom the people of Long Ampung had not seen in nine years, who brought news of loved ones in Long Segar, and who was committed to getting accurate research results proved invaluable.[11]

Migration histories were recorded on an eight-lined form with columns to indicate the relevant husband, when he went, where he went, what he did there, how long he was gone, what he took with him to sell, and what he brought home. The same questions were asked with regard to the previous year, in order to ascertain any differences in the present patterns in Long Ampung and Long Segar.

Most women were able to specify lengths of absence, destinations, kinds of work, and what the husbands brought home; but attempts to pinpoint years in which trips were taken were singularly unsuccessful. Dates carry little significance among the Kenyah. I was able to reconstruct enough dates, however, to ascertain that the pattern of circular migration was a longstanding, continuous one.

I succumbed to the temptation to ask several attitudinal questions that I would normally eschew, being somewhat sceptical about the reliability and interpretation of responses to queries of that sort. Two open-ended questions fell into this category: 'How is life when your husband is not here?' and 'How is it when your husband goes on an expedition? Do you help decide? Does he insist?' The yes-no question, 'Do you help decide how to use the money/things your husband gets from his own work?' also falls into this category. Since the responses to these questions conformed to my expectations based on participant observation, I report them here.

II. Circular Migration — Kenyah Style

The Uma' Jalan Kenyah recognise and discuss five major categories of human movement: *tuya*, *nuo'*, *tudo*, *tai selai* and *bolak*, each of which is discussed below in order to place circular migration, or *tai selai*, in perspective.[12]

Tuya requires leaving the house to engage in an activity with an uncertain economic pay-off. Hunting, fishing and looking for fruit in the forest are all *tuya* and carry elements of risk and some connotation of enjoyment.

Nuo' requires leaving the village for the day to engage in an activity with a very probable economic pay-off, like rice cultivation, gardening or wage labour.

Tudo refers to sleeping away from the village. It is most commonly done during busy agricultural seasons when people stay for a week or more at a time in their ricefields. However, staying overnight at a friend's house or a two-day hunting trip also qualify as *tudo*.

Tai selai, the form of movement with which this paper is concerned, is circular migration.[13] People, usually men, leave the village for extended periods, essentially in search of fame and fortune (most particularly crucial supplies to supplement what is available locally), with the intention of returning home.

Bolak is a permanent change of residence. Long Segar's residents' recent move from Long Ampung is representative of this category of movement. A few of the oldest residents of Long Ampung were born in Long Anye, about half an hour down the Kayan River from Long Ampung. In the mid-1960s, the whole village of Long Ampung moved back to Long Anye for one year, in an attempt to fool some evil spirits which had been bothering the people. Oldsters maintain that prior to the coming of the Dutch, who held a preference for settled peoples (1920s), major moves (*bolak*) were more common. Interview data on population movements from Lepo' Bem, Lepo' Tau, and Uma' Tukung Kenyah corroborate the ubiquity of this pattern in the region.

There is a sixth element of movement typically ascribed to the Kenyah, deriving from their practice of shifting cultivation. A common assumption — erroneous — is that if their fields 'shift', so must they. In reality, their dwellings are strong, well-built and intended to last many years. The relatively stable residential units are surrounded by a shifting patchwork of ricefields, secondary forest in various stages of regeneration, and primary forest.

Circular migration was traditionally surrounded by a host of customs and beliefs which were to some extent discarded with the people's conversion to Christianity, culminating in the 1960s. Prior to the arrival of the Dutch in the interior of Borneo in the early decades of this century, the Kenyah were fierce and wide-ranging head-hunters (as were the other ethnic groups in the area). Present-day Kenyah reminisce, somewhat sheepishly, about the exploits of their grandfathers, recounting tales of trips to distant places in search of heads. But the missionaries arrived, with the Dutch administrators, and Borneo was 'tamed'. The taming apparently, however, did not diminish the Kenyah males' sojourns out into the wider world. The Kenyah went to work for the Dutch as 'coolies'; they travelled into Malaysia to work on plantations and in timber camps; and during the Second World War they went to Irian Jaya (New Guinea), conscripted by the Japanese.

The most common reason for these journeys has traditionally been to procure goods that cannot be produced locally. Now these are cloth, tobacco, kerosene, sugar, guns, cooking-pots, and most importantly, *salt*. *Uman usen* is the name of the ritual, male get-together held on the return of a group of circular migrants, the purpose of which is to share the highlights and mishaps of the journey with those men who have stayed behind. *Uman usen* means 'to eat salt'. Salt is and has been the gold of the Apo Kayan.

But besides the persistent economic necessity for men to leave the Apo Kayan, there is an important symbolic reason. Being male and going on expeditions have long been linked. Expeditions have provided the opportunities for ambitious men to prove their courage and competence and to make a name for themselves throughout the region. Though few activities are the particular province of one sex or the other among the Kenyah, males are regularly associated with bravery and expedition-making, as females are reputed to be hardworking, rice cultivators. The importance of these affective aspects associated with human movements is discussed further in Peterson's forthcoming study of the Agta of the Philippines.

The current circular migration pattern in Long Ampung is essentially a traditional one. Groups of men regularly leave the Apo Kayan in search of trade goods and consumables. A group of about 15 men and one woman had just returned from a year-long expedition to Malaysia at the time of the survey there in May and June 1980. In April 1981, Lee Ndjau returned to gather more data, and found about 50 men gone. Their exact destinations and routes were variable.[14]

The Uma' Jalan Kenyah rarely take anything to trade other than their labour when they leave home. But Peluso and Jessup note a significant increase in expeditions made by the nearby Uma' Tukung Kenyah in 1979 and 1980, in response to the high Malaysian price they could obtain for the locally-available aloe wood.[15] Jessup, writing about the Uma' Tukung village, Long Sungai Barang (population c. 363), says: 'During the rice harvest in March 1980 . . . 55 men — about 65 per cent of the adult male population — were away from the village, in Sarawak (Malaysia) or on the Mahakam.'[16]

Circular migrants do a variety of kinds of work, including clearing plantations, logging, tapping rubber, planting and harvesting cash crops, making bricks, and collecting minor forest products, most of which are done in basically rural environments. Their visits to cities are usually brief and for the procurement of goods to bring home.

As a result of these sojourns out of the village, Kenyah men obtain various kinds of new information that they make available to other villagers. I found Kenyah villagers to be far more sophisticated and knowledgeable about technological advances and world events (for example, knowing about American kissing contests, Mohammad Ali, and trips to the moon, as well as more practical things like new methods of rice cultivation and the dangers of exploding 'empty' pressurised containers) than were the more sedentary villagers with whom I have worked and talked in the Middle East.

In Long Segar, the transitional village, the pattern of circular migration is somewhat different, with men going alone or in groups of two or three more often than in large groups. Long Segar men most typically work in the timber industry or on plantations, and tend to go for shorter periods to other parts of Indonesia.

Table 7.1 shows the destinations aggregated for all husbands of each woman, in both Long Segar and Long Ampung. The shift from Malaysian to Indonesian destinations, with the move to Long Segar, is even clear in these data, which include a great deal of life experience reported in Long Segar, but actually occurring in Long Ampung. The reason for this shift is that convenient transportation to Indonesia's lumber camps, factories, cities, and other islands is available from Long Segar, making the long trek to Malaysia by foot and canoe, with the accompanying potential for border problems, unnecessary.

Table 7.1: *Destinations for All Husbands of Each Woman, Long Segar and Long Ampung*

Destination	Long Segar		Long Ampung	
	No.	%	No.	%
Malaysia only	13	(5.7)	37	(33.0)
Indonesia only	110	(48.0)	9	(8.0)
Both	87	(38.0)	48	(42.9)
Not applicable[a]	14	(6.1)	18	(16.1)
Missing	5	(2.2)	—	—
Total	229		112	

Note: a. This includes both women who had no husband and husbands who never left home.

The destinations of husbands in 1979-80 were also recorded, in an attempt to portray more clearly the differences in current patterns of migration behaviour in the two communities. Table 7.2 shows that a higher percentage of women in Long Segar had circular migrant husbands in that year (36.2 per cent) compared to women in Long Ampung (20.6 per cent). The predominance of Indonesian destinations from Long Segar and Malaysian destinations from Long Ampung is also striking.

In fact, the ease of transportation from Long Segar has resulted in many more women leaving the village to go on expeditions themselves. In both villages women leave to seek medical attention if they are seriously ill, but they also occasionally accompany an expedition of men, particularly prior to marriage or the conception of children. There were several women, for instance, on the expedition that came down out of the Apo Kayan to Long Segar in 1963 in search of a place to resettle. In Long Segar, 50.2 per cent of the women reported having made a long trip, whereas only 12.5 per cent of the Long Ampung women had ever done so.

Table 7.2: *Destinations for Trips in 1979-80 from Long Segar and Long Ampung*

Destination	Long Segar		Long Ampung	
	No.	%	No.	%
Malaysia only	1	(0.4)	18	(16.1)
Indonesia only	82	(35.8)	5	(4.5)
Not applicable[a]	144	(62.9)	88	(78.6)
Missing	2	(0.9)	1	(0.9)
Total	229		112	

Note: a. This includes both women with no husband and those with husbands who did not leave home in 1979-80.

About 10 per cent of the women of Long Segar and about 8 per cent of the women of Long Ampung had experienced at least one husband's death on an expedition, or a failure to return. In Long Segar, 83 per cent of the women reported that all their husbands who had gone had returned, while 5.7 per cent reported no husbands having gone on an expedition. In Long Ampung all the migratory husbands of 71.4 per cent of the women returned, while 20.5 per cent either never had any husbands who had left or were awaiting an expected return.

Table 7.3 shows the total number of trips taken by all the husbands of each woman. The difference in the mean number of trips per husband (3.7 in Long Segar and 2.3 in Long Ampung) reflects the changes that occurred with the move to Long Segar. Traditionally, because of the necessity to cover great distances, through difficult terrain on foot, expeditions were almost never shorter than three months, and more typically lasted a year or more. Men went in groups and returned in groups, choosing a leader from among the traditional aristocracy (*Paren*).[17] The leader chose the route, secured work for group members at their destination, and was generally responsible for their wellbeing.

Although the prior importance of this pattern of circular migration is observable in Long Segar, important contextual differences exist. Long Segar is located within one foreign timber concession and is a half-hour by outboard-motor-driven canoe from another; wage-labour opportunities are also available a half-hour upstream at a pilot plantation project being undertaken by a

Table 7.3: *Number of Trips Taken by All Husbands of Each Woman, Long Segar and Long Ampung*

Number of trips	Women of Long Segar No.	%	Women of Long Ampung No.	%
0[a]	14	(6.1)	18	(16.1)
1	31	(13.5)	34	(30.4)
2	34	(14.8)	24	(21.4)
3	37	(16.2)	14	(12.5)
4	43	(18.8)	8	(7.1)
5	17	(7.4)	7	(6.3)
6	12	(5.2)	2	(1.8)
7	8	(3.5)	3	(2.7)
8	19	(8.3)[b]	—	—
9	3	(1.3)	1	(0.9)
10	2	(0.9)	1	(0.9)
13	1	(0.4)	—	—
[c]	8	(3.5)	—	—
	229		112	
Mean =	3.7 trips		2.3 trips	

Notes: a. Includes women whose husbands had not made any expeditions, and women who had not married. b. The interview form had eight lines, which may account for the over-representation here. c. Missing data.

foreign aid mission; and urban opportunities are available a couple of days downstream in Samarinda. Transport is not much of a problem, compared to the Long Ampung situation, so 'expeditions' take a form much more familiar in the circular migration literature.[18] Men go for shorter periods, returning home more frequently.

In the immediate Long Segar area, people of both sexes can work for an hourly wage of Rp. 1,000-1,500 per day doing agricultural labour, either for individuals or for the pilot plantation.[19] This rate is however considered to be very low, and those who are able to do so prefer to arrange contracts to supply such commodities as lumber, stakes, or rattan to passing longboats. The production of lumber is the most profitable option, bringing in Rp. 15,000 per cubic metre in the provincial capital of Samarinda. However, there is no mill in the area; such lumber is produced by very careful use of a chainsaw, meaning that only a few men are strong and skilled enough to take advantage of this income-earning opportunity.

Kenyah maintain they do not like selling stakes and rattan, and indeed other ethnic groups tend to monopolise the trade in these commodities. But Kenyah of both sexes do engage in the collection of rattan or the production of ironwood stakes when they are in need of money (or for home use).

Most Kenyah who work for the foreign timber compnay — all men — do so on a subcontracting basis as loggers. By working very hard they bring home as much as Rp. 150,000 in a month — though such loggers maintain that no one can sustain such a level of energy expenditure for more than a few months. There seems to be an informal agreement between the timber company and the local Kenyah that permanent employment of Kenyah is not mutually advantageous. The Kenyah maintain that the money they would receive (Rp. 800 per day) does not make their absence from home worthwhile, and they do not consider the timber company's daily wage to be worth the constraints on their freedom that go with regular daily employment. The timber company personnel maintain that Kenyah are unreliable workers because, being so close to home, they respond to the agricultural labour requirements during harvests and forest-clearing times by not coming to work. Instead the timber company prefers to hire Bugis, Banjars, and other ethnic groups from more distant parts of Indonesia. Interestingly, Peloso (personal communication, 1982) found the same reasoning applied in Malaysia, with companies preferring Indonesian Kenyah workers because, being far from home, they did not quit when the agricultural cycle required labour on their farms.[20]

III Meanwhile Back at the Farm . . .

Globally, knowledge of the impact of male migration on women left behind is beginning to accumulate. The literature consistently emphasises the hardships such migration puts on the women. Mullane's comments, for instance, are typical:

> In common with women throughout the developing world, the Jamaican farm woman is finding her resources dwindling while responsibilities mount. She is expected to feed and care for her

family, see to education when it is possible, and grow crops to sell and eat too, when there is enough. If her man is working abroad, she waits for what little money he can send home.[21]

Buvinic, Youssef and von Elm similarly stress the negative:

> The international data is [sic] compelling in showing the linkage between female family headship and poverty. It is women among the poor, be it in Central and South America, in sub-Saharan and North Africa, in Asia, who are increasingly becoming the sole or main economic provider of their families. In almost all these societies, this group of women are ill-prepared to assume such responsibility.[22]

Similar attention to the disadvantages of male migration can be found throughout the literature on this topic.[23]

However, in Long Segar, where I resided most of my time in Kalimantan, I was struck more by the general competence of women in providing the needs of their families than by the difficulties they experienced in their husband's absence. Indeed, my observations suggested that Kenyah women are not ill-prepared to deal with such responsibilities, and generally take on the additional work with good humour and aplomb. One could argue that this may have been a bit of showmanship (sic) for a guest/foreigner; however, living with two wives of circular migrants and observing many others on a daily basis over a 10-month period convinced me that I was not witnessing a drama staged for my benefit.

Additional, more verifiable evidence in support of women's competence included the fact that Kenyah women, unlike women in many places, continue to have equal access to farming land; they are socialised from early childhood to be involved in rice and vegetable production; they are used to making many kinds of decisions; they are knowledgeable about traditional agricultural practices, and can perform almost all the necessary stages in the agricultural cycle; and they expect to have to manage on their own from time to time.

It is not my intention to convey an overly rosy picture of life for women whose husbands are away. As can be seen in the ensuing discussion, there are certainly difficulties for women alone. However, my purpose is to provide a more balanced view, and to show some of the capabilities these women have that might be utilised in their husbands' absence.

In this section and the next, besides demonstrating the ubiquity of male circular migration, and the difficulties women experience as a result of it, I hope to convey something of the sense of independence and autonomy that Kenyah women manifest. The hardships women endure, like the problems encountered by men on their expeditions, are a source of pride and self-respect, proving competence and the ability to survive under adverse conditions. Independence, autonomy, competence — these are the traits that are important to identify and emphasise if we are concerned with development within a participatory framework.[24]

In some of the literature on circular migration, women's loneliness has been stressed as a major problem while husbands are away.[25] Kenyah ostensibly normally marry for love, so that women could be expected to miss their husbands. However, there is a definite reluctance to acknowledge missing one's husband. In numerous spheres, the Kenyah seemed to approach life with a more positive attitude than do Americans and Middle-Easterners, laughing at relatively major mishaps, dismissing minor problems with 'it doesn't matter' or 'don't worry', rarely complaining, and so on. Their response to the loneliness engendered by circular migration is no exception.

One factor that surely helped mitigate this problem was the integration of, and support available from, other members of the community. Different 'boundaries' relating to the continuum of physical expressiveness, from innocent touches to sexual intercourse, may also make apartness less difficult. Although sexual intercourse is forbidden between people who are not married, close friends of opposite sexes can sleep together, massage each other, and generally engage in a good bit of roughhousing that would definitely fit into an American's category of 'sexual behaviour'.

I was unable to ascertain any negative impact of paternal absence on the children. The Kenyah's kinship classification system involves categorising all male relatives one generation up as 'father' (*amai*). Of course, children know who their 'real' fathers are, but uncles make excellent father substitutes, often even living in the same household. Nor do the Kenyah have an authoritarian system of child-raising. There is a general expectation that children will respect their elders, and those who are not respectful meet with disapproval on all sides. But young children are allowed to run free; and only as they begin to approach puberty are they expected to contribute substantially to agricultural and household work. At this point they have a vested interest in appearing hardworking and easy to live with, since these are important traits that both potential marriage partners and the parents of such partners are seeking. Although marriages are based on mutual attraction, parents can apply strong pressures if they consider the chosen bride or groom to be genuinely unsuitable — lazy or difficult to live with. Disciplining of children seems to be as much in the hands of mothers, elder siblings, grandparents, and other community members as in the hands of fathers, and, on a daily basis, one actually observes very little disciplinary action directed at children.

I mentioned earlier my reservations about such attitudinal questions as 'How is life when your husband is away?' (*dalau taki ko' ra'un, kompin ga' pengudip kem panak*?) However, recognising that many researchers use this kind of data, the responses to this question are presented in Table 7.4. Here, 'difficult' usually meant a litany of the problems of building fences, fieldhuts, taking care of sick children, and being solely responsible for family subsistence and wellbeing. The simple statement that life was good (*tiga*) or an emphasis on the woman's ability to manage alone were categorised as 'good'. 'So-so' was used when the woman either mentioned both good and bad aspects, or modified their assessment (for example, not too bad, or good

Table 7.4: *Quality of Life in Husbands' Absence*

Quality	Women of Long Segar No.	%	Women of Long Ampung No.	%
Difficult	118	(51.5)	76	(67.9)
Good	57	(24.9)	18	(16.1)
So-so	29	(12.7)	5	(4.5)
Lonely	6	(2.6)	—	—
NA or missing	19	(8.3)	13	(11.6)
	229		112	

enough). A few young women mentioned missing their husbands, and these were called 'lonely'.

The greater proportion of Long Ampung women reporting a difficult life in their husband's absence may reflect the far more physically strenuous lifestyle in the Apo Kayan, where human energy is only supplemented by additional human labour. The availability of chainsaws and outboard motors in Long Segar renders certain repetitive agricultural tasks less consuming of human time and less exhausting.[26] This may, in effect, make male help from kin and friends more available to Long Segar women, even when their husbands are gone.

The kinds of difficulties women mentioned experiencing when their husbands were gone were predominantly related to agricultural labour, with tree-felling and fence and fieldhut construction most commonly mentioned. Many women also mentioned the difficulties of transporting small children to the fields, or caring for them when sickness struck. Women with no small children or who lived in extended families found their husband's absence least inconvenient. Women sometimes mentioned the perceived fertility-regulating effect of male circular migration, always with appreciation.[27]

Among the Kenyah, rice cultivation and gardening were recognised as critical features of a woman's role, just as expedition-making was seen as a predominantly male symbol. Men were also involved in agricultural endeavours, but a variety of kinds of study, using differing methods, showed women to be more central to the agricultural sphere.[28] Traditional male involvement in expedition-making was functionally congruent with the Kenyah emphasis on women's productive activity in agriculture.

Kenyah women found themselves alone by means of divorce, widowhood, or circular migration. In Long Segar, 3.9 per cent of the women were divorced, the comparable figure for Long Ampung being 2.7 per cent, while widowhood accounted for a larger percentage of women without husbands: 18.3 per cent in Long Segar and 10.7 per cent in Long Ampung.

The fact that men are very involved in circular migration soon becomes obvious to the participant observer, and is shown in Tables 7.5-7.9. Table 7.5 presents the number of husbands each woman reported having engaged in circular migration. The fact that more of the husbands in Long Ampung had never gone on an expedition reflects the greater difficulty of undertaking such an activity from the Apo Kayan as compared to Long Segar. The higher percentage of women reporting only one husband having gone from Long Segar may reflect the recent Kenyah acceptance of Christian teaching on the unacceptability of divorce, combined with an older adult female population in Long Ampung.

Table 7.5: *Number of Husbands Each Woman Reported Being Involved in Circular Migration*

Number of husbands making expeditions	Women in Long Segar No.	%	Women in Long Ampung No.	%
0[a]	15	(6.6)	18	(16.1)
1	180	(78.6)	83	(74.1)
2	25	(10.9)	10	(8.9)
3	2	(0.9)	1	(0.9)
4	1	(0.4)	—	—
[b]	6	(2.6)	—	—
	229		112	
Mean	1.4 husbands		1.4 husbands	

Notes: a. Includes women not yet married or who had never had a husband go on an expedition. b. Missing data.

Table 7.6 presents the time in years that women were alone due to circular migration in the two communities. The absences of all the husbands of any woman were combined, reflecting the total time each woman lived alone expecting a husband to return. Because of a certain arbitrariness about deciding when a man was no longer expected to return, the absences of men whom villagers considered permanent migrants were not included in these calculations, nor were those of men who died while on an expedition. Table 7.8 (discussed later) presents similar data by age. The data for Long Segar, of course, include many years of life experienced in Long Ampung, prior to the move to Long Segar. The time in total years women lived alone in the two communities do not appear to differ substantially.

In an attempt to ascertain differences in current patterns between the two communities and to tease out differences in duration of trips, the data portrayed in Table 7.7 were collected.

Table 7.6: *Time in Years Women Alone Due to Circular Migration*

Years women alone	Women of Long Segar No.	%	Women of Long Ampung No.	%
1	56	(24.5)	24	(21.4)
2	39	(17.0)	18	(16.1)
3	32	(14.0)	17	(15.2)
4	26	(11.4)	12	(10.7)
5	13	(5.7)	5	(4.5)
6	8	(3.5)	3	(2.7)
7	5	(2.2)	4	(3.6)
8	8	(3.5)	5	(4.5)
9	2	(0.9)	2	(1.8)
10	3	(1.3)	—	—
11	5	(2.2)	3	(2.7)
(out of range)[a]	32	(14.0)	19	(17.0)
	229		112	
Mean	3.3 years		3.1 years	

Note: a. Includes women not yet married, and those whose husbands made no expeditions, whose husbands were gone longer than 11 years, and those with missing data.

Table 7.7 shows the time husbands were gone in the 12 months preceding the survey (June-July 1980). Setting aside the large percentages making no trips that year, the largest category in Long Segar consists of husbands gone for one month (18.3 per cent). In Long Ampung the largest category (15.2 per cent) consists of those absent for the full year.

The current Long Segar pattern is for men to go alone or in small groups of two or three. However, larger groups of men were still sometimes organised to work on a subcontracting basis arranged by an entrepreneurial Kenyah villager — just as in the days of old. These more frequent but shorter trips were easier on the women because the men's presence in the village could often be arranged during the busiest agricultural seasons. The villagers joked somewhat forlornly about their increased fertility as a result of more frequent conjugal togetherness.

Table 7.8 provides the preliminary results of an on-going attempt to understand the relationship between male absence and

Table 7.7: *Time Husbands Gone in Months, 1979-80*

Number of months husbands gone	Women of Long Segar No.	%	Women of Long Ampung No.	%
0[a]	145	(63.3)	88	(78.6)
1	42	(18.3)	3	(2.7)
2	18	(7.9)	2	(1.8)
3	7	(3.1)	—	—
4	—	—	—	—
5	—	—	—	—
6	3	(1.3)	1	(0.9)
7	2	(0.9)	—	—
8	2	(0.9)	—	—
9	—	—	—	—
10	1	(0.4)	—	—
11	—	—	—	—
12	6	(2.6)	17	(15.2)
	3	(1.3)	—	—
	229		112	
Mean number of months (of those who were gone)	2.8		9.4	

Notes: a. 0 includes women not yet married or whose husbands did not go on any trips in 1979-80. b. Missing data.

fertility. The amount of time the husbands were gone can be contrasted with the number of children ever born, broken down by five-year age-groups. The pattern mentioned earlier of women marrying and reproducing later in Long Segar is reflected in the small number of Long Segar respondents in the youngest age category.

The 45-49 age-category in Long Segar, when contrasted with adjoining age-groups, provides the most interesting hint for further analysis. The men were gone more and fertility was lower. These are the women who would have been 30-35 during the exodus to Long Segar and during the Indonesian-Malaysian problems. Their husbands would still have been within the age-range (approximately 20-40) when men are most active in circular migration.

The people of Long Segar and Long Ampung remember the long absence of their men trapped in Malaysia during the

Table 7.8: *Fertility and Circular Migration, 1980*

Age-group of women	Mean time gone in years of husbands	No. of women	Children ever born	No. of women
Long Segar				
15-19	1.1	(8)	0.5	(8)
20-24	1.3	(29)	1.8	(30)
25-29	1.7	(31)	3.2	(32)
30-34	2.3	(29)	4.3	(32)
35-39	2.4	(22)	6.0	(24)
40-44	4.5	(24)	7.2	(27)
45-49	5.8	(15)	6.0	(18)
50+	4.4	(53)	7.2	(58)
Mean	3.1	(211)	5.1	(229)
Long Ampung				
15-19	0.7	(14)	1.1	(14)
20-24	1.9	(11)	1.6	(11)
25-29	2.6	(12)	3.2	(12)
30-34	2.6	(14)	3.1	(15)
35-39	2.6	(10)	6.0	(10)
40-44	4.3	(15)	6.1	(15)
45-49	3.9	(8)	6.2	(9)
50+	3.8	(26)	6.6	(26)
Mean	2.9	(100)	4.4	(112)

Confrontation. But Whittier, reporting on Long Nawang, a Lepo' Tau Kenyah village a day's journey down the Kayan River from Long Ampung, found a somewhat different situation:

> During the Confrontation, travel ceased and no trade took place. At the end of Confrontation, the Lepo' Tau had been without trade goods for several years except for the salt dropped in by the army. Massive expeditions set off for Sarawak, leaving Long Nawang a village of women, children and elderly. A labour shortage resulted and rice crops were poor. In 1970 large numbers of men returned home putting a bigger drain on already meagre rice supplies.[29]

Scattergrams were constructed correlating the number of adult person years (age minus 14) lived alone with the number of children ever born for women in both communities, by five-year age-groups. Interestingly, none of the correlations was particularly high, and indeed most showed a slightly positive relationship between number of years alone and number of children born!

Table 7.9 provides the best indicator of the actual percentage of adult time women spent without their husbands. The amount of time all of a woman's husbands were gone was divided by the woman's age minus 14. Age minus 14 gives a rough indication of the time the woman was exposed to the possibility of having a husband gone. The data were grouped into three age-groups: 15-29, 30-49, 50+. Differences in the experience of the youngest age-group can be said to represent differences in the traditional and transitional settings, since the oldest members of that age-group would have been just barely old enough to be exposed to a husband's absence when Long Segar was first settled. As can be seen, the young women in the traditional village were experiencing *more* male absence than were the young women in Long Segar. This finding has bearing on Zelinsky's widely-publicised mobility transition hypothesis: 'There are definite, patterned regularities in the growth of personal mobility through time-space during recent history, and these regularities comprise an essential component of the modernization process.'[30] Clearly, in East Kalimantan there had been changes in the pattern of personal mobility but there did not seem to be a general *growth* in personal mobility.

Table 7.9: *Percentage of Women's Adult Life When Husbands Were Gone*

Age of women	Long Segar		Long Ampung	
	%	No.	%	No.
15-29	17	68	22	37
30-49	15	90	14	47
50+	10	53	9	26
Total		211		110

The fact that Long Segar women aged over 30 lived a slightly higher proportion of their adult lives alone due to circular migration is probably a reflection of the fact that with travel so much easier, men can continue to leave, even into old age (when health problems encourage more frequent trips for medical care). Additionally, it may be that the choice to move to Long Segar is indicative of a propensity for movement throughout life, giving a built-in bias within the older age-groups.

IV. Women's Influence on Circular Migration Decisions

Because of the difficulties of life alone, and the fears women experience while their husbands are gone, it seemed important to ascertain how involved women were in decision-making about their husband's trips. Table 7.10 provides responses to another open-ended attitudinal question, 'How is it when your husband goes on an expedition? Do you help decide? Does he force the issue?' (*Kompin dalau laki ko' tai selai re? Iko' peteneng? Ia ase' tai?*) The tabulated responses do not seem inconsistent with women's observable involvement in decision-making of many kinds.

Table 7.10: *Women's Involvement in Decision-making about Their Husbands' Expeditions*

Response	Long Segar		Long Ampung	
	No.	%	No.	%
He forced the issue	14	(6.1)	5	(4.5)
She helped decide	154	(67.2)	84	(75.0)
Sometimes forced, sometimes helped decide	25	(10.9)	3	(2.7)
It's up to him	17	(7.4)	—	—
Not applicable	13	(5.7)	19	(17.0)
Missing data	6	(2.6)	1	(0.9)
	229		112	

This table provides the first of several clues that women's influence in the decision-making process may have diminished with the move to Long Segar. Of the women whose husbands had made an expedition from Long Ampung, 91 per cent reported having been involved in the decision, whereas only 73 per cent of the same group from Long Segar reported such involvement. The decision to leave Long Segar in search of additional income could be made individually, whereas this was more difficult from Long Ampung. Transport from Long Segar was easy, and men's ability to leave was sometimes observed in marital power plays there. This may also bear on the more widely expressed satisfaction among Long Segar women in their husband's absence, reflecting greater conflict between the sexes (though this is pure speculation).

Access by the women to goods brought home by their husbands seemed also potentially important in their attitude toward circular migration. I therefore asked, 'Do you help decide how to use the money/things your husband acquires from his own work?' (*Iko' mepoh pekimet kompin pakai uang atau inu inu ya' ko' ala' cen gayeng tengen?*) — see Table 7.11. This question seemed to make more sense to the women of Long Segar than to the women of Long Ampung. Some of the latter claimed that Kenyah generally had so little that decisions about how to dispose of it were rarely possible. The Kenyah attitudes about generosity also no doubt influence this. Stinginess is the most unacceptable characteristic, and 'Ask and ye shall receive' is the norm, for women as much as for men.

Table 7.11: *Women's Influence on the Disposition of Proceeds of Husbands' Expeditions*

Response	Long Segar		Long Ampung	
	No.	%	No.	%
Had *no* influence	16	(7.0)	6	(5.4)
Had influence	202	(88.2)	95	(84.8)
Not applicable	8	(3.5)	11	(9.8)
Missing	3	(1.3)	—	—
	229		112	

There did, however, seem to be a general tendency for a decline in women's status in Long Segar as compared to Long Ampung, related to the increased importance of money in daily life and the corresponding lack of opportunity for women (as compared to men) to acquire it. As the backbone of the agricultural system, women traditionally had a firm economic foundation for their observably high status. They were obviously productive, capable of subsisting independently, and the Kenyah had no ideology of female inferiority.[31] But the increasing importance of money in daily life had increased women's dependence on men, since most moneymaking opportunities were in logging and other timber-related industries requiring greater physical strength than women typically possessed as well as an ability to speak Indonesian, which women also rarely possessed. Additionally, moneymaking opportunities tended to be far from the village, introducing an incompatibility with child-care responsibilities not found with traditional agricultural activities within walking distance of the village.

A look at the kind of proceeds men brought back from their trips provided some insights into the material advantages women perceived from male circular migration, and also confirmed the increasing importance of money with the move to Long Segar. Table 7.12 provides the answers to the question, 'What did your husband bring home?' (*Inu laki ko' ngkin ule'*?), aggregated for all husbands of each woman over her total life-span (again remembering that a large part of Long Segar women's lives had been spent in Long Ampung). In Table 7.12 'Things' refers to salt, cloth, cooking pots, sugar, tobacco, kerosene and occasionally jewelry. In Long Ampung 'Machines' were mainly guns and

Table 7.12: *Proceeds from Circular Migration ('What Did He Bring Home?')*

Kind of item	Long Segar		Long Ampung	
	No.	%	No.	%
Money	33	(14.4)	—	—
Things	81	(35.4)	63	(56.3)
Machines	1	(0.4)	1	(0.9)
Money and things	28	(12.2)	—	—
Money and machines	16	(7.0)	—	—
Things and machines	20	(8.7)	22	(18.6)
All of above	19	(8.3)	—	—
Not applicable, or nothing	26	(11.4)	26	(23.2)
Missing data	5	(2.2)	—	—
	229		112	

Note: Responses aggregated for all husbands of each woman.

sewing-machines, with an occasional hand-cranked record player, cassette tape-recorder, or wristwatch; in Long Segar, outboard motors and chainsaws were the most common 'Machines', though sewing-machines, radios, wristwatches and cassette tape-recorders were not inconsequential booty. But the most interesting feature of Table 7.12 is that money was not mentioned once in Long Ampung, whereas 33.6 per cent of Long Segar's women reported their husbands bringing home money.

Table 7.13: *Proceeds from Circular Migration, 1979-80*

Kind of item	Long Segar		Long Ampung	
	No.	%	No.	%
Money	53	(23.1)	—	—
Things	8	(3.5)	10	(8.9)
Machines	1	(0.4)	—	—
Money and things	2	(0.9)	—	—
Money and machines	1	(0.4)	—	—
Things and machines	1	(0.4)	3	(2.7)
All of above	1	(0.4)	—	—
Not applicable, or nothing	158	(69.0)	99	(88.4)
Missing data	4	(1.7)	—	—
	229		112	

In an attempt to discover the *current* differences between the two communities, the same question was asked with regard to proceeds from circular migration in 1979-80. The number of Long Segar women reporting their husbands bringing back money dropped to 24.4 per cent (Table 7.13). But when the women whose husbands did not leave the village that year are excluded, the percentage rises to 85 per cent. In contrast, Long Ampung women still reported *no* money brought home by their husbands. The Long Ampung women's reports confirm the observation that men bring back what most people in the world would consider life's 'necessities', here meaning salt, cloth, kerosene, pots, and so on. The fact that such useful items are regularly available in Long Segar is one of its most important attractions. These data substantiate the ethnographic conclusion that money has been increasingly important in Long Segar as compared to Long Ampung.

V. Policy Recommendations

An obvious question at this point is, what, if anything, should be done on the basis of these kinds of findings? One could argue, for instance, for a whole restructuring of the economic base of the province (at present the timber and oil industries are dominated by foreign capital) so that the indigenous people could continue to control their own land and resources. However, there are powerful interests, both in other parts of Indonesia and abroad, that would resist such an effort. And few observers would go so far as to argue that the very small population of East Kalimantan should control all the natural wealth of that province when Java and Bali are so obviously in need. In any case, such a restructuring is unlikely at this time.

If one approaches the question within the existing context, including the apparently inexorable intrusion of a money economy, there are some clear implications for development activities in the area. The following suggestions recognise that any policy recommendations are based on personal judgements and values, but also that globally the personal judgements and values of women have been under-represented.

First, additional income-generating opportunities for women need to be developed. Since men have been and will probably continue to be away much of the time, since money is increasingly important in daily life, and since men are major suppliers of money, some mechanism should be developed to allow women greater access to money in their husbands' absence. Development of such opportunities would also provide some safeguard for women's traditional high status, dependent as it most likely is on their active role in production.

Second, in contrast to the current situation, agricultural training and inputs should be provided to women as well as to men. Agricultural training provided to men who subsequently leave the village is less useful from a production point of view than would be training provided to women who, by and large, remain in the village producing food. Furthermore, *not* providing such training and inputs to women can be expected to alter the traditional near-equality of access to resources in Kenyah communities, resulting in the typically adverse impact on women.[32]

Third, family planning services should be made available to

women. The women have expressed a desire for such services, a number of the difficulties expressed by women alone were related to their sole responsibility for child-care, a reduced birth rate is consistent with Indonesian national policy, and personal control of fertility could be expected, in the long run, to increase the likelihood of women's participation in formal employment activities, thus meeting the need for additional income-generating opportunities.

Fourth, nutritional information should be provided. The increasing importance of money has diverted people's energy from food gathering, vegetable cultivation and hunting to activities that have a more certain financial pay-off, such as rice cultivation and wage or contract labour. Yet people do not use their money to purchase daily foods (except sugar, tea, coffee, and an occasional package of noodles or tin of sardines). The result has been a decline in nutritional status in the community.[33] In the absence of men and the money they provide, women are even more constrained to focus their energies on rice cultivation rather than on gathering or growing other nutritious foods, to ensure a supply of the money on which they have grown to depend.

None of these suggestions is particularly unusual. But the major hurdle is the fact that they all require that development persons, mostly male, interact with a large number of villagers, in this case female. Certainly in Kalimantan, one would find that Dayak women are less educated and less likely to know the Indonesian national language than are the men. This fact is a significant and difficult hurdle.

However, other hurdles are largely in the minds of the developers and do not seem to be particularly troublesome in Dayak villages. Many educated Indonesians anticipate a substantial community antagonism for non-Dayak men interacting with Dayak women. However, Dayak men and women regularly interact quite openly, and development persons who displayed 'honourable' intentions would be quite free to talk and work with Dayak women.

In a similar vein, many developers have maintained that attempts to work with the women would be perceived by the local men as a threat to their own hegemony in the communities. I have discussed the near-equality of the sexes in Long Segar and Long Ampung elsewhere, suggesting that male domination is rather minimal in that context anyway.[34] Indeed, discussions in Long Segar of possible development projects directed at the women aroused enthusiasm among men and women, both of whom recognised the problems women had when their men were not around. In some areas, a simple solution to all these perceived dilemmas would be the use of female developers and extension workers.

Conversely, a hurdle apparently not recognised as such was the attitude of developers toward community persons. Dayaks are generally considered by educated Indonesians to be 'primitives'. Local people were frequently described as traditionalist, animist, irrational, and even as having tails. Dayak women were also considered promiscuous. Such attitudes were clear in interaction between developers and villagers, and did not encourage either participation or co-operation from village members of either sex. A related problem with existing development efforts in the area was the degree of centralisation of decision-making. Policies designed in central offices soon prove inappropriate in local contexts, but no mechanism had been developed for relaying such findings back to the policy-making centres. Such problems would be more dramatic in efforts to work with women, since Dayak women are even less experienced at dealing with bureaucracies and other formal institutions than are Dayak men. This of course is unrelated to migration, but would have to be addressed in any effort to implement the four policies outlined at the beginning of this section.

A wholesale approach that rejects everything about the status quo is not recommended, but enfranchising those who in a global perspective are disenfranchised may have genuinely radical implications. In sum, what is needed is a decentralisation of development efforts to benefit women, with development workers being trained in more effective communication and more constructive, collaborative attitudes. If possible, female development workers should be hired to work with village women to design projects that focus on income generation, agricultural training, family planning, and nutritional education.[35] Such efforts would directly address the problems women experience and provide some safeguard for their status. Indirectly, these efforts would benefit men by protecting them from the oppression of the sole economic responsibility for their families that one sees in traditional western settings. And their valued circular migration could continue, if desired.

VI. Conclusion

This analysis has essentially two conclusions. First, the Uma' Jalan Kenyah have been and continue to be involved in circular migration, the form of which is changing in response to the kinds of forces usually referred to as 'modernising'. The kinds of data reported here do not, however, support Zelinsky's well-known characterisation of 'pre-modern traditional society' as having 'Little genuine residential migration and only such limited circulation as is sanctioned by customary practice in land utilisation, social visits, commerce, warfare, or religious observances.'[36] My findings are closer to those of Watson, Hamnett, Hugo, and Chapman, who provide comparable evidence of considerable circular migration in 'traditional societies'.[37]

Second, the portrayal of women's fate in the presence of considerable circular migration has been one-sidedly gloomy, at least in this instance. Kenyah women recognise and complain about the hardships they undergo while their husbands are gone on expeditions. Indeed, life is observably harder for women alone, and all must cope with the possibility that a husband will not return. Focusing on these difficulties, however, has allowed development planners and programme implementers to overlook a critical and more important fact: women are demonstrably competent to manage on their own. As suggested in the previous section, this competence can be tapped in a beneficial manner.

That the women, both in Long Segar and Long Ampung, generally participate in decisions about their husbands' circular migration, often encouraging them to go, suggests that the women derive some benefit from such expeditions. These women are not the poor, desolate, powerless women abandoned by their greedy, money-hungry husbands often portrayed in the literature. They are actively involved in making circular migration decisions and in coping with the personal difficulties that result from such decisions. The women's knowledge that they can manage alone, as well as the experience of actually doing so, serve as important sources of the autonomy and independence that characterise Kenyah women.

Development literature focuses on the hardships women undergo and thereby encourages a climate of opinion that de-emphasises women's competence. The result is efforts to persuade men to stay home, to discourage circular migration, and to train men to take over women's productive tasks, in a misguided attempt to make men more responsible, following the western stereotype of men as breadwinners. But among the Kenyah there are no 'breadwinners', only rice producers — and there is no reason why these should not continue to include women.

Notes

1. I would like to thank the following for their careful critiques and suggestions for changes in an earlier draft of this paper: Murray Chapman, Dana Davidson, John Engel, Robert Gardner, Harold McArthur, Guy Standing, and Andrew P. Vayda. Additional ethnographic information, as requested, was also kindly provided to me by Lee Ndjau, a current and past Kenyah circular migrant. None of the above, however, bears responsibility for errors or shortcomings.

2. See, among others, N. Youssef, M. Buvinic and A. Kudat: *Women in migration: A Third World focus* (Washington, DC, International Center for Research on Women, 1979); E. Chaney: *Women in international migration: Issues in development planning*, report prepared for the Office of Women in Development (USAID, 1980; Ref. AID/OTR-147-80-46); E. Chaney and M. Lewis: *Women, migration and the decline of smallholder agriculture: An exploratory study*, paper prepared for the Office of Women in Development (USAID, 1980; Ref. AID/OTR-147-80/94/95).

3. M. Chapman: 'On the cross-cultural study of circulation', in *International Migration Review*, 1978, vol. 12, no. 4, pp. 559-69; S. Goldstein: *Circulation in the context of total mobility in south-east Asia*, paper No. 33 (Honolulu, East-West Center, Population Institute, 1978); G. Hugo: *Impermanent mobility in Indonesia: What do we know about its contemporary scale, causes and consequences?*, paper presented at the Population Association of America Meetings, Washington, DC, 26 March 1981.

4. For data substantiating female productive activity, see C.J.P. Colfer: 'Women as farmers in agricultural development', in *Benchmark Soils News*, 1981, vol. 5, nos. 1-2 (hereafter Colfer, 1981a); idem: 'Women, men and time in the forests of East Kalimantan', in *Borneo Research Bulletin*, 1981, vol. 13, no. 2, pp. 75-84 (reprinted by Environment and Policy Institute, Honolulu, East-West Center, reprint No. 25) (hereafter Colfer, 1981b); idem: 'Women of the forest: An Indonesian example', in Stock, Force and Ehrenreich (eds.): *Women in natural resources: An international perspective* (Moscow, Idaho, University of Idaho, 1982), pp. 153-82 (hereafter Colfer, 1982a); idem: 'Work and production among shifting cultivators of Borneo', address presented at Utah State University, Logan, Utah, June 1982; idem: 'Change and indigenous agroforestry in east Kalimantan', in *Borneo Research Bulletin*, 1983.

5. A.P. Vayda, C.J.P. Colfer and M. Brotokusumo: 'Interactions between people and forests in East Kalimantan', in *Impact of Science on Society*, 1980, vol.

30, no. 3, pp. 179-90 (reprinted as Reprint No. 13, Honolulu, East-West Center, Environment and Policy Institute); A.P. Vayda: *Progressive conceptualization: Method for integrated sociobiological research in the MAR program* (Honolulu, East-West Center, mimeo., 1982).

6. Long Gemar, Sentosa, Data Bilang, Long Segar, Tepian Buah, and Maura Satu.

7. By 1964, all people in Long Ampung had become Christian, but there was considerable controversy during the decade prior to that when people were generally worshipping Bungan — H. Whittier: 'Social organization and symbols of social differentiation: An ethnographic study of the Kenyah Dayak of East Kalimantan (Borneo)', PhD dissertation, Michigan State University, Department of Anthropology, 1973. There were three Christian sects in Long Ampung in 1980, and two in Long Segar.

8. Colfer, 1983.

9. Resettlement experience is discussed in C.J.P. Colfer, H. Soedjito and A. Azier: *On resettlement from the bottom up*, paper presented to the National Resettlement Conference, Samarinda, East Kalimantan, April 1980.

10. Final pre-testing of the financial questions in Long Ampung was impossible because of the lack of duplicating facilities and the complexities of transport.

11. Researchers who came to Long Segar for a two- or three-day survey went away with very inaccurate information; and I am sure my own results would have been comparable had I not had such help. Having lived in Long Segar for eight months by that time also helped me evaluate information more realistically than I might otherwise have been able to do.

12. For further discussion of Kenyah movement in the Apo Kayan, see T. Jessup: 'Why do Apo Kayan shifting cultivators move?', in *Borneo Research Bulletin*, 1981, vol. 13, no. 1, pp. 16-32.

13. The Kenyah translate *tai selai* into Indonesian *merantau*, which Naim defines as 'leaving one's cultural territory voluntarily whether for a short or long time, with the aim of earning a living or seeking further knowledge or experience, normally with the intention of returning home' — M. Naim: 'Voluntary migration in Indonesia', in A.H. Richmond and D. Kubat (eds.): *Internal migration: The new world and the Third World* (London, Sage Publications, 1976), p. 150.

14. Lee Ndjau, the research assistant on this project, had previously undertaken a 16-month trip between 1959 and 1961 and was group leader on a trip made in 1969-70 lasting ten months.

15. N. Peluso: *Interim report on Indonesian/US man and biosphere project, 'Interactions between people and forests'* (1980, mimeo.); also, Jessup, 1981.

16. Jessup, 1981, p. 24.

17. The Kenyah are however a pragmatic people, and if there were no competent *Paren* available for the trip, a competent commoner would serve as *de facto* leader of the group.

18. See, e.g., G. Hugo: 'Population mobility in West Java, Indonesia', PhD dissertation, Canberra, Australian National University, Research School of Social Sciences, 1975.

19. In 1980 the exchange rate was Rp. 623 to US$ 1.00.

20. See Colfer, 1983, for a more detailed discussion of wage-labour opportunities in the area.

21. L. Mullane: 'A new food supply at the doorstep', in *Agenda*, 1981, vol. 4, no. 2, p. 4.

22. M. Buvinic, N. Youssef and B. von Elm: *Women-headed households: The ignored factor in development planning* (Washington, DC, International Center for Research on Women, 1978), p. iii.

23. For example, Chaney and Lewis, 1980, Youssef *et al.*, 1979; Chaney, 1980.

24. See, for example, S.S. King: *Communication and agro-technology transfer*, paper presented at HITAHR workshop on Agro-technology Transfer (Honolulu, August 1980); K. Smith and C.J.P. Colfer: *Cooks on the world stage: Forgotten actresses/actors*, East-West Resource System Working Paper 83-5 (Honolulu, East-West Center, 1983).

25. E. Gordon: 'An analysis of the impact of labour migration on the lives of women in Lesotho', in *Journal of Development Studies*, April 1981, vol. 17, no. 3, pp. 54-76.

26. Chainsaws were owned by 28 per cent of the households, and 74 per cent of the households had outboard motors. The chainsaws available in the area were a large, commercial variety, too large for women and some men to handle — Colfer, 1983.

27. Preliminary analysis of the responses of 38 per cent of the women (86 out of 233) of Long Segar (non-random, but probably not particularly skewed either) showed that 64 per cent of all women (including those past menopause and having no husband) wanted birth control. In the Long Ampung part of this survey, the analysis of all women (100 per cent, or 87 women) showed that 66 per cent wanted birth control. Behaviourally substantiating these findings, I personally examined and provided birth control pills to 48 women in Long Segar — C.J.P. Colfer: *Report: Women of Long Segar*, prepared for the Women's Promotion Study, Transmigration Area Development Team, GTZ, Samarinda, East Kalimantan, Indonesia, 1980, p. 13. No effort was made to encourage the use of birth control pills; but I obtained and dispensed them once I discovered the local desire for them.

28. This was observed through participant observation, in a time allocation study (Colfer, 1981a, 1981b), in a cognitive mapping procedure called Galileo (Colfer, 1982a), and in uncoded responses in the survey reported here.

29. Whittier, 1973, pp. 133-4.

30. W. Zelinsky: 'The hypothesis of the mobility transition', in *The Geographical Review*, 1971, vol. 61, no. 2, pp. 219-49.

31. Colfer, 1982a; idem: 'Female status and action in two Dayak communities', in M. Goldman (ed.): *Gender, equity and integration* (in preparation).

32. See, for example, K. Staudt: *Tracing sex differentiation in donor agricultural programs*, paper prepared for the American Political Science Association Annual Meeting, Washington, DC, 1979; reprinted by the Office of Women in Development (Washington, DC, USAID).

33. C.J.P. Colfer: 'The importance of women to agroforestry in Borneo', in *Pacific Health*, 1971, vol. 14.

34. Colfer, 1983.

35. For a proposal outlining such an approach in the Kalimantan setting, see M. Thompson: 'Women to women, village developoment in East Kalimantan', a proposal for a women's development project in East Kalimantan, 1982.

36. Zelinsky, 1971, p. 230.

37. J.B. Watson: 'The precontact northern Tairora: High mobility in a crowded field', in M. Chapman and R.M. Prothero (eds.): *Circulation in population movement: Substance and concepts from the Melanesian case* (London, Routledge and Kegan Paul, forthcoming); M. Hamnett: 'Precontact movement among Eivo and Simeku speakers in Central Bougainville', in Chapman and Prothero, forthcoming; Hugo, 1981; Chapman, 1978.

8
The Process of Wage Labour Circulation in Northern India

SHEKHAR MUKHERJI

I. Socio-economic Processes and Labour Mobility

Most analyses of labour migration and circulation have failed to take account of socio-economic and political factors, or the social context in which movement occurs, and have overemphasised the decision-making of movers, whereas individuals only respond to the social conditions over which they have no control, some of which they cannot even comprehend. Little choice exists for most labourers, who are virtually compelled to move. For them, the choice lies between slow starvation in the city slums and quick death in the tottering villages. Despite the abundant literature, there have been few attempts to provide a model of labour circulation as a process in low-income countries, accounting for the 'circulation-inducing' influences of poverty and under-development.

This leads to an important issue in mobility research: what should be the level of investigation and what should be the domain of generalisations? Mobility studies using aggregated census data fail to unravel the decision-making processes; whereas micro-mobility studies, which succeed admirably in this, fail to capture the societal processes that impinge on the lives of individuals. The answer is to try to profit from both levels of investigation. This may require successive levels of generalisations, reasoning from micro-level findings to macro-level generalisations while applying the latter to the micro-level investigations.

With this approach, a basic issue is the identification of the socio-economic processes that determine the extent and form of circular mobility. Examples of such processes are the alienation and uprooting from cultivable land, growing land inequality, the concentration of economic power and means of production, distribution and consumption in a few privileged hands; and the draining of surplus from agriculture contributing to the concentration of resources and growth in a few cities and coastal ports. Such processes impose constraints on the activities of labourers, and induce movement.

The following views labour mobility in India in its historical context, specifically focusing on constraints that explain the circular mobility of wage labourers. As such, the study is divided into three parts. Section II briefly summarises findings from three surveys depicting wage-labour circulation in parts of northern India, supplemented by one investigation covering all India. Section III presents a tentative historical explanation that may be capable of identifying the social processes inducing wage labourers to circulate. Section IV considers the policy implications and the planning strategies necessary to alleviate the considerable wage-labour circulation induced by poverty and underdevelopment.

II. Findings from Mobility Surveys in Northern India

The first of the three surveys in northern India covered wage-labour circulation in districts of eastern Uttar Pradesh in 1973; the second analysed circulation of cycle rickshaw-pullers in Varanasi city in 1977; and the third studied circulation of seasonal agricultural labourers in the district of Birbhum, West Bengal during 1980-81. By employing a multi-stage selection procedure and detailed questionnaires with both open-ended and multiple-choice questions, each survey collected data on circular movements and the migrants' socio-economic-cultural attributes, personal stresses, and determinants and consequences of circulation.

1. Wage-labour Mobility in Uttar Pradesh (1973)

The first study used mobility field theory, which states that the attribute structure of individuals in a population and their perceived place-utility distances between places of origin and destination cause migration and circulation. These two forces and the mobility patterns are independent parts of the mobility field, a change in any one part causing corresponding changes in others. Crucial to this theory is the notion of 'co-existence'. It implies that only those combinations of attributes, utility distances and behaviour can be conceptually and mathematically identified that really *co-exist* in the mobility field. This enables one to specify causal links between the attribute structures of the individuals, their perceived place-utility distances, and their resultant mobility behaviour (migration, circulation and oscillation).[1]

The theory was tested with data from a survey conducted in April-November 1973 of 305 individuals who in all made 436 moves, circulating between Varanasi city and the adjoining districts of eastern Uttar Pradesh, and adjoining states of northern India. The study revealed that migration and circulation of labourers from eastern Uttar Pradesh mainly reflected the rural dispossessed moving in search of jobs and better living conditions. Being landless agricultural labourers, most were virtually forced to leave villages and accept any manual work they could find in the towns and cities. A great majority lived in urban squalor, hoping to acquire sufficient money to buy land in their home village or find a long-term livelihood in the town. Some had gone to the nearest town, but more had moved to Varanasi, the largest city within a distance of 100-150 miles. Many of them had travelled hundreds of miles to the country's largest metropolises (Calcutta, Delhi, Bombay), probably because they had a faint idea that the chances of obtaining manual jobs increase with city size. Many had experienced prolonged urban unemployment, and were forced to return to their village to look after their family or tiny parcel of land. One feels that many oscillated between the same village and town, their hopes never fulfilled, the next generation repeating the same miserable drama.

The structure of movers' attribute matrix. Through factor analysis of the attribute matrix of 436 moves and 44 variables, 10 principal components with eigenvalues greater than 1.0 were extracted, explaining about 66.6 per cent of the total variance (Table 8.1). These dimensions define the underlying social forces and describe the attribute structure of the sample. Briefly, the main migrants and their characteristics were:

1. the poor, economically deprived and socially disadvantaged;
2. young people, aspiring to social mobility;
3. persons with restricted awareness of opportunities at other places;
4. youths with little family burden;
5. persons with high job-income dissatisfaction;
6. educated unemployed looking for jobs;
7. high-caste, rich landowners;
8. landless, unemployed peasants and workers;
9. people in debt and familial stress;
10. people of scheduled and low castes severely affected by drought.

Of these ten components, the first dimension is the most descriptive of the precarious situation in which so many Indian people find themselves and within which their movements occur. The rest of the story of the proletariat is revealed mainly by components 8, 9 and 10. The socially advantaged are represented by components 2, 6 and 7. Dimensions 3, 4 and 5 are probably common to both. In sum, the poor are characterised by landlessness, real and disguised unemployment, debt, drought, familial stress, illiteracy, poverty, and lack of food and shelter, whereas the comparatively rich who migrate are characterised by job-income dissatisfaction, social aspiration, lack of facilities for vocational training, and educated unemployment.

Factor analysis of the movers' perceived place-utility matrix (of 436 moves and five variables) generated *three* main components (Table 8.2). These explained 89.4 per cent of total variance. The job-facility-urban-educational utility component indicates that in the region job opportunities were heavily concentrated in urban areas, and that the movers did not evaluate urban facilities of a location as much as the likelihood of employment; one interpretation is that movers would go to non-urban areas if jobs were available there. The second component, kinship proximity, confirms the important role relatives play in the movement decision and indicates that acquaintance-kinship fields are spatially arranged, decaying with distance. The third component was of little significance in the final canonical analysis.

Table 8.1: *Factor Analysis of Movers' Attribute Data*
(Variables — 44; factors = 10; variance explained — 66.6%)

No. Variable name	Communality	Factors: 1	2	3	4	5	6	7	8	9	10
Individual variance(%)		26.1	7.5	6.4	5.4	4.6	4.1	3.7	3.3	2.8	2.7
Cumulative variance(%)		26.1	33.6	40.0	45.1	50.0	54.1	57.8	61.1	63.9	66.6
1 Household size	0.69	.54									
2 Sudra caste	0.34	-.71									
3 High caste	0.57	(.34)					(.30)				
4 Scheduled caste	0.58										.62
5 Age	0.63				-.65						
6 Per capita income	0.84	-.47					.76				
7 Years of schooling	0.85	-.91									
8 No. of persons/room	0.62	.41									
9 Per capita land	0.77						.79				.50
10 Moved alone	0.69				.79						
11 Previous occupation index	0.89	-.86									
12 Desire for education	0.68	-.77									
13 Index of modernism	0.52	-.59									
14 Minimum social aspiration	0.85	-.88									
15 No. of dependants	0.54				-.59						
16 Income dissatisfaction	0.83					.83					
17 Job/income dissatisfaction index	0.87						.89				
18 Below subsistence level	0.77	.83									
19 Extent of life space	0.92		-.95								
20 Awareness of adjacent districts	0.83		-.90								
21 No. of towns known	0.91		-.95								

Variable	h²	1	2	3	4	5	6	7	8	9	10
22 Family in origin	0.65				.65						
23 Family in destination	0.72				-.78						
24 Degree of debt	0.50									.62	
25 Unemployed	0.53	(.33)									
26 Degree of underemployment	0.58	(.38)							.64		
27 Educated unemployed	0.65					.74			-.54		
28 Stress of no college	0.70		-.49			.43					
29 Nature of job-search	0.69		-.46			.58					
30 Places visited	0.51			.63							
31 News information	0.49			(.30)	(-.37)	(-.36)					
32 Move with no kin in destination area	0.53			.65							.44
33 Income gain from move	0.57				(.31)	.62					
34 Familial stress	0.57										
35 Drought effect	0.55							.63			
36 Degree of lack of money	0.56	.52									
38 Per capita land less than 0.5 acre	0.78	.84						.63			
39 Landless	0.46	.41							(.39)		
40 Days/month food available	0.67	.72							(.35)		
41 Income less than Rs. 100 per month	0.63	.79									
42 Occupation difficult due to move	0.79		.40						.58		
43 0-4 years schooling	0.62	.76									
44 Income-need difference	0.59					.65					

Factor name

1 Poor landless economically deprived people
2 Young, wanting vertical mobility
3 Restricted awareness
4 Young, no burden
5 High income-job dissatisfaction
6 Educated unemployed, for income gain
7 High-caste rich, landowner
8 Landless unemployed
9 People in debt, stress
10 Scheduled and low castes suffer drought

Note: Those figures in parentheses are not included in computing the factor concerned.

Table 8.2: *Factor Analysis of the Utility Matrix*

No. Variable name	Communality	Factor: 1 Job-urban utility	2 Kinship-physical nearness utility	3 Mentally perceived nearness
Per cent of total variance		36.989	32.712	19.749
Cumulative variance		36.989	69.701	89.449
1. Job utility	0.898	0.932		
2. Urban utility	0.989	0.939		
3. Physical distance	0.814		0.838	
4. Kinship utility	0.864		0.916	
5. Perceived nearness	0.998			0.952

The Movers' Structure of Mobility. Factor analysis of the mobility matrix (436 movers and 34 variables) produced *13* dimensions with eigenvalues greater than unity, explaining about 84.7 per cent of total variance (Table 8.3). These dimensions define the major alignments in the structure of mobility behaviour in the Indian situation.[2] The dimensions are as follows (some are bipolar in nature, the negative polarity shown in parentheses):

1. rural-to-urban migration in search of any manual job lasting more than one year (urban-to-rural circulation for one to three months for vacation);
2. transfer moves for security;
3. moves for university study;
4. urban-to-rural circulation to home villages for harvesting or family visits;
5. moves of the educated unemployed for professional jobs;
6. moves for monetary or occupational prospects;
7. short-distance rural-urban moves within 100 miles for no single purpose (medium-distance intra-urban moves of between 200 and 500 miles);
8. migration for more than one year, again for no single purpose (temporary migration for three to twelve months);
9. circulation to resume wage labour in the city;

10. oscillation — that is, repeated circulatory moves between places of origin and destination because destination is near to home village;
11. moves of the unemployed (moves of the underemployed);
12. long-distance intra-urban moves;
13. medium-distance moves of between 100 and 500 miles.

A major objective of the survey was to collect data on the *total* mobility of all movers, including *labour* migration and circulation. The data were then factor-analysed to reveal the main mobility patterns. The predominant pattern that emerged was labour-related. Indeed, most movements seem associated with poverty, unemployment, and the search for security and sustenance. Of these, the most significant consisted of moves of landless peasants and unemployed agricultural labourers to city slums, seeking any kind of manual job to ensure bare survival. They made up 48 per cent of the migrants. It is those who most often return to their villages, either to harvest some tiny parcel of land or to visit families (the fourth component). Their dual responsibilities, family disruption and unsettled economic position are apparent from such circular mobility.

Canonical Linkages between Attributes, Place-utilities and Mobility Behaviour. Finally, the canonical test of interdependence between the three matrices linked specific types of migration or circulation behaviour with a specific personal characteristic. Table 8.4 shows that the *trace correlation* is quite high, 0.518, indicating a significant overlap in the two matrices describing mobility behaviour and attribute/utility variables.[3] The analysis also generated *causal* canonical linkages, picking out only those components from behaviour and attribute sets that are maximally correlated or causally linked. The most important variables thus linked are underlined in Table 8.4; thus, the first canonical vector can be interpreted as follows:

0.610 (migration to search for manual job) = 0.815 (poor landless socio-economically deprived people) + 0.522 (job-urban utility distance between origin and destination)

Table 8.3: *Factor Analysis of Mobility Matrix*
(Variables — 34; factors — 13; variance explained 84.7 per cent)

	No. variable name	Communality	1 Search for manual job /circ. for vacation vacation	2 Transfer for security	3 Move for higher	4 U-R agric. educ. tion	5 Profnl. job for educated unempl.
	Indv. variance		18.7	10.8	7.6	6.8	6.4
	Cuml. variance		18.7	29.5	37.1	43.9	50.3
Dist-tance	1 1-100 miles	0.76					
	2 100-200 ml	0.76					
	3 200-500 ml	0.86					
	4 500 ml +	0.92					
Dura-tion	5 1-3 month	0.86	−.72				
	6 3-12 month	0.78					
	7 Stay 1 yr. +	0.77	.74				
Kind of Move	8 Migration	0.86	.62				
	9 Circulation	0.84	−.71			(−.33)	
	10 Temp. move	0.46					
	11 Oscillation	0.95					
Direc-tion	12 Rural-Urban	0.83	.50				
	13 Urban-Urban	0.65					
	14 Urban-Rural	0.96	−.52			−.68	
First Pur-pose of Move	15 Seek manual job	0.97	.46	(.33)	1.40		(.35)
	16 Profes. job	0.88					.96
	17 Promotion	0.85					
	18 Transferred	0.97		−.89			
	19 Higher study	0.88			−.97		
	20 Harvesting	0.90				−.93	
	21 Vacation	0.94	−.91				
2nd Pur-pose	22 Resume work	0.96					
	23 Unemployed	0.97	(.26)	(.19)	(.30)		(.21)
	24 Underemployed	0.87	(.28)	(.20)	(.28)		(.22)
	25 Big university	0.97			−.96		
	26 Family security	0.91		−.88			
	27 Educ. unemployed	0.86					−.98
	28 More earning. etc.	0.90					
	29 Family respons.	0.84				−.92	
3rd Pur-pose	30 Near native place	0.78					
	31 Native place	0.85	−.68			−.53	
	32 Friends in destn.	0.66					
	33 No kinship consid	0.66		−.52			(−.38)
	34 Recreation	0.88	−.92				

6 Move for Prospects	7 Short, R-U 1-100 miles /Med, U-U 200-500	8 Temp move 3-12 months	9 Circulation to resume work	10 Oscillate to native places	11 Move of unemployed	12 Long U-U move/ Short R-U move	13 Medium dist. move 100-200 miles short dist. move 1-100m
6.0	5.5	4.9	4.6	3.7	3.5	3.0	3.0
56.2	61.7	66.6	71.2	74.9	78.4	81.7	84.7
	.43					(.34)	−.75
							.95
	−.84						
						−.84	
	−.47	−.40					
		.53					
		.49	.43				
			−.46				
		−.89					
				−.54			
	(.39)					.47	
	−.45					−.58	
(.37)							
−.93							
			−.89				
					.77		
(.21)					−.80		
(.23)							
−.94							
				−.71			
				.79			

Table 8.4: *The Canonical Structure Matrix (Canonical Analysis of Indian Mobility, Utility and Attribute Data)*

Canonical variates	1[a]	2[a]	3[a]	4	5	6	7	8	9	10
No. Mobility behaviour variables										
1. Migration to seek manual job or for vacation	0.610[b]	−0.515	0.086	−0.060	0.411	0.103	−0.110	−0.178	−0.200	−0.113
2. Transferred for family security	−0.273[b]	−0.098	0.410	−0.354	0.327	−0.112	−0.236	−0.091	−0.107	−0.343
3. Moves for college-university study	−0.552	−0.447	0.410	0.372	−0.122	0.151	−0.091	−0.095	−0.060	0.040
4. Urban to rural circulation for harvesting and meeting family	−0.121	0.508	0.135	0.130	0.255	0.391	−0.464	−0.027	0.077	−0.277
5. Moves for professional job of unemployed	−0.178	−0.243	−0.849	0.145	0.073	0.320	−0.123	−0.121	0.131	0.071
6. Moves for prospects and more earnings	−0.320	−0.145	−0.073	−0.363	0.353	−0.127	−0.046	0.317	0.029	0.018
7. Short-distance move/medium-distance	0.151	−0.155	0.014	−0.018	−0.201	−0.132	−0.161	0.193	0.510	0.100
8. Migration for more than 1 year/temporary move for 3-12 months	−0.164	0.022	−0.028	−0.165	0.012	−0.274	0.336	−0.656	0.363	−0.305
9 Circulation to urban area to resume work	−0.067	−0.050	0.057	−0.321	0.054	−0.258	−0.383	0.044	0.243	0.458
10. Oscillation because near native place	0.039	−0.082	0.197	−0.035	0.295	0.432	0.414	0.291	0.561	−0.076
11. Moves of unemployed	0.025	0.050	−0.073	0.850	0.437	−0.558	−0.045	0.135	0.158	−0.081
12. U to U long distance/R - U short distance	−0.116	0.203	0.081	0.036	0.436	0.108	0.271	−0.287	−0.146	0.650
13. Medium distance moves/short distance moves	−0.175	−0.003	−0.155	−0.075	0.047	−0.116	0.399	0.424	−0.330	−0.165

Table 8.4 (continued)

Utility distances and attribute variables

Utility distances and attribute variables										
1. Job-urban utility distance	0.522	−0.655	0.037	−0.067	−0.153	−0.274	−0.072	−0.010	−0.044	0.291
2. Physical-kinship utility distance	−0.105	0.345	0.187	0.043	0.377	0.113	0.251	−0.427	0.236	0.594
3. Perceived nearness-utility distance	0.008	−0.112	0.040	−0.105	0.118	0.072	0.045	−0.358	0.022	−0.363
4. Poor, landless socio-economically deprived	0.815	0.390	0.161	−0.040	0.111	0.116	−0.128	−0.030	−0.047	−0.220
5. Want vertical social mobility	0.320	−0.875	0.137	−0.111	0.146	0.029	0.068	0.083	−0.058	−0.184
6. Small awareness space	0.036	0.053	0.054	−0.003	−0.127	−0.037	0.302	−0.053	0.269	−0.072
7. Young adult with no family burden	−0.012	−0.127	0.075	0.661	−0.353	0.530	0.099	0.021	−0.207	−0.016
8. Job-income dissatisfaction	0.091	0.083	−0.128	−0.126	0.380	0.290	0.260	0.620	−0.220	0.309
9. Educated unemployed wanting earning	0.178	−0.081	−0.952	0.092	−0.009	0.043	−0.034	0.128	0.128	−0.047
10. High-caste and rich landowners	−0.103	0.055	0.008	−0.074	−0.025	−0.158	0.659	0.220	0.205	−0.308
11. Landless and unemployed	0.103	0.023	0.035	0.706	0.380	−0.538	0.034	0.106	0.024	−0.041
12. In debt and stress	−0.264	−0.061	0.075	0.060	0.455	0.255	−0.451	0.143	0.482	−0.154
13. Scheduled castes suffering droughts	0.241	−0.029	0.083	0.066	−0.389	0.071	−0.033	0.303	0.685	0.156
Canonical correlation	0.912[c]	0.885	0.791	0.645	0.572	0.482	0.324	0.250	0.211	0.170
Chi-square	2,434.333	1,683.300	1,038.749	623.612	396.608	229.527	118.084	71.264	41.732	22.472
Degrees of freedom	169	144	121	100	81	64	49	36	25	16
Probability[e]										
Trace correlation	0.51760[d]									

Notes: a. Canonical variates are separate patterns of relationships between 'input' variables. b. Loading: degree and direction of relationship of the specific variables with this pattern. c. Canonical Correlation: the statistical dependence between each matched pair of variables. d. Trace Correlation: general overlap between Attribute/Utilities set and mobility behaviour sets. e. See Text

Likewise, eight patterns of canonical inter-relationships between the behaviour, utilities and attributes were successively identified, all statistically highly significant at the 0.001 level. They can be presented in the following propositions:[4]

1. The poorer an individual and the more landless and socio-economically deprived, the greater the chance of moving to an urban area in search of manual work, and from a place of less job facility-urban utility to one offering greater provision of such utilities. This canonical correlation is of such overriding power and statistical significance that it can be regarded as a rule of movement behaviour for the population of the study area of Uttar Pradesh (canonical equation 1).

2. The higher the gain in kinship proximity utility, the more frequent circulating moves to home places for harvesting or family visits (canonical equation 2).

3. If an individual were landless and unemployed, the younger the individual or the fewer the family burdens, the more chance of movement to seek employment outside the home village (canonical equation 4).

4. If an individual belonged to an upper caste, was elderly, had family responsibilities, was dissatisfied with job and income position, or was indebted, he had a relatively high probability of moving in search of employment, security or prospects (canonical equation 5).

5. The more an individual was underemployed, the more chance of moving in search of employment. Also, the younger an individual and the fewer family responsibilities, the greater the probability of frequent circulatory moves between village and city (canonical equation 6).

6. The greater an individual's debt or familial stress, the greater the probability of frequent circulatory moves from village to city (canonical equation 7).

7. The greater an individual's job-income dissatisfaction, the more chance of migrating for under a year, and the less chance of physical-kinship gains or losses (canonical equation 8).

8. If an individual belonged to harijan castes (untouchables), and if an individual was affected by drought and debt, the more chance of oscillating between village and city in search of employment for under a year (canonical equation 9).

The first canonical component simply reiterates the need for an attack on the roots of poverty and underdevelopment in India. The fourth, fifth and sixth canons emphasise that not only peasants and agricultural labourers need special attention; there are also multitudes of marginally employed or totally unemployed, even in non-agricultural sectors, whose survival demands nothing less than a change in the existing patterns of industries, investment and productive relations in favour of employment. The eighth canon shows the pitiable situation of the low castes and untouchables, and emphasises the need for social reforms to complement any changes achieved by economic growth.

2. Wage Labour Circulation of the Rickshawalas (1977)

The nature of labour circulation in India may be revealed in survey data on cycle-rickshaw pullers, known as 'rickshawalas', collected in Varanasi city in Uttar Pradesh during January-May 1977. The movers came from numerous villages in districts of Uttar Pradesh within 200 miles of Varanasi, and thus portray the situation in eastern Uttar Pradesh.

Of 1,940 rickshawalas surveyed, 51.6 per cent regularly circulated between village and the city, while 48.4 per cent did not circulate (including 12 per cent who were permanent migrants and 36 per cent who were born in the city). Table 8.5 indicates the mean monthly remittances by circulating and non-circulating

Table 8.5: *Monthly Remittances by Circulators and Permanent Migrant Rickshawalas, Varanasi, 1977*

Years of stay of rickshawalas in the city	Mean monthly remittances to home village (in rupees)	
	By circulators	By non-circulators (permanent migrants and residents)
0-1	90.5	112.5
2-4	99.0	102.5
5-9	108.0	146.0
10-14	106.8	128.0
15-19	99.6	78.5
20+	86.3	115.2

rickshawalas. Compared with permanent migrants and non-circulators, the circulators spent more in the city for sustenance, and were more indebted, often owing as much as 1,400 rupees. Moreover, they were unable to remit much to their village families, though this was the main purpose of their rickshaw-pulling; remittances were often not sufficient for productive use or for raising agricultural productivity.

The reasons for their comparatively disadvantaged situation were that they had to maintain two households, entailing both dual responsibilities and village visits. And because they maintained connections with rural life, they were exposed to its vicissitudes and were prone to fall prey to village moneylenders. Consequently, they incurred more expenditures and debt than those settled permanently in the city.[5] Arguably, such circulatory moves neither enhanced their standard of living nor promoted social development.

All the rickshawalas, both circulators and permanent migrants, were very poor, mostly of very low social status. Of the 1,940 rickshawalas, half belonged to untouchable castes, and another third belonged to low castes. Most were illiterate (67 per cent) or semi-literate (22 per cent), and were either landless (59 per cent) or owned less than 0.04 hectares per household (21 per cent). Thirty-five per cent of rickshawalas had to support five or six dependants, and another 13 per cent had to feed nine to sixteen dependants. Such a large dependency burden was a compelling reason for moving and taking up whatever manual work was available in the city.

A feature of the rickshawalas is that in 1977 there were 26,098 registered rickshaw-pullers but only 16,511 rickshaws. The survey data indicated that 78 per cent of all rickshawalas did not own rickshaws, having to rent them on a daily rental of 4 rupees, or about 40 per cent of their average daily income. Circulating rickshawalas had to leave rickshaws with their owners when they visited their villages, and then had to wait their turn for a rickshaw on their return. Some 16 per cent of circulating rickshawalas owned rickshaws, which they lent or rented to others when they visited their home villages.

Few circulating rickshawalas had been able to obtain a bank loan under the government's subsidy programme designed to subsidise and encourage self-employment, because few of them could find a local guarantor required to vouchsafe for the rickshawala for the full repayment of the loan.

Labour Circulation and Social Mobility. Social mobility is commonly measured in terms of occupational mobility and income gain, and both aspects were considered in this study of circulating rickshawalas. An examination of their former occupations in the villages (Table 8.6) tells the familiar story of pauperisation and rural exodus. Table 8.6 shows there were mainly three groups who took up rickshaw-pulling: formerly skilled and semi-skilled groups, the unemployed, and landless labourers and unskilled workers. As many as 36.2 per cent were previously engaged in skilled or semi-skilled occupations, including cultivation on own farms (13.7 per cent), weaving of silk saris (6.3 per cent), government service (2.0 per cent), private service (4.3 per cent), own business (5.0 per cent), and other semi-skilled work (4.9 per cent). These jobs were more skilled and desirable than the hard manual labour of rickshaw-pulling, but were lost for various reasons. The data show that small farmers, for example, were uprooted by land mortgage, litigation, debt and the land usurping tendency of big landlords, whereas skilled weavers were displaced by the low prices paid by monopolist silk merchants controlling local and national markets.

Some downward social displacement of skilled and semi-skilled workers is thus evident. Only 9.6 per cent were previously unemployed, for whom some improvement had occurred. But as many as 53 per cent (Table 8.6) were previously landless agricultural labourers or other unskilled labourers who had not been able to withstand pressures arising from manipulation of tenancies, bonded labour, debt and so on. For them, there was no change in socio-economic status; they moved from low-paid work to low-wage urban informal activity.

Table 8.6 also reveals that as many as 34 per cent of circulating rickshawalas had no income gain, while a further 18 per cent experienced little improvement (less than RS. 50 (US$ 5) per month. Thus, more than half did not benefit from circular mobility and occupational change.[6]

Comparison of Table 8.6 (circulating rickshawalas) with Table 8.7 (permanent migrant or local resident rickshawalas) also highlights the circulators' disadvantaged position. While 53 per cent of circulating rickshawalas previously worked as agricultural labourers or unskilled workers, only 35 per cent of non-

Table 8.6: *Degree of Improvement in Monthly Income of Circulating Rickshawalas Due to Change of Occupation (% distribution)*

Degree of improvement in monthly income	Previous occupation										Row Total	
	No job	Cultivation	Agricultural labour	Unskilled work	Weaving	Government service	Other service	Self-employment	Others	Data not available	Row	Total
1. None	10.2	11.6	33.7	19.5	4.4	4.4	3.5	6.0	3.5	2.2	34.3	(344)
2. Little (income gain below Rs. 50)	8.0	12.2	42.5	14.4	7.4	1.0	2.7	4.8	6.3	0.5	18.8	(188)
3. Fair (income gain between Rs. 50 and 149)	6.3	17.3	33.8	17.3	8.7	0.0	5.0	4.7	6.3	0.4	25.3	(254)
4. Much (income gain above Rs. 150)	9.6	12.2	41.0	14.4	6.3	1.6	6.3	3.2	4.2	1.0	18.8	(188)
5. Incomplete information	42.8	21.4	7.1	10.7	0.0	0.0	3.5	7.1	0.0	7.1	2.8	(28)
Column total	9.6	13.7	36.1	16.8	6.3	2.0	4.3	5.8	4.9	1.3	100.0	
	(96)	(137)	(361)	(163)	(63)	(21)	(43)	(50)	(49)	(14)	(1002)	

Notes: Figures in brackets show absolute numbers in row total and column total. Percentages may not add up exactly to 100 per cent due to rounding. Chi-square value was 197.2 with 36 degrees of freedom, which was significant at the 1 per cent level. Rs. 10 is equal to US$ 1, but in terms of local purchasing power one rupee is equivalent to one dollar.

Table 8.7: *Degree of Improvement in Mean Monthly Income of Non-circulating (Permanent Migrant or Resident) Rickshawalas Due to Change of Occupation (% distribution)*

Degree of improvement in monthly income	Previous occupation										Row	Total
	No job	Culti-vation	Agricul-tural labour	Unskilled work	Weaving	Govern-ment service	Other service	Self-employment	Others	Data not available		
	1	2	3	4	5	6	7	8	9	10	12	
1. None	11.7	3.1	10.7	21.0	24.1	2.8	8.3	12.4	4.9	1.0	30.9	(290)
2. Little (income gain below Rs. 50)	12.2	2.7	17.0	19.7	28.7	1.1	4.3	10.6	3.1	0.5	20.0	(188)
3. Fair (income gain between Rs. 50 and 149)	7.2	3.4	12.0	27.9	29.8	2.9	6.7	4.3	4.8	1.0	22.2	(208)
4. Much (income gain above Rs. 150)	10.2	4.2	18.6	16.7	24.2	3.3	6.5	2.8	8.8	0.0	21.8	(205)
5. Incomplete information	34.0	2.1	6.4	12.8	10.6	0.0	10.6	12.8	2.1	8.5	5.0	(47)
Column total	11.7	3.3	14.0	21.1	25.9	2.5	6.9	8.2	6.4	1.1	100.0	
	(110)	(31)	(131)	(198)	(243)	(23)	(65)	(77)	(50)	(10)	(938)	

Note: Chi-square value was 132.8, with 36 degrees of freedom. It was significant at the 1 per cent level.

circulating migrants or city-born rickshawalas were previously engaged in those activities. Similarly, only 3.3 per cent of non-circulators were formerly cultivators, as against 13.7 per cent of circulators. Thus, considerably fewer non-circulators had been landless. Among non-circulating rickshawalas, a majority were formerly skilled weavers, testifying to social displacement even among this group. Compared with circulation, more of the permanent migrants had benefited from spatial mobility and occupational change; for example, 21.8 per cent of them showed income gain above Rs. 150 per month, as against 18.8 per cent of circulators (Table 8.7). It appears that permanent migrants were better off than circulators, who also had dual responsibilities.

In contrast, then, to optimistic assessments of the role of circulation in mitigating individual poverty and fostering rural development, this study suggests that that kind of circular mobility only maintains — and often worsens — personal poverty. Circulation of wage labourers occurs within, and in turn reinforces, the syndrome of poverty and mobility.[7] A circulating rickshawala remains in a lowly position even after 20 or 30 years of intermittent urban residence. There is no evidence of significant upward social mobility.

3. Wage Labour Mobility of Seasonal Agricultural Labour in Birbhum District, West Bengal (1980-1)

Those findings have been corroborated by a survey in seven villages of Birbhum district of West Bengal between December 1980 and March 1981. The villages were selected on the basis of multi-stage sampling procedures, migrants and circulators were purposively selected in each of the villages, and very detailed data were collected.

These indicate that most circulators were landless or owned less than 0.05 hectares per household; they were illiterate or had been to school for less than two years, and were small-scale peasants, agricultural labourers or unskilled village operatives. A majority were idle for nearly nine months each year. Their fields were parched, water scarce, and agricultural productivity very low. Chronic unemployment and underemployment plagued these villages, which were characterised by a high degree of land inequality and pauperisation of the petty farmers and agricultural labourers. Ninety-five per cent of these workers' moves were in pursuit of jobs. Yet whatever temporary work they found in neighbouring villages, including land digging under the government's 'food for work' programme, was hardly adequate to overcome the vagaries of prolonged hunger and acute unemployment. Such circulatory moves were merely spatial manifestations of poverty and underdevelopment.[8]

4. Summary of Micro-level Studies

These investigations, based on individuals and statistical analyses of socio-economic factors influencing migration and circulation, demonstrate that labourers in India move from one area of acute stress to another, from rural poverty to rural poverty or from rural to urban poverty. They move from low-grade rural activities to low-grade rural or urban informal activities, all characterised by low levels of skill and technology, intense competition and extraction of super-profits through severely competitive wages. For such circulators, consumption is commonly below subsistence level, their remittances are inadequate, and escape from destitution is almost impossible. Such circulation in India is a spatial symptom of underdevelopment. It begins and ends in poverty, compounding involution and dependency, and results in a massive waste of human potential, both at places of origin and destination, for the movers themselves and for the country.[9]

5. Proliferation of Poverty-induced Urban Tertiary Sector and Migration to class I cities

In that context, the findings from one macro-level investigation are pertinent. This investigated urban in-migration to all Indian cities with over 100,000 population in 1971. A test of interdependence was performed by employing a canonical analysis of a dependent matrix of migration and the combined (independent) matrix of economic structure of Indian cities-cum-capital investment made there. This gave five pairs of independent and orthogonal patterns of relationship between the dependent and independent vectors that were statistically significant and meaningful. They showed a proliferation of poverty-induced tertiary sectors, especially low-grade service, industrial, petty trade and transport activities. Migrants from rural areas were absorbed in such poverty-induced informal activities and did not have any relationship with investment in the organised sector. The circulation of wage labourers between rural and urban areas thus occurred in a context of urbanward migration, where former peasants and agricultural labourers crowd into the cities, becoming absorbed into tertiary economic sectors, or returning if unabsorbed as less fortunate movers.[10] In this manner the weak economic base of Indian cities, their rapid growth, and the migration of former peasants and agricultural labourers are linked.

III. Towards Generalisations: Wage Labour Circulation in an Historical Context

Moving on to a tentative explanation incorporating socio-economic-political processes, we can make some generalisations about the causes and consequences of wage-labour circulation in India.[11] The survey findings demonstrate that circulation is linked to many inter-related processes, such as land inequality, both rural and urban poverty, the weakening of links between villages and towns, urban polarisation of resources and investment, the parasitic character of cities, and the proliferation of urban informal sectors. Some of these can be seen from the surveys, but others cannot be discerned from the study of individuals. The socio-economic processes can be captured in micro-level studies only to the extent that they are reflected in individuals' attributes and mobility behaviour in the form of various stresses and non-gratification of basic material needs. A survey might explain circulatory moves of poverty-stricken or unemployed persons in search of means of sustenance; it cannot fully explain the underlying causes of this circulation-inducing poverty, nor can it explain the stagnation of a previously 'condemned' circulator-source region. For a fuller explanation of the circulation process that takes account of these forces a more macro approach is required.

The Historical Context

Figure 8.1 depicts the salient features of an historical analysis. As the figure is schematic and capable of modification, it and the accompanying discussion should not be considered as a 'model' in the strict sense of the term; they only attempt to provide an approximate picture of historical phases and structural settings of the labour mobility process in an underdeveloped economy.

Figure 8.1: *The Structural Setting of the Process of Labour Circulation in Underdeveloped Economies*

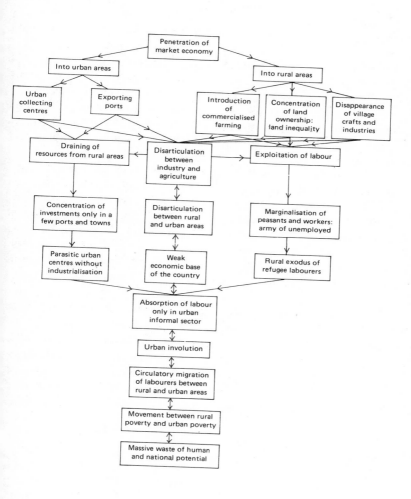

First, crucial to an understanding of the historical context of labour mobility in India is the notion that underdevelopment is not a lower stage of development, nor a lagging behind, but the product of colonialism. Coming first to coastal ports and foreign enclaves, the colonial administration reoriented the country's major economic activities to export promotion, neglecting development of indigenous industries that had provided a stable economy and that would have gradually promoted the development of an economic base. Instead, the country's peripheral economy became dominant. Cash-cropping, mining and plantations were emphasised, causing massive movements of indentured labourers into plantations, mines and export centres. As profits were not available, the condition of the movers scarcely improved. Today the same kind of export-oriented economy and the same kind of labour mobility persist.[12]

Second, India's spatial structure became increasingly disorganised as export-orientation created new ports and foreign enclaves while stunting the growth of old ports and settlements. Indigenous trade circuits, which had integrated the local economy, were severed. Furthermore, most investment and services were concentrated in a few cities, such as Calcutta, Bombay, Delhi and Madras, which grew rapidly at the expense of the vast rural interior and smaller towns (Table 8.8).[13]

Table 8.8: *The Nature of Capital-intensive Industrialisation in Indian Cities and Lack of Employment*

Metropolis	Capital invested in organised industries (1970-1) (million rupees)	New workers employed in that organised sector (1970-1) (in 000.'s)	Amount of capital investment required to create one job (rupees)
Calcutta	5,606	201.3	27,844
Bombay	2,765	402.8	6,864
Delhi	1,470	64.5	22,790
Madras	6,044	130.6	46,278
Ahmedabad	1,577	118.1	12,500
Hyderabad	1,508	29.7	50,000
Bangalore	1,414	54.9	25,755
Kanpur	489	55.5	8,630

Source: Central Statistical Organisation, Calcutta.

These cities were imperfectly related to their hinterlands, and consequently stunted their development.[14] Moreover, capital-intensive and export-oriented urban industrialisation meant limited employment generation. As a result, the millions of former peasants and agricultural labourers who crowded into the larger cities and ports could not be properly absorbed into the economy. Today, similar groups swarm to the metropolises in search of manual work, often eking out a miserable living in urban informal activities.[15] Frequently, they visit their home villages to see their families, to harvest tiny plots or to work on other farms. Such mobility is induced by underdevelopment, not development.

Third, during the colonial period, the cities and small towns were used as collecting points to extract resources and raw materials from agricultural regions, mines and plantations. Networks of railways and roads were constructed mainly to aid this draining of rural regions. The colonial economy thus gradually reached all parts of the countryside, where its adverse effects were primarily felt in three ways:

(a) Introduction of permanent land settlement and private land ownership. Land thus became a commodity; it could also be usurped or forcefully occupied.

(b) Introduction of commercial crops (such as tea, jute, indigo, opium, rubber) at the expense of essential food crops, leading to food shortage and imports.

(c) Neglect of traditional village crafts and industries, like weaving, oil-pressing, leatherwork, textile and silk industries, to facilitate evolving mercantile and monopoly capitalism.

These mechanisms in turn accentuated the marginalisation of cultivators and small farmers, many of whom were relegated to the status of sharecroppers or agricultural labourers. The exploitation of peasants, labourers and village artisans resulted in a massive and continuous flow of pauperised groups from the countryside to the slums of coastal ports and administrative capitals. According to unpublished census data of 1971 on lifetime migrants, about 53 per cent of Calcutta's residents and about 43 per cent of Greater Bombay's consisted of migrants, of which in Calcutta 34 per cent came from Uttar Pradesh and Bihar. Of the total *male* migrants, about 69 per cent of Calcutta's inflow and 54 per cent of Greater Bombay's were illiterate or had less than five years schooling. Most migrants are married men, forced by the housing shortage to live without their families. A vast majority make at least two or three return moves a year to their villages. The low wages and occupational status, the insecurity and stress of their urban existence, and the absence of any employment opportunities in their home villages, compel them to a lifetime of circular migration.

Fourth, village and urban small-scale industries, and cottage industries and handicrafts, that had served their local hinterlands by integrating a settlement hierarchy and territorial systems, were neglected. Numerous village artisans, craftsmen, masons, weavers, artists, and skilled operatives were squeezed out of age-old occupations and obliged to become agricultural labourers, thus increasing the already heavy pressure on the cultivable land. Eventually, they too found their way to the city pavements.[16] The pitiable condition of circulating rickshawalas of Lucknow city is a case in point.[17]

Fifth, the development of India's peripheral economy produced both social and spatial disorganisation.[18] Social disorganisation brought conflicting social relations between the land owning and non-owning classes and aggravated socio-economic inequalities. These led to the concentration of means of production, mainly land and capital, and released surplus labour as more peasants and workers were marginalised (Table 8.9). The same forces still induce widespread labour circulation.

The resulting disorganisation created three crucial distinctions of the spatial structure of India's economy:

(a) A shift to export activities which usurped the major part of investment resources (which were therefore not available to other important sectors), and consequent orientation of trade and transport-communication linkages to ports and metropolitan areas rather than to the interior.

(b) A growth of low-grade tertiary activities, both old and new. Thus the towns and cities of India characteristically developed a poverty-induced tertiary sector, which sheer population growth created; development of a strong industrial base did not occur (Table 8.10).

(c) A growth of light industries, with low-level technology.

Table 8.9: *Proliferation of Agricultural Labourers in India, 1961 and 1971 (rural only)*

	Proportion agricultural labourers	
	1961	1971
Andhra Pradesh	30.9	42.3
Assam	3.3	11.5
Bihar	21.0	44.9
Gujarat	17.2	27.6
Haryana	6.7	19.2
Himachal Pradesh	0.1	4.8
Jammu-Kashmir	2.4	1.7
Karnataka	14.0	35.2
Kerala	19.8	33.1
Madhya Pradesh	18.2	28.8
Maharashtra	27.7	39.3
Orissa	15.3	35.0
Punjab	13.3	23.5
Rajasthan	4.5	9.4
Tamil Nadu	20.8	38.4
Uttar Pradesh	8.3	24.1
West Bengal	21.6	33.5
India	17.5	31.1

Note: Conceptual differences with regard to workers between 1961 and 1971 censuses revolve around (a) a reference period of one week prior to enumeration was used to identify regular work in 1971 instead of two weeks in 1961; and (b) a dichotomy of persons into workers and non-workers according to labour time disposal in 1971, rather than gainful occupation irrespective of time spent on it as in 1961. To put the data on a comparable basis, the Census Office did a resurvey on this issue and collected comparable survey data during December 1971-April 1972. The data presented in Table 8.9 are extracted from that resurvey.
Source: Compiled from *Census of India, 1971*, Series I, India, *Report on resurvey of economic questions — Some results*, Paper I of 1974, tables 8-10, pp.21-45 (New Delhi, Registrar General's Office).

The links between agriculture and industry were severely disarticulated, as were those between rural and urban areas. Consequently, internal contradictions flourished. Urban growth occurred, but without development; parasitic urban centres grew and multiplied, but without industrial strength or strong economic foundation. These tendencies maintained regional and rural-urban inequalities because the coastal ports, foreign enclaves, and administrative capitals served as focal points of collection, rather than as poles of development to diffuse growth

Table 8.10: *Proliferation of Tertiary Activities in Indian Cities, Males, 1901-71*

City	Sector	Proportion of all male workers						
		1901	1911	1921	1931	1951	1961	1971
Calcutta	Secondary	21.8	18.7	17.5	16.3	29.1	34.1	35.6
	Tertiary	75.8	79.3	80.6	82.9	70.3	65.7	63.8
Bombay	Secondary	32.8	30.9	29.8	28.9	39.9	44.7	46.9
	Tertiary	64.5	66.3	68.9	69.1	58.8	53.6	51.6
Ahmedabad	Secondary	48.2	54.7	50.7	—	57.1	56.6	51.3
	Tertiary	48.5	41.7	45.9	—	41.3	42.8	47.1

Source: Censuses of India, 1901-71, economic tables.

to the hinterlands. Had such discontinuities been less pronounced, the spatial distribution of production and employment would have been more uniform and, consequently, there would have been less poverty-induced labour circulation.

Sixth, even after India's Independence, the situation did not improve much, and successive five-year plans have achieved only limited success in alleviating poverty, underdevelopment, spatial disorganisation, and socio-economic inequalities. The planning objectives are still not directly aimed at the poor, though they make up almost half of India's population.[19]

There has been a growing realisation that the benefits of economic growth, where achieved, have not reached the poor and to some extent, growth has accentuated their problems.[20] Most of the benefits of the so-called Green Revolution and related agricultural investments were gained by only 57 productive districts of Punjab and Haryana, at the expense of 225 less fortunate districts of India.[21] Thus, only a few privileged people in advanced regions have gained from economic growth; the benefits have reached neither the lower strata nor the neglected regions. Marginalised rural labourers continue to migrate and circulate to regions which, though favoured, could provide few opportunities for them. These huge streams of poor, illiterate and unskilled labourers could find employment only in urban informal activities (Table 8.11).

A recent series of studies has revealed that masses of landless agricultural labourers from neglected regions of West Bengal and Orissa were transported by private labour agents (*thikadar*) to

Table 8.11: *Absorption of Illiterate or Semi-literate Migrants in Low-grade[a] Urban Informal Sectors, India, 1971*

City	Proportion of lifetime migrants (male)				
	Rural origin	Urban origin	With 0-5 years schooling	Engaged in low-wage activities	Unemployed
Calcutta	61.78	38.22	69.33	87.70	12.33
Bombay	72.25	27.75	53.95	81.00	12.17
Delhi	49.83	50.17	46.87	71.76	12.22
Madras	42.73	57.27	42.78	73.70	16.65

Note: a. Low-grade sectors comprised unskilled production-process jobs, construction labourers, 'informal sector' services, transport workers, hawkers, vendors, porters, domestic servants, and so on.
Source: *Census of India, 1971 — Migration tables* (New Delhi, Registrar General's Office).

the agriculturally favoured and prosperous states of Punjab and Haryana.[22] They were compelled to work almost as bonded labour, often without wages. Yet rural unemployment is so widespread that labourers must migrate in search of even those jobs.

The concentration of resources and growth in a few regions and sections of the population has been increasing. For example, the concentration of economic power has increased in the corporate sector. Yet the expansion of large-scale industries has failed to absorb much of the circulating labour force, and has in some places undermined such cottage industries as textiles, leather and pottery. Consumer expenditure surveys show that in 1973-4 the lowest 20 per cent accounted for 9.5 per cent of rural consumption, while the top 20 per cent accounted for 38 per cent. For urban areas, the corresponding figures were 9.2 per cent and 40 per cent.[23] Thus, persistent inequalities between rich and poor continue to worsen.

Intra-rural socio-economic inequalities also persist, due partly to uneven distribution of natural resources, and partly to maldistribution of new investment in irrigation and fertilisers. Rural-urban inequalities are also exacerbated by the continued flow of resources to towns. And the scenario is repeated between small and large towns, since the major share of planned investment is concentrated in a few cities and ports, at the cost of stagnating small towns. These trends have gained momentum, further widening the gulf between rich and poor communities, and between growing and lagging regions.

Seventh, population growth in the context of meagre access to arable land has meant fragmentation, increasing land inequality, widespread unemployment, and a rise in the number of refugee migrants and circulators. A land-hungry proprietory class has accentuated land inequality, worsening frustration and misery among the petty farmers and agricultural labourers. According to an Indian Reserve Bank survey, the concentration ratio of assets (mainly agricultural land) owned by rural households was 0.65 in 1961-2, increasing to 0.66 in 1972.[24] In 1971-2 the poorest 10 per cent owned only 0.1 per cent and the richest 10 per cent more than 50 per cent of total assets (mainly land). The Gini concentration ratio of land inequality was 0.61 in 1953-4, which worsened to 0.68 in 1960-1 and to 0.67 in 1970-1 (Table 8.12).[25] From 1961 to 1971, while the Indian population grew by 22.5 per cent, the number of landless agricultural labourers increased by 50.7 per cent (from 30 million to 45.4 million), indicating growing landlessness. This was aggravated by widespread violence during 1971-81, causing further uprooting from the land. Inequality in land ownership facilitated the continued exploitation of small

Table 8.12: *Land Inequality in India, 1961-71*

Size of landholdings (acres)	1960-1		1970-1	
	Cumulative percentage of holdings	Cumulative percentage of area owned	Cumulative percentage of holdings	Cumulative percentage area owned
0.0-0.99	44.21	1.59	44.89	5.5
1.0-4.99	75.22	19.99	89.35	39.6
5.0-9.99	88.08	40.53	96.35	67.0
10.0-19.99	95.64	64.10	99.16	88.3
20.0-29.99	98.01	77.09	99.69	94.5
30.0-49.99	99.40	88.87	99.91	98.0
50.0 and above	100.00	100.00	100.00	100.0

Source: *Census of India, 1961* (New Delhi, Registrar General's Office, 1963); *Agricultural Census of India, 1971* (New Delhi, Board of Revenue and Directorate of Agriculture, 1975).

peasants and sharecroppers by landlords and the proprietory class.

India's economy continues to be oriented towards primary exports. Railways and roads still feed export centres or primary cities, so that internal trade circuits remain weak. There have been few vigorous attempts at rural or community development in all these years of planning. The 568,000 villages of India are therefore reeling under poverty; many lack irrigation, schools, health facilities or potable drinking water. The lack of rural employment opportunities forces many labourers to remain idle for nine months a year, leaving them no alternative but to circulate to other districts or nearby towns or cities to find any job, no matter how unskilled or low the pay.

The colonial export-oriented activities initially generated distortions in the spatial economic structure, inhibiting the emergence of a self-generating economic base. This is the historical context of wage-labour mobility in India. But the forces set in motion by colonialism still largely determine labour circulation, as government measures have not been sufficient to overcome the acute poverty in the country. Peasants and agricultual labourers are still moving into towns in search of any kind of job. But as the towns and cities have limited employment-generating capacity, the incoming labourers often only find work as porters, rickshawalas, domestic servants, vendors, hawkers, construction workers, bricklayers and the like (Table 8.11). Urban unemployment has been growing, the great metropolises lack proper urban facilities, and the inability of the urban centres to absorb this rural exodus has compelled labourers to circulate for long periods. The deep sense of belonging and commitment to home villages, where they are compelled to leave families, also has been a strong social force encouraging frequent urban-to-rural circulation.

Thus, wage-labour circulation is from rural poverty to urban poverty, from unemployment to underemployment, from one region of stress to another. But the phenomenon can best be understood in its historical setting, for such types of circulation are rare in developed economies; they are found primarily in the once-dependent countries of the Third World. Amin has argued that labour mobility in western Africa primarily arises as a response to politico-economic and structural changes caused by uneven penetration of capitalism and colonialism, generating widespread spatial, social and economic inequalities.[26] Forbes and Hugo, studying mobility in Indonesia, have also argued that circulation arises as a result of incomplete penetration of capitalism, in itself helping to maintain the inequalities so generated.[27] Such studies lend support to the findings from investigations in India and the historical considerations there.

IV. Policy Implications and Strategies for Development

1. Policy Implications

One important question is whether the circulation of wage labourers improves their socio-economic condition. A conclusive answer must await nationwide field research on the causes and implications of wage-labour circulation. Unfortunately, even exploratory studies on circulation in India are rare. However, in northern India the surveys suggest the answer is 'No'. There is no evidence that the circulation promotes upward social mobility, or permits escape from poverty and misery; neither are remittances adequate to foster agricultural development in the home villages. Circulation may lead to downward social mobility in some cases, where uprooted skilled workers must take unskilled jobs. In any case, rickshawalas in the city, agricultural labourers circulating to near or distant villages, and bonded circulators working in brick-kilns, are chained to the same lowly positions even after many years of such existence, circulation notwithstanding. In the meantime, their sons and grandsons join them in the new workplaces to repeat the same miserable drama. There is very little possibility of either vertical or intergenerational social mobility.

A related question is whether such circulation should be discouraged. Even if mobility does not improve the socio-economic position of wage labourers, this in no way implies that small farmers and agricultural labourers were much better off in their home villages. That such circulation does help to avoid starvation must be underlined; it is the only beneficial aspect of labour circulation, as it stands today. Judged from this perspective, labour circulation, even in its present form, should not be discouraged or stopped. It acts as a safety valve, providing whatever small means of livelihood and economic support is available for keeping alive the labourer and his family.

Nevertheless, circulatory movements from one low-income activity to another result in a massive waste of human potential for the individual and for the nation as a whole. It would be better to encourage permanent population movements that would result in greater economic security and social mobility.

A third policy question is whether such circulation will increase or decrease in the near future. The answer depends on structural changes in the processes that cause labour circulation, processes that collectively constitute a *syndrome of poverty and circular mobility*. If this continues, labour circulation will increase in the coming decades, especially if population growth remains rapid.[28] It is fast approaching an involutionary situation that will only allow increasingly circular migration between the rural peasant sector and the urban informal sector, and very little real population transfer to urban organised sectors. The main policy implication is simply that the structure underlying the poverty-mobility syndrome must be changed.

Another policy implication concerns socio-economic and spatial inequalities. If increasing circular migration of impoverished labourers accentuates those inequalities, an explosive situation will occur in which labourers can no longer be absorbed even in the peasant and urban informal sectors. Urban centres and rural destinations would then fail to act as safety valves, leading to politico-economic turmoil. Alleviation of these inequalities remains a top priority.

Another implication is the need to ensure a productive labour force and raise productivity through effective programmes, such as vocational training, for ameliorating the condition of wage-labour circulators. Freeing bonded labourers and providing them with minimum living conditions are prerequisites for augmenting productivity and socio-economic progress.

2. Strategies for Alleviating the Condition of Circulators

The best way to eliminate poverty-induced circulation is not by fostering other forms of mobility, such as permanent migration, commuting or long-term circulation, but by changing conditions in both village and city by reducing rural-urban disparities, rural indebtedness, and stagnation.[29] But as the majority of the Indian poor live in villages and as the countryside suffers from stagnation, unemployment and underemployment, planning must assist the rural poor. Programmes and policies are required that aim at rural reconstruction and the development of neglected regions and communities. Rural development must involve effective land redistribution for the landless, agricultural labourers and petty farmers; there must also be accelerated rural industrialisation, improved irrigation, massive employment generation in villages, and more growth in neglected areas. A few comments on some of these are pertinent.

Land Reforms. Intense land inequality in India not only militates against agricultural productivity, growth and social justice, but keeps large cultivable areas ill-used and unproductive. Land redistribution, coupled with the development of irrigation facilities, consolidation of scattered holdings, and more generous credit for small farmers will raise per capita and per acre agricultual productivity and enhance levels of living.[30] These programmes will benefit the communities as well as the landless labour circulators, who constitute the bulk of the rural poor.

Development of Irrigation and Generation of Employment. An extensive network of irrigation facilities (canals, tanks, deep and shallow tubewells, and river irrigation) should be the basis of India's rural regeneration and agricultural modernisation. A recent analysis of data from 281 districts of India has shown that food grain production depends primarily on the extent of irrigation, and not on chemical fertilisers, high-yielding varieties of seeds, tractors, pump-sets, and so forth. It was found that irrigation alone explained about 65 per cent of the variance in foodgrain production.[31] The provision of irrigation to all parts of the country, especially in dry belts and seasonally dry regions, would increase the number of man-days of work a year from its present level of 150 to as much as 300 days. It would raise agricultural employment and productivity, and thereby redress the serious rural unemployment and underemployment.

Elimination of Barriers to Mobility. There are many barriers to mobility that restrict choice and the attainment of basic needs.[32] They include the caste system, illiteracy, language difficulties, lack of information, the practice of restricting jobs to 'sons of the soil', and rural indebtedness that can bind villagers to serfdom. Sometimes, the government's actions against hawkers or squatters, or its reluctance to subsidise small-scale entrepreneurs, act as further barriers to mobility. Identification and elimination of these barriers is another prerequisite for individual, community and national development.

Rural Industrialisation. Novel development strategies may be necessary. For instance, unemployed workers could be transferred from agricultural activities to cottage, small-scale or agro-based industries, as well as livestock rearing and dairy development. Such industries existed in Indian villages for many centuries, but were neglected or allowed to die out. They should be revived, and the age-old occupational skills of the rural folk regenerated. In recent years, the government has become aware of the need for reviving such industries, and is encouraging their development.[33] These efforts should be strengthened and integrated into the government's other development programmes.

Mobility Planning and Spacial Restructuring. The need to plan for circulation and migration while integrating it with economic planning, has not been recognised.[34] Problems of mobility bear directly upon regional and national development, as movements mainly reflected regional imbalances in natural, economic, and social resources. Unless such disparities are corrected, the socio-economic problems associated with circulation and migration will not be solved.

Planning should take into account the migrants' employment, socio-economic welfare, security and assimilation, and should include:

(a) identification and development of backward areas;

(b) more effective steps to reduce socio-economic and regional inequalities through more equitable distribution of production and investment;

(c) programmes to enable villagers to derive more benefits from their labour and products, and to pay less for necessities;

(d) increased utilisation of human and natural resources, such that all possible avenues of employment are opened; and

(e) development of circulation origin and destination regions.

The last step emphasises the need for constructive planning programmes in both the countryside and in urban centres. In source regions, effective programmes are required to provide maximum possible employment for the rural masses. Construction of housing and of irrigation networks, and rural industries are the greatest employment generators. Raw materials should be processed within rural areas and only then exported, so that the rural poor receive their due share of benefits. The modernisation of agriculture, through such innovations as irrigation development, multiple cropping and intensive cultivation, coupled with the transfer of unemployed labourers to rural industries, would also create employment and discourage rural migrants and circulators from crowding into cities. Such measures would create village work opportunities, thereby raising consumption and productivity while ensuring that the countryside was no longer depleted of human and natural resources.

A development strategy is just as necessary for destination areas. Provision should be made for training to incoming circulators so that they gain access to skilled and productive activities, instead of urban informal activities like porterage, shoeshining, domestic service, and hawking. The numerous decaying small towns should be developed by setting up more productive units and services there and by channelling more investment into them. And the parasitic cities, ports and former foreign enclaves must be transformed so as to act as agents of change by diffusing development impulses to surrounding villages.

As discussed earlier, most Indian towns and cities have limited employment-generating capacity under capital-intensive industrialisation.[35] Thus, most incoming circulatory migrants remain unemployed or take up manual work in the urban informal sector. If this situation continues, it will create an involutionary urban condition.[36] In that context, restrictions on circulation and/or squatter settlements are not desirable. The alternative policies outlined above are more effective and desirable to reconstruct the village economy and reorient the functions of small towns and cities in favour of more labour-intensive industries with migrant-absorbing capacity.

The transformation of parasitic towns and cities will not be possible unless we realise that spatial economy is a consequence of political economy, and that serious efforts are needed to restructure the economy and create a national spatial organisation. This means less dependence on international market relations and more emphasis on internal markets and internal growth. It will require a reorientation of trade and transport links, resource use, investment and growth, credit services and subsidies, and functions of urban centres away from the present heavy reliance on export activities and a concentration of growth and development in rural and urban settlements neglected during the colonial and post-Independence periods. It also requires efforts to provide welfare for the poor and to raise their purchasing power. In short, it requires a more equitable distribution of income, wealth, and consumption.

When these requirements are met, and moves are made towards the strategies described earlier, India will have initiated self-sustained growth and development. This will result in structural changes in the systems that explain India's poverty-induced mobility, and the elimination of its syndrome of poverty and circular mobility.

Notes

1. Such links of interdependence between the three matrices are established by canonical analysis (a form of regression), which permits mapping of the bases of the mobility behaviour matrix and the attribute-utility distance matrix. Canonical analysis measures the statistical overlap (trace correlation) between the matrices, and generates successive causal linkages between the pairs of vectors from both the dependent and independent sets that are maximally correlated (canonical correlations). For details see, e.g., S. Mukherji: 'The mobility field theory of human spatial behaviour: A spatial-behavioural approach to the study of migration and circulation in the Indian situation', PhD dissertation, University of Hawaii, 1975, pp. 49-129.

2. S. Mukherji: 'The mobility field theory of movement dynamics: A pathway to generalisations for migration planning for underdeveloped countries', in *Geografiska Annaler*, 1980, no. 62, B, pp. 20-32.

3. These two matrices were defined and measured as independent variables.

4. Canonical equation 3 refers to movements of educated unemployed, and is not relevant here. S. Mukherji: 'The need system, place utilities and mobility behaviour in the Indian situation: Structures, dimensions, linkages and migration planning policies', in K.C. Eidt, K.N. Singh and R.P.B. Singh (eds.): *Man, culture and settlements* (New Delhi, Kalyani Publishers, 1977), pp. 281-324.

5. S. Mukherji: 'The syndrome of poverty and wage labour circulation: The Indian scene', in R.M. Prothero and M. Chapman (eds.): *Circulation in the Third World countries* (London, Routledge and Kegan Paul, 1978), pp. 1-30.

6. For details, see ibid.

7. See, e.g., K.C. Zachariah: *Migrants in Greater Bombay* (Bombay, Asia Publishing House, 1968), pp. 338-9.

8. S. Mukherji: *Circulation of seasonal agricultural labourers in Birbhum district, West Bengal*, Occasional Paper No. 6 (Santiniketan, Department of

288 Wage Labour Circulation in Northern India

Geography, Visva-Bharati University, 1981) pp. 1-32 (hereafter Mukherji 1981a).

9. Mukherji, 1978.

10. A. Mitra, S. Mukherji and R.N. Bose: *The Indian cities: Their industrial structure, inmigration and capital investment* (New Delhi, Indian Council of Social Science Research and Abhinav Publishers, 1981).

11. There exists widespread confusion and scepticism about generalisations from case studies. In this connection, Chapman's views in Chapter 13 are worth reflection.

12. S.L. Kayastha and S. Mukherji: 'Spatial disorganisation and internal migration in India: Some probable strategies for restructuring the space economy and development', in *Canadian Studies in Population*, 1978, vol. 6, pp. 45-61.

13. Government of India, Planning Commission: *Industrial planning and licensing policy* (New Delhi, 1967).

14. B.J.L. Berry: *Essays on commodity flows and the spatial structure of the Indian economy*, Research Paper No. 111 (Chicago, University of Chicago, Department of Geography, 1966), pp. 7-20.

15. S. Mukherji: *Mechanisms of underdevelopment, labour migration and planning strategies for India* (Calcutta, Prajna, 1981), pp. 11-65 (hereafter, Mukherji 1981b).

16. S. Mukherji: 'Labour migration, spatial disarticulation and regional planning in India', in L.R. Singh (ed.): *New perspectives in geography* (Allahabad, Thinkers' Library, 1981), pp. 232-44.

17. H.A. Gould: 'Lucknow rickshawalas: The social organisation of an occupational category', in M.S.A. Rao (ed.): *Urban sociology in India* (New Delhi, Orient Longman, 1974), pp. 90-100.

18. These aspects are discussed in greater detail elsewhere. See Mukherji, 1981b, pp. 10-45; S. Mukherji: 'A theoretical model of the process of labour mobility in India', in S. Mukherji (ed.): *Labour migration and regional development in India* (Allahabad, Thinkers' Library, 1982), pp. 15-60.

19. The percentage below the poverty line was projected to be 48 per cent in rural areas and 41 per cent in urban areas in 1977-8. The total so defined would be about 280 million. Government of India, Planning Commission: *Draft Five-Year Plan, 1978-83*, vol. I (New Delhi, 1978), pp. 1-7.

20. P.K. Bardhan and T.N. Srinivasan (eds.): *Poverty and income distribution in India* (Calcutta, Statistical Publishing Society, 1974), pp. 1-2.

21. Mukherji, 1981a, pp. 125-53.

22. R. Banerji: 'Exploitation of circulating labourers in Punjab and Haryana', in *Aaj-Kaal* (Calcutta), 22 August 1981.

23. Government of India, Planning Commission, 1978, pp. 3-7.

24. Reserve Bank of India: *All India debt and investment survey, 1971-72* (New Delhi, 1982), pp. 1-20.

25. Mukherji, 1981a, pp. 117-56.

26. S. Amin: *Modern migrations in western Africa* (London, Oxford University Press, 1974), pp. 10-45.

27. D. Forbes: *Mobility and uneven development in Indonesia: A critique of explanations of migration and circulation*, paper presented to the Development Studies Centre Conference on Population Mobility and Development, October 1980 (Canberra, Australian National University, 1980), pp. 20-2; G. Hugo: 'Circular migration in Indonesia', in *Population and Development Review*, March, 1982, vol. 8, no. 1, pp. 59-83, and Chapter 3.

28. S. Mukherji: *The demographic field theory: Population policies and demographic behaviour in India* (Allahabad, Thinkers' Library, 1982), pp. 1-40.

29. S. Mukherji: *Circular mobility, wage labour displacements and policy: A*

cross-cultural comparison of circulation in Hawaii and India (Varanasi, Banaras Hindu University, 1977; mimeographed), p. 5.

30. For details of land reforms, see Mukherhi, 1981a, pp. 155-88.

31. A. Mitra and S. Mukherji: *Population, food and land inequality in India: A geography of hunger and insecurity* (New Delhi, Indian Council of Social Science Research and Allied Publishers, 1980), pp. 12-65.

32. Mukherji, 1975, pp. 300-63.

33. S. Mukherji: *Essays on rural development* (Varanasi, Utsargo, 1982), pp. 1-66.

34. The need for such integrated development planning has been succintly expressed by Goldstein, who concluded a study of circulation by noting: 'The interests of these individual movers as well as of the rural and urban communities of which they are a part and toward which they make important contributions can best be met by policies that take account of the needs of the rural population, the needs of the urban population and the needs in both locations of those persons who move between them for shorter or longer periods' — S. Goldstein: *Cirulation in the context of total mobility in Southeast Asia* (Honolulu, East-West Center, Population Institute, 1978), p. 61.

35. Mitra, *et al.*, 1981, p. 182.

36. Mukherji, 1981a, pp. 44-70.

9
Circular Migration, Segmented Labour Markets and Efficiency

ALAN STRETTON

I. Introduction[1]

It is generally agreed that labour markets in Third World cities contain many institutional barriers. However, there is considerable debate over the success of different theoretical models in explaining the effects of such barriers. Neo-classical economists usually argue that while institutional factors often result in the segmentation of labour markets, competitive models are still a useful aid to analysis provided that adequate allowances are made for market imperfections.[2] This view is similar to the economic analysis of labour markets in western economies. Concepts such as occupational and local labour markets were developed as some of the more extreme assumptions of the competitive model were relaxed. According to this approach the labour market is segmented, at least in the short term, into non-competing groups, although competitive forces still operate within each segment. However, supposedly market forces would erode these institutional barriers, especially if governments adopted policies to remove imperfections in the system, such as in the areas of education and the capital markets. Recent neo-classical models of labour markets in Third World cities follow this tradition by including an informal or traditional sector in addtion to a modern industrial sector. In these dualistic models wage and productivity differentials are long-term phenomena because of restrictions on entry into the high-wage sector. Within this institutional setting, however, competition is still evident in the informal sector, and to some extent in the formal sector.

Others deny the importance of competitive forces and argue that the institutional setting has led to the emergence of a segmented labour market in which factors such as the supply and demand for labour, wages, and recruitment policies are determined independently in each submarket. This literature is often divided into institutional and structural approaches.[3] The former is content to describe the institutional setting of labour markets. The discrepancy between reality and the assumptions of the competitive model is thought to be sufficient grounds to dismiss neo-classical analysis. The structuralists, on the other hand, adopt a more radical approach and suggest an alternative analytical model. In one such model the number of jobs is determined by the level of output and technology and wages are set according to institutional and social guidelines. The mechanism for allocating people to jobs is decided by employers, and often results in a workforce segmented by age, sex, race or education.

Migration is known to play an important part in influencing the performance and structure of urban labour markets and is also prominent in the debate surrounding segmented labour markets. In most neo-classical models, migration is seen as an equilibrating factor as individuals respond rationally to the comparative incentives of different sectors. On the other hand, migrants are often seen as an identifiable group in the labour market who are either discriminated against or favoured. This discrimination is then one factor leading to the emergence of segmented labour markets.

Another scenario is that the migration pattern itself may raise barriers to competitive forces within urban labour markets and hence result in segmentation. It is this possibility which we will examine below. We begin by showing how repetitive circular rural-urban migration can result in the formation of segmented urban labour markets by introducing barriers to entry into particular occupations, by restricting access to training and by influencing wage determination. This process is illustrated by the building industry labour market in Manila. None of the standard models seems capable of adequately explaining the workings of this market. Usually, neo-classical economists regard barriers to competition as non-optimal, but in this chapter it will be argued that a 'closed' labour market increases the efficiency of the industry labour market. The reason is that many occupations in

Third World cities offer very insecure employment. Circular migration helps to reduce this uncertainty by restricting competition in the labour market and by allowing migrants to retain close links with their villages. Consequently, labourers exhibit a stronger commitment to the industry, which benefits from an experienced workforce it would not otherwise have. This point will be made by comparing the building industry labour market in Manila with that in Port Moresby, where circular migration is being replaced by long-term residence in the city.

II. Building Industry Labour Market in Manila[4]

Most labourers working on building sites in the Greater Manila area are migrants. Only about 15 per cent were born in the city. However, few of the labourers have moved permanently to the city or regard themselves as long-term residents of Manila. Most (approximately 60 per cent of the workforce) have adopted a repetitive circular migration pattern.[5] When they move to Manila, their families remain in their villages. Skilled labourers in particular move to the city specifically to work on building sites and migrate only when they are fairly certain that work is available. When the industry's demand for labour falls, they return to their villages. Labourers are able to move under conditions of relative certainty as they work and migrate as part of a small gang of workers led by a foreman or highly-skilled artisan. When the foreman or leader of the group finds work in Manila he informs his permanent labourers and they join him in Manila. For the duration of the project, labourers live on the building site and return to their villages for short visits. Remittances are sent to family members in the village. If by the end of the project the foreman has been unable to find more work, his labourers return to their villages and wait until they are called. Unlike the situation found in some countries, such as Mexico, their migration pattern is not seasonal.[6] Artisans regard themselves as building labourers who rely on the village economy when the industry's demand for labour is low, rather than rural workers who move to the city during slack agricultural periods.

The small group within which the labourers migrate and work is most clearly defined in the case of independent foremen who construct most low-income and middle-income housing and small non-residential buildings in the city. The foreman maintains a small group of permanent labourers (ranging in size from 3 to 15 men) whom he employs on all projects. The men are usually from the same rural district and in some cases are relatives of the foreman. The group includes a few unskilled labourers who receive training from the foreman or other tradesmen in the group. If the foreman requires additional workers for a particular job, men who approach the site are hired on a daily basis. *Pakiao* or subcontractors working on medium and large projects operate in a similar fashion. These small gangs are also found among the casual labourers of large contractors. They are led by a highly-skilled artisan but are less easily identified as each labourer is hired individually.

These groups are not only an integral part of circular migration but also play an important role in recruitment, training and wage determination in the industry. Indeed, we will argue that by restricting entry into the workforce, creating barriers to skills acquisition and reducing the influence of the supply and demand for labour on wages, the circular migration pattern tends to insulate the building industry labour market from Manila's labour market as a whole. It creates a segmented labour market.

Recruitment procedures vary with the type of contractor. Independent foremen and *pakiao* employ their permanent labourers on all their projects and only hire outsiders when the size or composition of their workforce is inadequate. Small and medium-sized construction companies usually delegate responsibility for recruitment to their foremen, who give preference to labourers they have known for long periods. Hence the arrangement is similar to that which exists between independent foremen and their gang of permanent labourers. Large contractors, on the other hand, often try to prevent strong ties developing between foremen and their workforce. They fear that if a foreman is 'pirated' by a competitor, most of their tradesmen will leave as well. Recruitment is often controlled, then, from a central office rather than on the site, and workers can be transferred to different projects so that they work under different supervisors. However, small gangs of labourers can still be found on large sites. The highly-skilled artisans who lead these groups rely on their contacts in the industry (foremen for whom they have worked previously) to inform them of job availability. Each member of the group then applies for work with the same firm.

Recommendation from a foreman is usually sufficient to ensure success. While the labourers may be hired as individuals by the contractor, they tend to work together.

Because of transportation costs and constraints, circular migration with frequent return visits is more likely to be adopted by persons living within a limited radius of the city. Most labourers on building sites in Manila come from central and southern Luzon. While migrants from other provinces search for work in the industry, their success is limited by the barriers to entry erected by these recruitment procedures. On small sites labourers who are not part of a foreman's permanent workforce will only be employed, if at all, for a short period. While large sites may appear more open, migrants without contacts in the industry will be at a disadvantge. As the screening procedures adopted by contractors are minimal, jobs usually go to the earliest applicants, especially if they have worked for the firm before or have been recommended by a foreman. Hence, those with the best information and contacts are more likely to secure employment. If a firm requires more labourers, its foremen will inform skilled labourers whom they have previously employed, and these tradesmen, in turn, will inform their gang of labourers. Labourers who are part of the circular migration network are more likely to be in the right place at the right time than a migrant who is searching for work independently. Hence, the circular migration pattern also operates as an informal but efficient information network.

Migrants from more distant provinces who manage to obtain a job on a building site find that their prospects for acquiring skills are thwarted by the fact that training occurs primarily within the circular migration network. Almost all manual skills are acquired informally through on-the-job training. Formal apprenticeship schemes and vocational schools are insignificant. On smaller sites carpenters (and other tradesmen) are instructed by the foreman or skilled labourers. The trainee is engaged on activities essential to the completion of the project and instruction usually takes the form of the demonstration of a particular technique followed by 'learning by doing'. Large contractors play virtually no role in training their workforce. They do not take on apprentices and their foremen are usually too busy to teach younger labourers. Any training which occurs on large sites is within the confines of a small group led by a *pakiao* or highly-skilled artisan. Foremen recognise three different classes of carpenter although no formal criteria exist. The time spent by an individual in each of these categories will vary with his ability and the attitude of his foreman. No payment is made for training received.

Obviously, some labour market conditions are more conducive to this type of informal training than others. It will be more efficient if the trainee can develop a long-term relationship with one instructor or group of instructors, otherwise he will spend much of his time searching for teachers on each site. Highly-skilled tradesmen must also be willing to engage in the scheme. They may do so because they expect their social standing to rise if they train village youths who might otherwise have difficulty in obtaining employment. Or instructors may expect some indirect economic benefit. An independent foreman is training his future skilled workforce without which he will find it difficult to obtain jobs. Also, while the foreman may not receive any immediate payment for his services, the trainee may be placed under an unwritten obligation to his instructor. If the foreman needs assistance at some future time, he can call upon those whom he has previously helped.

This discussion suggests that circular migration is an ideal environment for informal training if the apprentice is a member of the foreman's permanent workforce. It allows the two participants to work together for a long time despite the instability of employment offered by the industry. However, a highly-skilled artisan is less likely to train a labourer from a different district as the chances of the two working together on the same site for more than one or two projects are quite small. In addition, the incentives to an instructor will be less in this case. His social status in his village may not rise as much as when he assists local youths. Nor will the evidence of his generosity be visible. The economic benefits will also be less. A foreman desires a permanent workforce from the same district so that they can be easily contacted. Finally, if he wishes to call on past apprentices to honour their obligations to him, close proximity is likely to be an advantage.

Hence, if a migrant from more distant provinces secures a job as an unskilled labourer on Manila's building sites, the likelihood of his acquiring skills is quite remote. However, as unskilled labourers face low wages, arduous work and uncertain employment prospects, there is little incentive to remain in the industry.

The few skilled labourers from areas other than central and southern Luzon who were working in the industry had been trained in their home province and had migrated as skilled labourers.

The third way in which circular migration tends to insulate the industry from the wider urban labour market is through its effects on wage determination. One of the essential characteristics of neo-classical models is that wages are determined endogenously by supply and demand. If one relaxes the standard assumptions so as to permit a two-sector urban labour market and minimum wage legislation, these models usually predict a wage differential. The formal or modern sector is expected to comply with the regulations (partly because this sector utilises advanced technology, and therefore workers in it have a higher productivity), but in the informal sector an excess supply of labour will keep wages below the statutory minimum.

However, the situation in the building industry varies significantly from this prediction. Despite the apparent excess supply of labour in Manila, the legal minimum wage is observed even on small building sites. The stable employment relationship that exists within the small groups of labourers who engage in circular migration is an important contributing factor. The leaders of these groups face strong social pressures to maximise the benefits received by their labourers. In addition, independent foremen do not enter into fixed-price contracts with their clients. Rather, they are paid a daily wage to recruit and supervise a workforce. Most owners provide funds to cover wage costs and the purchase of materials. Hence, the foreman is able to pay his unskilled labourers the legal minimum wage and pass on the costs to his client. A second characteristic of the industry's wage structure is that there are no differentials among different sections of the industry. Contractors pay the same wage for the same skill irrespective of their size.[7] There are a number of reasons for this. Trade unions do not restrict entry into the formal section of the industry and skills are transferable from one site to the next. Large contractors do not offer higher wages to reduce labour turnover as they are not interested in retaining a committed workforce.

The above discussion suggests that the argument that wages are determined by institutional factors and social custom may be applicable to the building industry. At the very least one would expect minimum wage legislation, the types of contracts used in the industry, and the circular migration pattern to dampen the effects of supply and demand on wage levels. An increase in the level of urban unemployment or underemployment may not reduce wages on building sites because the new entrants to the wider urban labour market do not represent competitors to building industry labourers. The recruitment methods centred around circular migration can restrict entry into the industry's workforce. Similarly, a recession in the building industry would not lead to a lower urban wage, as most unemployed building industry labourers will return to their village rather than seek other jobs in Manila. Hence the effects of circular migration on recruitment, training and wages have created a building industry labour market that can be viewed as insulated (at least to a certain extent) from the rest of Manila's labour market. Any change in circumstances in the industry labour market is likely to result in an increase or decrease in the amount of migration rather than spilling over to affect the labour market of other industries in the city.

As is often the case, the peculiar set of circumstances found in the building industry labour market in Manila can be at least partially explained by both structural and neo-classical models. Structuralists could argue that the level of employment in the industry is determined not by wages but by the level of building activity and the choice of technology. In a competitive model techniques of production are primarily influenced by relative factor prices. However, the evidence to support this hypothesis is not very convincing. The output mix of the industry and the attitudes of architects, engineers and contractors seem much more important. Most large contractors prefer to use modern, western construction techniques and materials. This attitude has been nurtured by professional education based on American syllabuses and numerous professional and trade journals which contain information on the latest equipment and materials. Rarely, if ever, do they carry articles discussing labour-intensive alternatives. Hence during the early 1970s when wages fell relative to the price of capital, there was no move towards more labour-intensive construction methods. In fact, a shift in output mix combined with the attitudes of engineers to produce an increase in labour productivity.[8] Hence the structuralists could argue that wages play little role in determining the number of jobs created by the industry.

Furthermore, wages are not determined by supply and demand. Rather, they are set by institutional factors (minimum wage legislation) and social custom (as part of the circular migration network). Recruitment is then organised on a first come, first employed basis. One of the main purposes of the circular migration is to act as an information network so that participants in it are ensured of a place at the front of the queue.

The main difficulty in accepting this explanation refers to the actual process of segmentation. Structuralists usually argue that the mechanism for allocating jobs, and hence the means of discrimination, is controlled by employers. Segmentation is seen as largely a demand-side phenomenon. However, the circular migration network is in fact the outcome of employees' reactions to the conditions of employment presented by the industry. In order to protect their rather precarious position, longer-term employees have erected barriers to prevent outsiders from entering the workforce. Large and medium-sized contractors have not played an active role in establishing the industry's segmented labour market. It seems that contractors are 'exploiting' their labourers by not offering more-secure employment and so are ultimately responsible for the segmentation of the labour market. However, it is necessary to remember that contractors also face considerable uncertainty over the future demand for their services, the failure rate among firms being high.

It is also possible to partially interpret the industry's labour market within a neo-classical framework. Neo-classical models which have been modified to encompass some labour market institutions and imperfections, but which still attribute considerable explanatory power to competitive forces, exhibit a number of common characteristics. They argue that segmentation occurs because of institutional barriers or imperfections on the supply side of the market and view the segmented labour market as non-optimal so that removal of institutional barriers would result in improved efficiency in the labour market. Their analysis suggests policies which would eliminate market imperfections.

It is possible to argue that circular migration represents a rational economic response on the part of labourers. Fan and Stretton (see Chapter 11) demonstrate that under certain conditions it is rational for a migrant to circulate rather than move permanently to the city. If the family separates its decisions relating to income from those relating to consumption, under certain conditions it is rational for a migrant to circulate rather than move permanently to the city. If the family separates its decisions relating to income from those relating to consumption, under certain circumstances, the family will maximise earnings if the labourer spends much of his working time in the city whereas it will maximise utility from consumption by spending most of its income in the village. This spatial distribution of employment and consumption can be achieved through circular migration. Fan and Stretton also show that if the potential migrant is risk averse, circular migration can be a rational response even if the expected income from migrating permanently exceeds that from circulating.[9]

Contractors surely act rationally by not engaging in elaborate recruitment procedures. Because of fluctuations in their demand for labour, builders expect a high labour turnover. They are not interested in nurturing a long-term, committed workforce. Also, as they hire workers on a casual basis, recruits found to be unsuitable can be dismissed at little cost. Hence there is no need for contractors to adopt elaborate screening procedures, and their practice of hiring the first arrivals, especially if they are recommended by one of their foremen, seems optimal. Any labourer not measuring up to the required standards can be easily detected and fired. Contractors do not engage in training, as firm-specific skills cannot be taught. As most skills can be used throughout the industry, they feel that labourers should pay for their own training.

According to neo-classical models, the segmented labour market in the building industry has emerged because of imperfections on the supply side. The barrier to competition arises from advantages that accrue to circular migrants with contacts in the industry and information on job availability. By its nature circular migration can only be practised by migrants whose villages are close to Manila. Migrants from other areas, or residents of central and southern Luzon who have no contacts in the industry, are excluded from the informal information network. Hence their chances of securing employment are reduced. However, once allowance is made for this institutional barrier, competitive forces are still important in explaining the actions of both employers and employees. This analysis suggests the possibility of removing the barriers and creating a more competitive environment. First, it would be necessary to improve access to information on job vacancies. This would open the market to the urban unemployed, who are currently unable to obtain a job in the industry. However, this would not be sufficient. While the new entrants to the workforce might be able to secure jobs as unskilled labourers, they would still be excluded from the informal training programmes, which are part of the circular migration patterns. Hence it would also be necessary for the government to provide alternative training facilities, such as vocational schools.

The point at which the neo-classical view of the building industry labour market loses credibility is in the presumption that removal of the market imperfections would lead to an improvement in efficiency. In the present case this is far from obvious. The urban unemployed who are excluded from the industry would be made better off, as their employment prospects would improve. This must be balanced against the less secure position of the circular migrants. However, perhaps surprisingly, contractors may find that if the labour market becomes more open and competitive it might operate less efficiently from their point of view. As this is a rather important suggestion we will discuss it in some detail.

III. A More Open Labour Market

A more open labour market might be expected to increase efficiency in a number of ways. First, contractors could choose their labourers from a large and more diverse group of applicants, possibly resulting in a workforce of a higher calibre. Second, the supply of labour to the industry would expand so that future wages might increase at a slower rate than would otherwise be the case. In addition, the formal training facilities that would need to accompany the change in market structure might produce more highly-skilled artisans than the current informal arrangements. However, the benefits of informal training should not be dismissed lightly. Most contractors in Manila speak highly of their skilled labourers.[10] And in many respects the building industry is well suited to informal training. The trainee is performing useful tasks while undergoing instruction, and work on the site is not unduly disrupted while the foreman is assisting his apprentice. Nor is expensive equipment left idle. In addition, the skills the labourer learns on one site are useful on others.

The advantage of a more open labour market is that it might produce a less committed industry workforce. This would imply a higher labour turnover rate for the industry. While each contractor may not be interested in maintaining a stable workforce, he would prefer the casual labourers he employs to have experience in the industry. If the industry's (as opposed to the firm's) labour turnover rate is high, efficiency will be reduced.

A number of authors have suggested that because of the instability of employment offered by contractors, labourers remain in the building industry for only a short period.[11] They argue that building labourers, most of whom are recent rural-urban migrants, view employment in the industry as a stepping-stone from agricultural employment to a more stable and desirable job in the city. Labourers react to the insecurity of employment by leaving the industry as fast as they can.

This hypothesis appears to describe the attitude of unskilled labourers on Manila's building sites who are not part of the circular migration pattern. As they are unable to acquire skills or secure a job, they work in the industry for only a short period. In contrast, most skilled labourers have exhibited a considerable degree of commitment to the industry. Approximately 85 per cent of skilled labourers have worked in the industry for more than five years, and almost 40 per cent for more than 10 years.[12]

The most important factor in explaining this commitment of tradesmen is the extent to which circular migration is able to offset the insecurity of employment offered by contractors. It does this in three ways. First, the small groups within which labourers work and migrate provide a reasonably stable work environment. Without this support mechanism, labourers would have to change frequently not only their job location but also their working companions. This could place considerable stress on the individual. However, if a labourer moves to a new site together with other members of his group, this problem is less important.

Second, circular migration allows labourers to return to the social and economic security of their villages when they are unemployed. At the same time, they are kept informed of job prospects on building sites in Manila by their network of contacts in the industry. Hence, the periods of unemployment between jobs do not create as much hardship as they would if the labourer was forced to remain in the city. Third, a labourer who is part of the circular migration pattern is likely to receive training, so that he has the prospects of a more interesting and better-paid job in the future.

A workforce committed to the industry enables it to retain experienced labourers, despite the fact that contractors offer insecure employment. This improves the efficiency of the industry and its labour market considerably. As the quality of the workforce is higher it requires less supervision. This, combined with a lower wastage rate of materials, should reduce costs. At the same time the quality of the final product is improved. These considerations can be important even for unskilled labourers. Simple tasks such as mixing cement and collecting materials can be executed more efficiently by labourers with some experience in the industry than by complete novices. However, the major benefits accruing from an experienced workforce relate to training costs. If tradesmen worked in the industry for only short periods, the social (and possibly private) return to any formal training would be very low. Also, it is difficult to imagine any serious informal training occurring in the industry if labour turnover rates were high. By its very nature, informal training takes years to complete. In addition, the incentives for older artisans to pass on their skills would be reduced. So that a high labour turnover rate for the industry would increase training costs and/or lower the quality of instruction.

There can be little doubt that a committed workforce increases the efficiency with which the industry operates and that the circular migration pattern found in Manila helps to achieve this. However, is circular migration a necessary condition for the industry to retain an experienced workforce? If it is, attempts by governments to undermine the circular migration pattern and create a more open labour market would actually reduce the efficiency of the industry. This is a difficult question to answer, but we can gain some insight by examining the industry labour market in a different setting. Port Moresby in Papua New Guinea is a useful comparison, as in the past a circular migration pattern was followed by building labourers. However, there the industry labour market has experienced considerable changes in recent years, including a move away from circulation. By examining the effects of such changes on the efficiency of the industry we can assess the desirability of government policies to create a more open industry labour market in other settings.

IV. The Building Industry Labour Market in Port Moresby[13]

In recent years one of the most significant features of the building industry labour market in Port Moresby has been the change in the ethnic composition of the workforce. From the late 1940s until the mid-1960s most labourers working on the city's building sites migrated from the nearby provinces of Central and Gulf. These workers adopted an employment-migration pattern similar to the circular migration pattern found in Manila. They returned to their villages frequently, and an informal information network linked the villages and Port Moresby. Informal training was also an important feature of the arrangements.

There are a number of reasons for the early dominance of these ethnic groups in the industry. They were the first people in Papua New Guinea to receive rudimentary training in western building techniques. Village mission schools often taught basic carpentry skills and some men received informal training while working for the Australian army. After the war many men from these provinces remained in Port Moresby to participate in reconstruction activities. The close proximity of their villages to Port Moresby meant that they faced considerably lower transportation costs than potential migrants from other provinces. And so when the administration relaxed restrictions on rural-urban migration, they were among the first to respond.[14] However, by the mid-1960s young men from Central and Gulf Provinces were showing a strong preference for white-collar jobs. The number of such positions open to Papua New Guineans was increasing and, because of their higher educational qualifications, youths from Central and Gulf were the most succesful applicants. By that time vocational education had spread to other areas of the country and the distance over which people were willing to migrate had increased. So that while youths from Central and Gulf were searching for work outside the industry, migrants from more distant provinces were arriving in Port Moresby and seeking employment on building sites.

If we use the employment-migration patterns adopted by labourers as criteria, we can distinguish three groups of labourers currently working on Port Moresby building sites. The first are those from Central and Gulf Provinces, mostly older men who have exhibited considerable commitment to the industry, although some younger labourers unable to obtain white-collar jobs have used their contacts to obtain employment. Most of these labourers circulate or commute between Port Moresby and their villages. This group accounts for about half of the industry's skilled workforce, but they are proportionally less represented among carpenters aged less than 26 years than among older tradesmen. Very few men from these provinces work as unskilled labourers.

The second group of labourers are from the more distant Morobe and highland provinces. These migrants provide most of the industry's unskilled labourers and approximately 38 per cent of the skilled workers. Most of the industry's young carpenters are from this region. Few of the labourers in this group had experience in the building industry before they migrated. They moved to Port Moresby to seek a job and income, but they did not migrate specifically to work on building sites. Those who are now tradesmen acquired their skills while working in Port Moresby. High transportation costs prohibit a repetitive circular migration pattern from emerging among these labourers.

The third group of labourers, accounting for about 12 per cent of the skilled workforce, are tradesmen from distant provinces who have migrated to Port Moresby specifically to work in the industry. They received their training on building sites in their home provinces and seem willing to travel around the country to obtain work. While these men exhibit a certain commitment to the building industry it is not clear that they have a commitment to Port Moresby.

One consequence of the changing ethnic mix is that the circular migration pattern that was once a dominant feature of the industry's labour market has become less significant. About 40 per cent of the labourers interviewed in 1980 were separated from their families, but only 12 per cent of this group (7 per cent of the sample) returned to their village at least once a year.[15] Another 13 per cent of the labourers lived in Port Moresby with their families but visited their village at least annually. Most of the labourers who did visit their villages frequently were from Central Province. If daily commuters from urban and peri-urban villages are included, approximately 37 per cent of the workforce had regular contact with their village and should have been able to return during periods of unemployment. If the importance of Central Province as a source of building labourers continues to decline, the size of this group of circular migrants will also diminish.

The pattern that appears to be replacing circular migration is one of medium- to long-term residence in the city. About 56 per cent of the workforce moved to Port Moresby as single men, while 20 per cent were married but left their wives in their villages. Since migrating, labourers have consolidated their family ties in Port Moresby so that one-third were married migrants living in the city. About 35 per cent of the workforce had dwelt in the city for more than five years and were living with their immediate family. If we include migrants who had lived in the city for more than five years and those whose immediate family had also moved to Port Moresby, slightly more than 60 per cent of the workforce were covered. Another 17 per cent of the labourers were born in Port Moresby or villages within commuting distance. Hence, compared to Manila, the industry's workforce appeared to regard themselves as long-term (if not permanent) residents of Port Moresby.

The following paragraphs examine the effects on efficiency of these structural changes in the industry's labour market. Partly as a result of the changing ethnic mix of the workforce, the industry's labour market is quite open. An individual is unlikely to have difficulty in securing a job because he lacks contacts in the industry or because of his ethnic background. Slightly more than half of the workforce obtained their first job in the industry by approaching the foreman on a site on which they had no contacts. However, the more open labour market is also creating difficulties. The discussion of these will be divided into two parts, first analysing how the different migration patterns have influenced the commitment of labourers to the industry, and then turning to the effects of the changing ethnic mix on skill acquisition.

Building labourers in Port Moresby experience employment insecurity similar to that found in Manila. Almost half of the workforce of large expatriate contractors had been working for their current employer for less than six months. It was also estimated that in July 1980 perhaps as many as 45 per cent of the industry's workforce had experienced unemployment during the previous 18 months. The manner in which labourers react to periods of unemployment varies with their migration pattern and attitudes to residence in Port Moresby. Workers who commute from nearby villages return to their villages. They can easily keep themselves informed on job prospects, although those who work for small village-based builders often wait until their boss is awarded a new contract. Approximately 30 per cent of the labourers who had experienced unemployment fell into this group.[16] Some migrants who have retained strong links with their villages return to their rural homes when jobs are not available. Their ability to keep themselves informed of changes in the state of the labour market depends upon the number of migrants with a knowledge of the industry who return to the village or on the frequency of short trips that the unemployed labourers make to Port Moresby. Only 23 per cent of the unemployed labourers chose this option and most of these were without work for more than a year. One explanation of this long period of unemployment is that despite the fact that most of these workers live in villages in Central and Gulf Provinces, the information network that once linked these villages with Port Moresby building sites is disintegrating. Alternatively, once the labourers returned to their villages they may have been forced to remain for longer than they intended in order to fulfil social obligations, or they may have become involved in the village economy or have simply enjoyed the change.

By far the largest group of unemployed labourers are migrants who remain in Port Moresby. Almost half of the workers who had experienced unemployment chose this option. The implications of this coping mechanism will vary with the age and family responsibilities of the labourer. It is useful to distinguish four subgroups. Single men who are living with their parents probably face few hardships, as most can rely on their family for support. The second group comprises migrants whose families still live in their villages. Most of these men live with relatives or with *wantoks* and rely on their support while unemployed.[17] If the labourer contributed to the household budget while he was earning income, it is likely that his *wantok* would provide food and shelter, especially if it was agreed that he had lost his job through no fault of his own. However, it is unclear as to how long a family would be willing to support an unemployed *wantok*. If the labourer has difficulty in finding another job, he may be asked to leave. The effects of this might be cushioned by the fact that these labourers have no dependants living with them in the city, enabling them to cope with a fall in living standards.

Unemployed labourers whose families have also migrated to Port Moresby would appear to be in a more precarious position. Most members of this group said that they used past savings to support their families when they were not earning an income. However, it is useful to distinguish between young and old labourers in this predicament. An older man probably has children of working age on whom he can rely for support. In addition, during his life he has undoubtedly assisted many *wantoks* by contributing to their educational expenses and bride prices; if he needs assistance he can call on these people to repay obligations to him. However, a younger man supporting a wife and young children has few sources of support. Because of his age he is unlikely to have assisted others whom he could ask for help. Similarly, *wantoks* who would be willing to support a single unemployed man might baulk at the prospect of feeding and housing a whole family. It is this group which would appear to face the greatest hardship from unemployment.

We argued earlier that industry's efficiency would be adversely affected if the instability of employment it offered resulted in a high labour turnover rate. Unfortunately, we do not have data on labourers who leave the industry after losing their jobs, but several factors suggest that the number could be quite high in Port Moresby. The discussion above suggests that the coping mechanisms available to those who remain in the city while unemployed are far from adequate, so that labourers who lose their jobs on building sites might be tempted to accept employment in other industries. It was argued that married migrants living with their families were in the most precarious position. While this group represented 33 per cent of the workforce, they accounted for only 21 per cent of those who had experienced unemployment. One explanation of these figures is that members of this group are forced to leave the industry when they lose their jobs on building sites. Because of the pressures they face when not earning an income, these men are unable to wait for the industry's demand for labour to increase. If a job on another building site cannot be found quickly, they search for employment in another industry or return to their villages.

Unmarried migrants and those who have moved without their

wives and children are in the best position to cope with periods of unemployment in the city. While these men account for about half of the industry's workforce there are still grounds for concern. First, these labourers will face pressures from *wantoks* supporting them to search for employment in other industries if jobs on building sites cannot be found quickly. Second, the relative size of this group is likely to shrink. We have already mentioned the tendency for migrants to consolidate their family ties in Port Moresby as their period of residence in the city increases. Single migrants will marry, while those already married will ask their families to join them in Port Moresby. As this demographic process occurs, the labourers will move into the most vulnerable position in terms of dealing with unemployment in the city. Hence a pattern could be emerging in which young, recent migrants join the industry workforce and rely on *wantoks* for support during periods of unemployment. If they have not obtained a reasonably stable job with a large contractor by the time they must support their family in the city, they leave the industry for more secure employment. If this is correct, the industry's labour turnover rate will increase, and experienced workers will become scarce. Even the coping mechanism of returning to the village during periods of unemployment is not operating as effectively as it might, for labourers are remaining unemployed for longer than necessary. This places stress on the training arrangements, as a larger number of tradesmen must be taught.

We now turn to the effect of the changing ethnic mix and the openness of the labour market on skill acquisition in the industry. Informal training remains the most important means of acquiring skills, although some large contractors offer formal apprenticeships and a number of vocational schools provide courses of varying length and quality. During the 1950s and early 1960s the informal arrangements appear to have operated satisfactorily because most of the workforce came from Central and Gulf Provinces. But the current situation does not seem conducive to an effective informal training scheme. Most of the young men seeking training are from Morobe and highland provinces, while the older tradesmen are from Central and Gulf Provinces. For reasons discussed earlier, this may lower the incentives to artisans to pass on their knowledge. In addition, it can be difficult for an instructor and trainee from different ethnic groups to arrange to work together on the same sites for an extended period. The development of the scheme has also been hindered by a fall in the wage differential for skill and the attitudes of some of the large Australian-owned construction companies.

As a result of these pressures, the informal training arrangements seem to be deteriorating. Young men entering the industry who wish to acquire skills now tend to seek advice on a casual basis from carpenters working on the same site. Fewer trainees enter a long-term, intensive relationship with one or two instructors. Some labourers claimed they acquired their 'skills' simply by watching tradesmen performing their tasks. When they thought they could do the job they purchased or borrowed tools and tried to get a job as a carpenter. Discussions with foremen and site supervisors suggest that these arrangements are producing a large number of carpenters with basic skills but very few highly-skilled artisans. Of course, this trend will also impair the efficiency of the industry.

So it appears that the shift from circular to permanent (or at least long-term) migration in Port Moresby has reduced efficiency in the building industry and its labour market. While there are difficulties in drawing inferences from the Port Moresby experience for the situation in Manila, it is easy to imagine a similar process occurring in Manila if steps were taken to make the industry's labour market more open. An increasing proportion of the industry's workforce would come from more distant provinces. Hence they would need to remain in Manila during periods when work was not available on the building sites. However, they could not afford the luxury of remaining unemployed. While other family members may be employed, the cost of living in the city is high and a prolonged period during which the main income earner is without work would create considerable hardship. If the labourers are to remain committed to the industry and return to the building sites as soon as work is available, they would require at short notice 'fall-back' jobs for irregular periods. Such jobs would be difficult to find. Access to many informal-sector occupations is restricted in much the same way as on building sites. Even if labourers could gain access to the materials and equipment necessary to become, for example, hawkers, they would be forced to operate in more marginal locations. The fact is that Third World cities such as Manila offer very little support to labourers in insecure employment. Building labourers living in

Manila would, then, face considerable pressure to leave the industry as soon as more attractive alternatives become available. Consequently, the industry's labour turnover rate would increase and the efficiency of the labour market would be impaired.

V. Conclusion

Repetitive circular migration has evolved as a coping mechanism for labourers facing very difficult and insecure employment prospects in cities. I have argued that this migration pattern has created segmented labour markets within cities, but that contrary to the prediction of the usual neo-classical models, this has not inhibited efficiency. In fact, breaking down the barriers of these segmented labour markets would be disadvantageous. The reason for standard neo-classical models of labour markets failing to predict this outcome is that they ignore the problem of uncertainty. Employment in the building industry and in many other informal-sector occupations is very insecure.[18] As welfare schemes are virtually non-existent, labourers must fend for themselves. Circular migration represents one possible coping mechanism. It means that labourers can return to the support provided by their villages during times of hardship. In addition, the migration pattern acts to restrict entry into the occupation. In this latter sense circular migration is similar to one of the functions of trade unions in western countries. Of course, other coping mechanisms exist. Permanent or long-term urban dwellers might attempt to restrict entry into an occupation through informal information networks that could also be based on village ties.

These coping mechanisms result in the formation of segmented labour markets in many occupations in the city.[19] The disadvantages include the fact that some individuals are prevented from working in particular occupations even though they might be suitable for such jobs. This not only affects their wellbeing but also restricts the choice available to an employer. As competitive forces are reduced, *ceteris paribus*, efficiency will be impaired. The advantage of the segmented labour markets is that they reduce the risk and uncertainty facing individual labourers. Consequently, they are willing to remain in the industry for much longer, creating an experienced workforce. The greater security also means that labourers and the self-employed will be more willing to invest in both training and equipment, so improving the quality of the services they offer. If the advantages conferred by the segmented labour markets outweigh the disadvantages, this state of affairs is desirable, and there is no need for government intervention to remove the barriers.

Notes

1. The views expressed in this paper are those of the author and not of the BLMR or the Australian Government. Most of the work for this paper was done while the author was a member of the Economics Department, University of Hong Kong. Helpful comments were received from Guy Standing.

2. Labour market segmentation has been defined as 'the historical processes whereby political-economic forces encourage the division of the labour market into separate submarkets, or segments, distinguished by different labour market characteristics and behavioural roles' — R. Loveridge and A.L. Mok: *Theories of labour market segmentation* (The Hague, Martinus Nijhoff, 1979), p. 27.

3. G.G. Cain: 'The challenge of segmented labor market theories to orthodox theory: Survey', in *Journal of Economic Literature*, December 1976, vol. 14, no. 4, pp. 1215-57; G.B. Rodgers: *Migration and income distribution* (Geneva, ILO, 1981; mimeographed World Employment Programme research working paper; restricted).

4. This discussion is based on fieldwork conducted by the author in 1975. For a more detailed discussion see A.W. Stretton: 'The building industry and employment creation in Manila, the Philippines', PhD thesis (Canberra, Australian National University, 1977); idem: 'The building industry and urbanization in Third World countries: A Philippine case study', in *Economic Development and Cultural Change*, January 1981, vol. 29, no. 2, pp. 325-9.

5. Stretton, 1977.

6. D.A. Germidis: *Labour conditions and industrial relations in the building industry in Mexico*, Employment Series No. 11 (Paris, OECD Development Centre, 1974).

7. Consideration of fringe benefits would not change this conclusion. The major fringe benefit offered by employers is on-site shelter, and this is provided by all contractors.

8. For a more detailed discussion of these issues, see A.W. Stretton: 'Construction activity and employment creation in the Philippines', in *Philippine Economic Journal*, 1979, pp. 121-47.

9. Ibid.

10. This impression was gained from discussions with contractors and from articles in trade journals.

11. UNIDO: *Construction industry*, Monographs on Industrial Development No. 2 (New York, 1969); Germidis, 1974; P. Sylos-Labini: 'Precarious employment in Sicily', in *International Labour Review*, March 1964, vol. 89, no. 3, pp. 268-85.

12. Stretton, 1977.

13. This section is based on a study conducted by the author for the Papua New Guinea Institute of Applied Social and Economic Research. Fieldwork was undertaken in 1980. For a more detailed analysis, see A.W. Stretton: *The*

building industry in Port Moresby: A study of the industry's structure and labour market (Port Moresby, IASER, forthcoming).

14. This discussion of migration patterns of building labourers during the 1950s and 1960s is based on N.D. Oran: 'The Hula in Port Moresby', in R.J. May (ed.): *Change and movement: Reading on internal migration in Papua New Guinea* (Canberra, Australian National University Press, 1977); and D. Ryan: 'Toaripi in Port Moresby and Lae', in May, 1977.

15. About two-thirds were unmarried.

16. The survey methodology was such that only unemployed labourers who had returned to the industry were covered.

17. A *wantok* is someone who speaks the same dialect and therefore comes from the same village or district.

18. The income of hawkers, for example, can vary daily, depending on factors such as their location, the weather, holiday periods and the activities of the police and other officials.

19. This paper has concentrated on the building industry but there is a growing amount of evidence that shows circular migration operating in a similar way in many other occupations — S. Goldstein: *Circulation in the context of total mobility in southeast Asia* (Honolulu, East-West Population Institute, Paper No. 53, 1978).

10
Temporary Work in Brazilian Agriculture: 'Boia-fria' — A Category under Investigation

CHEYWA R. SPINDEL

I. Introduction

In rural Brazil, the increased use of non-resident day-workers, or 'boias-frias', essentially occurred in the 1960s, but it was only at the end of that decade and in the early 1970s that it became a subject for academic study.[1] It was also at that time that the issue became one of journalistic interest, the press devoting considerable space to the 'boias-frias', descriptions of the risks and exploitation to which these workers were subjected having moved their readers and attracted the attention of politicians. It was considered a politically strategic area, and one of 'proposed' government action. The object of this chapter is to summarise the information acquired over the past decade on the 'boia-fria' phenomenon, highlighting points that seem to be the most relevant with a view to understanding the development and continuation of this form of production.

We shall begin by discussing the operational nature and the explanation of certain concepts; second, we shall analyse the convergence and inter-relationship of the factors responsible for the rise and development of this form of social labour relations; third, we shall outline the living conditions and the conditions of exploitation to which these workers are subjected; and fourth, we shall consider the limitations and/or contradictions of proposed policies aimed at reducing and/or eliminating these problems.

II. 'Boia fria' — Tentative Conceptualisations and Definitions

The basic characteristic identified in early studies was the fact that this rural worker lived in an urban area, generally on the outskirts of a town or city, and depended for his reproduction as an urban dweller on temporary work in the rural area. Other elements were added in this connection, in an endeavour to be more specific, making a distinction between this and other forms of temporary worker used in agriculture. The principal feature distinguishing this type of worker from other temporary workers in agriculture is his constant practice of daily urban-rural migration for the purposes of his work. This type of worker is a 'daily cycle migrant', as described by Silva and Rodrigues.[2]

The importance of the rural-urban movement as a distinguishing characteristic has been stated in several studies. Gonzales and Bastos endeavoured to define the limits and scope of the various temporary-work relationships.[3] First, they divided the temporary-work category into mobile and seasonal workers. The basic dichotomy is access or lack of access to land. Seasonal workers sell their labour temporarily but live within the rural area, maintaining some kind of access to the land, whereas the mobile worker is defined as 'an agricultural worker who lives outside the estate, in general on the outskirts of the town or city, and who is continually moving about to do work in rural areas'. There are two variants of the mobile worker category, viz. 'itinerant' and 'rurban'. Itinerant workers are those who 'temporarily live at the place of agricultural work, periodically moving from one farm to another . . . as a function of the duration of the job', while 'rurban' (or 'boias-frias') differ from 'itinerants' only in their characteristic of moving daily from a fixed urban location to work at various rural properties. The common factor distinguishing them from other rural workers, according to these authors, is that as direct producers, they live exclusively from the sale of their labour, or are a proletarian worker population. In this way, workers having access to the land, whether as tenants, share-croppers, homesteaders or owners of small landholdings, form a different category from seasonal workers.[4]

However, these conceptual dichotomies, both within the proletarian population and between the proletarian and non-proletarian population, hardly allow identification of these various forms of labour in agriculture. For this reason, in trying to understand the evolution and crystallisation of certain types of labour relationship, this approach seems inadequate. This is partly because the reality under investigation is not inherently dichotomised; it is in the process of evolution that categories evolve, are crystallised and/or disappear. Therefore, to understand the phenomenon, the limits defined as an area of observation can hardly be restricted to the space occupied by the subject; it is necessary to go beyond these limits, since we are considering a phenomenon that is the result of a process of which the dynamics, governed by capital, affect all social production relationships. Most fundamentally, historically the seasonal employment of sharecroppers, smallholders, homesteaders, and so on, is generally the first step in the direction of their total proletarianisation.

Secondly, these 'seasonal' workers, during certain periods of the year, swell the numbers of 'boias-frias', selling their labour on a daily basis as a way of obtaining the additional money necessary for their reproduction as rural dwellers.

The difficulty in dealing with these dichotomies between a 'landed boia-fria' and 'non-landed boia-fria' is that the latter, as a labour supply, does not have any qualitative distinction. All supply to the same market, and participate or are exploited in it under equal conditions. Consequently, it must be remembered that the 'seasonal' workers represent an additional and highly significant supply of temporary labour, contributing to an extension of the elasticity of labour supply, liable to affect the working and wage conditions of other temporary workers.

A further situation of which little mention has been made in the literature is that it is not only the sharecroppers, homesteaders and owners of small landholdings, or the *landed* 'boias-frias', that swell the number of rural day-workers in the periods of greatest demand, but also members of the family of the *unlanded* 'boias-frias', those normally working in permanent or temporary urban activities, or unemployed, and/or those who do not work, both adults and children, who enter the rural labour market at peak periods.

It is important to stress the lack of knowledge with respect to these so-called 'seasonal' workers, sporadically but systematically joining the 'boias-frias' group. The importance of studies of the landed 'boias-frias' rests in the fact that these workers maintain social relations of production that could be regarded as hybrid —

that is, the protagonists play a number of roles, at times wage earner, at times owner and/or tenant. In the other case, the situation is one of unification of the labour market, with the disappearance of any dividing line between the supply of urban labour and rural labour.[5]

A deeper analysis of the situation of these workers could provide a better understanding not only of the processes that caused the emergence of the current 'boia-fria', but also of extrapolations of their extent, use and characteristics. However, bearing in mind the importance of all types of temporary labour in agriculture for understanding the 'boia-fria' phenomenon, this discussion is limited to a consideration of those who are urban dwellers and rural workers.

Silva and Rodrigues, using various concepts acquired from studies by Bombo and Bruneli, Vassimon, Santos, Gonzales and Bastos, Martinez-Allier, and D'Incao and Mello, proposed a 'globalising concept' which endeavours to incorporate all the basic elements in the different conceptualisations encountered.[6]

In this definition, the term 'boia-fria' is understood to mean:

> The rural worker, residing outside the agricultural property, *generally* on the outskirts of a town or city, *registered or otherwise*, paid by the *piece*, *job* or *day*, *recruited by a gang leader or otherwise*, and who *generally* moves to the place of work each day, *almost always* by truck.

This relatively flexible conceptualisation embraces a wide variety of situations arising in different parts of the country, in which reference is made to the most frequently used empirical evidence of location of residence, rural-urban movement, form of regimentation, selection, labour contract, and form of payment.

In the majority of the studies, concern has centred on the urban-rural movement. In other words, the subject of study has been the rural worker who is also an urban dweller, whose frequency of urban-rural movement is governed by the demand for labour in agriculture, and whose stay in the rural area is limited to the working day. It is this worker whom we shall consider in this study.

First, however, we must give some idea of the numbers involved in order to have an idea of the magnitude of the problem. Although it is not possible to determine the exact number of 'boias-frias', we can obtain an order of magnitude from some approximate calculations. Census statistics provide information with respect only to the place of residence of the active population in farming and cattle-raising. The criterion for calculating the number of temporary workers is based on the hypothesis that all those declaring an urban residence may in theory be included in this category. On the basis of this assumption, with respect to 1970, the proportions of temporary labour in the total labour force employed in agriculture were estimated for the following states: Pernambuco, 13 per cent; São Paulo, 26.6 per cent; Paraná,, 7.4 per cent; and Goias, 14.5 per cent. This is equivalent to 630,000 workers, or 16 per cent of the total number employed in agriculture in these states.[7]

Another study, using statistics from the Instituto Nacional de Crédito Agrícola (INCRA) survey, gave a tentative estimate of the *maximum number* of temporary wage earners, obtaining the results shown in Table 10.1. We believe these data, even bearing in mind peaks in demand, are rather on the high side. Our suspicion is based not only on the fact that these numbers are very much higher than the estimates based on the 1970 Population Census, but also, considering the State of São Paulo only, are very much higher than those provided by the IEA in 1970 (Instituto de Economia Agrícola, secretaria de Agricultura de São Paulo), as will be seen from Table 10.2.

An important point, evident from Table 10.2, is the growing use of this type of worker in agriculture in the State of São Paulo

Table 10.1: *Estimate of Temporary Rural Workers, by State, Brazil, 1972*

State	Total number of rural temporary workers	% of total number of rural workers
Minas Gerais	1,807,310	72
Paraná	796,116	49
São Paulo	770,170	58
Goias	557,037	75
Rio Grande do Sul	311,867	25
Pernambuco	504,868	47
Brazil	6,844,849	55

Source: INCRA survey statistics, 1974, as in Silva and Rodrigues, 1982.

Table 10.2: *Resident and Non-resident Workers Employed on Agricultural Estates, State of São Paulo, 1970 and 1980*

Labour force	1970 No.	%	1980 No.	%
Resident	1,351,498	83.4	717,418	61.9
Non-resident				
Mobile	194,957	12.05	292,800	25.26
Others	72,257	4.46	148,846	12.84
Sub-total	267,214	16.51	441,646	38.10
Total	1,618,712	100.00	1,159,064	100.00

Source: Instituto de Economia Agrícola.

from 1970 to 1980. In spite of the reduction in absolute numbers of all workers employed in agriculture in the State of São Paulo (from 1,618,712 in 1970 to 1,159,064 in 1980), the number of 'boias-frias' increased by 100,000, totalling 300,000 workers. Other estimates produced for São Paulo suggest the average number of mobile workers in 1980 was about 400,000, or even 500,000, according to statements made by the Secretary for Agriculture in São Paulo.[8]

With respect to other states, it was not possible to obtain more recent information, but it may be stated with some assurance that demand for this type of worker must have increased, considering that all states in the country experienced agricultural commercialisation to a greater or lesser degree over the decade.

III. Economic, Political and Social Processes in the More Widespread Use of 'Boia-fria'

The phenomenon of 'boia-fria' in Brazil is another form by which capital has adapted labour relations to changes in the seasonal character of agricultural production. These changes derive from a combined process of increase in the scale of production and increase in productivity, in turn the result of an economic policy aimed at encouraging the more widespread use of modern technology, directed primarily towards the production of exports, products to be used as raw materials for industry, and the large-scale production of foodstuffs, transforming agriculture into a major user of modern inputs and in this way ensuring greater demand for industrial production.

This policy has been implemented via the abundant and cheap supply of machinery and related inputs for agriculture, through the institutionalisation of rural credit since 1965, when the National Credit System was created, offering capital to rural enterprises at interest rates below the level of inflation.[9] In addition to credit facilities, new types of tax incentive were offered, attracting industrial, financial and commercial capital to agricultural production.

In 1969, the government allocated 6.5 billion cruzeiros to financing agriculture and cattle-farming, and 10 years later this had risen to 33 billion in 1969 constant values (449 billion in current cruzeiros).

Comparing rural credit with the agricultural product in current value terms, the latter showed a thirty-sixfold increase, while the resources allocated to institutionalised rural credit showed a sixty-ninefold increase.[10] Data on the development of rural credit in Brazil from 1971 to 1977 reveal a growth of 1,900 per cent.

This volume of funds offered by the State at interest rates below inflation produced an artificial relative reduction in the price of modern inputs, fertilisers, pesticides and machinery. With respect to machinery, Silva and Gasques noted that in 1960 Brazil had one tractor for every 468 hectares tilled, the figure in 1970 having moved to one to every 217 hectares.[11] In São Paulo, where the ratio in 1960 was already one tractor to every 175 hectares, the ratio in 1970 was 1:73 hectares.[12]

In Pernambuco, in the north-east of the country, the sorghum economy in 1960 used 687 tractors, as compared to 1,048 in 1970. This increase is all the greater if we take into account the difficulties of a rugged terrain, accounting for approximately 70 per cent of the land suitable for sorghum farming in the Zona da Mata.[13]

In Brazil, the use of fertilisers showed one of the highest growth rates in the world, having grown from 221,000 tonnes in 1959 to 2,361,000 tonnes in 1976, the consumption of pesticides having increased from 16,193 tonnes in 1964 to 101,057 tonnes in 1974.

The subsidies offered by the government in the case, for example, of fertilisers (in spite of the increase in prices as a result of the oil crisis in 1974) made it possible for prices in 1976 to be held equal to those in 1970, in real terms.

In a general manner, one of the principal results of this subsidy policy on social labour relations in the field was to render the low wages received by the rural workers 'more expensive' than their machine or weedkiller substitutes.[14]

Although the programme of subsidised credit to agri-businesses was basically aimed at small and medium proprietors, in reality it favoured the large producers from the beginning. As regards the credit to agriculture, in 1966 large producers shared less than 0.5 per cent of signed credit contracts, although their contracts shared 20.3 per cent of the total credit funds available. In 1976, larger producers shared 3.3 per cent of all contracts, making up 53.5 per cent of the total credit allocated. With regard to the livestock subsector, the situation was similar.[15] In this fashion, the government accelerated the changes in the social relations of production in rural areas.

However, the increase in resources available via institutionalised rural credit has been only one factor within the general policy of promoting and encouraging economic growth and achieving major changes in the country's production structure, in which rural production plays a new role in accumulation.

Guedes Pinto listed a series of structural changes, to which sparse reference has also been made by other authors, resulting from the economic measures taken by the government.[16] The changes include: (a) progress in the internationalisation of the economy, with the penetration of foreign capital in various sectors previously controlled by local capital; these sectors are generally the more dynamic in the economy, also affecting certain sectors related to farming and cattle-raising; (b) a concentration of income and wealth, including land ownership; (c) an acceleration in industrial development, within a new scheme of capital accumulation; (d) stimulation for capital concentration and centralisation; (e) reform of the financial system; and (f) rapid urbanisation, due primarily to rural-urban migration. It should also be added that these changes, resulting from the economic policy adopted in the country, are an essential prerequisite for the feasibility of the guiding economic model — that known as 'industrialisation of the countryside'.

Within this new technical level in agriculture, the need for labour for land preparation, planting and hoeing has been declining, and the seasonal nature of agricultural work has increased. This situation derived not only from the increase in productivity as a function of the combination of machinery and other modern inputs, but also from the changing range of products, since modern technology was channelled towards an expansion of 'modern' produce. These crops, particularly sorghum, soya and oranges, require an extremely high number of workers for harvesting in relation to other phases of production.

Between 1967 and 1975, the area devoted to these crops almost doubled, leading to major changes in the seasonal volume of employment. But there was also a tendency in commercial agriculture towards specialisation, transforming multiple-crop areas into single-crop areas, and making the seasonality of employment even more marked, intensifying the use of labour for shorter periods.

During this period, other conditions also favoured the expulsion of rural labour and increased seasonality. The policy of eradicating coffee plantations between 1962 and 1967, particularly in the states of São Paulo and Paraná, led to this crop being replaced by cattle-rearing and soya, wheat and fruit. Not only did cattle-rearing reduce the use of labour, its penetration and expansion also reduced subsistence activities, thus producing a mass of landless rural workers. But above all, the 'modern' crops involved only seasonal use of the majority of workers required for their production.

The seasonality in agriculture was not an invention of economic policy. What happened is that it became uneconomic to maintain sharecroppers on the estate, whereby they had been given not only a place to live but also the right to plant subsistence crops.

However, certain requirements relating to the laying out and spacing of plants to assist mechanisation and the use of weedkillers made the system of intercalary subsistence farming unworkable from a technical viewpoint. In addition, investment in the land, even where of poor quality, by the use of financed inputs, made it possible for the entire area to be used for farming, rendering it uneconomic for land to be assigned to workers for subsistence farming. On the other hand, the monetary payment received by the rural worker who lived on the estate was not sufficient for his own and his family's survival without his subsistence 'roça' (the popular name for subsistence-farmed land). A number of 'boias-frias' interviewed in São Paulo and Pernambuco, in research carried out for the Ministry of Labour in 1977-8, categorically stated that they would not return to living on the roça, 'because now you can't plant anything in the roça to live from'.

In addition to the changes in economic policy, there have also been major changes in the laws governing work in the countryside. Considering labour legislation for the countryside, one usually focuses on the Rural Worker's Statute, passed in 1963. It should, however, be remembered that laws were passed from 1943 onwards, gradually extending to the rural worker rights already acquired by other workers in the Consolidation of Labour Laws — the 'CLT'. Minimum wages, annual paid leave, and notice of dismissal first became compulsory in 1943, being subsequently supplemented by the right to stability in rural property, compensation for unfair dismissal, the prohibition of wage deductions for excessive harvesting, the rural labourer's right to housing for his family, and compulsory free schooling for his children. In practice, however, all this legal cover remained without effect, because there was no government control to ensure it was applied and the workers had no competent channels through which to direct their claims, since the formation of rural unions was illegal. However, at the end of the 1950s and beginning of the 1960s, disputes occurred between workers and employers with respect to the implementation of the labour laws, though most statements in the literature, and made to us in the field, show that these related more to a group of lawyers with particular interests, known as 'paqueradores' who offered their services to the rural workers, convincing them to take legal action to obtain compliance with the law, to which employers were not adhering.[17] In the majority of cases, these lawyers took in fees a large proportion of the compensation received by the workers.

With the passing of the Rural Worker's Statute in 1963, a set of laws was introduced defining the occupational classifications, and duration of working day, supported by legislation protecting women and children, specifying the individual contract of employment and the collective contract, and so on. The 'Funrural' (the Fundo de Assistência e Previdência ao Trabalhador Rural, the Rural Workers' Assistance and Welfare Fund) was created, related regulations were passed, and the decision was taken to create an Arbitration Council, that being a matter mainly of union organisation.

Much of the literature — particularly works published in the early 1970s — reveals a marked tendency to deny any causal correlation between the establishment of the Rural Workers' Statute (the 'ETR') and the expulsion of resident workers from rural estates. The basic criticism of these analyses is that they used 'discussions' with the protagonists — employees and employers — without working through them critically.

In statements collected from employers and employees in various regions of the State of São Paulo, there was a constancy in the replies given by the employers in referring to the ETR as a propelling factor in the changes made with respect to work in the fields.[18] With respect to dismissals of employees from the estates, the employers generally justified these as a reaction, based on the alleged feeling of fear and annoyance at a situation they considered unjust. It is, however, important to note that economic grounds, or the burden on the cost of production represented by compliance with the legislation imposed by ETR (obligation to pay minimum wages, thirteenth month wage at the end of each year of employment, holidays, weekly paid rest day, and so on), did not appear on the employers' statements.

In reality, the importance of the ETR has been felt only when associated with worker disputes arising in the context of the rural unions. The opening of these channels enabled rural workers to demand compliance with rights contained in the ETR, and when legal action was taken, in most cases they won.

Winning their action usually meant receiving the compensation requested on grounds of unfair dismissal, calculated on the basis of all entitlements stipulated by the ETR. In some cases, that meant small and medium-sized estates incurring extremely heavy costs.

One rural landowner interviewed in Ribeirao Preto, São Paulo, summed up the situation as follows:

> the tendency on the part of the employer was to want to get rid of employees (labourers, unskilled sharecroppers), a kind of revulsion, he didn't want problems, because he wasn't equipped to have a regular 'written agreement' with his employees . . . and because he normally regarded himself as doing right by his employees.[19]

In other statements, one factor frequently mentioned as a

reason for dismissing workers was the legal imposition of equality between employer and employee. It was said to be humiliating for the employer, in the presence of the public attorney and the president of the worker's union, to have to talk on an equal basis with an employee who until a matter of days beforehand had been his subordinate. The situation, according to declarations made by one owner, was 'as if a general had to converse with a private soldier and listen to what the soldier was saying without being able to stop him'.

That workers should start to be heard by the union and to win legal actions, objectively and subjectively reduced the status of the employer, measured on the basis of the political, economic and social power he held over his workers. The psychological effect of this loss, or apparent loss, of strength and the reactions to this situation were not considered in analyses dealing with the problems of change in labour relations in the countryside.

This point is significant, since this sector of society is tied to norms and values that are deeply rooted, and according to which right is always on the side of the landowner, never on that of the employee, and the former's power is measured by his capacity to subjugate and exploit his employees. It cannot be denied that to some extent the law had the strength to balance belief in the impunity of this behaviour with limiting the employers' freedom of action.

However, for the ETR to have been able to unleash an entire situation of fear and uncertainty to explain the release of manpower in the rural area, it would be necessary for a large number of rural workers to have settled their employment situation at law — for a large majority of the workers to have taken their claims to court. Clearly, this did not occur. The 'demonstration effect' may have played a part as a factor in the extent of change, but in itself it would not have caused the change that occurred.

We believe in the notion that a law cannot create a new labour relationship. It merely endeavours to 'govern' a relationship already established, in such a manner as to facilitate its dissemination, using the legal shield of the State.[20] But there is a lack of empirical study to allow deeper reflection, of research endeavouring to understand the implications of legal changes with respect to labour and the rural worker at different times in Brazilian history.

By way of an example, we might mention the changes in the 'rural worker' concept in the laws, as granted to rural workers at different times. When, from 1943 onwards, some of the rights already acquired by the urban worker were extended to rural workers, the rural worker was defined as: 'any individual who renders services to the rural employer on rural property or a rustic estate, for a wage paid in money or *in kind* or part in kind and part in money'.[21] and as specified by law by Decree No. 6,969 of 1944, the rural worker was defined as a worker providing labour services on a *permanent, periodic or transitory* basis. This definition was maintained until Law 5,889 of 1973, which still governs rural labour in the country, and which revoked the ETR, which defined as rural workers only 'individuals who, on a rural property or rustic estate, provide services of a *non-casual* nature to the rural employer, being answerable to him, and being paid a wage'. This transformed the 'boia-fria' into a worker without legal protection. Denial of the status of 'rural employee' to the temporary worker may have facilitated the expulsion of the former 'sharecroppers' and led to their reintegration into the rural production process as 'boia-fria'. This may support the hypothesis that legislation strengthened an established situation.

However, it may be wondered why it was only in 1973 that a decision was taken to exclude certain categories of worker from State protection, and why, in this 'cleaning-up operation', both landless temporary workers and those having some labour link giving them access to land were excluded. The situation of rapid economic growth during the 'Brazilian miracle', together with the change in the level of productive forces, led to an increase in surplus labour. The Minister of Labour at the time acknowledged that it was the wording of Law 5,889 which 'transformed more than 6,000,000 Brazilians into institutionally unemployed', by excluding them from the category of rural worker.

Nevertheless, we must take care not to simplify highy complex processes by assuming a linear determinism causing certain developments, or the chance character of historical 'coincidences' causing situations favourable to the emergence of new social relations of production. We have to consider all the various factors and situations outlined in this study, and possibly others, in order to obtain a better approximation of the emergence and continuation of the 'boia-fria' in the context of capitalist accumulation in agriculture.

IV. Regimentation of the 'Boia-fria' and the Maintenance of this Category of Worker

The pattern of daily movement of the 'boias-frias', according to information from studies carried out in São Paulo (SEPLAN) and Pernambuco (IJNPS), shows that the distance travelled each day between the place of the 'boia-fria', or some place such as a square or bar in their district, and the workplace varied from 20 to 50 kilometres. Some owners at peak times consider it economically viable to look for workers over a radius of 80 to 100 kilometres. The distance covered by the worker from his place of residence to the place of work on group trucks can go beyond the limits of a municipality, a region, or even a state.

For this process to occur, there has to be an organised system of selection, sorting, payment and transport. In addition, for this to be transformed into a labour force of interest to capital, there must be a guaranteed regular labour supply to meet demand in accordance with its requirements at various stages of production, without major fluctuations in labour costs.

As use of this category of worker becomes more generalised, an intermediary assuming these tasks is introduced into the capital/labour relationship. In general, this agent is a person known to the owner, popularly termed the 'gato' (the cat).[22] He is the person who selects the workers, agrees the daily or job rate,[23] transports them by truck, which may or may not be his own, and also generally controls the production in cases of payment by the job.

According to Stein, the 'gato' endeavours to pay the minimum possible to the 'boias-frias'.[24] He lives from the difference in price he agrees with the landowner and the price paid by him to the 'boia-fria', retaining a share that varies between 20 and 50 per cent of the total.

One might ask why the owner of the farm does not undertake the intermediary task himself. The primary reason is that in this way his direct link with the contract of employment is removed. Even though the temporary or casual worker was not taken into account in the rural worker concept, Law 5,889 still applies, with its regulating decree in Article 14. This requires application of the conditions relating to the working day (eight hours, with a maximum of two hours' overtime) and other conditions relating to work at night and by minors, to casual workers and other rural workers who, without an employment link, render services to rural employers. It also requires the advantages of the 'thirteenth month' to be applied to such workers, who cannot be paid less than the equivalent of the minimum daily wage for the region.

The importance of the 'gato' does not lie simply in his capacity to discipline the workers, but also in his role of dissimilating the existing labour relationship, enabling the employer to adopt a strategy to protect himself from the legal obligations imposed on him as a user of labour.

It should also be stressed that part of the temporary work is supplied by 'fixed gangs', or groups of 'boias-frias' working for the same 'gato' or for the same set of estates in the region.[25]

In reality, as stated by Silva, if they are working on a property as part of a fixed gang, it is relatively easy to identify their status as rural workers and thus their rights to receive all benefits legally stipulated.[26]

In other cases, where 'boias-frias' have been incorporated only at harvest time and in discontinuous periods, working on different properties, whether alternating between rural and urban work or working only in the rural area at times of peak demand, it becomes more difficult to legally identify the labour tie. But this type of arrangement has released the employer from responsibility for any accident at work on the property and particularly in transporting the 'boias-frias', many of whom have been in truck accidents involving a number of deaths.

Considering the process of agricultural work in the context of the lower rate of incorporation of machinery in harvesting, and the rise in productivity resulting from increasing use of more modern techniques in planting and treatment, it can be expected that the demand for temporary workers will continue to rise. As such, it has been noted that the temporary worker, supported by 'an employment relationship made and unmade at short and irregular intervals, cannot constitute an adequate basis for the "normal" reproduction of labour'.[27] But also, that intermediation, supported on such a precarious and informal basis, can signify a major risk for producers.

It is in this sense that we should understand the growing spread of fixed gangs, restricting seasonal work by women, children and other workers to specific periods. At the same time, the growth of registered rural labour contractors ensured more regular supplies of labour at stable cost. As corporate bodies, these could be sued by the Ministry of Labour for the payment of benefits owing to the 'boia-fria'.

This concern reflects the existence of a large number of workers pursuing claims relating to their labour dues under the law, and the fact of the public prosecutor's office not only having found in favour frequently for the workers, but also having sued the owner directly, the gang-leader being regarded purely as his agent.[28]

These problems have been partially overcome by the common practice of settlement proposals made by employers or estate owners. Since the worker is either unaware of how much is due to him, or is unable to question the sum offered, the settlements are always well below what the 'boia-fria' could be awarded in court. Frequently, they choose to accept the settlement because they regard bureaucratic requirements as complicated or because they prefer to receive a little rather than go through the long procedure of the courts.

It can be predicted that as the 'transitory nature' of 'boia-fria' labour is perpetuated, the 'gato' will be of declining interest to the owner, primarily because of the need for a more formal, structured organisation corresponding to the new level of productive forces, capable of responding in a more systematic manner to market demand fluctuations.

V. 'Boia-fria' — Living Conditions, Exploitation

If we compare the indices for production and use of the 17 principal agricultural products in the State of São Paulo with the development of salaries of rural workers, we find that from 1948 to 1980, agricultural production increased from an index of 100 to 224, while agricultural employment dropped from 100 to 25. Dividing the former by the latter, we find that labour productivity increased by 770 per cent. Comparing this with the evolution of wages, deflated by the price index received by farmers, we find that in relation to the resident worker category, there had been an increase of 10 per cent in wages in relation to 1948, and for the mobile worker only 8 per cent.

This difference between wages and productivity indices, accentuated in the 1970s, was shown by high income concentration indices. The bottom 50 per cent of the rural poor, who in

1970 received 22.4 per cent of the income generated in agriculture, by 1980 received only 14.9 per cent, while the top 1 per cent of the richest increased their share from 10.5 to 29.3 per cent.[29]

Whatever the labour relations in which rural workers become involved, their wages in no way kept up with or benefited from the increases in productivity. In the case of the 'boia-fria', his impoverishment as a rural worker has been aggravated by his situation of instability and uncertainty with respect to the possibility of regular work throughout the year. There are no statistics on the number of months work per year for a 'boia-fria'. Calculations based on data in the 1970 Population Census on the number of months of hoeing worked in the State of São Paulo show that more than 5 per cent worked a maximum of six months in the year, 15 per cent between six and nine months, and the remainder from nine to twelve months. These statistics refer to all workers, including sharecroppers, permanent employees and mobile workers.

We believe that for the latter the amount of work would have been a smaller number of months. In general, the wage earned by the 'boia-fria', when calculated on a daily basis, was higher than that obtained by other unskilled rural workers, although the difference varied from one region to another and in different periods of the year. In 1977, in the area of Mata em Pernambuco, during the harvest period, the 'boia-fria' earned almost double the wage of the sharecropper per tonne of cane cut.[30] In 1976, comparing the minimum wage with the wage of a fixed or mobile day-worker, it was found in São Paulo that while the daily wage for a worker on the minimum wage was Cr.$ 2.60 a day, the fixed daily wage worker earned Cr.$ 3.01 and the mobile worker Cr.$ 3.74.[31]

A few authors have stressed that these wage differences signify an improvement in the life of the mobile worker, and an alignment with the living conditions of other rural workers. Others consider that, in general, the differences in living standards of the various categories of rural workers are insignificant, 'whether or not they are covered by labour legislation, whether they live on the properties on which they work or away, on the outskirts of the towns'.[32]

Table 10.3, prepared by da Silva and Rodrigues, covers certain living situations of the 'boia-fria' as witnessed in some of the field

Table 10.3: *Living Conditions of the Mobile Worker*

Authors: Indicator	Bombo and Brunelli (1965) — Piracicaba	Copercotia (1968) — Jau, São Paulo	Santos (1972) — Votuporange-S. Paulo	D'Incao and Mello (1973) — Alta Sorocabana — SP
Diet	Deficient due to economic and educational characteristics and to nature of the work.	'Work all day and eat at night'.	Extremely poor, below rustic.	Poor, children suffering from malnutrition.
Housing	'most precarious possible. Extremely rare for them to own their houses.'		3.3 rooms/house. 3.5 people per room; 35% with own cheap housing.	Precarious.
Education	Generally illiterate.		50% illiterate. 45% semi-literate.	70% illiterate. 16% semi-literate.
Health	36% of the mentally deficient class are children of mobile workers. Physically exhausted. Verminous. High infant mortality, malnutrition.		Risk of illness and death, particularly among children, higher than among the rest of the population.	Adults sick. Some bedridden.

Source: Silva and Rodrigues, 1982.

studies, conveniently avoiding the need to repeat the descriptions of misery and poverty contained in the literature.

The result of their living conditions and exploitation with respect to the conditions of reproduction was stated in a valuable study by the biologist, Angeleli, between 1976 and 1977, in Ribeirao Preto, São Paulo, a region in which the 'boias-frias' rates are the highest in the state. It is clear from this that the living and working conditions make the nutritional and health situation of these workers worse than that of other rural groups. Clinical nutritional examination revealed the 'boia-fria' to be a thin individual who, on weight, would be classified as grade 1 undernourished. The mean calorific intake was 2,000 calories, considered low for the age group in question and the activity performed. Their physical ability, measured by the ergometric cycle, was deemed lower than that of rural workers living in the field.

Another means of checking the conditions of inferiority of the 'boia-fria' was the picture that other rural workers have of them. According to one study in Pernambuco, the 'parceleiros' (owners of small plots, mainly received from the government) pity the 'boias-frias' when comparing their own situation with theirs and feel that the clandestine worker, particularly with respect to food, is much worse off than themselves. Job instability, the risks in the trucks run by the gangs, the lack of prospects, and alcoholism, were other characteristics of the mobile workers that the 'parceleiros' regarded as disadvantages. 'The result is that they [the mobile workers] are nobody, they have no future, and no expectations of life. The days on which they work they eat, and on the days they do not earn they are deprived.'[33]

The 'boia-fria' himself is conscious of his disadvantaged situation vis-à-vis other rural workers. He or she does not like to be called 'boia-fria', since this expression has a connotation of inferiority. In the local language there is a song popular among rural workers that captures the outstanding features of the itinerant worker's psychology:

My boss quarrelled with me;
He called me a boia-fria.
I didn't hit his face
So I wouldn't lose a day's pay.

VI. Proposed Solutions

In the literature the proposed solutions may be divided into those endeavouring to resolve the problem with clearly palliative measures, and those proposing policies of a more organisational character, emphasising co-operativisation and unionisation.

In the first case, the most frequently mentioned are those relating to improvements in the transport of such workers and their diet. In the case of diet, experiments have been carried out in organising a food programme for a control group, consisting of providing the 'boia-fria' with an insulated container with his customary food, but with a better balance of calories and proteins. The container was prepared at a boardinghouse in town, issued to the truck in the morning and returned at night. After three months on this programme, workers were re-examined and tested on the ergometric cycle, which showed their physical capacity to have improved.

One might question the use of human guinea-pigs in experiments for which the results are well known in advance, and one might also wonder who would benefit most from such a policy. The field study that led to this experiment clearly showed that the workers' requirements were quite different.[34] We reiterate the pleas made by the workers, as stated in the research report: 'better working and wage conditions, equivalent rights to those of the city workers, to have someone defending their rights, or at least showing what these rights are'. To summarise, one said: 'We're asking for someone to fight on our behalf, because we know nothing other than working.' In the face of such pleas, why was the experiment undertaken?

The only realistic explanation is that this would respond to a plea by employers and administrators of estates, who constantly call for greater productivity from these workers. As stated in the report, employers considered the 'boia-fria' an inferior worker, and stated that the work formerly carried out by one man now required two or three 'boia-frias'. The report added that 'these workers cannot work continuously, they have to stop frequently, and even so, many showed signs of frailty, and shake'. The report concluded that there was a need to 'break the vicious circle: inadequate diet, low physical ability, low wage, poor diet'.

This being the understanding of the problem, or rather the understanding of the sequence of events, the solution proposed could only be that of providing dietary aid and education to the workers in the social centres at the outskirts of the city, thereby ensuring maintenance of the status quo and socialising the cost of producing more productive labour for capital.

With respect to transport, the news in the press of disasters, always involving death, from accidents with the trucks transporting the 'boias-frias', in addition to vivid descriptions in field investigations, has led to the introduction of control measures in some regions, mainly designed to regulate the form of daily movement of these workers.

In the report of the research carried out in Zona da Mata in Pernambuco, it was noted:

> that trucks transporting livestock from Sergipe to Pernambuco were constantly being intercepted by the police for routine inspections, checking whether the grating was sufficiently safe and whether they conformed to requirements for animal transport. However, the trucks carrying mobile workers, in addition to being overcrowded, also carried women and children, with no protective grating or seats, failing to offer the minimum safety for passengers. In spite of this, they passed in front of police posts without being intercepted, because, according to one of the policemen, this fact was not against the law.[35]

The so-called 'Operation Boia-fria', as published in the press, was set up in 1980 after eight mobile rural workers had died in a road accident.[36] The operation consists of ensuring compliance with federal regulations, requiring high-sided trucks similar to those used to transport cattle, seats, roofing, and the carriage of tools in a special compartment, the reason being that in various accidents, the tools, loaded together with the workers, have caused mutilation and other extremely serious injury. We do not know to what extent this supervision is being carried out, and under what terms of reference. But we do know that it could do a great deal to reduce the number of deaths and enable workers to begin the working day somewhat less exhausted.

With reference to programmes for 'temporary labour co-operatives', these were insistently promoted for a long time, not only by the government but also by well-intentioned planners and researchers. But criticisms were made of the implications of a

Temporary Workers' Labour Co-operative, both with respect to the ideological aspects and to the question of whom the State would be rendering a service to, the employee or the employer. The basic criticism was that the co-operative is an employer-oriented method of achieving organisation and structuring of the labour market, minimising the problems of labour fluctuations, thus reducing situations of inflexibility in supply likely to create bargaining power among temporary workers. As one observer concluded, 'The advantages presented, with benefits for the worker, endeavour to dissimulate the ideological political aspect of this magic proposal of the temporary labour co-operative. It may change in form, but the essence of the problem remains: low remuneration and the temporary nature of mobile work.'[37]

In the investigations carried out by ourselves in São Paulo the proposed solutions endeavoured to highlight the economic reality and, in a less radical manner, provide a more realistic solution, combining co-operatives and the union.[38] The appraisal of the situation and the proposals made at the time still seem valid, since although the 'boia-fria' is not a very topical subject of interest for academic and planning studies and newspaper reports, the misery and exploitation in which they live is unchanged, as is the apparent lack of caring on the part of the authorities.

We thus reiterate our statements at the end of 1977 and beginning of 1978, when the establishment of temporary worker co-operatives throughout the country appeared imminent. The co-operatives expressed the official recognition by the State of the specific situation of the mobile worker. It has been endeavouring through them to form a labour exchange, that is, an organised temporary labour market, which could provide employers with labour to suit the peaks and troughs of the productive cycle, and operatives with continuity of employment, better working conditions, guaranteed compliance with labour laws, courses, training, schools and crèches for their children.

These co-operatives are run by a management-and-consultative board comprising representatives of the State organisations participating in the project; the board has an orientational function, checking compliance with directives, to the extent of supervising the management elected by the members.

The law distinguishes co-operatives from the unions. The co-operative is a legal organisation for the provision of services, while the unions are class defence bodies. For a legal organisation to function, it is necessary for it to be based on society itself, and not only the government. In this way, a co-operative could only be properly implemented if it represented an association of mobile workers, protecting their specific interests. Only the union, as a body of a large number of people devoid of means of production who have only their labour to exchange, would be capable of binding together the mobile workers in the face of their greatest challenge — the confrontation with the employers for the purpose of agreeing a contract of employment. For this reason, the functioning of the co-operatives will depend on how the workers organise themselves outside them, and how, independently of the management and consultative board, supervision is exercised over the conditions of use of their labour, and its price.

The question of mobile labour in agriculture falls into broader perspectives relating to the method of organisation of labour in Brazilian society. Obviously a union of rural workers would need to have freedom and independence of organisation, these being essential conditions for the performance of a political activity differing from the assistance and corporative tradition of our traditional organisations. We see no other way by which mobile workers would find the means capable of ensuring a minimal subsistence, at least not as labourers of the type required by the new form of agricultural production in Brazil.

Notes

1. 'Boia-fria' (literally, 'cold rations') is the term used primarily in the southeast and south of the country, particularly in São Paulo and Paraná, and refers to the fact that the worker has to eat his meals cold. In Pernambuco, this category of workers is known as 'clandestine', as opposed to registered or official workers. Other terms less widely used, such as 'pau de arara' (truck) and 'pilao' (crusher), refer to the means of transport, which is generally extremely precarious, or to the vehicle that transports the workers from the urban area to their work in the fields. All of these descriptions are pejorative. Among academics and planners, the common term used to describe temporary rural workers, in addition to the popular conceptual regionalisms stated above, is 'mao de obra volante' (literally, 'mobile/flying labour'), the Portuguese term 'volante' being defined in the dictionary as roving, nomadic, vagrant, and also passing, transitory or ephemeral.

2. J.G. Silva and V.L.G.S. Rodrigues: 'A problemática do "boia-fria" ', in Department of Rural Economics, FCA, *Mao de obra volante na agricultura* (Botucatu, CNPQ/UNESP, 1982).

3. N. Gonzalez and M.I. Bastos: 'O trabalho volante na agricultura brasiliera', in ibid.

4. José Graziano de Silva terms this category 'temporary wage-earners' — "boia-fria", entre aspas e com os pingos now is', in ibid.

5. It was verified in a study carried out in São Paulo in 1976-7 by biolog Valter Angeleli, that approximately '42 per cent of the "boias-frias" in the region Ribeirao Preto did not previously live in the rural area; they were primary urb dwellers' — V. Angeleli, in J.E. Dutra Oliveira: ' "Boia-fria" é antes de tudo u forte', Legislative Assembly of the State of São Paulo, Special Committee Inquiry into the Situation of the 'Boia-fria' Mobile Worker, September 1981.

6. Silva and Rodrigues, 1982; see also M.C. D'Incao and A. Mello: *Reflexc sobre o estudo do 'Boia-fria' no Brasil*, Publication Series No. 3 (Rio de Janeir Noel Nutels Study Centre, 1976).

7. Gonzalez and Bastos, 1982.

8. In an interview published in *O Estado de São Paulo* on 22 January 198 given by José Gomes da Silva, current Secretary of Agriculture and Supply for t State of São Paulo.

9. In 1970, when inflation was 19.3 per cent, the mean rate of interest f government finance was 11.3 per cent; in 1980, with an inflation rate of 110.2 p cent, the mean rate of interest on subsidised capital was 20 per cent — L.C. Guedes: 'Notas sobre a políticas de crédito rural no Brasil', Legislative Assemb of the State of São Paulo, Special Committee of Inquiry into the Situation of t "Boia-fria" Mobile Worker', September 1981.

10. According to data submitted by Guedes to the Special Board of Inqui into Boias-frias, in the São Paulo Legislative Assembly, 1981.

11. J.G. Silva and J.G. Gasques, 'Diagnostico Incial do Volante em S. Paul in Dept of Rural Economics FCA, *Mao de Obra*, 1982.

12. The advantages offered for machinery were substantial, in addition to t negative real rates of interest, and 100 per cent financing of the value machinery purchased; the debt repayment period was five years, consisting of per cent in the first year, 15, 20, 25 and 30 per cent consecutively up to the fi year — Silva and Gasques, 1982. The tractor industry has been almost tota dependent on rural credit, and any change in incentive policy would affect prof in these industries. Massey Ferguson, in its 1977 year-end world-wide accoun identified the decision to reduce funds available for investment in agricultu taken by the Brazilian authorities as a cause for the decline in their profits for th year — Guedes, 1981.

13. Instituto Joaquim Nabuco de Pesquisas Cociais, Ministry of Labour: *trabalhador rural volante na zona de Mata de Pernambuco*, vol. 2 (Reci Pernambuco, 1978).

14. Silva and Gasques, 1982.

15. Comissao Coordenadora da Política Nacional de Crédito Rural COMCRED (Banco do Brasil, various dates); Guedes, 1981.

16. Guedes, 1981.

17. The verb 'paquerar' in Brazilian slang means to approach someone wi vested interests.

18. C.R. Spindel (ed.): *Trabalho volante na agricultura Paulista*, Study a Research Series No. 25 (São Paulo, SEPLAN, Secretaria de Planejamento de S Paulo, 1978).

19. Ibid.

20. Silva, 1982; Gonzalez and Bastos, 1982.

21. L.L. Burmeister: 'Guia do Empregador e Trabalhador rural', Legislati Assembly of the State of São Paulo, Special Committee of Inquiry into Situation of the 'Boia-fria' Mobile Worker, September 1981.

22. In the literature and in fieldwork, I was unable to find an explanatioon this name. The only explanation that occurs to me is the most obvious, and a

the most invidious and humiliating, being that a cat is a good rat catcher.

23. These two methods of payment are in general specific to different times of the production cycle. The daily rate is generally used at times of planting, when the rate is determined by the machine, that is, the speed at which the tractor works and the rate at which the plough opens the trenches. Payment by production is effected in the harvesting and cutting work.

24. L. Stein: *Gatos e 'boias-frias'*, Publication Series No. 3 (Rio de Janeiro, Study Centre Noel Nutels, 1976).

25. The use of this form of temporary worker is only viable in multiple-crop regions, and where peaks in demand for labour do not temporarily coincide. On the basis of field surveys, one analysis calculates regional estimates in which the proportions of permanent 'boias-frias' of the total number of mobile workers varied between 15 and 40 per cent — Silva, 1982.

26. Ibid.

27. P. Singer: *Economia politica do trabalho* (São Paulo, Editora Hucitec, 1977), p. 84.

28. Silva, 1982; L.H.F. Saboia: 'O mundo do volante, trabalhadores rurais de Cravinhos', Master's dissertation (São Paulo, UNICAMP, 1978; mimeographed).

29. Published in *Jornal a Folha de Sao Paulo*, 2 March 1982, in an article signed by Eduardo M. Suplicy, relating to statistics produced by Professor José Gebara, in his doctoral thesis.

30. Instituto Joaquim Nabuco, 1978.

31. Silva, 1982.

32. H.O.M. de Barros: 'A Caminho de "Rua" — Condicoes de vida e trabalho no meio rural da zona da Mata de Pernumbuco' (Recife, Pernambuco, FUNDAS, 1981; mimeographed).

33. Instituto Jaoquim Nabuco, 1978.

34. J.E.D. Oliveira.

35. Instituto Joaquim Nabuco, 1978.

36. State of São Paulo, 12 January 1983, and 15 January 1983.

37. Silva, 1982.

38. Spindel, 1978.

11

Circular Migration in South-East Asia: Some Theoretical Explanations

YIU-KWAN FAN AND ALAN STRETTON

I. Introduction[1]

Until recently research on migration in South-East Asia supported the view that most rural-urban migratory movement is of a permanent nature. This view is challenged by recent empirical studies, which reveal evidence of a sizeable volume of repetitive, circular migration in many South-East Asian countries. Although there are inter-country variations in the region, a stylised pattern of circular migration seems to emerge from these studies. A typical family that practises circular migration has one or two members working in the city while the remaining members continue to live and work in the village. The migrant spends extended periods working and living in the city but makes frequent return visits to see his family.

Circular migration has long been observed in other parts of the world. For example, much of the empirical work on rural-urban migration in African as well as in Pacific Island countries has emphasised the importance of non-permanent migration.[2] Elkan argued that a large proportion of urban residents in Uganda and other East African countries could not be regarded as permanent town dwellers.[3] Many migrants intend to return to their village after some period of wage employment. He also postulated that this behavioural pattern was best explained in terms of economic forces, rather than by social or cultural factors. First, urban wages were generally too low to support a labourer and his dependants in the city. Second, the family could maximise its income by combining wage employment with farming. In addition, urban employment provided little security in times of sickness or old age. Hence it was necessary to retain contacts with rural society which was thought to offer more assistance in times of difficulty.

Some of Elkan's explanations may still be applicable to circular migration in South-East Asian countries. Other hypotheses have also been suggested. However, few attempts have been made to develop theoretical frameworks for analysing the circular pattern of migration and the conditions under which such migratory movements can be expected to occur. This task we endeavour to do in this chapter.

Two models are presented to provide theoretical explanations of circular migration. The first seeks the explanation in the decision of the family to maximise income as well as utility from consumption. The second shows that circular migration can result from the behaviour of income maximisation-cum-risk aversion. The models are complementary rather than competitive. The first considers the spatial allocation of family labour resources, whereas the second compares the alternatives of the family and shows that a risk-averse decision-maker prefers circular migration to permanent migration even if the latter promises higher expected income.

The remainder of the paper is arranged as follows. The next section discusses the incidence of circular migration in South-East Asia and outlines the main characteristics of this type of movement. In section III we build a model that shows that under certain circumstances, circular migration is consistent with income and utility maximising behaviour by the family. The influence of attitudes towards risk-bearing on choice of migration pattern is examined in section IV. We conclude by using the analysis to examine some of the consequences of circular migration. Finally, some observations on the policy implications are briefly discussed.

II. Circular Migration in South-East Asia

In recent years a number of researchers who have collected data on migration have found evidence of circular migration in South-East Asian countries. Their investigations have been of two types — village studies of migration and urban occupation studies.

Both of these provide valuable information about migration patterns which normally cannot be extracted from census data. As Hugo and Goldstein argue, the types of question asked during a census interview and the definitions used during the analysis of such data will prevent the detection of short-term circular migration.[4] Questions such as 'usual place of residence' become quite confusing if a person maintains his family in the village while spending most of his time in the city. As well, census data are unlikely to provide information on moves made within the geographic regions specified in the questionnaire (for example, province) or on return moves completed within the interval between censuses. An individual may have been in his village at the time of two consecutive censuses but have travelled many times between his village and the city in the intervening period. An analysis of census data may not detect such movement. Also, in many countries permanency is used as a criterion in determining whether migration has 'officially' taken place. Hence it is not surprising that this type of analysis has found little evidence of temporary movement.

Many of these village studies of migration and urban occupation studies are reviewed by Goldstein.[5] The discussion that follows does not attempt to duplicate these references, but rather outlines some of the main characteristics of circular migration as found in Asia, and presents some additional findings not included in the Goldstein review.

The most detailed examination of circular migration in Asia is that undertaken by Hugo.[6] In a study of migration out of 14 villages in West Java, he found that villagers made a clear distinction between permanent movement away from the village and a migration pattern that involved a number of cyclical moves between the village and city without any intention of a permanent change of residence. In the latter case, the family of the migrant invariably remained in the village while he was working in the city. The limiting case of this type of migration is commuting, which was also significant in villages very close to towns. In 11 of the 14 villages that Hugo studied, temporary migration accounted for 50 per cent or more of all movement, and in 9 cases circular migration was the dominant type of movement.

In another study of population change in a village in Central Luzon, in the Philippines, Anderson found that most labourers working outside the village 'choose to maintain their households in Sisya and to return two or three weekends a month for visits rather than establish their households in the urban areas where they work'.[7] Goldstein discusses similar studies conducted in Thailand, Indonesia and Malaysia.

Urban occupational studies, especially in industries that form part of the so-called informal sector, have also detected the practice of circular migration. The majority of samlor drivers in Bangkok,[8] ice cream hawkers in Jakarta,[9] and skilled and unskilled building labourers in Manila[10] have adopted a circular migration pattern. This occupational grouping of circular migrants is an indication of the strong network of contacts that appears to form an integral part of the circulation migration process. A potential migrant is likely to adopt a circular migration pattern partly because other members of his village have done so. On his first trip to the city he is accompanied by a relative or friend who provides the introductions necessary to ensure employment and housing. Hence a migrant who can become part of this established network will know before he leaves the village that he can obtain employment in the city as well as his likely income and expenses. As a result, there is more certainty attached to the variables affecting the decision to move than is often thought to be the case.

Circular migrants from the same rural area and working in the same occupation tend to live together in the city. This not only provides social support but also lowers the cost of staying in the town and hence increases the remittances that the migrant can send to his family. Stretton also found that circular migration could form a barrier to entry into an occupation. Small groups of labourers led by a foreman or highly-skilled tradesman formed the basis of recruitment and skill acquisition on most building sites. These groups were usually composed of individuals from the same region, all using a circular migration pattern. An individual who lacked a contact to provide entry into such a group would find it very difficult to obtain training from the skilled labourers and would tend to remain an unskilled labourer or leave the industry.

It may be thought that this type of migration is merely a preliminary stage before the migrant and his family move permanently to the city. However, the evidence from the studies discussed above suggests that this is not the case. Less than 2 per cent of the temporary movers interviewed by Hugo indicated that they intended to move permanently to the city.[11] Only 10 per cent of the building labourers interviewed by Stretton had decided to move permanently to Manila.

What seems to emerge from these studies is a pattern of repetitive, circular migration being adopted by many families in South-East Asian countries. A typical circular migrant family has one or two members working and living in the city. The migrants frequently return to the village to see the family and to maintain their work contacts. In the city they generally find accommodation among their fellow circular migrants from the same and nearby villages, sharing very modest housing facilities to minimise living costs. Most of their savings are remitted to the family in the village.

It is this stylised pattern of circular migration that we attempt to explain using the following models.

III. Spatial Allocation of Family Labour

The first model stems from Fisher's theory of investment, in that we separate the family's income-earning decisions from its consumption decisions. The family members allocate their labour between the urban and rural sectors so as to maximise their income, which in turn is allocated between urban and rural goods so as to maximise utility. As a result, the permanent migration pattern implicit in most models of migration does not necessarily emerge.

1. Family Income Maximisation

Consider the case of a rural family with its income earners facing the opportunity of working both in the city and the rural area. Through some decision-making procedure, the family distributes its labour resources between the village and urban centre so as to maximise family earnings. Assume that it has knowledge of the rates of return one unit of labour can obtain in both the rural and urban sectors. This assumption is not as unrealistic as it appears. Evidence from surveys of circular migration suggests that the migrant moves with friends or relatives from the village into an established employment-migration pattern. He knows, before migration, that he can obtain employment in the same occupation as his fellow-villagers and he knows the approximate income he can expect.

The family will maximise its income if it distributes its labour, which is assumed to be divisible by the number of man-days, between the rural and urban sectors such that the marginal returns are equated. This is illustrated in Figure 11.1. For simplicity of exposition, transport costs are ignored for the moment. The horizontal axis AB represents the number of man-days in a given period (say, a year). ST shows the marginal return from working in the rural sector, assumed to be diminishing, for man-days counting from B to A. VW gives the same information for the urban sector. The diagram is drawn to illustrate the situation in which the migrant's daily earnings do not change with the number of days worked in the city, although in some urban informal sector occupations, a concave curve might be more appropriate. The family will maximise its earnings if it allocates Ax man-days working in the city and xB man-days in the village. Its total income is representd by the area SZVAB, and denoted by Y.[12]

Figure 11.1: Earnings Decision

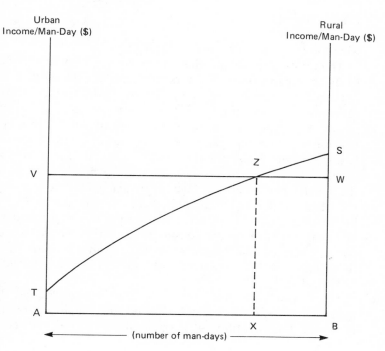

2. Utility Maximisation

Given this income, the family maximises its utility (family welfare) by allocating it between 'village goods' (consumed in the village), and 'city goods' (consumed in the city). How and by whom the utility-maximising decisions are made in the family are not important in the present context. It is assumed that the village goods and the city goods are in some way different.[13] Hence the family's preference ordering is represented by a utility function of the type

$$(1) \qquad U = U(x_1^u, x_2^u, \ldots, x_k^u, x_1^r, \ldots, x_n^r)$$

where $x_1, \ldots, x_n$ are different goods and the superscripts u and r denote whether the commodity is available in the city (u) or village (r). If we allow for the possibility that all of the city goods $(x_1^u, \ldots, x_k^u)$ can be replaced by a composite basket of goods, C_u, and that C_r is a corresponding bundle of village goods, we can rewrite the utility funciton as

$$(2) \qquad U = \phi(C_u, C_r)$$

where ϕ is assumed to be well-behaved.

The utility a family attaches to a particular level of C_u or C_r is likely to depend on two factors, the absolute standard of living obtained by consuming these goods and services and the satisfaction gained from living and consuming in a particular place. A family may have a bias toward rural consumption because it prefers the quality of life in the village (the pace of life is slower, there is less pollution and congestion, traditional values are more prevalent, and so on). Stated in a slightly different way, the family may attach satisfaction to living (and consuming) in the village so that the utility attached to a particular level of C_r is higher than might be expected solely from the physical standard of living provided by the consumption of the goods. Hence C_u^* and C_r^* may be bundles of goods that imply the same physical living standard, but for a family who prefers to live in the village, $U(C_r^*) > U(C_u^*)$.

Given family income, composite price indices P_u and P_r for commodity bundles C_u and C_r and the family's preference ordering, family utility is maximised at $(\bar{C}_u, \bar{C}_r)$ where the marginal rate of substitution between the two commodity bundles equals the ratio between their composite prices or the urban-rural terms of trade. This is illustrated in Figure 11.2 which shows that to maximise family utility, OM of city goods and ON of village goods are purchased.[14]

Figure 11.2: Consumption Decision

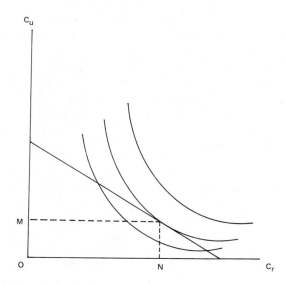

3. Conditions for Circular Migration

As the diagrams are drawn in Figures 11.1 and 11.2, the family will maximise its income if it allocates most of its labour resources to the city and maximises its utility by consuming primarily village goods. This situation can be achieved if the major income earner works in the city for most of the year while the majority of the family remain in the village. While the conditions represented in Figure 11.1 produce a circular migration pattern, it is obvious that this will not always emerge. From the diagrams it can be seen that the distribution of employment and consumption activities between urban and rural sectors will depend on

(a) the relative rates of return to working in the two sectors;

(b) the relative price of urban and rural goods; and
(c) the consumption preferences of the family.

A set of sufficient conditions for a circular migration pattern to emerge is that the rate of return in the urban sector is relatively higher than in the village (at least for a large part of the year) *and* either living costs are higher in the city than the village $(P_uC_u > P_rC_r)$, or the family has a rural-biased consumption preference, or a combination of both. The migrant's family may remain in the village either because the costs of living are so high in the city that its income would be insufficient to support the family there and/or because the family prefers to live in the village. Hence even a family with a strong urban-biased consumption preference may be forced to adopt a circular migration pattern if the income earned is insufficient to support the family in the city.

4. Transport Costs and Return Visits

So far we have assumed that transportation costs are insignificant. If the migrant makes only one round trip during the period, this is a reasonable assumption. In this case the income available for consumption is reduced by the cost of a return journey. However, our discussion of the literature suggested that most circular migrants return frequently to their villages. Obviously they wish to be with their families as often as circumstances allow, and there is also the need to transfer urban savings to the family for rural consumption.

One would expect the number of return journeys to be influenced by the enjoyment which the family gains from being reunited and the cost of the journey.[15] If we incorporate these factors in the utility function, the family's decision problem becomes

(3) $\max U = U(C_u, C_r, F)$
        subject to $Y = P_uC_u + P_rC_r + P_fF$

where Y is the family income determined by the labour allocation decision, F is the number of return visits and P_f is the round-trip fare.[16] The number of return journeys would be such that the last monetary unit spent on fares gives the same marginal utility as the last monetary unit spent on urban and rural goods. If the return fare is a proxy for distance and time spent travelling, as these variables increase the number of return journeys will fall.

This analysis assumes that there are no institutional barriers that prevent the migrant from taking time off work to return home. However, this will depend on the type of job the migrant obtains in the city. If he obtains formal sector employment, he will be required to work set hours, usually six or even seven days per week. If the employee were to take time off to make return visits, he would incur the opportunity cost of income forgone and face the risk of dismissal. In this case the cost of visiting his family would be much greater than the return fare. Hence return visits would be restricted primarily to holidays. Under these conditions a family which places high value on being together is unlikely to adopt circular migration. This is true generally, but is made even more important if frequent return visits are impossible. In this case the whole family may move to the city and return to the village as a group as often as possible.

In contrast, if the migrant undertakes informal sector employment, the institutional constraints are likely to be minimal. In many cases he will be self-employed and determine his own working hours.

IV. Income Maximising-cum-Risk Aversion

The second model complements the income-utility maximisation model just presented by approaching circular migration from a different perspective. It examines the options open to the potential migrant, and shows that under certain reasonablé assumptions, if he aims at maximising income and is risk-averse, then he would favour circular migration to other options. Income maximising behaviour is consistent with the observation that the migrant tends to minimise his living expenses by maintaining very modest living conditions for himself in the city. Risk aversion provides an additional reason for keeping a home base in the village. If plans fail to materialise, the family can always fall back on its existing mode of livelihood. By keeping his contacts, the circular migrant goes to the city only when work is available, thus eliminating to a great extent the uncertainties of job-hunting. Compared to permament migration, circular migration may not promise as high expected returns, but it allows the migrant to avoid most of the risks of migration and offers the family a sense of security and flexibility. Thus circular migration is a rational choice of risk-averters, as demonstrated in the following by applying the Friedman-Savage utility analysis of choices involving risk.[17]

1. Maximising Above-subsistence Family Income

Consider a rural household head whose decision, however reached, applies to his family. His family income varies from year to year, being affected by exogenous factors such as weather conditions, fluctuations in agricultural prices and the like; but over the years, he has learned to expect that on the average his yearly family income is Y_r. Let the yearly cost of supporting the family on subsistence level be E_r.[18] The average above-subsistence family income for a year is

$$(4) \qquad S_r = Y_r - E_r$$

which is assumed to be non-negative for survival. The concept of above-subsistence income is used in order to emphasise the difference in family-support costs between rural and urban areas.

Suppose that an opportunity arises for the household head to work as a circular migrant in the city. As recruitment is made in the village through the existing contact network, he is certain of employment and is fairly well informed of the income he can earn. Let this annual income be Y_c^i. This will supplement rural earnings by other members of the family, Y_r^f. Assuming positive marginal productivity of labour, the rural earnings of the remaining family members would be less than the previous family income level, should the household head decide to migrate:

$$(5) \qquad Y_r^f < Y_r$$

Let the living cost of the household head in the city be E_u^i, which includes the cost of travelling between his rural and urban homes, and let the cost of supporting his family in the rural area be E_r^f. Then if he should decide to take the job and be a circular migrant, the family income above subsistence would become:

$$(6) \qquad S_c = Y_c^i + Y_r^f - E_u^i - E_r^f$$

If the head of this rural household tries to maximise above-subsistence family income, he will choose the alternative of circular migration if

$$S_c > S_r$$

that is,

(7) $Y_c^i - (Y_r - Y_r^f) - (E_u^i + E_r^f - E_r) > 0$

It is reasonable to assume that $E_u^i + E_r^f > E_r$. Then what (7) says is that the increase in income must exceed the increase in costs for circular migration to occur. It also follows that the migrant will minimise his own cost of living in the city to maximise $Y_c^i - E_u^i$.

2. Circular Versus Permanent Migration

But instead of practising circular migration, the household head may decide to migrate to the city with his family permanently. There are a few forces, however, that weigh against this alternative, even if we ignore the less tangible factors such as traditional values, sense of belonging to the village community and problems of assimilation to the urban way of life.

First, job uncertainty is a serious problem facing potential permanent migrants. This problem is aggravated by the institutional and traditional inflexibility which characterise the labour market in most less-developed countries. In many cases contacts are necessary for obtaining jobs. But the system of contacts tends to be contained within some specific group of workers, so that one has to be a group member to have access to the contacts. Permanent migration would mean breaking away from old contacts. Before the migrant can establish new contacts, the threat of unemployment is very real. In contrast, circular migrants always maintain their contacts. Indeed, circular migration is practicable only because migrants have their contacts in the city who will inform them when work is available.

Another factor acting against permanent migration is the relatively high cost of supporting the family in the city. The difference between urban and rural cost of living is so large in most cases that the cost of keeping the whole family in the city, denoted by E_u, is greater than the total cost of supporting the income earner in the city while keeping the rest of the family in the rural area. In such a case

(8) $E_u > E_u^i + E_r^f$

How the decision-maker responds to this choice depends on (a) his subjective assessment of the expected income which can be realised if he migrates permanently, versus the more or less certain income realisable through circular migration; and (b) his attitude towards risk.

To illustrate this, consider a potential migrant who is deciding whether to move to the city permanently. He would like to get a job in the urban formal sector.[19] The above-subsistence incomes derivable from these prospective jobs are $(Y_m - E_u)$ and $(Y_t - E_u)$ respectively. If the subjective probability of obtaining a job in the formal sector is σ_m, and that of getting an informal sector job is $(1 - \sigma_m)$,[20] the expected above-subsistence income for the permanent migrant family would be:

(9) $\Sigma(S_u) = \sigma_m(Y_m - E_u) + (1 - \sigma_m)(Y_t - E_u)$

which may or may not be greater than the above-subsistence income obtainable by practising circular migration, S_c, given by (6). σ_m is likely to be small.

For purposes of exposition, suppose that $\Sigma(S_u) > S_c$, that is,

(10) $\sigma_m(Y_m - E_u) + (1 - \sigma_m)(Y_t - E_u) > Y_r^i - E_u^i - E_r^f$

Can we then predict that the decision-maker, who is assumed to prefer more expected income above subsistence to less, will choose permanent migration instead of circular migration? To put the question another way, does the observed fact that circular migration is practised imply that the inequality (10) is reversed? The answer, in general, is negative. It depends on the decision-maker's attitude to risk.

3. Choice Involving Risk

This can be illustrated by a straightforward application of the Friedman-Savage utility analysis of choices involving risk. Let the decision-maker's preference ordering be represented by a von

Neumann-Morganstern utility function U. Define a 'prospective outcome' L to be

(11) $\qquad L \equiv \Sigma(S_u) = \sigma_m(Y_m - E_u) + (1 - \sigma_m)(Y_t - E_u)$

then

(12) $\qquad U(L) = \sigma_m U(U_m - E_u) + (1 - \sigma_m) U(Y_t - E_u)$

Assume that the decision-maker is certain of the incomes and expenditures that are involved in circular migration. Then we can define a 'sure outcome' A to be

(13) $\qquad A \equiv Y_c^i + Y_r^f - E_u^i - E_r^f$

which has been interpreted to be the family above-subsistence income realisable if circular migration is practised.

It is reasonable to assume that $A > (Y_t - E_u)$. Empirical evidence suggests that many jobs open to circular migrants (for example, construction jobs) pay higher wages than the average earnings of urban informal sector workers because of labour market imperfections and the closed contacts system. But even if equilibrating forces were at work so that $Y_c^i + Y_r^f = Y_t$, A would still be greater than $(Y_t - E_u)$ if $E_u > E_u^i + E_r^f$, as in (8). It is also reasonable to assume that $(Y_m - E_u) > A$ because the modern sector labour market in developing countries is generally protected from competition and income for modern sector workers tends to be high.

Given the assumption that $(Y_t - E_u) < A < (Y_m - E_u)$ and $_m$ is close to zero, a risk-averse person would always prefer circular to permanent migration. This is illustrated in Figure 11.3. Indeed, the decision-maker would consider permanent migration only if σ_m is sufficiently high such that $\sigma_m \geq \sigma_m$ where σ_m is that probability for which

$$U(L') = \sigma'_m U(Y_m - E_u') + (1 - \sigma'_m U(Y_t - E_u) = U(A)$$

Conversely, a risk-loving person would prefer permanent migration to circular migration as long as his subjective probability of getting a job in the formal or modern sector is not too small. His utility function is convex over the range between

Figure 11.3: Risk-averse Situation

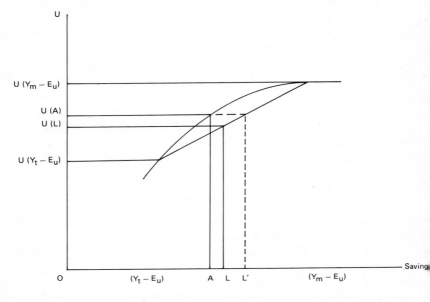

$(Y_t - E_u)$ and $(Y_m - E_u)$, as shown in Figure 11.4. He would choose circular migration only if $\sigma_m \leqslant \sigma_m''$, where σ_m'' is that probability for which

$$U(L'') = \sigma_m'' \, U(Y_m - E_u) + (1 - \sigma_m'' \, U(Y_t - E_u) = U(A)$$

For a major decision such as rural-urban migration, there is every reason to be cautious and risk-averse. If we accept that risk-aversion is the predominant attitude among potential migrants, then even if $L \geqslant A$, that is

$$\Sigma(S_u) = \sigma_m(Y_m - E_u) + (1 - \sigma_m)(Y_t - E_u)$$
$$\geqslant Y_c^i + Y_r^f - E_u^i - E_r^f = S_c$$

which is equivalent to saying that the expected above-subsistence income from permanent migration is no less than that from circular migration, it may still be rational for the decision-maker to choose circular migration.

Figure 11.4: Risk-loving Situation

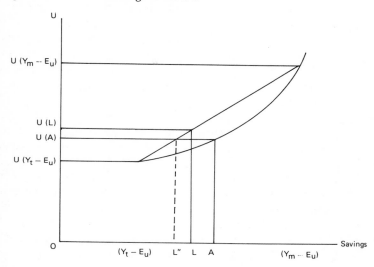

V. Consequences and Policy Implications of Circular Migration

If circular rather than permanent rural-urban migration is the prevailing pattern in South-East Asia, as suggested in recent empirical studies, then the consequences of migratory flows in the region may be quite different from those generally perceived by researchers and policy-makers who tend to treat all migration as permanent. While some possible consequences have been noted in the literature, others are yet to be discovered.

For instance, circular migration is likely to have different consequences for sectoral development than those of permanent migration. As the migrant's family remains in the village the increase in urban population is less rapid and hence the pressure on the social and economic infrastructures that governments need to provide in the cities is reduced. The urban area gains the benefit of the migrant's labour without the expense implied by an increased demand for housing, transport, health and education facilities. But remittances from the migrant to his family represent a leakage from the urban economy, so that the multiplier effects of increased activity will be reduced.

From the point of view of the rural sector, remittances represent an important benefit of circular migration. While permanent migrants may also send funds to their villages, the amounts are unlikely to be as large or as regular. Money not used to support the subsistence of village members may be invested in housing, projects to raise agricultural productivity, or small businesses. Obviously, circular migration will affect the demographic balance of the village although frequent return visits may minimise the effects of fewer working-age males on agricultural output and birth rates.

Circular migration may act as an important vehicle to strengthen the linkages between the rural and urban sectors. Indeed, regular remittances and the repetition of the circular pattern emphasise the lasting nature of the links between rural and urban areas. This means that policies aimed at the urban modern sector will often have a significant impact in villages quite removed from the target group. For example, government restrictions on credit for building and construction in Manila will reduce the level of employment in the industry, which in turn will harm the villages that supply the industry's workforce. Not only will remittances cease but also labourers will return to their villages in need of employment, food and shelter. If building labourers were primarily permanent migrants, a reduction in the level of construction activity would increase the level of urban unemployment. However, as they are circular migrants, the laid-off labourers return to their villages and the burden of adjustment is placed on the rural sector.

Temporary rather than permanent migration may also carry different social and political implications. One would expect the separation of the household head from his dependents to create strained and less stable relations in the family, although Nelson argued that temporary migration 'disrupts extended family and clan ties less than would the permanent departure to the city of segments of the family or clan'.[21] Circular migrants may be less likely to integrate socially into the city. They may mix only with fellow migrants from the same rural district and be less willing to join formal associations and clubs, including political movements. However, from the village viewpoint, circular migrants may disseminate ideas and attitudes gained in the city which will influence change in the village.

The policy implications of different types of migration pattern for development strategies have not been fully explored in the literature. Further research is required before such questions as whether circular migration leads to a more optimal allocation of resources from the perspective of the economy can be answered. Hence we cannot conclude that governments should attempt to reduce the flow of migrants.[22] But if those policies that have been advocated to reduce permanent migration were to apply to situations where circular migration is prevalent, then undesirable effects might result. For example, a legal ban on permanent movement to the cities, which has been suggested as a means of reducing migration, may actually increase the number of circular migrants, as Hugo observed in the case of Jakarta.[23] Potential migrants unable to obtain permanent resident status have sought visitors cards which permit the holder to live in Jakarta for six months. On expiry, the migrant can return to his village and apply for another. If he is still regarded as a member of his village (for example, his family resides there) his application is likely to be successful. Obviously, this situation encourages the use of circular rather than permanent migration.

Notes

1. The authors have benefited from comments by Guy Standing, R. Scott Moreland and Peter V. Schaeffer.

2. For a review of studies on circular migration in these countries see J. Connell, B. Dasgupta, R. Laishley and M. Lipton: *Migration from rural areas: The evidence from village studies* (Delhi, Oxford University Press, 1976).

3. W. Elkan: 'Migrant labor in Africa: An economist's approach', in *American Economic Review*, May 1959, vol. 49, no. 2, pp. 188-97; idem: 'Circular migration and the growth of towns in East Africa', in *International Labour Review*, December 1967, vol. 96, no. 6, pp. 581-9.

4. G.J. Hugo: *New conceptual approaches to migration in the context of urbanisation: A discussion based on Indonesian experience*, paper prepared for a seminar organised by the International Union for the Scientific Study of Population's Committee on Urbanisation and Population Redistribution, 30 June-3 July (Bellagio, Italy, 1978); S. Goldstein: *Circulation in the context of total mobility in Southeast Asia*, Papers of the East-West Population Institute No. 53 (Honolulu, East-West Center, 1978).

5. Goldstein, 1978.

6. G.J. Hugo: *Population mobility in West Java, Indonesia*, PhD dissertation, Canberra, Australian National University, Department of Demography, 1975. He also found that most circular migrants from a particular village were engaged in only one or two occupations — Hugo, 1978.

7. J.N. Anderson: *Social strategies in population change: Village data from central Luzon*, Southeast Asian Development Advisory Group (SEADAG) Papers No. 72-15 (New York, 1972).

8. R.B. Textor: 'The northeast samlor driver in Bankok', in UNESCO, Research Centre on the Social Implications of Industrialisation in Southern Asia

(eds.): *The social implications of industrialisation and urbanisation* (Calcutta, UNESCO, 1956).

9. L. Jellinek: 'Circular migration in the *Pondok* dwelling system: A case study of ice cream traders in Jakarta', in P.J. Rimmer, D.W. Drakakis-Smith and T.G. McGee (eds.): *Food, shelter and transport in South-East Asia and the Pacific* (Canberra, Australian National University, Department of Human Geography, 1978).

10. A.W. Stretton: *The building industry and employment creation in Manila, the Philippines*, PhD dissertation, Canberra, Australian National University, Department of Economics, Research School of Pacific Studies, 1977; idem: 'Instability of employment among building industry labourers', in R. Bromley and C. Gerry (eds.): *Casual work and poverty in Third World cities* (Chichester, John Wiley & Sons, 1979); idem: 'The building industry and urbanisation in Third World countries: A Philippine case study', in *Economic Development and Cultural Change*, January, 1981, vol. 29, no. 2, pp. 325-39.

11. Hugo, 1978, p. 23.

12. It is possible that VW might lie entirely above ST, in which case the migrant will maximise his income by working only in the city.

13. The goods and services available in the village and city may be of a different type or quality. While goods such as housing, health care, education, transport, water supply, sanitary services and entertainment are available in both sectors, the quality of the goods is sufficiently different to regard them as separate goods between which the differences may not be so great; some individual items (for example, coca-cola) may be exactly the same in both centres. However, for a large number of goods the differences are sufficient to justify the assumption. The implication is that while labour and money can move between the two sectors, goods cannot. The alternative is to discuss the process in real terms and assume that there is a market in which city goods can be exchanged for village goods. In this case we have the problem that many goods (for example, the different standards of housing, utilities and health care) are not exchangeable in this manner. The final solution is similar irrespective of which assumption is made.

14. We have reformulated the consumption decision from

$$\max U = U(x_1^u, \ldots, x_k^u, x_1^r, \ldots, x_n^r)$$

Subject to
$$Y = \sum_{i=1}^{n} P_i x_i$$
to
$$\max U = (C_u, C_r)$$
subject to $Y = C_u P_u + C_r P_r$
where
$$C_u = C_u(x_1^u \ldots, x_k^u) \colon {}_k^u)$$
$$C_r = C_r(x_1^r \ldots, x_n^r) \colon {}_n^r)$$
$$P_u = P_u(P_1^u, \ldots, P_k^u)$$
$$P_r = P_r(P_1^r, \ldots, P_n^r)$$

This will determine the expenditure on urban goods, Z_u. This expenditure will be allocated among the different city goods by

$$\max C_u = C_u(x_1^u, \ldots, X_k^u)$$

Subject to $Z_u = \sum_{i=1}^{n} P_i^u x_i^u$

A similar procedure will give the distribution of expenditures on rural goods, Z_r.

These two methods of utility maximisation will be consistent if the prices or the quantities of goods in each category are in fixed proportions or if the utility function is homogeneously separable. This last condition requires the elasticity of demand of each good in a category with respect to expenditure on that category to be unity — H.A.J. Green: *Consumer theory* (Harmondsworth, Penguin, 1971).

This grouping of commodities into two categories, C_u and C_r, is done primarily to simplify the exposition. The general results of the model would remain even if the assumption were thought to be too strong and consumption decisions were made by maximising the original utility function.

15. Return visits needed to fulfil village obligations could be included here.

16. This methodology assumes that return visits do not affect the income decisions of the household head. In effect, we are saying that the migrant will divide the total working days in a period between urban and rural employment so that the marginal productivities are equal. This will leave a number of days for leisure, which he may spend in the city or village. An alternative would be to build a simultaneous equation model in which the number of days of leisure is determined endogenously by, among other factors, income forgone. In such a model it might be possible to determine the length of each return visit as well as the number of such visits.

17. M. Friedman and L.J. Savage: 'The utility analysis of choices involving risk', in *Journal of Political Economy*, August 1948, vol. 56, no. 5, pp. 279-304.

18. For simplicity, it is assumed that E_r is the strictly necessary cost for supporting the rural family, and hence is independent of Y_r. This assumption applies to all family-supporting costs in the model (that is, E_r^f, E_u^i, E_u) to be introduced later.

19. The transportation cost involved in permanent migration is not introduced explicitly. This one-shot expenditure can be accounted for by deducting from the yearly income an appropriate amount which would be the yearly instalment of repayment should the trip be financed from a loan.

20. Subjective probabilities à la Fan are used instead of objective probabilities à la Todaro because to a large extent migration decisions are based on the migrant's perception and interpretation of information channelled to the village through friends and relatives in the city or other villagers with friends and relatives in the city. In many cases, the information itself or the interpretation of it is not accurate, so that the migrant's subjective assessment of job opportunities is significantly different from the objective picture as reflected by unemployment rates. The implication is that in empirical research a survey of migrants' attitudes towards job opportunities is preferred to calculations based on unemployment statistics in determining the probabilities of finding jobs in different urban sectors. See Y.-K. Fan: 'The dynamics of structural change: A model of economic development and urbanization', in *Regional Science and Urban Economics*, September 1978, vol. 8, no. 3, pp. 249-70; idem: 'Emigration and growth: A model for small developing economies', in *Journal of Economic Development*, December 1979, vol. 4, no. 2, pp. 141-54; M.P. Todaro: 'A model of labor migration and urban unemployment in less developed countries', in *American Economic Review*, March 1969, vol. 59, no. 1, pp. 138-48.

21. J.M. Nelson: 'Sojourners versus new urbanites: Causes and consequences of temporary versus permanent cityward migration in developing countries', in *Economic Development and Cultural Change*, July 1976, vol. 24, no. 4, pp. 721-57.

22. Cf. J.R. Harris and M.P. Todaro: 'Migration, unemployment and development: A two-sector analysis', in *American Economic Review*, March 1970, vol. 60, no. 1, pp. 126-42.

23. Hugo, 1978.

12
Household Labour Mobility in a Modern Agrarian Economy: Mexico

KENNETH ROBERTS

I. Introduction

In pronouncing the 'End of the Age of Innocence in Migration Theory', Abu-Lughod recognised that the preponderance of evidence no longer supported many of the propositions developed in the income-maximisation model that had dominated migration theory for at least a decade.[1] Patterns of labour mobility were much more complex than the parameters of that model would suggest; in less-developed countries, circular migration was found to be the prevalent form of mobility in many regions.[2] Moreover, evidence is accumulating to suggest that rural development in these countries is often *positively* associated with migration from rural areas. These anomalies have led to the generation and examination, from a multidisciplinary perspective, of many hypotheses that are beginning to take the shape of a major reformulation of migration theory. This paper develops a model that incorporates and extends several of these recent contributions in order to specify the differential effects of various aspects of rural economic development upon labour mobility in four rural areas of Mexico.

II. Development, Risk and Peasant Household Labour Mobility

The process of economic development in less-developed countries presupposes migration from rural to urban areas. Lewis's influential model of a dual economy emphasised the pull of increasing job opportunities in the urban sector, and attributed a relatively passive role to the rural agricultural sector.[3] In order to explain high rural-urban migration in the face of high levels of urban unemployment observed in less-developed countries, Todaro generalised this economic approach to include the probability of unemployment in urban areas.[4] And Harris and Todaro framed it as 'a simple extension of traditional two-sector neo-classical trade models', with urban and rural expected incomes endogenously determined by the relative quantities of the basic factors of production — land, labour and capital.[5] Todaro later claimed that 'its fundamental contribution — i.e. the idea that migration proceeds primarily in response to differences in "expected" urban and rural real incomes . . . remains widely accepted to this day as the "received theory" in the literature on migration and economic development'.[6]

The Todaro model, although often empirically estimated at the macro level of average rural and urban wage rates and urban unemployment, is framed at the micro level of the individual migrant's decision process. It is its linkage with neo-classical theory which allows macro processes to be translated into signals to the migrant at the micro level with regularity and predictability. Specifically, capital accumulation in either sector will raise the marginal productivity of labour and therefore the expected wage in that sector, while capital accumulation and technical change in the agricultural sector will raise farm incomes.[7] In contrast to the earlier dual economy models, the rural sector no longer plays a passive role, which has important implications for development policy. Banerjee and Kanbur recognised this model's pervasive influence: 'the current orthodoxy . . . is that rural development, in the sense of increasing the incomes and standards of living in the rural sector, will have to be the major policy instrument in reducing rural-urban migration'.[8]

This brief summary shows that the widely-held view that migration is inversely related to rural development depends critically upon two elements: the linkage between agricultural development (equated within the neo-classical model to the application of capital to agriculture) and a rise in rural incomes, and the theory that expected income is the primary determinant of migration. The first is a necessary condition for agricultural development to cause rural incomes to rise, while the second is necessary for that rise to decrease migration.

The neo-classical linkage has been the subject of intense debate (an examination of which is outside the scope of this paper), which shows that only under certain very special circumstances are 'relative factor prices' and 'relative factor supplies' inversely related to one another.[9] However, this critique only tells us what economic development *may not* do, but it does not help us to determine what it *will do* to labour mobility.[10] This paper will argue that the focus of migration theory on expected income is incomplete, and that in order to understand labour mobility in less-developed countries, not only must the effect of agricultural change on rural incomes be examined, but also its effect on the risk of this income stream and on agricultural employment.

The first step in this examination is to broaden the scope of the analysis from rural-urban migration to labour mobility, and to focus on the factors causing this mobility to take one form or other. Evidence from studies in developing countries is accumulating to show that the rural landholding population works off its own farms in a variety of occupations, and engages in types of labour mobility that span a spectrum from commuting to permanent migration.[11]

The next step is to define with greater precision the meaning of what has been loosely referred to as 'agricultural development', 'rural development', or 'agricultural capitalisation'. Essentially, what is being described is the process of monetisation of the peasant economy, both at the level of consumption and production, resulting from the substitution of manufactured for traditional goods, commercial for subsistence crops, and wage labour for family labour in agricultural production. This process has been examined in Mexico[12] and many other countries, and is graphically described for a village in central Mexico by Arizpe:

> By 1973, 80 per cent of the production costs of maize had to be paid for in cash, compared to 30 per cent a decade before . . . During this same period local cottage and crafts industries greatly declined. Manufactured products poured into rural areas; some were cheaper or more durable than their local counterparts, or had greater prestige. Bottled beer swept away locally brewed beverages such as *pulque* . . . while junk foods and soft drinks have done away with women's sales of tortilla savories. *Tule* raincapes were replaced by plastic

sheets, leather sandals by plastic shoes, *zacaton* (brushes) by those made with synthetic fibres — the list can go on and on, region by region.[13]

While this process is occurring everywhere, it proceeds with different degrees of intensity depending on the suitability of the region's soils for commercial crops or mining, the availability of irrigation, the transportation network, the level of industrial and commercial development of nearby urban areas and, in countries with large indigenous populations such as Mexico, cultural factors affecting the household and its position in the community.

Having expanded the definition of migration and concretised the process of agricultural change motivating it, the analysis may turn to the question of the effect of this process on labour mobility. Hugo frames this question in the context of Indonesian mobility: 'How do the external forces of colonial penetration and the resultant uneven and distinctive pattern of capitalist penetration evince themselves at the level of the village, family or individual and impel migration of a particular type or encourage stability?'[14] The nature of the effect of the penetration of capitalism into rural areas on labour mobility of landholding households will be shown to depend upon two factors: what it does to farm incomes and what it does to the level of risk faced by the household. It is this latter component that has been comparatively ignored in empirical analysis, and which may reverse any potentially positive effect of increased 'agricultural development' on labour mobility, particularly circular migration.[15]

The application of the economic theory of behaviour under uncertainty to migration analysis is not a novel idea, but the analysis, in part because of its complexity when rigorously developed, has not been comprehensive concerning the impact of agricultural change upon risk. A certain conception of risk — the probability of failure — is incorporated in the Todaro model as the risk of unemployment, but only as it affects expected income, a single-valued parameter. Fan and Stretton in Chapter 11 extend this analysis to circular migration. They hypothesise that circular migration is usually directed toward the informal sector of urban areas, where the migrant faces a lower probability of unemployment than in the formal sector. The risk of this alternative, which combines farm income with wage income from jobs in the urban informal sector, is lower than that of permanent migration to the urban area. Goodman examines the role of information flows on the perceived probability distribution of urban wages, and how rural socio-economic status affects these information flows.[16] David presents a rigorous and suggestive approach to incorporating the effect of the risk of urban income upon migration, focusing upon the trade-off facing the potential migrant in the allocation of funds between migration and job search.[17] The significant contribution of these approaches is the incorporation of the distribution of potential income into the decision process, either as it actually exists in the urban areas or as it is perceived by the decision-maker through information and job search.

Risk in the rural sector has also received attention. Many authors have referred to the peasant's primary motivation as being to ensure that basic subsistence needs are met, which implies a different allocation of resources than the goal of income maximisation. Guillet called this goal 'reproductive maximisation: the goal of security and survival of the household'.[18] Roumasset and others have rigorously developed this concept as it applies to the adoption of new agricultural technologies.[19]

The goal of the reduction of the risks associated with farm production and off-farm labour has been related to labour mobility by Hugo. In Indonesia he found, 'A circulation strategy kept the mover's options in the village completely open so that the risk of not being able to earn subsistence is reduced by spreading it between village and city income opportunities.'[20] His focus is on the migrant's expected income flow, the risk of which is reduced by maintaining a foothold in the rural community.

When the emphasis is upon risk in the rural area, there is both theoretical and empirical support for the proposition that a more inegalitarian distribution of rural income would increase migration. David's model predicts 'higher frequencies of migration to appear in more thoroughly urbanised societies (with a higher dispersion of income), at least by comparison with settled, predominantly rural societies where the mass of the working population were hired in markets characterised by relatively low dispersion of wages'.[21] In India, Connell et al. found that 'migration from villages was positively associated with unequal distributions of incomes and with commercialisation'.[22]

This brief overview indicates that migration theory appears to incorporate adequately the effect of risk, perceived as the variability of potential incomes in sending and receiving regions, upon the *individual*, in either the role of agricultural producer or migrant. However, it is the relevance of the individual as the appropriate unit of analysis in peasant societies that is increasingly being called into question. Standing's recent review found that 'typically, the survival of the community or family has relied upon the complementary efforts of its various members. That has meant complex ties of customary obligations, thus making emigration much more than an act of personal independence.'[23] This paper adopts the view that the household is the appropriate unit of analysis for studying labour mobility in developing countries. With this perspective and the focus upon risk, labour mobility emerges as one element of a strategy of household labour allocation under uncertainty.[24] This viewpoint broadens the concept of risk beyond the variance of potential incomes to the correlation among these incomes, and confers theoretical significance to the concept of the household as more than the sum of individuals pursuing their separate goals.

The hypothesis of this paper, developed more fully in the following section, is that the household, when its size and composition allow, engages in a strategy of risk minimisation through the allocation of its labour to different economic sectors and regions. The commercialisation of agriculture increases monetary costs of production, the variability of farm income and, when combined with the substitution of manufactured for traditional consumption goods, the risk that this income will fall below a certain minimum level. The potential for local agricultural wage labour might also be decreased by changes in crop composition and mechanisation.[25] Faced with these changes, the rural household will compensate by 'spreading risk across economic sectors and geographical space and securing alternative sources of income'.[26] The household will seek to minimise the risks associated with its portfolio of farm income and off-farm wage labour by diversifying its labour supply among these activities.

This view has received theoretical and empirical support. Stark and Levhari developed a model in which the increased risk associated with a new agricultural technology is offset by permanent migration of a family member to an urban area.[27] In her study of two areas in Mexico, Arizpe found that 'as the deficit in maize cultivation grew, *minifundio* [small farm] households turned to multiplication and diversification of wage earnings'.[28]

Connell *et al.*'s review of Indian village data concluded: 'The evidence for many areas suggests that migration is related to the distribution as well as the extent of opportunities within the village and is often used to increase not individual but household income, and to reduce household risk by increasing the variety of income prospects.'[29]

This portfolio approach to household migration presupposes an extended family structure in which household income and its potential variability are important considerations in where its individual members work. In that context, Nelson discussed the importance of rural social structure on circular labour mobility in developing countries.[30] And Dinerman observed in two Tarascan communities of Michoacan, Mexico, a division of labour in which the women sold vegetables to supplement cash income while their husbands worked in the United States, with all cash income pooled into a common household budget.[31] Larger, more established households tended to send more migrants to the United States, as discussed in a study of migration from five Mexican cities by Selby and Murphy.[32]

Weist suggested that household size should not be considered a fixed constraint to labour allocation, but that individuals in nuclear households will fuse together when faced with low and unreliable farm income; he found support for this hypothesis in a Mexican village in Michoacan.[33] Dinerman concurred: 'Migration tends to maintain, if not create, a preference for a particular form of household organization, the extended household.'[34] Holding other factors constant, the more persons of working age in the household, the more diversification can occur for any income level, or a higher income can be expected for any level of risk to household income.

This focus on risk should not be taken to imply that the effect of agricultural capitalisation on farm income can be ignored, simply that this effect cannot be determined outside a specific rural context as easily as can its effect upon risk. Apart from the direct interaction of farm income and its variability in determining the allocation of household labour between farm and off-farm pursuits, higher farm incomes may affect labour mobility *within* the category of off-farm labour by providing a fund to finance migration. Banerjee and Kanbur developed a model in which farm income is a resource for migration, and in applying it to Indian data found 'a non-monotonic relationship between migration propensity and origin income'.[35] Migration increases with wealth in David's theoretical model because more funds are available for job search and migration.[36] And migration to the United States was curtailed from the poorer of the two villages Dinerman studied because of the lack of local funds that could be borrowed to finance the cost of crossing the border.[37]

III. A Model of Household Labour Allocation

The variables discussed above can be incorporated into a simplified graphical exposition of household labour allocation. Figure 12.1 presents the income side of the story. The household is assumed to have a fixed number of work-months $(L_h)^*$ that can be allocated to farm and off-farm labour. This will vary according to each household's size and its composition among adult members and dependants.

Figure 12.1: Income and Costs of Household Labour Alternatives

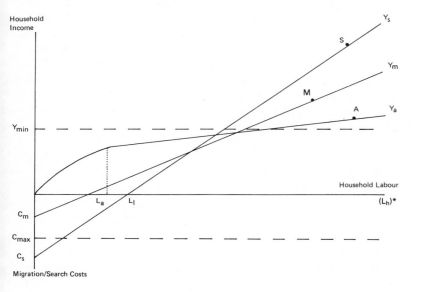

Three different types of off-farm labour are shown in Figure 12.1 (more options are of course open, but these are representative of those open to most rural Mexican households). If all available labour were allocated to work in the United States, expected household income would lie along the income line Y_s, its exact position at S depending upon the amount of time the household could expect to earn wages if it chose this option — that is, taking account of the expected unemployment. If all household labour worked in urban Mexico, expected income would lie at point M on the line Y_m. In both cases expected income is the mean of a distribution of potential household incomes in a particular locale and job, weighted by their respective probabilities of occurrence. Higher rates of unemployment lower this expected value by moving the point of expected income back along the income line from the point of full employment of household labour.

The third type of labour shown is a combination of work on the household plot and local off-farm agricultural wage labour. Under this alternative the household is assumed to use its available labour to meet all seasonal demands of farm production to the capacity of its members, to hire labour at the local wage rate for periods of intense work, and to work themselves as agricultural day-labourers during periods of slack on-farm labour. As the household works more on the farm, the marginal product of labour in farm production falls until L_a, where the household substitutes off-farm wage labour for more work on-farm. The expected income of this combination will lie at point A along line Y_a if the household allocates all of its labour to this alternative.

Each of these types of labour also has an associated level of migration and search costs: local agriculture is assumed to have zero cost; migration to urban Mexico would involve expenses of transportation and job search (C_m); and migration to the United States would include these costs and a substantial fee charged by *cayotes* who help them cross the border (C_s).

The slope of each income line represents the expected wage of that type of employment less the excess of living costs at the destination over living costs at the household residence. Thus a household allocating all of its labour to the USA would have to plan on working at least L_1 just to break even on the expenses of migration and job search. If a lower proportion of household labour were allocated to US labour, the income line would pivot on L_1, reducing both migration/search costs and expected income.[38]

Two constraints are defined for the household. The level of subsistence income, below which the household would suffer severe economic hardship, is set at Y_{min}. This subsistence income is composed of both consumption and production requirements of the household, for if there were a crop failure the household must have enough income to survive after paying the cash costs of production.[39] C_{max} defines the maximum level of migration and search costs the household can afford. This will depend on past levels of income, which may be used either in the form of savings or serve as a sign to other members of the community of the household's ability to repay a loan.[40]

As formulated, a household attempting to maximise expected income would allocate as much labour as possible to the highest-paying alternative within the constraints of migration and search costs. Unless it was due to particular circumstances which would dramatically lower the household's perceived ability of its members to migrate or get a job, pushing the household back along the income line Y_s below its intersection with Y_a, there would be little reason to expect a household to prefer local employment or internal migration to the United States.[41]

Without yet considering the effects of diversification, risk enters this model in several ways. The probability distribution of wages affects the slope of the income line, while the probability distribution of unemployment affects the position of expected household income along the income line. In addition, the lower tail of the distribution of potential incomes around Y_a may fall below Y_{min}. The area in this part of the distribution, measuring the probability of obtaining a combined level of farm income and income from agricultural wage labour that is below subsistence, would play an important part in determining the allocation of household labour.

Figure 12.2 presents the other side of the story. Variability in the distribution of occupational income, measured by its variance, is made explicit on the vertical axis, so that corresponding to each level of expected household income from allocating all household labour to one occupation there is a particular level of risk. Utility functions U_1 and U_2 represent household preferences between higher levels of expected income and higher risk, with positions on U_2 preferred to those on U_1. Thus, the household would prefer a certain agricultural income of Y_{min} to a higher expected agricultural income of Y_a with its associated

Figure 12.2: Variance in Expected Income of Household Labour Alternatives

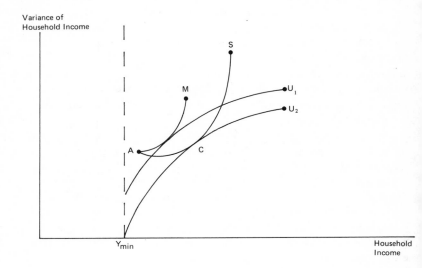

uncertainty. The concavity of the utility function in Figure 12.2 shows the household to be risk-averse; it will accept increasing uncertainty only if expected returns increase more than proportionately.[42]

The household will allocate labour by two criteria: the lowest degree of uncertainty for any expected level of income, and diversification among activities that react differently to change. The first is incorporated into the utility function, while the second follows from the combination of occupations within the household's income portfolio. If the returns of A (which is already a portfolio consisting of farm income and local agricultural wage labour) were perfectly correlated with those of working in urban Mexico, any combination of these two would lie along the straight line connecting A to M. In this case, diversification does not provide risk reduction, only risk averaging.

Diversification reduces risk when the returns of two occupations are not perfectly correlated with one another. In this case, the variance of a portfolio consisting of a mix of occupations can actually be less than that of either of the corresponding occupations. As shown in Figure 12.1, combining agricultural income with circular migration to urban Mexico may provide a lower risk for the same level of expected income as does working in local agriculture. But the combination of local agricultural income with US migration, two occupations with relatively uncorrelated returns, is the dominant strategy in this example, for it maximises household utility. The household would choose occupational mix C, defined by the point of tangency of the income-risk relationship with utility curve U_2, and allocate labour between local agriculture and circular US migration in order to achieve this expected income level.

This is shown more clearly in Figure 12.3, which combines the income/cost side of Figure 12.1 with the income/risk of Figure 12.2. For a household with two working members, one of whom is sent to work in the United States and the other works on the household's land and in local agricultural wage labour, migration/search costs would be half of those resulting from choosing the alternative of allocating both workers to the US. Expected household income would be Y_c, the sum of the separate expected household incomes resulting from allocating half of total labour to each option. The distribution of this expected income has a variance of σ_c which is considerably lower than that of working entirely in the United States and only slightly higher than that of working entirely in Mexico. The relationship among the actual incomes, costs, and risks of these three occupations may of course be very different from those presented for illustrative purposes in Figure 12.3. Nevertheless, the model allows separation and derivation of the different effects of agricultural development upon household labour mobility developed in the previous section.

The monetisation and commercialisation of the local economy will increase Y_{min}, both through the increased consumption requirements of the household and by increasing the monetary costs of agricultural production. Moreover, any resulting change in crop composition or mechanisation may reduce the amount of income that could be expected from local agricultural wage labour (a movement back along Y_a), and make the potential distribution of this wage-labour income wider. Higher fixed costs would also make agricultural income more variable; the combined effect of these factors would be to increase the probability that household income from local agriculture would fall below Y_{min}.

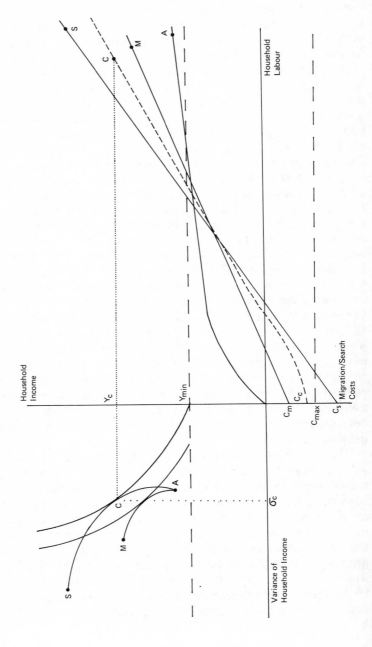

Figure 12.3: Household Labour Allocation Under Uncertainty

Farm income may also be affected by agricultural capitalisation, though the direction of this effect cannot be determined *a priori*. It is probable that through machinery rental resulting from mechanisation of local agriculture, even households with smaller plots of land can produce the same level of farm income with less labour, shifting the farm income curve up, at least to a certain level of farm labour. If agricultural income were to be increased by this change throughout its range, for any given level of income the probability that Y_a would fall below subsistence would decrease. But it would also increase C_{max}, for reasons discussed earlier.

Thus, without considering the effect on risk other than on the potential distribution of local agricultural income, the effect of agricultural development on labour mobility would depend primarily upon the relative effects of a given change in agricultural income on C_{max} and Y_{min}. If agricultural income were increased substantially, agricultural development might reduce the need to work off-farm, though it would probably increase the time the household had available to do so. However, the increase in C_{max} would allow the household to finance more costly forms of mobility such as circular migration. If Y_{min} were increased more than proportionally to agricultural income, the household might reduce the resulting higher probability of falling below Y_{min} by circular migration to urban Mexico or to the USA. Were agricultural change not to cause an increase in expected agricultural income, the increase in Y_{min} would merely force the household to work off-farm in non-agricultural occupations, either locally or elsewhere in Mexico, for it could not afford the more costly alternative of US migration.

Larger, more mature households would have more labour to allocate to all occupations, thereby increasing expected income, and more than compensating for the increased consumption needs of a greater number of household members. This is because the extended household would enjoy economies of scale in living expenses due to the presence of fixed costs such as housing. Households with more working members could also engage in greater diversification of income sources, thereby decreasing the risk of the household income portfolio.

From this analysis it follows that long-distance circular migration could be expected to emerge among larger households in areas in which agricultural development has increased the risk of local agricultural income while also increasing the average level of income, thereby providing funds to finance the relatively high migration/search costs. The risks of the total income portfolio might actually be reduced by allocating some labour to this alternative. If farm incomes were not increased by agricultural change, the ability to finance costly forms of circular migration would be curtailed, and the household would attempt to diversify local income sources to offset the increased risks of commercialisation.

No such diversification of income sources would be expected in areas of traditional agriculture. If farm incomes were relatively high due to favourable local conditions there would be little reason for labour mobility, though that which did occur could involve high-cost circular migration. If farm incomes were low, the lack of commercialisation of the local economy would imply few possibilities for off-farm work other than as an agricultural day-labourer in low-wage, traditional agriculture. For households which could not subsist on farm income, and which were restrained from costly circular migration by a lack of resources, permanent migration might offer the only viable alternative.

IV. Agrarian Structure and Labour Mobility in Four Areas of Mexico

This last section will briefly examine data collected in four rural areas of Mexico in 1974 to determine the applicability of the concepts developed in the previous section. The areas studied were Las Huastecas in San Luis Potosi, the Mixteca Baja in Oaxaca, Valsequillo in Puebla, and a part of the Bajio that lies in the state of Guanajuato.[43]

The survey regions represent almost the entire spectrum of agriculture found in Mexico. The Mixteca Baja, located in the mountainous coastal region of the state of Oaxaca, certainly occupied the lower end of the socio-economic spectrum. The area had no large towns, and transportation within the zone and from it to other regions was severely limited by poor roads. There were few local opportunities for off-farm labour, and farm techniques had remained substantially unchanged from the pre-Conquest period, employing the slash-and-burn method to clear the mountain jungles for corn cultivation. The Bajio occupied the other end of this spectrum, having undergone a dramatic process of agricultural change in the 1960s and rapid growth of the urban areas and infrastructure during the 1970s. A variety of commercial crops, employing improved inputs and mechanisation, dominated agriculture in the Bajio.

However, the concept of a linear progression from traditional to commercial agriculture breaks down when the other two zones are examined. Las Huastecas exhibited many aspects of traditional agriculture, employing a lot of family labour and few purchased inputs, but subsistence crops were mixed with commercial crops, while farm incomes were relatively high. Valsequillo, on the other hand, was intimately linked with the commercial and semi-urban economy in the Puebla area, agriculture was partially mechanised, yet corn, the primary subsistence crop in Mexico, was predominant and farm incomes were low for most households.

Table 12.1 presents summary data on agricultural production, farm labour and off-farm labour in the four regions. It is apparent that off-farm labour and income, which included remittances from migrants, were important in all the regions, contributing the majority of household labour in the commercially-developed regions of the Bajio and Valsequillo, and one third of household labour and one half of household income in the most isolated zone of traditional agriculture, the Mixteca Baja. Only in Las Huastecas was the importance of off-farm labour relatively low; in this zone a monetary income would be earned by growing coffee and sugar cane, utilising low levels of purchased inputs, especially hired labour, because women and children could participate in many tasks required by these labour-intensive crops. Thus, these households work more on their land and less off-farm than in other zones.

But the *type* of off-farm labour in the commercial zones — the Bajio and Valsequillo — differed significantly from the zones of more traditional agriculture. Almost all of the off-farm labour in the traditional areas was in local agricultural work, while in the Bajio and Valsequillo there was a great deal of labour in other occupations. In particular, in the Bajio, a highly-developed area with several large towns, there was a wide diversity of types of off-farm labour.

Farms in all four areas hired a significant amount of their total farm labour input. Households in the zones characterised by

Table 12.1: *Major Characteristics of Farms and Households in the Four Survey Areas*

	Mixteca Baja (67 households)	Las Huastecas (98 households)	Valsequillo (99 households)	Bajio (98 households)
Agricultural production				
Average farm size (hectares)	2.8	7.1	6.1	10.4
Cultivated land in subsistence crops (%)	76	66	87	46
Corn production sold (%)	10	14	37	88
Value of agricultural capital/ha (pesos)	907	285	1,789	4,070
Value of farm production/ha (pesos)	1,234	3,273	2,218	4,250
Farm income (pesos)	2,639	16,816	21,487	22,306
Farms with incomes less than $5,000 pesos (%)	79	20	65	23
Agricultural labour (days)				
Household farm labour	172	275	78	86
Hired farm labour	68	52	87	85
Total farm labour	240	327	165	171
Total farm labour/ha cultivated	118	75	37	22
Household farm labour in corn production	127	105	58	30
Household income (pesos)				
Farm	2,639	16,816	21,487	22,306
Off-farm	2,239	4,211	12,293	12,257
Total	4,968	21,027	33,780	34,563

	Mixteca Baja (67 households)	Las Huastecas (98 households)	Valsequillo (99 households)	Bajio (98 household
Household labour (days)				
Farm	172	275	78	86
Off-farm	88	139	253	101
Total	260	414	331	187
Off-farm labour days as *journalero* (%)	72	100	63	23
Average number of adults per household	3.1	3.3	3.7	5.4

Note: The population data are from the 1970 Censo de Población, Mexico. All other data are from the household surveys.

modern agriculture, the Bajio and Valsequillo, hired more than half their total farm labour input. And farms in the Bajio used more hired labour per hectare than in any other zone, even though far less labour was used per hectare than in the other areas. For the two regions for which monthly labour data are available, household farm labour inputs in peak months exceeded *total* farm labour inputs in all other months. Even so, the household hired labour even in months of slack agricultural activity.
months of slack agricultural activity.

Further investigation of seasonal patterns showed that monthly off-farm labour in the Bajio did not vary much, so that households there did not subordinate off-farm labour to farm work demands. Thus, hired farm labour played a pivotal role in total household labour allocation — households worked a rather constant amount of time off-farm each month, and during months of high farm labour input hired labour to enable them to maintain the continuity of off-farm activities.

Farm incomes were high in the Bajio and Las Huastecas, low in the Mixteca Baja, and low for the majority of households in Valsequillo (about two-thirds of the farms there earning less than 5,000 pesos, or $400 at the exchange rate prevailing at the time). Seventy-five per cent of total income was earned off-farm for four of every five households in Valsequillo.

Varied patterns of labour mobility emerge in the four survey areas. Households in the Mixteca Baja, with extremely low levels of farm income and few local opportunities for off-farm labour, could not afford to sponsor circular migrants. Instead, the predominant pattern of labour migration from the zone, noted in several studies, was permanent migration to Acapulco, Oaxaca City, or Mexico City, where migrants from the local region maintained networks to ease the transition from traditional Indian communities to urban life.[44]

In Las Huastecas, farm production yielded a relatively high income with few purchased inputs. The need for wage labour was reduced by the low commercialisation of agriculture, and heavy inputs of household labour left little opportunity for extended stays away from the farm. Clearly farm income played an important role in determining migratory patterns in these two zones of traditional agriculture. Were the analysis to stop there, it might be concluded that agricultural development, equated with farm income, would decrease migration.

Valsequillo and the Bajio provide little support for this conclusion. Both were much more commercially developed than the two indigenous zones, though farm incomes were low in Valsequillo and high in the Bajio. The increasing monetisation of production in both zones had increased the relative importance of off-farm labour and the diversification of this labour to different types of off-farm activity. However, circular migration was not an important part of the off-farm labour mix in Valsequillo, while in the Bajio circular migration, especially to the United States, was quite common. Around one-fourth of all agricultural wage labour done by members of Bajio households was worked in the United States, and over 5 per cent of household members lived in the USA at the date of the interview — more than lived in Mexico City (3 per cent) and almost equal to the number of the two major local cities, Calamanca and Celaya (7 per cent).[45]

The influence of farm income on the risk of not producing a subsistence income is central to understanding the different patterns of labour allocation in these two zones. While households had to work off-farm in Valsequillo to earn an adequate level of income, they could not afford to undertake the substantial investment needed to support a circular migrant, and the accompanying risk that he would not quickly obtain a job and send remittances. Therefore, they worked locally for extended periods in a variety of occupations.

Households in the Bajio used higher levels of farm income to support circular migrants, and thereby reduced the risk associated with their much greater dependence upon monetary sources of income. The total portfolio of income-producing activities is the important consideration — higher farm incomes permitted the relatively risky alternative of US migration, while this activity produced high cash income and could reduce the variability of the total income portfolio.

The model suggests that circular migration to the United States would only be undertaken by households with multiple sources of income, so as not to be too dependent upon this risky income source. This hypothesis is supported by the survey data, which showed that the only statistically significant difference between the characteristics of farms and households of US migrants and others in the Bajio was that the labour force of the former was larger, permitting a diversification of income sources to offset the increased risks of US migration.

Moreover, Table 12.1 shows households in the Bajio were larger than in the other zones. The higher level of farm income permitted more members to share in the income of farm production, stimulating the incorporation of adult members into an extended household. The larger household labour force, combined with low farm labour requirements resulting from the mechanisation of agriculture, allowed one or more household members to work almost entirely off-farm. With the security of the extended household, which provided care for dependants and continuity in the production of agricultural income, household members could leave the community for extended periods.

In conclusion, it seems the variables and concepts developed in the model adequately differentiate patterns of labour mobility observed in these four rural areas of Mexico. While the effect of agricultural change on farm income has depended on the context of its introduction, in both the Bajio and Valsequillo commercialisation of agriculture increased the riskiness of agricultural income, decreased agricultural employment, and caused a diversification of household labour among types of off-farm employment. In the short run, higher levels of farm income in the Bajio permitted more allocation of household labour to long-distance circular migration, while in the long run it may have stimulated the formation of larger households, further expanding the possibility of household income diversification.

Notes

1. J. Abu-Lughod: 'The end of the age of innocence in migration theory', in B.M. Dutoit and H.I. Safa (eds.): *Models and adaptive strategies* (The Hague, Mouton, 1975), p. 201-6.

2. G. Hugo: *Impermanent mobility in Indonesia: What do we know about its contemporary scale, causes and consequences?*, paper presented at the Annual Meeting of the Population Association of America, Washington, DC, March 1981.

3. W.A. Lewis: 'Economic development with unlimited supplies of labour', in *The Manchester School of Economic and Social Studies*, May 1954, vol. 23, no. 2, pp. 139-92. The 'classical' variant of this model developed by Fei and Ranis, emphasising an institutionally determined rural wage, competed with the neoclassical version by Jorgensen, and resolution was sought in the determination of the marginal productivity of rural labour. See J. Fei and G. Ranis: *Development of the labor surplus economy: Theory and policy* (New Haven, Yale University Press, 1964); D.W. Jorgensen: 'The development of a dual economy', in *Economic Journal*, June 1961, vol. 71, pp. 309-48.

4. M.P. Todaro: 'A model of labor migration and urban unemployment in less developed countries', in *American Economic Review*, March 1969, vol. 59, no. 1, pp. 138-48.

5. J.R. Harris and M.P. Todaro: 'Migration, unemployment and development: A two-sector analysis', in *American Economic Review*, March 1970, vol. 60, no. 1, pp. 126-42.

6. M.P. Todaro: *International migration in developing countries* (Geneva, ILO, 1976), p. 45.

7. Greenwood, in his study of Mexican migration, explicitly assumed the neoclassical relationship: 'because the labour-capital ratio is relatively high in L (the low-wage region) and relatively low in H (the high-wage region), the rate of return on capital tends to be relatively high in the low-wage region and relatively low in the high-wage region' — M.J. Greenwood: 'An econometric model of internal migration and regional economic growth in Mexico', in *Journal of Regional Science*, April 1978, vol. 18, no. 1, pp. 17-31. Hayami and Ruttan developed a model based on the neo-classical relationship in which technical change in labour-abundant rural areas will absorb labour, reducing the necessity for rural out-migration — see Y. Hayami and V.W. Ruttan: *Agricultural development: An international perspective* (Baltimore, Johns Hopkins University Press, 1971). King utilised this relationship to define surrogate variables for the empirical estimation of migration parameters, noting 'density is usually interpreted as a proxy for the marginal product of labour on the land and is thus taken to be inversely related to the wage rate in the rural sector of the state' — J. King: 'Inter-state migration in Mexico', in *Economic Development and Cultural Change*, October 1978, vol. 27, no. 1, pp. 83-101. For a selective survey, see R.E.B. Lucas: 'Internal migration and economic development: An overview', in A.A. Brown and E. Neuberger (eds.): *Internal migration: A comparative perspective* (New York, Academic Press, 1977), pp. 37-60.

8. B. Banerjee and S.M. Kanbur: 'On the specification and estimation of macro rural-urban migration functions, with an application to Indian data', in *Oxford Bulletin of Economics and Statistics*, February 1981, vol. 43, no. 1, pp. 7-29.

9. D. Harris: 'Capital, distribution and the aggregate production function', in *American Economic Review*, March 1973, vol. 63, no. 1, pp. 100-13. For an application to agriculture, see J.S. Metcalfe and I. Steedman: 'Reswitching and

primary input use', in *Economic Journal*, March 1972, vol. 82, no. 325, pp. 140-57.

10. The evidence on the effect of higher agricultural incomes on migration in Mexico is contradictory. Unikel, Chiapetto and Lazcano found that rural out-migration correlated positively with agricultural productivity, and Greenwood, Ladman and Siegel supported this conclusion; Silvers and Crosson, however, concluded that higher agricultural income retarded migration — L. Unikel, R. Chiapetto and O. Lazcano: 'Factores de rechazo en la migracion rural en Mexico, 1950-1960', in *Demografia y Economia*, 1973, vol. 7, no. 1, pp. 24-57; J. Greenwood, J.R. Ladman and B.S. Siegel: 'Long-term trends in migratory behaviour in a developing country: The case of Mexico', in *Demography*, August 1981, vol. 18, no. 3, pp. 369-88; A. Silvers and P. Crosson: *Rural development and urban-bound migration in Mexico*, Research Paper R-17 (Washington, D.C. Resources for the Future Inc., 1980).

11. For a summary, see D. Anderson and M.W. Lwiserson: 'Rural nonfarm employment in developing countries', in *Economic Development and Cultural Change*, January 1980, vol. 28, no. 2, pp. 227-48.

12. C.H. de Alcantara: *Modernizing Mexican agriculture: Socio-economic implications of technological change, 1940-1970* (Geneva, United Nations Research Institute for Social Development, 1976).

13. L. Arizpe: 'The rural exodus in Mexico and Mexican migration to the United States', in *International Migration Review*, Winter 1981, vol. 15, no. 4, p. 638.

14. Hugo, 1981, p. 23.

15. The effect of a reverse link between circular migration and agricultural production is less clear. Robichaux found that money earned in circular US migration from Tlaxcala, Mexico, was often invested in agricultural improve-ments, while Cornelius saw little evidence of this in Jalisco — see D. Robichaux: *El significado de la articulación entre la agricultura y otros sectores económicos en una comunidad de la Meseta Central de Mexico*, paper presented at the Annual Meeting of the Cibola Anthropology Association, University of Texas, 1978; W. Cornelius: *Mexican migration to the United States: Causes, consequences and US responses*, paper presented at the Brookings Institution/El Colegio de Mexico symposium, Washington, DC, 1978.

16. J.L. Goodman: 'Information, uncertainty and the microeconomic model of migration decision making', in G.F. de Jong and R.W. Gardner, *Migration decision making* (New York, Pergamon, 1981).

17. P.A. David: 'Fortune, risk, and the microeconomics of migration', in P.A. David and M.W. Reder (eds.): *Nations and households in economic growth: Essays in honor of Moses Abramovitz* (New York, Academic Press, 1974), pp. 21-88.

18. D. Guillet: 'Surplus extraction, risk management and economic change among Peruvian peasants', in *The Journal of Development Studies*, October 1980, vol. 18, no. 1, pp. 3-24.

19. J.A. Roumasset (ed.): *Risk, uncertainty and agricultural development* (New York, Agricultural Development Council, 1979).

20. Hugo, 1981, p. 70.

21. David, 1974, p. 49.

22. J. Connell, B. Dasgupta, R. Laishley and M. Lipton: *Migration from rural areas: The evidence from village studies* (Delhi, Oxford University Press, 1976), p. 10.

23. G. Standing: 'Migration and modes of exploitation: Social origins of immobility and mobility', in *The Journal of Peasant Studies*, January 1981, vol. 8, no. 2, pp. 173-211. See also S.F. Harbison: 'Family structure and family strategy

in migration decision-making', in de Jong and Gardner, 1981.

24. This perspective is identical to that of Wood, in which 'migration is conceptualised as an integral part of the sustenance strategies the household adopts in response to the opportunities and the limitations imposed by conditions that lie beyond the household unit' — C.H. Wood: 'Structural change and household strategies: A conceptual framework for the study of rural migration', in *Human Organization*, Winter 1981, vol. 40, no. 4, pp. 338-44.

25. Rendón found that a change in crop composition was the greatest contributor to the decline in the demand for Mexican agricultural labour between 1950 and 1973, followed by mechanisation — T. Rendón: 'Desarrollo agricola y absorbsion de mano de obra', in *Marxhi-Nanda*, 1977, vol. 3, pp. 26-35.

26. Guillet, 1981, p. 12.

27. O. Stark and O. Levhari: 'On migration and risk in LDCs', in *Economic Development and Cultural Change*, October 1982, vol. 31, no. 1, pp. 191-6.

28. Arizpe, 1981, p. 640. In the book from which her article was drawn, she noted that 34 per cent of the households in the area having undergone rapid monetisation had two or more people in different occupations — L. Arizpe: *Migración, etnicismo y cambio economico* (Mexico City, El Colegio de Mexico, 1978), p. 154.

29. Connell *et al.*; 1976, p. 30.

30. J.M. Nelson: 'Sojourners versus new urbanites: Causes and consequences of temporary versus permanent cityward migration in developing countries', in *Economic Development and Cultural Change*, July 1976, vol. 24, no. 4, pp. 721-57. Solien de Gonzalez recognised the importance of family structure at a much earlier date — N.S. de Gonzalez: 'Family organization in five types of migratory wage labor', in *American Anthropologist*, December 1961, vol. 63, no. 6, pp. 1264-80.

31. I.R. Dinerman: 'Patterns of adaptation among households of US-bound migrants from Michoacan, Mexico', in *International Migration Review*, Winter 1978, vol. 12, no. 4, pp. 485-501.

32. H.A. Selby and A.D. Murphy: *The role of the Mexican urban household in decisions about migration to the United States* (Austin, University of Texas, Institute of Latin American Studies, 1980).

33. R.E. Weist: *Wage labor migration and household maintenance in a central Mexican town*, PhD dissertation, University of Oregon, 1970, p. 126.

34. I.R. Dinerman: *Migrants and stay-at-homes: A comparative study of migration in two communities in Mochoacan, Mexico*, Monographs in US-Mexican Studies No. 5 (La Jolla, University of California-San Diego, 1982), p. 76.

35. Banerjee and Kanbur, 1981, p. 19. They concluded: 'nothing can be said *a priori* about the influence of growth of rural incomes in migration. The outcome will depend on how growth has affected rural income distribution . . . if there has been a development programme aimed exclusively at raising the living standards of the lowest income groups, migration is likely to increase' — ibid., p. 16.

36. David, 1974, p. 54.

37. Dinerman, 1982, p. 52.

38. There would be discontinuities in these relationships arising from the fact that migration and search costs depend upon the number of household *members* allocated to a particular job market, not the proportion of labour months. Although for any particular household the preferred allocation of labour will be affected by these discontinuities, the argument does not depend upon a linear relationship.

39. The ability to borrow from local sources may lower Y_{min} in any particular year, but the household would eventually have to pay off the loan, raising subsistence needs in another year.

40. Dinerman found that 'each household attempts to create a large network of economic allies' to maintain economic viability through reciprocal loans; migration to the US was a major means of obtaining the cash to participate in this network — Dinerman, 1978, p. 496.

41. The inability of some indigenous peoples of Mexico to speak Spanish may be an example of such a circumstance, for it would make the trip through Mexico, the negotiation of the border crossing, and communication on the job difficult.

42. An alternative formulation would be the 'safety-first' criterion developed by Kataoka, who suggests income maximisation subject to the constraint that the probability of a return less than predetermined limit is not greater than some predetermined value. If distributions of expected returns are normal, safety-first criteria usually lead to the same outcome as mean-variance approaches like the one utilised here. For a review of the extenisve literature on portfolio analyses in investment theory, see E.J. Elton and M.J. Gruber: *Modern portfolio theory and investment analysis* (New York, John Wiley and Sons, 1981).

43. For a more thorough discussion of the agricultural characteristics of these regions and their effect on household labour mobility, see K.D. Roberts: 'Agrarian structure and labour mobility in rural Mexico', in *Population and Development Review*, June 1982, vol. 8, no. 2, pp. 299-322.

44. For instance, D.S. Butterworth: *Tilantongo: Communidad Mixteca en transicion* (Mexico City, Instituto Nacional Indigenista, 1981).

45. These data may understate the importance of US migration for households in the Bajio, for they only capture circular migration if the household member was absent at the interview date and had sent remittances to the household, or had worked in US agriculture. The surveys were designed mainly to capture the influence of agricultural conditions upon employment, and as a result the migration data are incomplete.

13

Policy-makers and Circulation at the Grass Roots: South Pacific and South-east Asian Examples

MURRAY CHAPMAN

> One of the difficulties Pacific administrators frequently encounter is inadequate basic information upon which to formulate policy. Research workers come and go, yet to tease any applications from their published statements is both a delicate and time-consuming task.[1]

I. Introduction[2]

Since the late 1960s, many micro-studies of population movement have been conducted in South-East Asia and the islands of the Pacific. Few have directly addressed policy issues, and the epigraph above, which more than 10 years ago prefaced a report to a colonial government, today needs little modification. There is the common feeling that results from village or community research are too particularistic to be of use to policy-makers. Despite such disheartening beliefs, this chapter attempts to demonstrate that both academics and planners have been needlessly cautious about what can be learned from micro-studies.

To critics, the minuscule size of the population under investigation and the time and energy spent within the confines of an encampment, a village, or an urban enclave make the term 'case study' self-evident. In fact, local-level studies of population mobility proceed from several points of reference and employ a surprising variety of field methods. Some take a holistic approach and view the hamlet or village as both points of origin and ultimate destination for movers. Others focus on the city destination of different ethnic groups or of particular occupations, such as construction workers or ice-cream vendors. Others are concerned with community reactions to national issues, such as transmigration. In this chapter several studies of circulation, a particular form of mobility, will be selected to exemplify how micro-level research can illuminate policy issues far beyond the limits of the particular group or local community.

II. Communities in Circulation: Two Villages of South Guadalcanal

A holistic approach to population movement was taken in a study of two communities in the Solomon Islands carried out during the mid-1960s.[3] Focused on Duidui and Pichahila, coast and inland communities of south Guadalcanal (Figure 13.1), the dominant concern was the interplay of social and economic factors in mobility behaviour. These people, isolated from north Guadalcanal and the capital of Honiara, are subsistence cultivators, generally have adequate land for food gardens and cash crops, earn money from wage labour and local coconut groves, and are noted for their independence. To discuss research undertaken 16 years ago would seem highly questionable in a paper about policy implications, were it not for the fact that subsequent study and revisits in 1972, 1974, 1978 and 1980 have shown the patterns of circulation to be remarkably durable. Perhaps even more surprisingly, the practical aspects of such recurrent mobility are not basically different from those reported in 1967 to the former Western Pacific High Commission.[4]

Observers, such as Allan, have commented upon the residential stability of Solomon Islanders.[5] If by stability is meant how firmly rooted they were to their home village, wherever it might be, then this is clearly correct. But given the emotional and practical ties to their community, the people of both Duidui and Pichahila were far more mobile than would have been anticipated from stereotypes then prevalent in the social sciences. Field enquiries revealed two different kinds of circulation. Younger persons, and predominantly men, moved for durations of as little as 10 days and as long as a year. The principal reasons were to earn money in the main town of Honiara (Figure 13.1), at district

Figure 13.1: South Pacific Locations

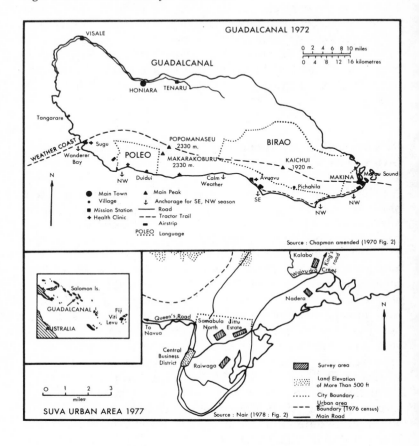

Sources: Chapman, 1970; S. Nair, 'Population mobility from the rural areas of Fiji to the urban area of Suva', MA thesis, University of Hawaii at Manoa, 1978.

(now provincial) centres, on European-owned plantations, or working for Solomon Island entrepreneurs; to visit Honiara and district and mission stations for retail, educational, medical, and administrative services; and to leave for other villages, either to go to school or because of a serious local dispute.

The pidgin 'go walkabout' summarised the second form of circulation, which mainly involved families, was highly spontaneous, meant an absence of less than eight days, and rarely extended beyond the language boundary of Poleo (Duidui) and Birao (Pichahila). Such journeys were made to other villages to visit kinsfolk, discuss clan and church business or attend a feast; to live temporarily in shelter at the edge of food gardens, to hunt wild pig or trap fish, or to quit the community briefly out of shame or by way of social protest.

There are two ways in which knowledge of such practices could assist the local administrator. One is specific to the communities or their immediate hinterlands, since people's mobility could influence the siting of community development schemes, the location of extension or social services, the spread of information and even when to schedule important official tours. Patterns of circulation are also relevant to larger questions that apply to hundreds of Solomon Island villages and not simply to Duidui and Pichahila, namely labour stability, vocational training programmes and the quality of education from the standpoint of the local community.

As Solomon Islanders are the overwhelming source of labour in their country, one practical question is how to reduce the high mobility at places of employment. The heart of this problem is the basic reason for the persistent ebb and flow, which is the largely polarised distribution of the village-dwelling population and the prevailing sources of employment, as well as the people's need to earn cash not only to pay their local taxes and school fees but also to obtain items of a money economy, and the fact that housing at many workplaces is still only available for single men, without women and children.

If employers throughout the Solomons were to offer family housing, then the wives — and particularly the younger and frequently more sophisticated — would be willing to accompany their husbands to most workplaces, at least within their own island. In such cases, a family would padlock its house, leave its pigs in the care of close relatives, and possibly even transfer the use of its garden land. More importantly, there would be a greater willingness to stay away for two to three years. Although this absence would not imply a permanent departure from the village, from an employer's standpoint it would mean a more stable workforce and thereby reduce the high rate of labour turnover.

The converse of this argument is that unless carefully implemented such programmes could have a negative impact upon village society. The local community can and does adjust to the loss of able-bodied males for periods of less than a year. When, in the first three months of 1966, 18 out of 51 men aged between 21 and 54 left Duidui for wage labour, young children, the elderly, and the infirm were widely used to carry water, prepare vegetables, nurse infants and keep the village swept and weeded. Yet a point can be reached where the number of families accompanying their menfolk would be too great to permit a community to function, as indicated by reports of chiefs, big men, and peers pressurising men to remain in the village until some absentees returned.[6]

The difficulty of reducing the mobility of wage labourers is complex but, given the prevailing nature of circulation, it can be resolved. Even if labour turnover cannot be reduced in the near future, as for instance through the provision of married quarters, then its distinctive seasonal character suggests that changes in vocational training might help to achieve the same goal. Employers depend upon the village for their manpower; while few married men are prepared to remain continuously at wage work, because August to February are busy months during which new food gardens must be cleared, root crops harvested and planted and leaf dwellings built or repaired. Particularly in Honiara, employers do not feel inclined to put much effort into training for even minimal skills, when they are lost the moment the villager quits his job to return home, frequently never to be seen again.

This seasonal availability points to a compromise beneficial to both parties, provided that employers adopt a long-term view. On-the-job training could begin the moment a man was hired for the months February to August, which could be regarded as a trial period leading to an annual but seasonal association between employer and wage-earner. At the end of the period both parties could, if mutually satisfied, come to an arrangement whereby the Solomon Islander guaranteed his labour for the next year, in return for family housing and subsequent training in more difficult tasks. Were this to occur for three to seven years, then the cumulative experience and on-site training would about equal the non-apprenticeship programmes currently available for many of the manual trades. Such a scheme would be feasible, for example, for the training of painters, carpenters, plasterers, bricklayers, plumbers, linesmen, electricians and mechanics.

As envisaged, the arrangement between employer and wage-earner would be based on mutual understanding, with the migrant losing an assured job and family housing should he not return the following year. Obviously, employers would only be interested in such an annual seasonal association with workers judged to be energetic, trustworthy and manually dexterous. Solomon Islanders would be similarly unwilling unless impressed by the treatment received during the initial weeks of what to them would have been 'just another job'. Such arrangements might appeal most to small employers, whose scale of operation means closer and more personal contact with employees. But the major point is that programmes of vocational training could be evolved to mesh with the markedly seasonal flow of labour.

The fact that throughout the Solomons comparatively few schools are in the villages means that most children board away from home. Their annual return at Christmas is not only an exciting time for the community but also provides parents with evidence of the education received. And the onlooker's view is the sharper because of the children's absence for many months, compared with their much briefer vacation of four to six weeks. Particularly in Duidui, the older adolescents were often said not to know how to work properly, to be lazy and to want only to play. Intermittent comments were made about particular pupils not learning well and that it would be wasted money for them to continue. As time away increased, the children tended to become scornful of many village activities, an attitude that might have been less evident had they been attending local schools. More regular contact with their homes would facilitate the acquisition of local skills, along with more academic information. It would also considerably alleviate the boredom observed, especially among older adolescents, on completion of schooling.

Upon return, the children's most obvious accomplishment was simple English, which could be used, for example, to read letters from absent kinsmen, the local administration or mission authorities. But for the most part, it was not the knowledge of English that was most impressive but its marginal utility in the village and how pupils with less than four years training preferred Solomons' pidgin in conversation with outsiders. It is not surprising that parents were heard sometimes to remark that schooling was 'not much good', as the skills children might learn to help improve the community were not those with which most returned: for girls, simple nutrition and hygiene, first aid, sewing, gardening methods and handicrafts; for boys, crop improvement, carpentry, carving, simple accounting, fashioning tin or metal and mixing cement. In the Solomons, as in most Third World countries, the capacity of its human resources will remain underutilised until most villagers possess a wider range of manual skills, a greater awareness of nutrition and health care, a literacy based upon a lingua franca and the local language, and an awareness of communities beyond their own.

An interventionist philosophy has coloured this discussion of what patterns of circulation mean for labour turnover, programmes of vocational training and the quality of village education. It has been assumed that some authority — national, provincial, mission, or private — would construct family housing at places of employment, alter methods of vocational training and implement a curriculum more attuned to a rural society. Since the late 1960s, low-cost housing has become available in Honiara, and concerted, if sometimes controversial, attempts have been made to evolve a school curriculum more attuned to the needs and aspirations of village communities. But of what relevance is all this to local groups who have no academic mouthpiece and whose institutional environment may be neutral, apathetic or perhaps even hostile? To what extent does circulation represent an adaptation to such circumstances, and what can the policy-maker learn from it?

III. An Occupation Group in Circulation: Peasant Farmers in Bangkok

During 1978-9 a geographer, Paul Lightfoot, and a sociologist, Ted Fuller, undertook collaborative research in six Thai villages on what has become known as 'the north-eastern problem': the persistent outflow of peasant farmers to Bangkok.[7] Located in Atsamat District, Roi-et Province (Figure 13.2), these communities have a long history of men and women leaving farm households to seek urban employment. This practice has intensified since 1976, with the inauguration of a twice-weekly bus service, that put the capital within ten hours of the district centre, as well as the extension of laterite roads in rural areas, which permitted villagers to use vehicles in all seasons. Sceptical

Figure 13.2: South-East Asia Locations

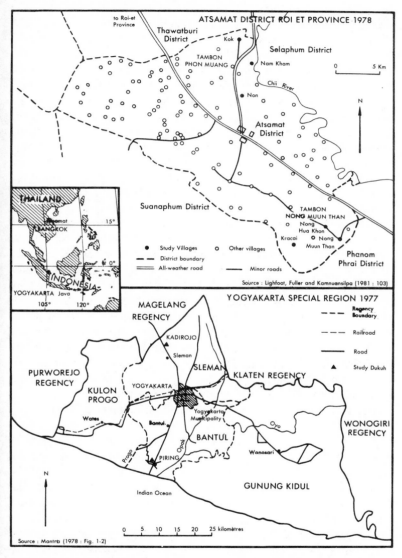

Sources: P. Lightfoot, T.D. Fuller and P. Kamnuansilpa, 'Impact and image of the city in the northeast Thai countryside', in *Cultures et Développement*, 1981, vol. 13, pp. 97-122; I.B. Mantra, 'Population movement in wet rice communities: A case study of two dukuh in Yogyakarta Special Region', PhD thesis, University of Hawaii at Manoa, 1978.

that the flow of people along these routes was overwhelmingly in one direction, Fuller and Lightfoot approached mobility as a process of territorial and social interaction linking places spatially distant and culturally and economically distinct. Since city destinations are as important to this process as villages of origin, a parallel survey of north-easterners in Bangkok was made by a Thai colleague and social demographer, Peerasit Kamnuansilpa.[8]

In terms of gross provincial product, Roi-et is the second poorest province in Thailand but the most densely settled in the north-east. For subsistence, peasant farmers in the study communities rely on glutinous rice cultivated by traditional methods, without benefit of irrigation or high-yielding varieties: only in favourable years is a surplus for sale. Some cash may be obtained from growing upland crops. Critical to survival are the various social, economic and political networks within which farmers and their families are enmeshed: the immediate household, peers, household labour exchanges, and between patrons and clients. Such interpersonal networks were originally confined to the village where they provided local opportunities, but they have been territorially extended through the processes of monetisation and population movement. Since rural-urban networks have emerged to serve new functions, as well as complement traditional ones, various questions arise for the policy-maker. What is the relationship between rural-urban networks and the circulation of peasant farmers? What opportunities and obligations, at home and abroad, exist with different kinds of network and how are their competing claims resolved? Apart from the individual migrant, what collective impact does mobility behaviour have on rural communities of origin?

In the six Roi-et villages studied, 23 per cent of those aged 10 or over had made a visit of at least 24 hours in town during the three years 1977-9. Such movement, involving 77 per cent of the households, was heavily oriented towards Bangkok and was recurrent. Most villagers had left and returned more than once; for any one absence, almost a third had been away for 30 days or less. Circulation had become such an integral part of community life that specific links had been forged between particular rural households and precise urban destinations, including both job sites and places to stay. In the absence of village information about employment opportunities in Bangkok, most persons do not leave until assured by contacts or compatriots in town of the availability of wage work — for men, on construction sites, at factories or driving taxis; for women, in domestic service or on assembly lines of small factories. The research team concluded:

> Regardless of the actual distribution of jobs and other opportunities, prospective movers almost always follow their friends and relatives to the same towns, if not the same jobs, unless other equally credible information networks are established to link them with alternative destinations.[9]

Despite the popular impression that every year peasant farmers time their absences in Bangkok to mesh with slack periods during the agricultural calendar, this is only partially true of movement from Roi-et. Cultivation of wet rice requires heavy inputs of labour in July-August for planting and in December for harvesting. Reinforced by the small size of farm holdings and their inability to produce dependable cash incomes, this permitted adults to take up city jobs without depleting the household labour force at critical points in the farm cycle. While about twice as many villagers were absent in the six months following harvest as against when it was in progress, between 1976 and 1979 only 9 per cent (40 out of 442 movers) followed a strictly seasonal pattern.[10] Furthermore, this minority was demographically and economically distinct, being composed of heads of household in early stages of family formation, to whom both supplementary income and their physical presence during planting and harvest were essential.

That more than half of all Roi-et movers had been absent during an agricultural season had negative implications for the rural households of which they remained part. Loss of farm labour and its impact on the production of subsistence and emergent cash crops was viewed most seriously, not simply for its disruption of the family workforce but also for an inability to honour agreements (*long khaek*) to pool household resources for burdensome tasks, such as threshing rice, or for larger projects, such as building a house. Lack of locally available labour was also reported to be the most critical constraint on the introduction of cash crops and new farm techniques.[11] Even so, numbers away were not so great nor lengths of absence so prolonged that a household consistently forfeited its workforce to Bangkok over several seasons, and fathers often sanctioned the departure of sons on condition that they returned, in particular for the rice harvest.

A widespread belief that Roi-et villagers moved to the capital because they and their communities were poor is equally simplistic. As almost all households owned the land they cultivated, and as rice farming was the primary occupation and source of income, individuals were not driven to leave for Bangkok in response to acute socio-economic deprivation. On the contrary, propensity to move was not related to area of farmland per person, although household heads who judged their holdings 'adequate' were a little more likely to have been away than those who did not (76 versus 69 per cent).[12] The undoubted strength of economic factors inducing rural-urban circulation was articulated through varying levels of personal aspiration, under-pinned and reinforced by networks between peers and patrons. The poorest households, commonly without connections and unaware of urban opportunities, were disinclined to jeopardise slender resources by having a member seek supplementary income, whereas the relatively well-off could bear the cost of bus transport and withstand the loss of some family labour, or could hire temporary replacements if necessary. Persons from compar-atively wealthy families were able to capitalise on jobs secured and guaranteed through being clients of a city patron, perhaps a previous employer, the foreman on a construction site or an enterprising villager long resident in Bangkok.

The north-eastern Thai concept of *phuuk siaw* — solidarity and loyalty among friends — means that peer groups were facilitators of such repetitive mobility, notably among younger adults aged 15 to 39. Friends often left the village together, were more likely to have received family aproval than if moving alone, could stay on arrival in Bangkok with peers who had jobs and provided shared comfort in a forbidding city whose inhabitants are thought to be unfriendly, cunning, unreliable, deceptive and selfish. Overall, urban experience reinforced the feeling of being peasants and of rural background, the desire to maintain regular contact with Roi-et households, the practice of making occasional visits should time away extend beyond several months, and the fact that the primary purpose of being in the capital was to earn cash to augment family incomes.

Remittances were an important source of money for rural households. Interviews conducted in 1979 with 788 north-easterners in Bangkok established that on average migrants sent back US$ 30 (614 *baht*) every month.[13] This represented 37 per cent of their monthly earnings and, for north-east Thailand as a whole, equalled 48 per cent of the total mean income available to farm households. Proportionately greater amounts were remitted by the youngest (10-19) and oldest adults (40+). The former did so because of higher incomes and a sense of obligation to parents (*bun khun*) who often subsidised their journeys; the latter because many were household heads on whom distant families remained dependent. Increasingly, Roi-et peasants have viewed intermittent wage labour in Bangkok as the only realistic strategy to improve their lot, and in this they mirror the Filipino construction worker of Greater Manila, for whom circulation 'represents a means by which he can maximise his living standards'.[14] Given such personal and familial goals, remittances were used predominantly for household consumption rather than for farm improvements and were spent on urban items such as clothing, appliances, materials for upgrading dwellings or constructing new ones. Thus, the constant exchange of Roi-et labour between village and city results in short-run gains for particular families at the long-term expense of enhancing the productive capacity of the local and regional economy.

This casual work by peasant farmers, unlike that for wage-labourers from south Guadalcanal, has evolved gradually rather than from administrative fiat or employment regulations. As Lightfoot *et al.* noted,

> In the same way as Bangkok's residents have no maps, those outside Bangkok have no access to the monthly reports on jobs and housing; their image of Bangkok is constructed from their own experiences, and from the letters, anecdotes, and personality changes of their acquaintances who have been in the city.[15]

If this were so, according to the Roi-et research team, why could not these circuits be redirected toward regional centres and local towns, where presumably the flow of labour would benefit north-eastern development rather than subsidise the primacy of the nation's capital?

From this provocative question arose an experiment to transmit details of job vacancies to selected villages and monitor whether that information affected the destinations to which peasant farmers went in search of wage employment. Interviews were conducted in six communities on two occasions a year apart. In between, starting December 1978, lists of jobs available in towns throughout Thailand were sent every month to three villages in Nong Muun Than commune (Figure 13.2) but not, quite deliberately, to the three others in Phon Muang commune. Such lists, routinely compiled by provincial departments of labour but normally displayed only on departmental premises, were placed on special notice-boards, and their content was also advertised by local committees constituted for this purpose. From December 1978 until July 1979, village headmen received information of 6,974 vacancies, information that included name of company, type of work, rates of pay, and categories of employee needed. Of those, 40 per cent were located in the north-east, about half of which were restricted to men and another third to women only.[16]

Despite the experiment's brief duration, it had the desired effect of encouraging higher rates of movement toward north-eastern towns while those to Bangkok remained fairly constant. Within the three communities of Nong Muun Than, adult circulation was appreciably more frequent after job lists were supplied than in the previous two years — a difference that was statistically significant for each community, as well as when compared in aggregate to the three villages that did not receive details of vacancies. Leaving for a regional centre rather than for Bangkok was most pronounced for those who took urban employment for the first time, notably the younger and most able-bodied. Among inhabitants of the three 'experimental' villages who had gone away during the two previous years, the preference for north-eastern towns over Bangkok was 153 to 100, in striking contrast to 30 to 100 for the three 'control' villages.[17] Hence, the long-established practice of choosing Bangkok as a likely place for wage work persisted in the latter communities but was dramatically changed in the former.

Despite this evidence, it was not possible to establish that these shifts in mobility pattern were a direct and unequivocal consequence of the information programme. Partly this reflected its brief and deliberately small-scale nature, but more especially the fact that 30 per cent of those who left for north-eastern towns were absent at the time of resurvey. None the less, if villagers present in the study communities had read the notice-boards, they were far more likely to have been away to work in regional centres. Fuller and his associates argued that a policy of routinely providing details of jobs elsewhere to distant or isolated rural communities would be administratively simple, since that information could be channelled through labour officers at provincial headquarters or development workers operating at the level of the commune. Expenditure in time, effort and money would be low; over six months, the field experiment involved two days at the outset in local meetings, plus time needed by three labour officials mailing job lists every month, village headmen putting them on notice-boards, and a mid-period check by a clerical assistant. In short, the Roi-et study has helped demolish a cherished myth, that people's mobility, unlike their mortality and fertility, cannot be managed for both individual and collective well-being.

IV. Ethnic Groups and Circulation: Fijians and Indo-Fijians in Suva

Proximity of origin communities, defined in terms of both kinship ties and distance, ensured the ethnic homogeneity of migrant workers and school pupils in south Guadalcanal and north-east Thailand. But when the frame of reference is shifted to urban destinations, people who circulate are more varied in their attributes as are the regions from which they come. To what extent does ethnicity affect the intensity of circulation and links between urban domiciles and natal places? If it does have an effect, might this indicate that comprehensive national policies would be less effective than those that are to some extent regionally or culturally specific?

Late in 1977 a geographer, Shashikant Nair, began a study of Fijians and Indo-Fijians who, although born in rural areas, had lived for at least six months in the capital city of Suva.[18] The 400 heads of household interviewed were divided equally between the two ethnic groups, and their range in both duration of stay and socio-economic position was reflected in the residential areas chosen for investigation (Figure 13.1). Nair, himself an Indo-Fijian, was concerned initially with how long people lived in Suva, their residential intentions, and the kinds of socio-economic linkages maintained between rural and urban places. However, so many implications emerged from his research that it provided rare documentation of how far the ethnicity of movers must be incorporated in framing policy.

Six out of ten Fijian heads of household were born in the distant islands of eastern Fiji, which have scanty resources and are prone to hurricanes. A similar proportion of Indo-Fijians came from the main island, Viti Levu, where sugar cane is grown and where the problems of a steadily-rising population and diminution of available land per capita have been compounded by the expiry of native leases. Contrary to the image of Fijians as a village people, considerably more of them than Indo-Fijians had resided in town for ten or more years. Conversely, seven times as many Fijians as Indo-Fijians expected eventually to return to their villages or rural settlements of origin.

The bilocality of people in town having various degrees of commitment to their natal place was sustained by a cross-flow of visitors, goods and cash. Indo-Fijians visited their rural communities more often but for shorter periods than Fijians, a pattern reflecting differential accessibility rather than increasing length of residence. Kinship was the dominant reason for most visiting: to take holidays with relatives, attend weddings or funerals, or console the sick. Festivals, enshrined in both customary and religious belief, also stimulated return. Thus, Hindus celebrate *Diwali* and Muslims *Eid*, and Fijians must formally introduce a newborn child to their father's village (*mananigone*).

Apart from visiting, there is an illuminating contrast in the ways in which Fijian and Indo-Fijian heads of household interacted with their places of origin. For Fijians, the extended family, the village and the province command different kinds of support and attention. As Nair noted,

> Whereas links with the extended family in the village are primarily spontaneous, those with the larger village community are somewhat spontaneous but often sanctioned by tradition, while most of those with the provinces are mandatory and may be enforced by administrative authority.[19]

Indo-Fijians, having no residential unit of reference comparable with the Fijian village and not being bound by provincial regulations, maintained exclusive links with close kin, most usually through the remittance of money.

Fijians sent cash and manufactured goods to the extended family, while traditional products (woven mats, scented coconut oil) and fresh food (root crops, fish, mangoes) flowed in the opposite direction. The dominant form of contribution to the entire village was money collected in town for some communal project, either through direct donation or participation in benefit games such as *kati*. Reciprocal help, although less frequent, occurred during traditional ceremonies, especially before and after burials. At such times, village relatives assisted with ceremonial procedures, provided labour, supplied food and materials for the funeral feast and, most critically, represented those Suva residents unable to attend the ceremonial sequence. Compared with rural-urban interaction at the level of the family and the village, payments made to the province represented head tax or land rates which, although buttressed by official sanction, were ignored by about half those living in Suva.

The differential weight Fijians and Indo-Fijians gave to their rural heritage, while masked by the many years in town and the generally skilled nature of their employment, was summarised by their self images. Fijians overwhelmingly felt they were village people (83 per cent), whereas almost half the Indo-Fijians viewed themselves as townsfolk and a further fifth were either ambivalent or unsure.[20] How ethnic differences affect movement can be captured by scoring the number and recency of visits to natal communities, the kinds of socio-economic links maintained with them, plus intentions about future residence. On the scale of origin-destination links thus derived, Fijians ranked from high to moderate but Indo-Fijians quite low; for the former, circulation between town and country was quite intense, for the latter comparatively weak.

Culture, history and social conditioning, rather than the attributes of movers, explain this instructive result. Given the hierarchical nature of Fijian society, there existed a certain communalism at all levels of socio-political organisation down to the village, and reciprocity was emphasised. In Nair's words:

All Fijians who wish to retain their group identity . . .identify strongly with the village, which is the hearth of all tradition, where their roots lie. Fijians who live in urban areas consequently must do far more than simply say they are of the village — their declarations have to be translated into such actions as contributing to village projects. Beyond this, Fijians are taught both formally and informally that their traditions and lifestyles must be retained at all costs, even though this often results in conflicting ideals.[21]

Reinforcing such customary mechanisms is the fact that most land was owned communally, managed at the village level, and legally could not be sold. Understandably, such vested interest in rural land made it impossible for any Fijian to renounce all links with the natal place. This is in contrast to Indo-Fijians who, being of immigrant descent, did not 'necessarily identify their rural settlements with a cultural heritage or view them as the anchor of their whole existence. Above all, there is no traditionally sanctified system of exchange among kin and no conditioned expectation to contribute to settlement affairs'.[22]

In broadest perspective, there exists a complementarity between Suva and the rural areas, of which circulation is the most visible manifestation. Thus Nair disagreed with attitudes evident in Fiji's Seventh Development Plan (1976-80), in which movement from rural places was conceived of as an exodus that created problems of congestion in urban destinations and depression in the origin communities. On the contrary:

For the Fijians in particular, urban centres are regarded as locations of employment and modern amenities, and rural communities primarily as locations that offer opportunities for a better social and cultural life and a chance for peaceful retirement. Consequently, people move between urban and rural places to maximise their satisfactions.[23]

This explanation is identical to that offered by Fuller and Lightfoot for the peasant farmers shuttling between village households and Bangkok.

Based on this practice, Nair argued for policies to help Suva residents maintain their rural interests and ultimately to implement their desire to return at or before retirement. Rural investment should also aim to facilitate and reinforce the links with natal communities while delaying the outward movement of young people, so that they could experience meaningful aspects of local life and find eventual return less burdensome. Improved shipping services to the outer islands, for instance, would permit more frequent return and more active participation in village affairs, while better roads and bus services to areas tributary to the capital would facilitate employment in town without a parallel transfer of domicile. More junior and senior secondary schools strategically located in rural areas would not only help children remain but also lead to a fuller experience of local lifestyles, especially given that many Fijians and Indo-Fijians have relocated for education.

Availability of money-earning opportunities in or near villages would confer upon returning Fijians the dual advantage of a quiet life and basic needs being met. While the introduction of cash-producing activities would be no simple matter, better transport services could be integrated with cultivation of high-value or off-season cash crops, or the establishment of suitable cottage industries. The sensitivity throughout Fiji about access to land could be alleviated, Nair argued, were government to reclaim forest and coastal swamp for subsequent lease or sale to Fijian and Indo-Fijian farmers, as well as to encourage underutilised or idle land to be planted with a greater variety of cash crops. Such agricultural policies would attract more rural Fijians into the cash economy and provide landless Indo-Fijians with the opportunity to settle outside urban centres.

Irrespective of the rural focus of these suggestions, Nair emphasised the paramount need for balanced development throughout Fiji and for planners to understand that reinforcing rural-urban links would also have implications for urban growth. As the Roi-et team noted for Greater Bangkok, people who circulate make different demands on city services from those intent on lengthy residence. Many Fijians and some Indo-Fijians preferred temporary quarters upon arrival in Suva, which suggests that authorities ought to encourage the construction of low-cost rental units and maintain a lenient attitude towards squatter settlements. If the cross-flow of people between complementary places is acknowledged, then an obsession with rural-urban drift can be avoided.

V. Local Participants in National Policy: Transmigration and Two Javanese Dukuh

In Indonesia, a vast literature exists on transmigration, which has been the primary instrument by which successive governments since 1905 have tried to ease population pressure in Java. From the outset, the transmigration programme encountered difficulties. Yet little is known about the transmigrants in the context of their origin communities: who found success through resettlement in southern Sumatra, whether close links were maintained with their natal places on Java, or how many became disenchanted and returned. Could it be that sensitive discussion with transmigrant families would isolate factors explaining success and failure in such a national policy?

In the mid-1970s, Mantra undertook a detailed study of population movement in two *dukuh* (hamlets) in central Java.[24] Both communities, Kadirojo and Piring, are in the most densely-settled regencies (Bantul and Sleman) of Yogyakarta Special Region (Figure 13.2). Both depend on wet-rice irrigation for their livelihood and, since the 1970s, both have experienced a dramatic increase in short-term and short-distance mobility through the extension of rural roads and the appearance of the minibus. Although Mantra's research was not primarily concerned with transmigration, he became aware of and reported the opinions and experiences of *dukuh* participants.[25]

During the fieldwork from May 1975 to January 1976, 11 heads of household left *dukuh* Kadirojo and Piring for south Sumatra. Only two of them participated in the government-sponsored programme and, as with former transmigrants, most made their own arrangements and paid their own expenses. This disinclination to relocate under official auspices reflected both complicated administrative procedures and a preference for areas where relatives or friends had already settled. Within the *dukuh*, stories abounded of officially-sponsored migrants being told to prepare for departure, and then, having sold their ricefields and basis of subsistence, being forced to wait for several weeks for transport.

Perhaps even more important was that meeting one's expenses to Sumatra left open the option of eventual return to Kadirojo and Piring, so that the decision to resettle became a gradual rather than a peremptory one. A common sequence has been to visit a relative, who had previously relocated, stay for a few months working as farm labourer or trader and then, if favourably impressed, attempt to purchase some agricultural land. Thus, spontaneous transmigrants have not been bound by government regulations, which accounts for their higher average age. Nor have they officially transferred their residential status from the *dukuh* to the new settlement. So, it has been simple for them to return if they so choose.

Both previous and potential transmigrants from Kadirojo and Piring have favoured long-settled areas in southern Sumatra, despite the likelihood that other parts of the island would offer better employment opportunities and lower transport costs. Quite simply, the dominant attraction has been the presence of relatives in such areas, compounded by the relatively short distance from central Java that reduces the expense of both relocation and return visits to their natal communities. In Mantra's words:

> Clusters of kinsfolk in transmigration areas can be regarded as preferred residential destinations and demonstrate that the greater the number of related people who stay . . . the greater the flow of transmigrants to that destination.[26]

The gradual and cumulative process of the decision to transmigrate, as well as the critical links of kinship, are summarised in the life history of a Kadirojo family.[27] In 1967, after four years in Tanjungkarang, south Sumatra, one brother returned to the *dukuh* to visit relatives and responded to questions about life in a colonisation area, the nature of landholdings, the local people, and systems of transport. A younger brother, asked to accompany the elder to help work his ricefields, soon learned that their cost was about one-third that in Kadirojo. In addition, the settlement was close to a main road, and nearby householders were friendly. Within a year the younger brother had returned to the *dukuh*. His wife agreed to accompany him provided that their home was located in the same area as the older and longer-resident brother's, and that the family's transfer be delayed a year until the daughter completed primary school.

In the interim, the husband sold some of the family ricefields and, accompanied by his son, returned to Tanjungkarang to buy land and build a semi-permanent dwelling. As soon as the daughter had finished her elementary education, the entire family migrated to Sumatra and left their remaining possessions in the care of the husband's youngest brother. Since 1967, as a result, close links have existed between two communities, one in Sumatra, the other in central Java. Letters to the *dukuh* from the two families contain many details about their fate and the mother was sometimes sent money, which conveyed the impression that the relocation was already a success. Such positive impressions might stimulate other people to migrate from Kadirojo — an act which, as with the two brothers, would be preceded by visits to establish that sufficient agricultural land was still available at reasonable cost.

Unfortunately for policy-makers, channels of communication do not discriminate between good information and bad. Thus the negative experiences of villagers in officially-sponsored programmes have also flowed back to the Javanese *dukuh*, whose inhabitants have not been slow to draw unfavourable comparison. One Kadirojo family, having arrived at a resettlement area where crops could not be cultivated because of deep tree roots that bound the soil, wrote to parents to send money and promptly returned. For a local community, such facts translate into a marked reluctance to participate in official schemes of transmigration.

Given the views of *dukuh* residents, Mantra advocated new tactics in the transmigration programme. What was first needed in pioneer areas, he argued, was 'a small nucleus of "successful" migrants, reinforced by better logistics and improved transportation'.[28] In turn, this would stimulate the flow of spontaneous migrants from Javanese communities. Volunteers willing to act as such a pioneer group, and sought from among friends and relatives, would expand the range of destinations that transmigrants would be willing to consider and anticipate the desire of potential settlers to live among their own people. Without friends or relatives in resettlement areas, *dukuh* inhabitants would remain uninterested in moving in spite of national policy or, if sufficiently courageous to participate, would feel anxious about their allotment of land upon arrival or their reception from existing residents.

In general, priority should be given to the links that exist and might evolve between the settlements and the origin communities of prospective participants, a conclusion parallel to that reached in Nair's study of Fijians and Indo-Fijians living in town. One method used by the Dutch in colonial Indonesia, which could be copied, was to encourage successful migrants to return periodically to their natal communities. Such visits, especially at celebrations like *Lebaran* and *Ruwah*, would enable kin to demonstrate their improved socio-economic position. Government could also encourage voluntary transmigrants by meeting transport costs and subsidising other relocation expenditures.

VI. Tying the Threads Together

> The most important discoveries of the laws, methods and progress of Nature have nearly always sprung from the smallest objects which she contains (Lamarck).

Individuals, families and small groups that make up encampments, villages and urban enclaves constitute the elementary particles of society. Consequently, what is known about two small communities of south Guadalcanal, peasant farmers in Bangkok, ethnic groups in Suva, and potential transmigrants in central Java can illuminate policy issues at several levels of consideration: the hamlet or village, the town or city, the region and the country.

Pointing to the links between the results of local enquiries and their broader implications reveals 'the connexions between the large-scale expressions of human action and what is taking place in the micro-spaces where the actors actually handle their tools and materials and cooperate face-to-face'.[29] Again, in a comment that could apply equally to village parents dissatisfied with their son's education, the household head sending cash and goods to his natal place, the peasant farmer awaiting news of a temporary job in town, and the *dukuh* family's disinclination to transmigrate, Hägerstrand noted:

> Individual feelings and opinions contain the seeds of further real-world changes in the aggregate. The give and take of costs and benefits in a society are so strongly associated with minute locational acts that it is necessary for . . . analysts to apply the best magnifying glass in order to detect them.[30]

In these days of strong philosophies and remorseless hypotheses, the evidence in case studies can be variously interpreted. Circuits of movement described by schoolchildren of south Guadalcanal, wage labourers of Bangkok, Fijian sojourners to Suva and transmigrants of central Java may all be viewed as the structural result of origin communities that lie at the margins of the world capitalist system. Alternatively, they may be seen as the family's attempt to spread risk or as a response to the complementary nature of different places or circumstances. Such differing explanations are the heart of intellectual discourse. More critical for the policy-maker, however, are details of what is happening on the ground, before the gloss of an explanation that is conceptually defined and theoretically inspired.

For population movement, such details are relatively simple but frustratingly difficult to collect on a large scale. Who moves where, how far, and for what dominant reasons? With whom is the movement made, how often, and with what success? Does mobility recur, and at what points in time? Between what communities of origin and destination do links exist, and what is their impact? Answers to such questions, if available at the micro-scale, can inform the nature of people's mobility at several levels of consideration beyond that of the particular group or community to which they most immediately refer.

Yet there is a deep and abiding scepticism in the literature about such a prospect. The social demographer, Sidney Goldstein, wrote:

To obtain [mobility] data in adequate depth, with appropriate information on motivation and impact, necessarily restricts the researcher to a few communities. This limitation, in turn, inevitably raises the question of the extent to which those communities are typical of the more general patterns characterising a region or country as a whole, given the unique ecological, economic, and social conditions that probably typify most villages.[31]

However well meaning, such concern indicates a misunderstanding of the micro-study and manifests what might be termed the myth of uniqueness and typicality. The village and town communities studied are neither unique, in the sense of being idiosyncratic, nor typical, in the sense of representing some statistical norm. Rather, they have been selected according to some specific criteria, that in turn reflect the kinds of theoretical, substantive or practical questions to which the field research was addressed.

Conclusions based on a given village or urban neighbourhood may consequently be generalised to other places which can meet the same set of contextual conditions, that is, the original criteria that defined the selection of the study communities. Such generalisations do not derive from statistical extrapolation but from an astute mix of intuition and a detailed awareness of the inner workings of a piece of social reality. According to J. Clyde Mitchell, a social scientist who throughout his career has been much concerned with the 'widespread confusion about the role of the case study in systematic enquiry':

> The basis of inference from a single case is not that the particular case is deemed to be 'representative' or 'typical' of all cases, as is the basis of statistical inference, but that . . . the logical connection between its constituent parts makes relationships apparent which were formerly obscure. Generalisation from the case study is premised upon the universality of the theoretical propositions relating relevant aspects of the case to one another.[32]

While planners and policy-makers are understandably little concerned about such esoteric matters, they have their practical ramifications. First, results from micro-studies reveal far more common ground, and consequently a much greater ability to generalise, than is usually assumed. Second, careful comparison of field investigations and their particular context can identify different mobility reactions to changing sets of socio-economic conditions — and in a way not possible from more aggregative research. The Roi-et study of north-east Thailand is a too rare example of these conclusions being taken a step further by means of controlled experiment. To understand the circulation of individuals, groups and whole communities, and to deploy that understanding for the benefit of the locality and the region, is not nearly as intractable as conventional thinking would have us believe.

Notes

1. M. Chapman: 'A population study in South Guadalcanal: Some results and implications', in *Oceania*, 1969, vol. 40, no. 2, pp. 119-47.

2. Thanks are due to Ted Fuller (Virginia Polytechnic Institute and State University), Paul Lightfoot (University of Hull) and Ida Mantra (Gadjah Mada University) for helpful comments on an earlier draft. This paper was reworked while a visiting research associate at l'Office de la Recherche Scientifique et Technique Outre-Mer, Centre de Nouméa, New Caledonia. A related paper, with different case studies, has appeared in G.W. Jones and H.V. Richter (eds.): *Population mobility and development: Southeast Asia and the Pacific*, Development Studies Centre Monograph 27 (Canberra, Australian National University, 1981).

3. M. Chapman: 'Population movement in tribal society: The case of Duidui and Pichahila, British Solomon Islands', PhD thesis, University of Washington at Seattle, 1970.

4. Chapman, 1969.

5. C.H. Allan: *Customary land tenure in the British Solomon Islands Protectorate*, report to the Special Lands Commission, Western Pacific High Commission, Honiara, 1957, p. 117.

6. Chapman, 1969, p. 137.

7. P.T. Lightfoot and T. Fuller: 'Circular rural-urban movement and development planning in north-east Thailand', in *Geoforum*, 1983, vol. 14, no. 3, pp. 277-87.

8. T.D. Fuller, P. Kamnuansilpa, P. Lightfoot and S. Rathanamongkolmas: *Migration and development in modern Thailand* (Bangkok, Social Science Associaton of Thailand, 1983); P. Lightfoot, T.D. Fuller and P. Kamnuansilpa: 'Impact and image of the city in the northeast Thai countryside', in *Cultures et Développement*, 1981, vol. 13, pp. 97-122; idem: *Circulation and interpersonal networks linking rural and urban areas: The case of Roi-et, northeastern Thailand*, Paper No. 84 (Honolulu, East-West Population Institute, 1983).

9. Lightfoot, *et al.*, 1983, p. 23.

10. Ibid., Table 10.

11. Lightfoot and Fuller, 1983, p. 281.

12. Lightfoot, *et al.*, 1983, p. 29.

13. Ibid., Table 12.

14. A. Stretton: 'The building industry and urbanization in Third World countries: A Philippine case study', in *Economic Development and Cultural Change*, 1981, vol. 29, no. 2, p. 335.

15. Lightfoot, *et al.*, 1981, p. 101.

16. Fuller, *et al.*, 1983, pp. 134-40.

17. Ibid., p. 164.

18. S. Nair: 'Population mobility from the rural areas of Fiji to the urban area of Suva', MA thesis, University of Hawaii at Manoa, 1978; idem: *Rural-born Fijians and Indo-Fijians in Suva: A study of movements and linkages*, Development Studies Centre Monograph No. 24 (Canberra, Australian National University, 1980).

19. Nair, 1980, p. 46.

20. Ibid., Table 19.

21. Ibid., pp. 57-8.

22. Ibid., p. 60.

23. Ibid., pp. 75-6.

24. I.B. Mantra: 'Population movement in wet rice communities: A case study

of two dukuh in Yogyakarta Special Region', PhD thesis, University of Hawaii at Manoa, 1978; idem: (Yogyarkarta, Gadjah Mada University Press, 1981).

25. Ibid., pp. 192-7, 232-5, 279-80.

26. Ibid., p. 196.

27. Ibid., pp. 233-5.

28. Ibid., p. 197.

29. T. Hägerstrand: 'The domain of human geography', in R.L. Chorley (ed.): *Directions in geography* (London, Methuen, 1973), p. 75.

30. Ibid.

31. S. Goldstein: *Circulation in the context of total mobility in Southeast Asia*, Paper No. 53 (Honolulu, East-West Population Institute, 1978), pp. 46-7.

32. J.C. Mitchell: 'Towards a situational sociology of wage-labour circulation', in R.M. Prothero and M. Chapman (eds.): *Circulation in Third World countries* (London, Routledge and Kegan Paul, in press), ms. p. 37.

Notes on Contributors

Murray Chapman, East-West Population Institute, East-West Center, and Department of Geography, University of Hawaii, Honolulu, USA.

Carol Colfer, Women in Development Programme, University of Hawaii, Honolulu, USA.

Yiu-Kwan Fan, Division of Business and Economics, University of Wisconsin-Stevens Point, USA.

Graeme Hugo, School of Social Sciences, Flinders University of South Australia, Australia.

Julian Laite, Department of Sociology, Manchester University, UK.

Christopher Lwoga, Churchill College, University of Cambridge, UK.

Shekhar Mukherji, Department of Geography, Visva-Bharati University, Santiniketan, West Bengal, India.

Kenneth Roberts, Southwestern University, Georgetown, Texas, USA.

Cheywa R. Spindel, Pontifical Catholic University of São Paulo, Brazil.

Guy Standing, Senior Economist, International Labour Office, Geneva, Switzerland.

Allan Stretton, Bureau of Labour Market Research, Canberra, Australia.

Kenneth Swindell, Department of Geography, University of Birmingham, UK.

Veena Thadani, formerly, The Population Council, New York.

Index

This excludes authors' name cited in the notes.

409